HOMOSEXUALITY: A EUROPEAN COMMUNITY ISSUE

International Studies in Human Rights

VOLUME 26

HOMOSEXUALITY: A EUROPEAN COMMUNITY ISSUE

Essays on Lesbian and Gay Rights
in European Law and Policy

Edited by

KEES WAALDIJK and ANDREW CLAPHAM

Coordinated by
European Human Rights Foundation

MARTINUS NIJHOFF PUBLISHERS
DORDRECHT / BOSTON / LONDON

Library of Congress Cataloging-in-Publication Data

```
Homosexuality : a european community issue. Essays on lesbian
  and gay rights in European law and policy / Kees Waaldijk,
  Andrew Clapham, eds.
     p.   cm. -- (International studies in human rights ; v. 26)
  ISBN 0-7923-2038-7 (HB : acid free paper)
  1. Homosexuality--Law and legislation--European Economic
Community countries. I. Waaldijk, K.  II. Clapham, Andrew.
III. Series.
KJE5144.G39H66      1993
346.401'3--dc20
[344.0613]                                            92-34502
```

ISBN 0-7923-2038-7 (HB)

Published by Martinus Nijhoff Publishers,
P.O. Box 163, 3300 AD Dordrecht, The Netherlands.

Sold and distributed in the U.S.A. and Canada
by Kluwer Academic Publishers,
101 Philip Drive, Norwell, MA 02061, U.S.A.

In all other countries, sold and distributed
by Kluwer Academic Publishers Group,
P.O. Box 322, 3300 AH Dordrecht, The Netherlands.

Printed on acid-free paper

Printed in the Netherlands

General Table of Contents

List of Contributors

Contributing Editors:

Kees Waaldijk
Andrew Clapham

Editorial board:

David Geer
Anya Palmer
Micha Ramakers
Jennie Wilson

Authors:

ASHMAN, Peter
European Human Rights
Foundation, Brussels

BETTEN, Lammy
University of Utrecht

BYRE, Angela
London Policy Institute

CHILD, Russell
University of Bradford

CLAPHAM, Andrew
European University Institute,
Florence

DERCKSEN, Adrianne
University of Utrecht

DE WITTE, Bruno
University of Limburg,
Maastricht

EMMERT, Frank
Academy of European Law,
Florence

JESSURUN D'OLIVEIRA,
Hans-Ulrich
European University Institute,
Florence

SNYDER, Francis
University College, London
European University Institute,
Florence

TANCA, Antonio
University of Florence

VAN DER VEEN, Evert
University of Utrecht

VAN DIJK, Pieter
Council of State of the
Netherlands
Netherlands Institute of Human
Rights (SIM)

WAALDIJK, Kees
University of Utrecht and
University of Limburg,
Maastricht

WEILER, Joseph H.H.
Harvard Law School,
European University Institute and
Academy of European Law,
Florence

Acknowledgements

This report was commissioned from the European Human Rights Foundation by the Commission of the European Communities. Three bodies coordinated the studies, the European University Institute, Florence, the Interfacultaire Werkgroep Homostudies of the University of Utrecht, and The Stonewall Group, London.

Many people have contributed to the production of this report, the following deserve particular thanks:

Tim Barnett of the Stonewall Group and Lisa Power, Secretary General of the International Lesbian and Gay Association (1988-1992), for persuading the EC Commission of the need for the study; Colin Kotz of the Socialist Fraction of the European Parliament for his invaluable assistance; Mel Read and Marijke Van Hemeldonk, Members of the European Parliament for their support; members of the Staff of the Department of Gay and Lesbian Studies of the University of Utrecht for research, criticism and secretarial services: Aart Hendriks, Jelle Martens, Astrid Mattijssen, Judith Schuyf, Rob Tielman, Willem-Jan Bogaarts, Loes van de Pavert; secretarial staff at the Department of Public Law, University of Limburg: Netty Litjens and Joke Oud; Brian Clapham for invaluable editorial assistance, the European University Institute in Florence and its Academy of European Law for technical and editorial assistance, in particular Angelika Lanfranchi; and members of the Directorate General V of the EC Commission for their help and cooperation, particularly Mme. M. Michèle Teirlinck-Thozet.

The contents reflect the views of the individual authors and should not be regarded as representing in any way the views of the Commission of the European Community or of the Board of the European Human Rights Foundation.

Glossary

AEL	Collected Courses of the Academy of European Law
A.E.L.E.	Association européenne de libre échange
AFDI	Annuaire français de droit international
AIDS	Acquired Immune Deficiency Syndrome
AJIL	American Journal of International Law
All ER	All England Law Reports
Appl.	Application (European Commission of Human Rights)
ArchVR	Archiv des Völkerrechts
ASDI	Annuaire suisse de droit international
Bull.EC Suppl.	Bulletin of the European Communities, Supplement
BYbIL	British Yearbook of International Law
Camb.L.J.	Cambridge Law Journal
CanYIL	Canadian Yearbook of International Law
CDDH	Comité directeur des droits de l'homme
CDE	Cahiers de droit européen
CMLR	Common Market Law Reports
CML Rev.	Common Market Law Review
Colum.J.Trans.L.	Columbia Journal of Transnational Law
Corte Cost.	Corte Costituzionale
CSCE	Conference on Security and Cooperation in Europe
DB	Der Betrieb
Declaration E.P.	Declaration of European Parliament
Dec.	decision; décision
Dir.	directive
DR	Decisions and Reports of the European Commission of Human Rights
DS	Recueil Dalloz Sirey
EBRD	The European Bank for Reconstruction and Development
EBU	European Broadcasting Union
EC	European Community
ECHR	European Convention for the Protection of Human Rights and Fundamental Freedoms
ECJ	European Court of Justice
ECOSOC	Economic and Social Council
ECR	European Court Reports (Reports of the Court of Justice of the European Communities, Luxembourg)
ECU	European Currency Unit
EEC	European Economic Community (Treaty)
EFTA	European Free Trade Association
EHRF	European Human Rights Foundation

EHRR	European Human Rights Reports
EIB	European Investment Bank
EIRR	European Industrial Relations Review
EJIL	European Journal of Interntional Law
ELR	European Law Review
EMS	European Monetary System
EP	European Parliament
EPC	European Political Cooperation
EP Doc.	European Parliament Document
EP Debs	European Parliament Debates
EPIL	Encyclopedia of Public International Law
ERTA	European Road Transport Agreement
ESA	European Space Agency
EuGRZ	Europäische Grundrechte Zeitschrift
EUI	European University Institute
EuR	Europarecht (Zeitschrift)
Eur. Bus. L. Rev.	European Business Law Review
Eur Court H.R.	European Court of Human Rights
Eur Comm H.R.	European Commission of Human Rights
EuZW	Europäische Zeitschrift für Wirtschaftsrecht
EWS	Europäisches Wirtschafts- und Steuerrecht
FAO	Food and Agriculture Organization
FIDE	Fédération internationale pour le Droit européen
Fordham Int'l. L.J.	Fordham International Law Journal
Foro it.	Foro italiano
Foro pad.	Foro padano
Fs.	Festschrift
G.A. Res.	General Assembly (of the United Nations) Resolution; Résolution de l'Assemblée Générale des Nations Unies
GATT	General Agreement on Tariffs and Trade
Ga.J.Int'l. & Comp.L.	Georgia Journal of International and Comparative Law
Gazz Uff	Gazzetta Ufficiale
Giur. Cost.	Giurisprudenza Costituzionale
GRUR Int.	Gewerblicher Rechtsschutz und Urheberrecht, Auslands- und internationaler Teil
GYIL	German Yearbook of International Law
Harvard Int'l L.J.	Harvard International Law Journal
Harvard L. Rev.	Harvard Law Review
HCR	UN High Commissioner on Refugees
HIV	Human Immunodeficiency Virus
HRLJ	Human Rights Law Journal
HR Rev.	Human Rights Review

ICCP	International Covenant on Civil and Political Rights
ICESC	International Covenant on Economic Social and Cultural Rights
ICJ	International Court of Justice
ICJ Reports	International Court of Justice Reports
ICLQ	International and Comparative Law Quarterly
ILC	International Law Commission
ILGA	International Lesbian and Gay Association
ILM	International Legal Materials
ILO	International Labour Organization
ILR	International Law Reports
IYIL	The Italian Yearbook of International Law
J. Common Mkt. Stud.	Journal of Common Market Studies
JCP	Jurisclasseur périodique
JDI	Journal de droit international
JOCE	Journal officiel de la Communauté européenne
JORF	Journal officiel de la République française
Journal of the ICJ	Journal of the International Commission of Jurists
JWT	Journal of World Trade
Law.Soc.Gaz.	Law Society Gazette
LIEI	Legal Issues of European Integration
LQR	Law Quarterly Review
MEP	Member of European Parliament
Mich.J.Int'l L.	Michigan Journal of International Law
Mich. LR	Michigan Law Review
MLR	Modern Law Review
NGO	Non-governmental organization
NILR	Netherlands International Law Review
NJ	Nederlandse Jurisprudentie
NJW	Neue Juristische Wochenschrift
NLJ	New Law Journal
NYIL	Netherlands Yearbook of International Law
OECD	Organization for Economic Cooperation and Development
OJ	Official Journal of the European Community
ÖJZ	Österreichische Juristen-Zeitung
PCIJ	Permanent Court of International Justice
PCIJ Reports	Permanent Court of International Justice Reports
QB	Queen's Bench (U.K. Law Reports)
RabelsZ	Rabels Zeitschrift für ausländisches und internationales Privatrecht
RAE	Revue des affaires européennes

RBDI	Revue belge de droit international
RdC	Recueil des Cours de l'Académie de droit international de la Haye
RDE	Rivista di diritto europeo
RDH/HRJ	Revue des droits de l'homme/Human Rights Journal
RDI	Rivista di diritto internazionale
Reg.	regulation
Res.	resolution
RGDIP	Revue générale de droit international public
RHDI	Revue hellénique de droit international
RIDC	Revue internationale de droit comparé
RIW	Recht der Internationalen Wirtschaft
RMC	Revue du marché commun
RMT	Rechtsgeleerd Magazjin Themis
RSDIE	Revue suisse de droit international et de droit européen
RTDE	Revue trimestrielle de droit européen
RUDH	Révue universelle des droits de l'homme
SEA	Single European Act
SEW	Social-Economische Wetgeving
Stb	Staatsblad van het koninkrijk der Nederland
Syr.J.Int.L. and Comm.	Syracuse Journal of International Law and Commerce
UN	United Nations
UNCTAD	United Nations Conference on Trade and Development
UNESCO	United Nations Educational, Scientific and Cultural Organization
UNTS	United Nations Treaty Series
UNY	United Nations Yearbook
U.S.C.A.	United States Courts of Appeals
Va.J.Int'l.L.	Virginia Journal of International Law
Vand.J.Trans.L.	Vanderbilt Journal of Transnational Law
WEU	Western European Union
WIPO	World Intellectual Property Organization
WHO	World Health Organization
WuW	Wirtschaft und Wettbewerb
YB	Yearbook of the European Convention on Human Rights
YEL	Yearbook of European Law
ZaöRV	Zeitschrift für ausländisches öffentliches Recht und Völkerrecht
ZERP	Zentrum für Europäische Rechtspolitik
ZHR	Zeitschrift für das gesamte Handelsrecht
ZRP	Zeitschrift für Rechtspolitik

Preface

This report is a result of many years of work by the International Lesbian and Gay Association (ILGA) towards the recognition of discrimination against homosexuals as a concern of the European Community.

The ILGA was founded in Coventry, England in 1978 by 13 lesbian and gay organisations to co-ordinate action in the light of the first direct elections to the European Parliament. In the intervening 14 years, the organisation has grown into a global federation with 410 group members in 60 countries. Its activities range from stimulating grass-roots action to lobbying the United Nations and other international bodies. Its basic goal, however, has stayed the same since its inception. This is, according to the ILGA's Constitution, 'to work for the liberation of lesbians, gay women and gay men from legal, social, cultural and economic discrimination'.

Since its foundation the ILGA has undertaken to fight discrimination at the EC level. From early on it has found a willingness in the European Parliament to consider the concerns of lesbians and gay men, which led to a number of resolutions and other positive actions. The other European institutions showed less openness. It was not until the beginning of the current decade that progress started to be made. In 1990 a meeting with the Commissioner for Social Affairs, Mme Vasso Papandreou, for the first time led to tangible results: lesbians and gay men were explicitly mentioned in the EC Commission's 1991 Code of Practice Protecting the Dignity of Women and Men at Work, a contact person in the EC Commission was appointed, and funds were made available for this report to be written.

Obviously, this is just a beginning. But the concerns of lesbians and gay men have started to gain recognition, and a base has been laid for future work towards ending discrimination against lesbians, gay men and bisexuals in the European Community.

It is clear that the experiences of lesbians and gay men are not identical. In addition to discrimination suffered on account of their sexuality lesbians are also discriminated against because of their gender. For lesbians sex discrimination may have particular adverse consequences. Within society at large women are often valued not for themselves but because of their connection with a man (as wife, mother, etc.). Since lesbians are often not associated in this way with men, they generally suffer the additional disadvantage of being undervalued and therefore invisible. Even within the lesbian and gay communities lesbians suffer from invisibility and, as a result, lesbian issues are sometimes accorded second place in terms of the lobbying agenda.

Nonetheless, in this report, lesbians and gay men are, on the whole, mentioned together because the discrimination they face – where it is based on their sexual orientation – is similar. Both homosexual women and men are discriminated against by heterosexual society because of their sexual orientation and accompanying lifestyles. Both lesbian and gay male couples suffer a number of identical legal disadvantages as they are denied social benefits which are accorded to heterosexual couples, be they married or not. Both lesbians and gay men are insulted, abused and even attacked because of their sexual orientation.

It is our hope that this report may prove an important contribution to understanding of the consequences of ignorance, irrational fear and prejudice. With this knowledge we may develop effective ways of improving the situation of lesbians and gay men, thus contributing to the creation of a Europe in which all can live free from discrimination.

Micha Ramakers,
Information Secretary
International Lesbian and Gay Association
Jennie Wilson,
The Stonewall Group

Chapter One
Introduction

by

PETER ASHMAN[*]

*   Director of the European Human Rights Foundation.

In the huge diversity of peoples who make up the human race, there are a number of universal constants which have always been part of the human condition. One is that people who are different inspire fear which often leads to prejudice; another is that a proportion of the human race is homosexual. In Europe, homosexuality has almost invariably met with prejudice. In its most extreme manifestation – the degradation and slaughter of countless homosexuals wearing pink or black triangles in the Nazi concentration camps of the 1930s and 40s – prejudice against homosexuals demonstrates how bigotry and irrational hatred can so warp the human mind as to chase from it every scintilla of decency and justice.

In the Europe that emerged from those dark days, great efforts have been made to control prejudice and the injustice which it engenders. Among the tools fashioned for this purpose has been the creation of a legal order, based on respect for the human rights of individuals and the rule of law, which transcends the traditional barriers such as nationality, language, race and religion. The framework for this is to be found in the European Convention on Human Rights and Fundamental Freedoms. Another of these tools has been the creation of new international institutions in which, it is hoped, other constants of the human condition, such as the desire for prosperity, security and happiness, might be harnessed to create a better world for all.

The European Community (EC) is one such institution. According to the 1987 Treaty establishing the Single European Act, the EC is intended to be a union of States:

> determined to work together to promote democracy on the basis of the fundamental rights recognized in the constitutions and laws of the Member States, in the Convention for the Protection of Human Rights and Fundamental Freedoms and the European Social Charter, notably freedom, equality and social justice.

This follows a joint declaration of 5 April 1977, in which the constituent political organs of the EC, the European Parliament, Council and Commission, had stressed the prime importance which they attached to the protection of fundamental rights, and that in the exercise of their powers and in pursuance of the aims of the European Communities they respected and would continue to respect these rights. This approach was re-affirmed in the recent Maastricht Treaty on European Union.

In democracies where the majority rules, the treatment of minorities is one of the principal tests of how far respect for human rights and the rule of law is observed. The most important indicator here is the claim to equality before the law.

What that means, in practice, is that difference in treatment is permitted when it can be justified by the criterion of justice, or reasonableness. It is the principle of treating the equal equally and the unequal according to their inequality, so that factual inequality is recognized and suitably dealt with.

There is in the EC, as elsewhere, a proportion of the population which is homosexual. This report is the first ever study of the situation of lesbians and gay men in the EC. It examines how the EC has succeeded in its declared aims of respecting fundamental human rights and freedoms in its treatment of its homosexual minority.

In the European Community, it is the European Parliament which has shown the greatest concern to promote human rights, both for the citizens of the EC as well as others outside it. Its concern has included the homosexual minority. In 1984, the European Parliament passed a Resolution on Sexual Discrimination in the Workplace which called for an end to *de facto* and *de jure* discrimination against homosexuals both at national and Community level. The Parliament has re-affirmed these views on several occasions in the intervening years, most recently in promoting an amendment to draft Community legislation on tendering, as well as adopting a Resolution on the Rights of the Child, in both of which it demanded an end to discrimination on grounds of sexual orientation.

The absence of political will in the other organs of the EC has led these to ignore the views of Parliament. However, the last twenty years have seen the growth of non-governmental organisations dedicated to ending discrimination against homosexuals. One of these, the International Lesbian and Gay Association (ILGA), acting as a confederation of national and local NGOs, pressed the EC for a more positive response. As a result, the EC Commission in May 1991 agreed to fund this report in order to establish the factual and legal situation. The European Human Rights Foundation (EHRF) was invited to be the contractor and was happy to undertake this task. Since its inception in 1980, the EHRF has given special emphasis to protecting the human rights of those most vulnerable to abuse and persecution – children, prisoners, indigenous peoples and unpopular minorities like homosexuals. It has, over the years, given much support to the ILGA in its world-wide efforts to combat discrimination against homosexuals.

The report demonstrates, perhaps not surprisingly, that discrimination against homosexuals is still rife in Europe. In most Member States, there is still no true equality before the law and popular prejudice against homosexuals remains at levels powerful enough to inhibit democratic leaders from courting unpopularity by providing equality. The chapter on homosexuals and the European Convention on Human Rights suggests that even those entrusted with interpreting and enforcing human rights law in Europe are fearful of being too bold in this area, and look for reasons to justify discrimination rather than to condemn it. This situation demonstrates the practical limitation of law. One cannot legislate away prejudice; only the persistent appeal to reason and to justice against the powerful pull of irrationality and bigotry can achieve that. The history of the struggles against slavery, religious intolerance, sexual inequality and racial discrimination gives ground for believing that reason and justice eventually triumph over the darker side of human nature.

This report casts a clear light on a continuing injustice. The only reasonable conclusion is that the European Community, which professes noble aims, cannot hope to achieve them if it turns a blind eye to prejudice, discrimination and sometimes even to the oppression of some 5% of its citizens.

The ending of discrimination, and the achievement of equality, is a challenge not just for the institutions of the EC but to all those who care about universal human rights and the progress of the human race.

Although HIV and AIDS are a major threat to the health situation of gay men, in particular, and to the social situation of both gay men and lesbians, reasons of space prevented much attention being devoted to these issues. However, AIDS, HIV and the situation of HIV-positive people, i.e. people who are 'seropositive' or HIV-antibody positive, are mentioned where relevant to the subject.

Chapter Two
Lesbians and Gay Men
in the European Community Legal Order

by

ANDREW CLAPHAM[**] and J.H.H. WEILER[***]

---

[*]   Article 1, Declaration of Fundamental Rights and Freedoms, European Parliament, 12 April 1989.

[**]   Formerly Executive Director of the Academy of European Law, European University Institute, Florence

[***] Professor of Law, Harvard Law School; Director, Academy of European Law, European University Institute, Florence.

8

Table of Contents

I. Preliminary Perspectives: History, Perceptions, Strategy

Typically, the *Turn to Europe* by women and minorities suffering discrimination and exclusion is propelled by several strategic considerations: Working effectively at the transnational level requires the forging or the strengthening of links with groups beyond one's own immediate local and national environment, a process which in and of itself augments solidarity, diminishes feelings of isolation and helplessness and, through the pooling of resources, enhances a sense of strength. It is not only subjective self-empowerment which this process may yield. Self-empowerment can translate into real power and concrete gains. A 'victory' in Europe, legislative or judicial, can be very effective. It may, as has been amply demonstrated in, say, the field of gender discrimination, have a direct and legally binding impact throughout the legal order of the European Community thus obviating the need for specific campaigns in each of the twelve Member States.[1]

Then there is the question of resources. The Community, which has its own interest in 'de-nationalizing' economic and social forces, sometimes is, and almost always is perceived to be, rich and generous in helping to mobilize at the European level. There is, too, a symbolic allure in 'Europe'. The European Community, it is often felt, is new. It is in the making, a polity yet to be molded. It is as if it has no History – only a Future – a future in which one can grab for a stake, make it one's own.

Thus, in his pioneering book, Peter Tatchell sets the strategy for lesbians and gay men as follows:

> [T]he trend towards a united Europe is an unmistakable fact. It is happening whether we like it or not... We can, however, adapt the unification process to our advantage and influence the character of the new Europe in a progressive direction. Through political alliances and campaigns it is possible, indeed essential, to ensure that lesbian and gay equality is an integral part of a united Europe. The political project of winning 'Equality in Europe' is going to become increasingly important in years to come, as more and more of the decisions which affect our lives are taken at the European level.[2]

There is, surely, much to be said for this strategy. Not surprisingly, it is one shared by just about all interest groups – be they farmers, consumers, ecologists and numerous others – who increasingly find in Brussels an important pressure point. Much of what we shall do in this Essay will be to review the legal elements of such a strategy in terms of what is already available under existing Community law and can already be used in the

---

1   This is an allusion to problems of implementation etc. but those problems emanating from Community law based rights are not qualitatively different from rights derived from national measures. If anything, sometimes community remedies are more effective.

2   Tatchell, 1992, 12.

interest of lesbians and gay men and what may be promising avenues for future praxis.

It would, however, be unfortunate, indeed wrong, if the Community-Lesbian and Gay *problematique* were construed, and presented, purely in utilitarian and clientalistic terms, identifying how Europe may be utilized to protect and advance lesbian and gay interests now and in its future evolution. After all, the underlying issues clearly cut in some ways far deeper than, say, the level of price support for mutton.

Another important layer is the discourse of Human Rights. The European Community is committed within its sphere of competence to ensuring the observance of fundamental human rights.[3] These rights, of which there is no direct mention in the original Treaties setting up the Community, go beyond the specific norms, duties and entitlements of Community law. They constitute, or at least are meant to constitute, an overarching canopy of protection which is an important part of the values that the new Europe professes.[4] Framing issues as human rights highlights their ethical dimension, converts transient interests into foundational claims and, often, forces a debate which is explicitly self-defining: Not simply a debate about who gets what in the Community, but one which defines what the Community is about.

This is a process which is not without its dangers. Prejudice and opposition towards lesbians and gays is frequently presented – and at times genuinely held – as a matter of moral conviction with the same self-defining commitment. To present the issue in foundational terms is to invite foundational opposition. It would be pointless, in an essay such as this, to rehearse the fundamental debate about homosexuality. But we shall devote considerable attention to the legal dimension of human rights claims, exploring, in the context of lesbian and gay issues, the reach and limits of available guarantees as well as the reach and limits of Community competence within which these guarantees must be found to be operational.

But even framing the issue in human rights terms may be limiting.

In the first place there is the by now well-established critique of rights philosophy which argues that rights philosophy is often premised on an atomistic, anti-communitarian view of the individual and society.[5] To those to whom the debate about the place of lesbians and gay men in

---

3   For a recent comprehensive analysis and description of the theme of human rights in the European Community see Cassese, Clapham, Weiler (eds), *European Union – The Human Rights Challenge* (1991).

4   On 12 April 1989 the European Parliament adopted a Declaration of Fundamental Rights and Freedoms, lending concrete expression to existing Community law. In its Preamble, the human rights discourse is stated as reaffirming '... the existence of a common legal tradition based on respect for human dignity and fundamental rights.'

5   See, e.g., Gabel, 1984.

society is not simply one of eliminating discrimination in the existing polity but of reconceiving human relations more generally, a rights-based discourse, whatever its short term gains, might be an uncomfortable strategic plank. Whilst we acknowledge the power and insight of this critique, we do not plan to deal with it in this programmatic essay. At the present stage of lesbian and gay legal protection in Europe, classical rights discourse and mobilization seem to us the most promising.[6]

But there is something else that does have a special European hue to it. One of the driving forces and advantages of, say, the Community's Cooperation and Development Policy towards the Developing Countries is its supposed 'newness', the Community as an historical *tabula rasa,* not encumbered by a colonial past, by a heritage of domination and exploitation. The rights-based discourse is similar. In some sense it is both universal – transcending space, and a-historical – transcending time. In this mode of thinking the lesbian and gay rights claim to equality, to inclusion on a same footing among other participants in the European construct, is couched in 'rational', principled, universal terms. And the Community, unencumbered by the heritage of prejudice and hatred and exclusion, is meant to respond because of the compelling, universal power of this rationality.

But this is only part of the picture. The 'newness' of Europe is a notion that can be taken only so far. The Community is distinct from its Member States. But at the same time it is its Member States. And there is a darker history and tradition which is as much a part of Europe's heritage as is, in the language of Parliament's Declaration of Fundamental Rights and Freedoms, the common '...tradition based on respect for human dignity and fundamental rights.' Consider the most dramatic dimension of this other tradition.

If one visits the museum currently situated in what was once the Auschwitz concentration camp one can see tables and matrices explaining the various combinations of coloured triangles which prisoners were required to stitch onto their striped pyjama-like uniforms. The Yellow Star of David is the most notorious. But there are others. For example, a pink triangle inverted over a red triangle denoted that the person incarcerated had been classified as both 'homosexual' and a 'political'; a yellow triangle together with an inverted green triangle would denote a 'criminal Jew'. These multicoloured Stars of David were tabulated so as to cover a large number of possible combinations including other categories such as Jehovah's Witnesses (purple), gypsies (brown) and antisocials (black). These badges were visible reminders of one's status in the camp. Top of the pile were usually

---

6   We perceive our essay as within the law reform tradition, a perception which has dictated both the structure and the genre of arguments we adopt.

green triangles (criminals) and apparently bottom of the heap were pink triangles (homosexuals).[7]

Let there be no confusion: we do not wish to suggest that today's
Community, nobly composed of yesteryear's enemies, indeed that anyone
in today's generation, has moral responsibility for those atrocities. Con-
structs which seek to confuse the oppressors, the torturers and the murderers
with their victims are alien to us.

But today's community and today's Community do have a responsibility which emanates from that past but which is rooted in our own actions
and inactions. It is the responsibility of recognition – of breaking a common tradition of silence, of *disrespect* of human dignity.

This responsibility has often been recognized. The human rights instruments adopted in the wake of the Second World War – and central among
them the entire apparatus of the European Convention on Human Rights –
are part of our response to that past. They contain explicit provisions protecting religious freedom, trade union and political activity, and ethnic minorities. And yet, no mention is made of sexual minorities – not surprising
if we consider that homosexuality (between men) remained for years a criminal offence in several European countries, the United States and Soviet
Russia. These particular victims of the holocaust remained relatively invisible.[8] Only in 1988 did the German Federal Government offer compensation
to homosexuals who had suffered in the concentration camps.

In the 1990's homosexuals are perceived less as a criminal class and
more as a non-ethnic minority. Nevertheless, very few international or constitutional instruments mention discrimination on grounds of sexual orientation.[9]

7   See Heinz Heger's account of life inside concentration camps such as Sachsenhausen
    (Heger, 1980) 'But the lowest of the low in this 'scum' were we, the men with the pink
    triangle', 33. See also Boisson, 1988. Although lesbians were not given pink triangles
    they were sometimes interned as 'anti-socials' and were similarly stigmatized both by
    the Nazis and some of the other prisoners. Schoppmann, 1991.
8   See Boisson, *supra*; only in 1984 was a plaque installed in the Mauthausen concentra-
    tion camp; In 1990 a monument commemorating the fate of homosexuals under the
    Nazis was unveiled in Bologna, see *Babilonia* June 1990, 'Un monumento gay', 28-9.
9   Explicit prohibitions against discrimination on grounds of sexual orientation can be
    found in the Quebec Charter of Human Rights and Freedoms, the Manitoba Human
    Rights Code and the Yukon Territory Human Rights Act. For a recent interpretation of
    the Canadian Charter of Rights and Freedoms which outlawed discrimination on
    grounds of sexual orientation see below section III.C.2.e. The draft Constitution for East
    Germany included a ban on disadvantage due to sexual orientation. The new Constitu-
    tion for the Brandenburg land now includes a similar ban. The Dutch Constitution in-
    cludes a ban on 'any grounds whatsoever' a phrase apparently inserted to include dis-
    crimination on grounds of sexual orientation.

The same silence is present in most governmental reports on the human rights situation in the world.[10] This is partly due to the impossibility of achieving consensus at the international level on this issue; religious and cultural differences across the world should not be underestimated.[11] But another factor is the way in which homosexuality is hidden, suppressed and *invisible.*

10   D.Y. Rist has pointed to the absence of any mention of 'terrorism' against homosexuals in the Country Reports on Human Rights Practices produced by the Department of State and submitted to the Committee on Foreign Relations of the US Senate and the Committee on Foreign Affairs of the House of Representatives. The State Department together with non-governmental organizations such as Amnesty International, the World Council of Churches and Human Rights Watch have apparently seen this subject as falling outside the scope of international norms. 'Homosexuals and Human Rights', *The Nation,* 9 April 1990, 482 ff. However, in its September 1991 International Council Meeting in Yokohama, Amnesty International expressly interpreted its mandate so as to include calling for the release of individuals who have been imprisoned solely because of their homosexuality, including the practice of homosexual acts in private between freely consenting adults; see *ILGA Bulletin* 4/91. According to a recent external document issued by an Amnesty International delegation to the Isle of Man 'Amnesty International has for many years opposed the violation of the fundamental human rights of homosexuals through its work to stop torture, cruel, inhuman and degrading treatment or punishment, the death penalty and extrajudicial execution by calling for the release as prisoners of conscience of people because of their advocacy of homosexual equality.' (EUR 45/WU 01/92 External, 21 February 1992). Most recently Amnesty International and the International Lesbian and Gay Association both took up the case of Vladimir Mironov, a Russian gay man, who had been sentenced to 3 years imprisonment for having sexual relations with a man. His appeal was successful on 17 March 1992. It is noteworthy that Amnesty International sent two delegates to the Isle of Man in the wake of a series of arrests and suicides related to the criminalization of homosexual relations there. *Gay Times,* March 1992, 5-6.

11   In 1991 the International Lesbian and Gay Association applied for consultative status (grade II) with the United Nations Economic Council. At the hearings before the 19 member committee Libya and Oman refused to vote in favour thus effectively blocking approval. The decision has been postponed for two years. However ILGA has now received consultative status with the UN Department for Public Information.
United Nations reports on sexual minorities have yet to be debated. The Economic and Social Council has called for a study of the legal and social problems of sexual minorities, Resolution 1983/30. The Sub-Commission on Prevention of Discrimination and Protection of Minorities requested the Secretary-General of the UN to make a study in resolution 1987/31. See the report prepared by Fernand-Laurant E/CN.4/Sub.2/1988/31, 13 June 1988. One might expect that the UN World Conference on Human Rights (Vienna, June 1993) will be confronted by the issue of lesbian and gay rights.
Note the partially dissenting opinion of Judge Walsh in the *Dudgeon v. United Kingdom* case, Series A, No. 45, paras. 14 and 15 as well as the dissenting opinion of Judge Zekia which starts: 'Christian and Moslem religions are all united in the condemnation of homosexual relations and sodomy.'
See also Jakobovits (former Chief Rabbi of Great Britain and the Commonwealth) 'Compassion, but we cannot condone evil', *Times,* 9 November 1987, 16: 'The Jewish view is plain and uncompromising. All the authentic sources of Judaism condemn homosexual relations as a heinous offence.' Jakobovits was speaking for the classical Orthodox tradition in organized Judaism. In the Conservative and Reform movements to which the vast majority of affiliated Jews in the United States belong, a different perspective prevails.

This *invisibility* affects both the reluctance of members of the legislature and judiciary to promote actively 'lesbian and gay rights' and the hidden nature of the victim's disadvantages. Lesbians or gay men are no longer 'branded' with the pink triangle of homosexuality. But to campaign actively may mean inviting enquiries or suppositions about one's own sexual preferences and private life. By contrast, if a *legislator* promotes special measures to protect children's, women's, Black or Asian interests they project their political or policy preferences, but no one questions whether or not they are a man or a woman, Black or White and so on.

On the other side of the fence the lesbian and gay *victims* of discrimination or other abuse may be forced to parade their private life in a sea of publicity in order to obtain redress. If a Black person is a refused a job on grounds of race, any ensuing complaint does nothing to publicize information about his or her love life. If a lesbian is refused a job because of her private life, the act of complaining may render more visible her 'handicap' in the employment sector, thereby reducing her chances of future employment with another employer.

The importance of the role of this visibility factor is currently highlighted by the controversial practice of 'outing'. American lesbian and gay-rights groups such as Queer Nation and Outpost have been publicizing the names of public figures who these organizations claimed were secret or closet lesbians or gay men.[12] The fact that 'outing' has been rejected in Europe as a useful tactic is one indication of the differences between the lesbian and gay movements in the United States and in Europe.[13] It also reminds us of the 'paradox' of being an 'invisible minority': 'gays cannot fight for the right to be open about being gay, unless gays are already open about it; and gays cannot reasonably be open about being gay, until gays have the right to be openly gay.'[14] Moreover, the feature about which one is talking about being open is an especially personal one – one's sexuality – not necessarily easily discussed in public. Other interest groups do not need to reveal their sexual preferences before gaining representation in the public world of politics.

12   See 'Out and About', *The Economist*, 27 July 1991, 37-8. In the United Kingdom one gay group threatened to publish the names of gay public figures. This threat, which was not carried out, was designed to highlight the level of hypocrisy surrounding the public approach to these private matters. Outing in the United States has named a Defense Department official and others but seems to have centered more on Hollywood names in order to promote positive images and role models for younger gays. Of course the radical gay movement has been triggered by the AIDS pandemic and the perceived inadequacy of society's and the government's response to it as it affects gay men.
13   For a suggestion that high-profile campaigning can have counterproductive effects, at least in the United Kingdom, see Jeffery-Poulter, 1991.
14   Mohr, 1988, 187.

The relationship of the Community to 'its past' is an altogether more complex matter than a *tabula rasa*. At its very formation we find a classic rendition of the mutual relationship between past and future. In the Preamble to the Treaty of Paris the Framers wrote:

> Resolved to substitute for age-old rivalries the merging of their essential interests, to create ... the basis for a broader and deeper community among peoples long divided by bloody conflict...

The Community *is* new and forward looking, but it is clearly directed by an acknowledgment of 'its past' – the past of its peoples.

We are acutely aware, as shall transpire, of the need of the Community to respect its proper province of activity. But, officially to toe the standard line that lesbian and gay concerns 'do not relate to spheres in which the [Community] is required to exercise its powers'[15] constitutes formidable self denial.

Our point now becomes clear. The deep reason and motive for a Community posture of inclusion, recognition and equality is not only because lesbian and gay men can claim Community based entitlements under, say, the provisions for free movement; nor because, as the guarantor of human rights within the sphere of application of its legal order, the Community owes a duty of protection to lesbians and gay men.

The deepest duty is of the Community to itself. Europe must respond, not simply to outside claims, when well founded, of gay men and lesbians, but to a deeper claim which emanates from within.

The reaffirmation of the common tradition based on respect for human dignity on which the Community justly prides itself, and which found expression in the very Preamble to Parliament's Declaration of Fundamental Rights and Freedoms, has no credibility if it is not accompanied – in word and deed – by an acknowledgment of a common tradition of continued oppression. The Pink Triangle is the sharpest reminder of this past oppression, but the oppression still persists in a present where silence, invisibility and exclusion pervade.

---

15   Written Question to the Council No. 2134/83, OJ 1984 C 152/25, 12.6.84.

II. The Legal Landscape

The landmass of lesbian and gay rights under Community law is not large and its boundaries are fuzzy and hard to map.

Crucially, at the time of writing, there are no Community provisions explicitly prohibiting discrimination on grounds of sexual orientation and other homophobic practices. The terrain of existing legal rights is, so to speak, submerged, embedded in a variety of Community law principles and legal provisions which, whilst not explicitly directed at lesbians and gay men may indirectly apply to them.

Our first task, therefore, will be to explore this submerged terrain and to map the potential of the existing law for vindicating lesbian and gay rights. Once the 'map' is in place, we shall pick some, but only some, of its central features for further in-depth analysis, especially where we feel the need to dispel misconceptions.

The importance of the 'map' is not, however, simply or even primarily, in providing a framework for the subsequent more detailed analysis in our own essay. The 'map' is really intended as a guide which, we hope, will help those active in the field who, both by research and by praxis – in litigation, lobbying and legislation, will be fixing real sign posts on the legal landscape.

A. The Existing Matrix of Community Law: The 'Map'

In this section we shall simply list the potential sources of Community law with which lesbians and gay men may seek directly to combat discrimination and homophobic practices. Then we shall review some of the linkages between the various sources. It is likely that these linkages will prove to be the most promising. The map of potential rights deriving from existing law will thus be established. The reader should be warned that, unfortunately, there is no 'neat' or 'tidy' schema for this presentation. The various provisions are messy; they are, typically, qualified by exceptions and derogations. Indeed, the principal justification for engaging in the tedium of such a listing is to try and put at least some order in the mess. Furthermore, when we say that these are *'potential* sources' we are not guilty of excessive lawyerly caution. None of these sources has yet been forged in the crucible of European Community authoritative judicial proceedings. And one can safely anticipate that anti-homosexual prejudice – conscious and subconscious – will also play its role and take its toll in the EC context as it has in other national and transnational legal and judicial fora.[16]

1. The Internal Market Provisions (Negative Integration)

At the core of Community law are those provisions – in the Treaty and secondary legislation – designed to ensure free movement of labour, services and establishment, goods and capital. These are the classical features of negative integration: They interdict Member State restriction on the movement of factors of production.

Lesbians and gay men who qualify as Community 'workers' or come under the freedom of establishment provisions, or are providers of services should be guaranteed free movement among the Member States. This would clearly apply in situations where homosexuality is incidental to the principal economic activity of the worker or provider of services, etc. Additionally, where homosexuality constitutes in itself an economic activity it should also qualify under the free movement provisions. Thus, for example, homoerotic goods, including publications and cinematographic materials, should be allowed free access to all Member State markets and, say, lesbian and gay commercial dating services should enjoy transnational access in the same way that heterosexual services enjoy these freedoms.

In some cases secondary Community legislation has amplified the basic Treaty rights. Most relevant in this context are the rights of workers to be joined by their spouses and dependents.[17] Unlike the 'principal' worker, the spouse or dependent need not qualify as a Community worker, by reference to nationality (they may be non-Community nationals) or by economic activity.

Whether or not lesbian and gay partners may qualify as spouses or dependents will surely be a hotly contested legal issue some aspects of which we shall explore later. The importance of this 'battle' for gay rights is double: Not only as a protection for individual cases, but also as a principled affirmation of the nature of homosexual relationships. The thrust of the argument for recognition will rest too, in its turn, on a double reasoning: first, that such affirmation is necessary to ensure the objective of free movement of workers, some of whom are lesbian and gay and to whom their partners stand in a similar relation as a traditional spouse or dependent; and second the argument will rest on human rights grounds.

---

16   For a very critical view of national judicial attitudes and also by the European Commission and European Court of Human Rights, see Betten, Chapter Fourteen, and Van Dijk, Chapter Six.

17   See discussion *infra*. See generally Burrows, 1987, esp. Part II.

The free movement provisions are not absolute: In the absence of Community harmonization measures, the Member States are allowed to derogate from them on the grounds of, for example, public morality, public policy, public health and the like.

Member States might thus seek to bar homoerotic goods on the grounds that they conflict with public morality; they might seek to interfere with the free movement of gay workers, as Bavaria attempted to do, on the grounds of public health; and they may seek to deny access of partners on the grounds of public policy.

This right of derogation is not absolute and is subject to restrictions under Community law and scrutiny by the European Court of Justice. In some cases, for example the free movement of workers, there are Community measures which set parameters for the usage of broad notions such as 'public policy'.[18] Even in the absence of such specific regulation, the usage of the derogation is subject to broader principles of Community law, most importantly the prohibition on discrimination on grounds of nationality, the doctrine of proportionality and, most recently violation of fundamental human rights.

Thus, for example, a Member State could not prohibit the commercial importation of homoerotic goods from another Member State on the grounds of protecting public morality if similar goods, of a national origin, may be marketed on the domestic market. We shall deal with the human rights restrictions below, after explaining the position of human rights within the Community legal order.

2. Community Social and other Policies (Positive Integration)

EC law is not limited to negative integration. The Treaty empowers the Community to set in place a whole range of policies the purpose of which is to further its broader socio-economic and political objectives.

(a) Equal treatment for men and women

Most pertinent, but ultimately probably illusive, are measures designed to combat gender discrimination. Whereas the Treaty itself only interdicts discrimination in pay between men and women, secondary legislation extends this protection to a much broader context of gender discrimination in the workplace. Most recently the Community adopted a non-binding code designed to combat sexual harassment in the workplace.[19]

---

18   See e.g. Council Directive 68/360/EEC OJ Sp. Ed. 1968 (II) p 485.
19   See Burrows, *op. cit.*, and see Commission Recommendation of 27 November 1991 on
       the protection of the dignity of women and men at work OJ 1992 L 49/1, 24.2.92 and

Council Directive 76/207 EEC[20] puts into effect in the Member States the principle of equal treatment for men and women as regards access to employment, including promotion, vocational training and working conditions. Though far from perfect, if its provisions were applicable to lesbian and gay discrimination it would represent a major advance. The provisions of the Directive clearly apply to trans-sexuals whose change of sex has been recognized legally.[21] At face value these provisions do not apply to anti-homosexual discrimination and whilst arguments can be made for interpreting them in a way which would cover such discrimination, we are not sanguine about the outcome should this ever be tested before the Court. The stakes are extremely high, since, after all, it is in the workplace that lesbians and gay men face the most widespread and economically devastating discrimination. Probably, the most important aspect of this Directive, for our purposes, is the fact of its enactment and the precedent it creates as regards Community competence to enact a similar provision to protect lesbians and gay men. The Directive goes well beyond an implementation or even amplification of the equal pay provisions in the Treaty. Significantly, the legal basis for the Directive is not drawn from the Social Policy of the Treaty but from Article 235 – its 'elastic clause'. As we shall argue, it would seem difficult to argue that ensuring equal treatment for men and women at the workplace is, in the language of Article 235, '... necessary to attain, in the course of the operation of the common market, one of the objectives of the Community...' and that ensuring similar equality for lesbians and gay men is, by contrast, outside the competence of the Community.

(b) Data protection

The Commission has proposed a Draft Council Directive concerning the protection of individuals in relation to the processing of personal data and a further draft Directive concerning the protection of personal data and privacy in the context of public digital telecommunications networks and public digital mobile networks.[22]

The economic logic of the Directives is classic: The functioning of the internal market requires

> ... not only that personal data should be able to flow freely, regardless of the Member States in which they are processed or requested, but also that fundamental rights should be safeguarded in view of the increasingly frequent recourse in

---

Council Resolution of 29 May 1990, OJ 1990 C 157/3, 17.6.90 and Council Declaration of December 19, 1991, OJ 1992 C 27/1, 4.2.92.

20 OJ 1976 L 39/40.

21 Written Question No. 1276/83, OJ 1984 C 24/39, 30.1.84.

22 COM (90) 314 final SYN 287 and 288 respectively. 13 September 1990.

the Community to the processing of personal data in the various spheres of economic and social activity.[23]

It is also acknowledged by the Commission that the right to privacy forms
part of '... the general principles of Community law.'[24]

We are unqualified to determine the extent to which the provisions of
the Draft Directives do indeed offer adequate protection for individuals in
this context. But the following should be noted: In its Explanatory Statement the Commission acknowledges that:

> ... there is a broad consensus among the Member States that there are certain cat-
> egories of data which, by virtue of their contents – quite irrespective of the con-
> text in which they are processed – carry the risk of infringing the data subject's
> right to privacy.[25]

Consequently, Article 17 of the Draft Directive classes as sensitive certain
categories of data concerning racial origin, including information on skin
colour, political opinions, health information and 'data concerning ... sexual life.'[26]

Articles 12 and 13 of the Proposal for the Directive concerning telecommunications networks, contain detailed provisions concerning the calling
line identification problem. These Articles provide for the operators of such
networks to allow the possibility of eliminating caller identification features because '... among other reasons, callers making calls to and from ...
[a variety of services] AIDS hot line' might '... have a legitimate concern
that this service feature may compromise their anonymity.'[27] The desire for
anonymity of callers to AIDS crisis centres often stems from the stigma of
homosexuality which is attached to AIDS in the public perception.

In our view the importance of these provisions goes beyond the specific
protection they may, if adopted, provide lesbians and gay men. In the first
place we have here a specific measure of Community law covering sexuality which incontrovertibly applies to lesbians and gay men. Secondly, there
is an acknowledgement that discrimination based on sexual life should feature alongside the more classical 'suspect classes' of race, religion, colour

---

23   COM (90) 314 final SYN 287 at 45.
24   At page 46.
25   COM (90) 314 final SYN 287 at 35.
26   Article 17 of the Draft Directive. The proposal also includes a Draft Resolution of the
      Representatives of the Governments of the Member States of the European Communities
      Meeting within the Council to the effect that the same principles should govern the in-
      ternal laws of the Member States in the field of Data Protection which fall outside the
      scope of Community law as well as a draft Commission Declaration about the applica-
      tion of the same principles to the Community institutions themselves. This latter Decla-
      ration is probably not strictly necessary from a juridical point of view, though as a mat-
      ter of policy and consciousness raising is important.
27   SYN 288 at 86.

and the like. The importance of this cannot be overestimated especially since the Commission brackets all of these under the category of privacy and explicitly states that this forms part of the general principles of Community law.

Once again the question of competence is important. In this respect there is something of a breakthrough: The proposed measure is enacted on the basis of Articles 100a and 113 – the classic provisions for achieving the internal market and the Common Commercial Policy. For the most part it deals with harmonizing disparate Member State regulations in this sphere. It recognizes that in this context human rights might be violated. It does not, then, leave such violations to be corrected by a complaint of an individual before the courts. The Commission accepts that in 'Communiterising' the field it has a responsibility to acknowledge the danger and legislatively act against it. Hence the reference to the sensitive classes, including sexual life. The very same rationale could and should apply to all other aspects of internal market policy where in the sphere harmonized by the Community (such as aspects of labour law, social security and the like) a potential for violation of human rights – including discrimination based on sexual life – may be encountered.

3. Fundamental Human Rights and Freedoms[28]

The Treaty – the Constitutional Charter of the Community – contains no 'bill of rights' which would act as a formal check on human rights abuses under Community law.[29] But, in an evolution which dates back to the 60s, fundamental human rights have been recognized by the Institutions of the Community as forming an integral part of the corpus of Community law. In particular, the Court of Justice has asserted repeatedly that part of its duty is to ensure observance of fundamental rights in the field of Community law. The judicial commitment is important since it hardens what could have been thought of as political hortatory statements into binding norms susceptible of juridical vindication.[30]

---

28   See Weiler, 'Methods of Protection: Towards a Second and Third Generation of Protec-
     tion', in Cassese, Clapham, Weiler (eds), *supra* note 6, 555-642; Gaja, 'Aspetti prob-
     lematici della tutela dei diritti fondamentali nell'ordinamento comunitario', *Rivista di
     diritto internazionale* (1988) 574-589; Foster, 'The European Court of Justice and the
     European Convention for the Protection of Human Rights', *Human Rights Law Journal*
     (1987) 245.
29   In its Preamble, the Single European Act provides:
     Determined to work together to promote democracy on the basis of the fundamental
     rights recognized in the constitutions and laws of the Member States, in the
     Convention for the Protection of Human Rights and Fundamental Freedoms and the
     European Social Charter, notably freedom, equality and social justice.
30   Whether or not the Court has actually lived up to its commitment to human rights is a
     matter of some controversy.

How does this broad commitment to human rights translate into concrete concepts which may be relevant to lesbian and gay rights?

The following is an itinerary which has to be traversed in order successfully to invoke the human right source.

(a) The sources of human rights protection

Given that the Treaty itself contains no explicit human rights protection, to which 'external sources' may one turn in seeking to come within those rights the observance of which the Court sees its duty to ensure?

The European Convention of Human Rights constitutes one clear bench mark which the European Court of Justice will always accept as binding within the field of Community law. Thus, any practice which violates the European Convention and especially those practices which the Convention organs – the Commission and Court of Human Rights in Strasbourg – have found to violate the ECHR will *ipso facto* be prohibited in the field of Community law. Examining the jurisprudence of the ECHR organs becomes critical.

Unlike the European Court of Justice, the Strasbourg organs, Commission and Court, have had the opportunity to pronounce directly on matters pertaining to lesbian and gay rights. The jurisprudence has been disappointing and regressive and has been criticized very severely by the leading authorities in the field of human rights.[31] We shall revisit some of this jurisprudence in a later section of our essay.

What, however, is the situation if discriminatory or homophobic practices are found, as indeed has been the case, by the ECHR organs *not to constitute a violation of the Convention*?

This need not necessarily be negative for the Community human rights issue. In the first place it would appear that whilst parties to the Convention may not apply it in a more restrictive way than the Strasbourg organs, they may, within their own legal order, give the Convention a more extensive interpretation than the Commission or Court of Human Rights. This principle should apply to the Community and the Court of Justice as well.

Secondly, on its own terms,

[n]othing in [the] Convention shall be construed as limiting or derogating from any of the human rights and fundamental freedoms which may be ensured under the laws of any High Contracting Party or under any other agreement to which it is a party.[32]

---

31   See Chapter Six by Van Dijk.
32   Article 60 ECHR.

The European Court of Justice too has made it clear that it does not see itself limited to the protection afforded by the European Convention on Human Rights. One may thus also look to the other sources of the European Court of Justice's human rights jurisprudence, principally the constitutional traditions common to the Member States and other international instruments binding on the Member States and, implicitly, on the Community. These may provide protection or guarantees which are not to be found in the ECHR.

While no easy demarcation of these rights is possible, a useful and recent codification, already cited approvingly by an Advocate General of the Court in a recent case,[33] is the Declaration of Fundamental Rights and Freedoms adopted by the European Parliament on April 12, 1989 which on its own terms is an expression of the human rights which derive from the Treaties themselves, the constitutional traditions common to the Member States and other international instruments in force binding the Member States and, implicitly, the Community.[34]

(b) Human rights rationae materiae

What is the material content of rights which may be relied upon in countering homophobic practices? Can such practices be construed as constituting violations of fundamental human rights?

Lesbian and gay rights have usually been explored under the right to privacy and its various derivatives. Privacy is clearly fundamental. We have seen some of its ramification in the field of data protection and we shall explore some of its further contours below. But privacy, at least in its classical formulation, has certain limitations. Typically it will protect behaviour – frequently considered deviant – which the State or other public authorities are called upon to 'tolerate' on the principle that obnoxious as it may be it should not be the subject of public regulation because it is 'private' or takes place in 'private'.

Protection rooted in such a rationale is considered only as a first step. It is often followed by a demand for a positive affirmation rather than toleration of the emancipating group. It is thus important to explore the more modern conceptions of privacy. Thus, for example, the European Parliament Declaration encapsulates such a modern conception in its right to privacy which reads:

33   Case C-159/90, *The Society for the Protection of Unborn Children (SPUC) v. Grogan* [1991] 3 CMLR 849.
34   'Le Parlement européen adopte la Déclaration suivante en tant qu'expression de ces droits...' Preamble. [The European Parliament, lending expression to these rights, hereby adopts the following Declaration].

1. Everyone shall have the right to respect and protection for *their identity*.
2. Respect for privacy and family life, reputation, the home and private correspondence shall be guaranteed.[35]

We shall return in the last section of this essay to the problematics of defining the rights by which homophobia should be countered. In addition to privacy, general non-discrimination clauses, gender discrimination clauses, family rights, and freedom of expression may prove useful. We shall also examine some of these other rights in greater detail below.

(c) Does Community law protection against violations of human rights apply merely to Community acts and agents or may the protection be extended vis-à-vis the Member States?

The formulation used by the European Court is that human rights may not be infringed in the field of Community law. In its most recent formulation, the European Court seems to have widened the formula:

> [M]easures which are incompatible with respect for human rights, which are recognized and guaranteed [under Community law] could not be admitted in the Community.[36]

The question thus is what may be included within '... the field of Community law' or 'in the Community.'

Clearly this formula covers any direct action taken by the Community itself, its institutions, organs and agents. Increasingly it may afford protection under acts taken by the Member States or their organs.

Thus, Member State acts implementing Community obligations or a Community policy will clearly be covered.[37] Even more importantly, the formula covers acts of Member States when operating within the Treaty derogations to the 'Free Movement' provisions of goods, labour, service, establishment and capital. In this respect protection against violations of human rights is like the principle of non-discrimination on grounds of nationality which we discussed above.

As mentioned, the Treaty prohibits (in varying degrees of strictness) state interference in the movement within the Common Market of these factors of production. It does allow, however, derogations to the Member States on grounds of public order, public security, public health and the like. In the recent *ERT* case, the Court stated that

---

35   Article 6 (emphasis added).
36   Case C-260/89, *Elliniki Radiophonia (ERT)* of June 18, 1991 (not yet reported) at para. 41 (unofficial translation).
37   Case 5/88, *Wachauf* [1989] ECR 2609 and Joined Cases 201-202/85, *Klensch* [1986] ECR 3477.

[w]hen a Member State invokes [derogations to free movement provisions] in order to justify rules which hinder the free movement ... this justification, which is provided for in Community law, must be interpreted in the light of general principles of law, notably fundamental rights. The national rules in question may only benefit from the [derogations] insofar as they are compatible with funda - mental rights, the observance of which the Court ensures.[38]

4. General Principles of Law

A further, hybrid, source of protection, often fruitful, is the concept of general principles of Community law. Some of these are explicit in the Treaty such as the aforementioned principle of non-discrimination on grounds of nationality which is mentioned in the Treaty itself. Others, such as *ne bis in idem, nulla poena sine lege,* non-retroactivity, legitimate expec- tation, legal certainty and the like are 'judge-made', culled from the legal traditions of the Member States and public international law, and as such resemble the human rights law *stricto sensu.*[39] The most interesting and in- tricate is the principle of non-discrimination. The Court has stated that the '... principle of equality ... is one of the fundamental principles of Commu- nity law. This principle requires that similar situations shall not be treated differently unless differentiation is objectively justified.'[40]

As with human rights, the critical issue here will be to define the sphere of application of Community law within which this principle is to operate. It does not apply in the private sphere if not specifically covered by a Community norm (such as the gender discrimination directives) nor does it apply to acts of Member States, including discrimination against lesbians and gay men, if the Member State is not applying Community law or op- erating within one of the derogations to free movement.

B. Competence of the Community to Legislate Specifically Against Discrimination of Lesbians and Gay Men

How far may the Community go in introducing legislation against discrim- ination of lesbians and gay men, especially in the workplace? The follow- ing reply, quoted *in extensu* and typical of many similar replies,[41] was

---

38 *ERT* at para. 43 (unofficial translation).
39 See generally, Schermers & Waelbroeck, 1992, 36 et seq.
40 Case 117/76, *Ruckdeschel* [1977] ECR 1769, para. 7.
41 For Council view see, e.g., Reply to Written Question 2134/83, OJ 1984 C 152/25, 12.6.84 'The question ... does not relate to the spheres in which the Council is required to exercise its powers.' It could be argued that in this question at least the possibility of action, even if not required, was not excluded.

given in May 1990 to just this issue raised by a question to the Commission in the European Parliament:[42]

> The Community has no powers to intervene in possible cases of discrimination practiced by Member States against sexual minorities. The powers deriving from the Treaties allow the Community to intervene only in respect of discrimination on the grounds of nationality or in order to ensure equal treatment for male and female workers in the fields of labour relations and social security.
>
> The preamble to the Community Charter of Fundamental Social Rights of Workers recalls that, in order to ensure equality of treatment, discrimination in whatever form should be combated, 'particularly discrimination on grounds of sex, colour, race, opinion or creed.'
>
> In the Action Programme it submitted in December 1989 following the adoption of the Social Charter, the Commission stated that: 'while it is not making a proposal in respect of discrimination on the grounds of race, colour or religion, it nonetheless stresses the need for such practices to be eradicated, particularly at the workplace and in access to employment, through appropriate action by the Member States and by the two sides of industry.'
>
> The fundamental rights of sexual minorities are protected by other international instruments. Since all the Member States are members of the Council of Europe and signatories to the European Convention on Human Rights, the Commission and the Court of Human Rights are best able to guarantee the protection of sexual minorities against discrimination.

In many of its aspects, some of which we have already alluded to above, this statement is an inaccurate account of the law, in particular the assertion that '[t]he powers deriving from the Treaties allow the Community to intervene only in respect of discrimination on the grounds of nationality or in order to ensure equal treatment for male and female workers in the fields of labour relations and social security.'[43] The powers deriving from the Treaty allow the Community to do a great deal more – should the political will exist.

The response is, nonetheless, an important statement since it illustrates a prevailing view in Community circles. The reluctance of the Council to espouse lesbian and gay rights in their legislative programme cannot be simply attributed to personal and institutional prejudice, though this clearly may be a part of the story. Neither can this reluctance be explained simply by the politicians' fear of being associated with gays and lesbians – though this too will be part of the explanation. There is a broader political

---

42   Question No. 121 (H-594/90), Debates of the European Parliament No. 3-390/258, 16.5.90.

43   One could perhaps try and read the Commission reply as meaning that the 'actual' powers which have been exercised under the Treaty do not allow intervention, without excluding the possibility of exercising further powers. But given that the Question specifically asked whether the Treaty '... provide[s] a legal basis for outlawing discrimination against lesbians and gay men in the workplace' this benign construction is hardly tenable. It would seem as if the Commission, at that time at least, excluded the possibility of direct action.

dimension here that lesbian and gay rights activists must take into account and which we must present as part of the general 'map.'

The question of Community intrusiveness into the social and political fabric of the individual Member States is an issue which has emerged with increasing acuteness since the adoption of the Single European Act and in the process leading to the conclusion of the Maastricht Treaty and its ratification in the Member States. The sensitivity to intrusiveness derived, in part, from the shift to majority voting which excluded the control, or the feel of control, of individual Member States over the Community legislative output. The feeling that Community intrusiveness must be controlled led to the enactment of Article 3b in the new Maastricht Treaty – the famous *subsidiarity clause*. We shall deal shortly with the legal aspects of subsidiarity in relation to lesbian and gay rights, but the main thrust of the concept is not its legal limits but the expression it gives to a widely shared opposition to excessive Community intervention and activism.

Independently of the merits, it is our view that specific legislation to counter anti-homosexual discrimination will be perceived, and touted, as an example of Community legislative excess. For better or for worse, a vigorous campaign for anti-homosexual legislation will put those who prosecute such a campaign very clearly on one side of the debate between minimalists and maximalists of European Community power. This does not mean that such a campaign should not be undertaken. (Especially since in fact and in law such Community legislation will not be exceptional compared to other provisions of Community law.) But its political implications should be understood.

Has, then, the Community the legal competence to legislate against anti-homosexual discrimination?

When legislation is not directly mandated by the Treaty, as, for example, in the area of Competition, the Community is empowered to act when it can be shown that such legislation is necessary to further the realization of Community objectives. If specific powers are not available, legislation may be based on Article 235. Over the years, the Community and its Member States have taken a broad and expansive approach to the question of competence, an approach which has been sanctioned by the Court.[44] Whatever one may think about the wisdom and desirability of the expansive approach, it would be unacceptable to apply a different, more strict, legal test to the question of lesbian and gay rights.

If Maastricht eventually enters into force, there will be a second hurdle to pass. Even where the Community could be shown to have the competences to act in a certain field as a means of furthering its objectives,

---

44   See Weiler, 'The Transformation of Europe', 100 *Yale Law Journal* 2403-2483.

legislation will have to be subject to the test of subsidiarity. Article 3b (Maastricht) provides:

> The Community shall act within the limits of the powers conferred upon it by this Treaty and of the objectives assigned to it therein.
> In areas which do not fall within its exclusive competence, the Community shall take action, in accordance with the principle of subsidiarity, only if and in so far as the objectives of the proposed action cannot be sufficiently achieved by the Member States and can therefore, by reason of the scale or effects of the proposed action, be better achieved by the Community.
> Any action by the Community shall not go beyond what is necessary to achieve the objectives of this Treaty.

We shall have to see therefore what type of legislation may satisfy the requirement of Subsidiarity.

1. Objectives of the Treaty

In the Preamble to the proposed Data Protection Directive to which we have already alluded, the Commission usefully summarizes the objectives of the Community for the purpose of legislative enactments. These include

> ... establishing an ever closer union among the peoples of Europe, fostering closer relations between States belonging to the Community, ensuring economic and social progress by common action to eliminate the barriers which divide Europe, encouraging the constant improvement of the living conditions of its peoples, preserving and strengthening peace and liberty and promoting democracy on the basis of the fundamental rights recognized in the constitutions and laws of the Member States and in the European Convention for the Protection of Human Rights and Fundamental Freedoms;

The European Court of Justice has given an even broader definition of objectives in the context of legislative competence including among them the creation of a citizens' Europe.[45]

More specifically, there is the economic objective of establishing and rendering functional the internal market in which there will be, in accordance with Article 8a of the Treaty, the free movement of the factors of production. It is now accepted that, in that sphere, fundamental human rights must be safeguarded.

Finally, it is already part of Community orthodoxy to accept that the 'Social Dimension' of Europe as embodied in such instruments as the 1974 Social Action Programme and the more recent Community Charter of the Fundamental Social Rights of Workers, is as important a part of the Community agenda as is the economic objectives narrowly defined.

---

45   Case 242/87, *Commission v. Council (Erasmus)* [1989] ECR 1425, paras. 29 and 35.

How does this translate into legislative competence for anti-lesbian and gay discrimination?

Although the very broad definition of objectives listed above seems almost open-ended and able to include any statal activity, practice has been to relate novel Community policies, even indirectly, to its core socio-economic functions.[46] Thus, barring Treaty amendment, the Community does not have the competence to enact a *global* measure interdicting discrimination against lesbians and gay men. Such a measure would have to be situated within the sphere of objectives and activities of the Community however broadly defined. But it is relatively easy to show that it does have competence to enact such legislation within the reach of its activities.

Lesbians and gay men are part of the workforce of Europe. Discrimination against them in the area of free movement obstructs and deters their mobility in exactly the same way that gender discrimination obstructs and deters the mobility of female workers. Additionally, if, indeed, discrimination against lesbians and gay men is a violation of their rights, then, to the extent and within the boundaries that Community law governs their mobility and other economic activity within Europe, the Community would have a clear competence to protect them against violation of these rights.[47] A similar logic would apply across the internal market landscape. If the Community harmonizes in the field of professional training, recognition of diplomas, driving licenses and the like, thereby bringing these under the canopy of Community law, it could surely outlaw such discrimination against homosexuals that affects the substantive objectives of each of these policies and compromises fundamental rights – if that indeed be the case.

We have already mentioned that it would be difficult to construe Directive 76/207/EEC on Equal Treatment for Men and Women as Regards Access to Employment, Vocational Training and Promotion and Working Conditions as applying to lesbians and gay men. Be that as it may, we cannot see any reasonable argument which could explain why the Community would have the competence to enact legislation implementing the principle of equal treatment to men and women in the workplace, and to issue a Commission Recommendation, Council Resolution and Council Declaration[48] on the protection of the dignity of women and men at work,

---

46   As a matter of legal realism, there is a greater credibility and chance of acceptance for expansion arguments which link to the core, rather than those which rest solely on the meta-political objectives.

47   In reply to Question No. 14 (H-245/85), Commissioner Sutherland affirmed the Commission view that '... dismissal on the grounds of any aspect of an employee's private life is unacceptable in principle.' Debates of the European Parliament No. 2-328/164, 11.7.85.

48   Commission Recommendation of 27 November 1991 on the protection of the dignity of women and men at work, OJ 1992 L 49/1, 24.2.92; Council Resolution of 29 May 1990 on the protection of the dignity of women and men at work, OJ 1990 C 157/3, 27.6.90;

including a code of practice to combat sexual harassment, and not to include, in these instruments, on the same footing, protection against unequal treatment and harassment of lesbians and gay men. In particular it cannot be argued that gender discrimination is mandated because of Article 119 EEC, since that Article is quite clearly limited to the notion of equal pay. As we mentioned, this was acknowledged by the choice of legal basis for the Equal Treatment Directive, namely Article 235. Extending protection against discrimination against lesbians and gay men would not constitute a major constitutional expansion of Community competences. The important constitutional move took place decades ago with the adoption of the 1974 Social Action plan when it was accepted that certain features of the working environment are a legitimate matter for Community legislation. Putting protection against lesbians and gay men in the workplace on an equal footing to protection against gender discrimination may be politically more sensitive, but legally it would be as mundane as an inclusion of protection for the disabled or the aged.

2. Subsidiarity

The philosophy of subsidiarity is that even if the Community would have legislative competence, this should be exercised only if and in so far as the objectives of the proposed action cannot be sufficiently achieved by the Member States and can therefore, by reason of the scale or effects of the proposed action, be better achieved by the Community.

There is of course no hard legal experience with the operation of this principle. Many regard it as juridically unenforceable and a mere platitude.[49] This is not the place for a lengthy exegesis of Article 3b as inserted by the Maastricht Treaty. We would limit ourselves to one fundamental point. Subsidiarity should not be used as a foil, a ploy, to justify inaction in the field of lesbian and gay rights. There should, in other words, be no discrimination in the use of subsidiarity itself. The scale of discrimination against lesbians and gay men in the workplace and in other spheres of economic activity is a common place. Indeed, what is known and documented[50] is probably the tip of the iceberg. Our argument thus is simple, and reflects our previous reasoning in relation to objectives: If it is acceptable, also in terms of subsidiarity, for the Community to act in the field of sexual harassment, or disability, or youth, lesbian and gay rights should

Council Declaration of 19 December 1991 on the implementation of the Commission recommendation on the protection of the dignity of women and men at work, including the code of practice to combat sexual harassment OJ 1992 C 27/1, 4.2.92.

49   For discussion see Snyder, Jacqué & Weiler, 'On the Road to European Union – A New Judicial Architecture: An Agenda for the Intergovernmental Conference', 27 *CML Rev.* (1990) 185.
50   Cf. Betten, Chapter Fourteen.

not be considered as somehow different and left to action or inaction by the Member States.

We can take this point one step further. Set against a heightened awareness of the Social Dimension of Europe and the drive of the Community to redress the social as well as the economic balance, the pointed exclusion of any explicit Community commitment towards lesbian and gay rights contributes in itself to a legitimation of discrimination and harassment. Not to act, is to act.

III. Going Beyond the Map: Cases and Controversies

Having set out the schematic 'map' of lesbian and gay rights under Community law, we wish to examine, in greater detail, some of the principal landmarks on that 'map'. Whilst some repetition is unavoidable, we hope that in the concrete and detailed analysis of some of the concepts we shall be able to enrich discussion and set aside misconceptions and possible objections to the directions which the map points to. In particular the following analysis will help show how the different elements of the map actually translate into concrete legal rights.

A. Rights Which Can be Used Against the European Community

1. Rights for Community Employees and their Dependents

Until now, we have presented the matrix of Community law in a kind of hierarchical vacuum. But it is probably fair to state that there exists a hierarchy of protection in the Community legal order depending on who the violator of the rights is. One can expect, in theory, the highest protection when complaining against the Community itself. Community employees have been granted anti-discrimination rights which go beyond the rights enumerated in the Treaty of Rome and the various pieces of secondary legislation which cover discrimination.[51] Therefore, there is room for generous interpretations so as to minimize discrimination against Community employees with same-sex partners. Allowances such as those benefits paid following the death of a Community employee may be extendable to the partners of lesbian and gay staff members. The actual acquired rights will depend on the particular provision of the Staff Regulations etc. at issue, and whether the relevant Community Court is prepared to extend its

---

51 For a judgment by the European Court of Justice (ECJ) which went beyond the rights derived from 'written Community law' see Joined Cases 75 and 117/82, *Razzouk and Beydoun v. Commission* [1984] ECR 1509, paras. 16-19. This case concerned widowers' benefits where the deceased had worked for the Commission.

commitment to protecting sexual equality beyond the limits of Article 119 EEC so as to cover equality in questions of sexual orientation.

The point is that in this area there is no need for the Court to allow Member States a margin of discretion. Nor does the Court need to consider arguments based on limitation clauses in provisions such as Articles 48(3) and 56(1) EEC. These clauses are designed to allow States some discretion over matters of *national* concern, and, where moral and cultural standards have been in issue, the European Court of Justice has veered towards allowing Member States an important area of discretion though, as indicated above, even in this area the European Court will scrutinize for violation of fundamental human rights.[52] This has certainly been the approach of the European Court of Human Rights,[53] which, of course, only deals with applications against states. This last court never deals with the rights of employees of the Council of Europe or the compatibility of Council of Europe 'legislation' with the Convention. So its case-law only reflects the burden it is ready to place on a Contracting State of the Council of Europe rather than on an intergovernmental organization. But, although the European Court of Human Rights has shown states some deference when the issue of a European standard of obscenity has appeared,[54] the European Court of Human Rights has not permitted States to carve out matters of homosexuality as a no-go area. In two cases, *Dudgeon v. United Kingdom,*[55] and *Norris v. Ireland*[56] the European Court of Human Rights found that criminalizing legislation for homosexual sex among two consenting adults over the age of 21 violated Article 8 of the European Convention on Human Rights (ECHR).

Therefore, should a case concerning discrimination by the Community against a Community employee on grounds of that person's homosexuality come to be considered by the Court of First Instance of the Community, and eventually by the European Court of Justice, those Courts could afford to offer the highest level of protection in this area. There is no need to follow the path of cautious federalism for fear of treading on the toes of Member States. There is no need to find consensus or evidence of common constitutional traditions. Nor is there a need to allow any sort of margin of discretion as there is no risk of usurping a Supreme Court or national

52   See the ECJ's approach in Case 41/74, *Van Duyn v. Home Office* [1974] ECR 1337 (attempted entry to UK of a practising scientologist).
53   See generally Macdonald, 'The Margin of Appreciation and the Case-Law of the European Court of Human Rights', *Collected Courses of the Academy of European Law* (1990) Vol. I Book 2 95-161. Note the discussion of the Court's case-law regarding Article 8 ECHR 130-139.
54   See the *Müller and Others case,* Series A, No. 133, and the *Handyside case*, Series A, No. 24.
55   Series A, No. 45.
56   Series A, No. 129.

legislature. But the standards which the Community's institutions will seek to apply are, as yet, rather underdeveloped. The introduction of an Article in the Treaty on European Union demanding that the European Union respect fundamental rights can only serve to bolster the European Court of Justice's resolve to afford the highest form of protection in this field.[57]

2. The Community's Joint Declarations on Human Rights (1977) and Racism and Xenophobia (1986)

There is very little indication as to the Community's *own* policy on human rights. However, the commitment of the Commission, Parliament and Council of Ministers to be bound by 'fundamental rights' contained in their Joint Declaration of 5 April 1977 states in its second paragraph:

> In the exercise of their powers and in the pursuance of the aims of the European Communities they respect and will continue to respect these rights.[58]

Similarly, in a second Joint Declaration, on racism and xenophobia, these Community institutions joined with the Representatives of the Member States meeting within the Council to:

1. *vigorously condemn* all forms of intolerance, hostility and use of force against persons on the grounds of racial, religious, cultural, social or national differences;
2. *affirm their resolve* to protect the individuality and dignity of every member of society and to reject any form of segregation of foreigners;[59]

The Declaration finishes by stressing the 'need to ensure that all acts or forms of discrimination are prevented or curbed'. Although these statements are made in the context of racism and xenophobia, the reference to the 'individuality and dignity of every member of society' is worth recalling, as is the condemnation of all forms of intolerance, hostility and use of force against persons on grounds of cultural or social differences.

---

57   Article F(2) of the Treaty states: 'The Union shall respect fundamental rights as guaran-teed by the European Convention for the Protection of Human Rights and Fundamental Freedoms and as they result from the constitutional traditions common to the Member States as general principles of Community law.'
The Union Treaty is expected to enter into force during 1993 following ratification by all 12 Member States. For examination of the issues of competence and subsidiarity under the new Union Treaty see Chapter Eight by Snyder, Somsen and Hoyer.
58   The first paragraph reads: 'The European Parliament, the Council and the Commission stress the prime importance they attach to the protection of fundamental rights, a derived in particular from the constitutions of the Member States and the European Convention for the Protection of Human Rights and Fundamental Freedoms.' OJ 1977 C 103/1. See also the European Council Declaration of 7 and 8 April 1979. Both Declarations are re-produced in Clapham, 1991, 154, 160.
59   OJ 1986 C 150/01, also reproduced in Clapham, 1991, 163.

Considering the apparent rise in attacks on gay men and lesbians, another Joint Declaration may now be appropriate. Such a Declaration could build on the Parliamentary Declaration which 'deplores all forms of discrimination based on an individual's sexual tendencies'.[60] Such a Joint Declaration could be more than merely symbolic. First, action against discrimination and homophobia could be followed up in the same way that the Community's response to racism and xenophobia is.[61] Secondly, such a Declaration could eventually serve as a point of reference for either the Court of First Instance or the Court of Justice.[62] But even in the absence of such a Declaration, the judicial organs of the Community could well find that Human Dignity and the individual's right to respect for his or her identity – two basic concepts which receive expression in the European Parliament Declaration of Fundamental Rights and Freedoms, are sufficient to hold the Community and its organs to the highest standards in this respect.

B. Review of Community Provisions for Conformity With General Principles of Law

To what extent may one use the principle of equality under Community law in a concrete situation of anti-homosexual discrimination? The most promising prospect would be in the case of discrimination by the Community itself. The general principle of equality, as explained above, only operates in the sphere of application of Community law. Demarcation problems would be complex if applied to action of Member States, but absent if applied to the Community itself.

A successful challenge to a Community provision on the grounds that it treats gay men or lesbians in an unequal way from heterosexuals would have to show that the difference in treatment had no objective justification which was proportionate to the end to be achieved. Therefore, a challenge under the general principle of equality would not have to point to a specific Community provision which offered protection against discrimination on grounds of sexual orientation. If in staff regulations, or elsewhere, lesbians and gay men received different treatment, the Community would be pressed to explain why their homosexuality constituted a meaningful justifiable

---

60　Paragraph 2 of the Resolution adopted at the time of the Squarcialupi Report. OJ 1984 C 104/46. See also the European Council Declaration on Racism and Xenophobia, 9-10 December 1991.

61　See the Evrigenis Report, OJ C 36/142; the Ford Report, Parl doc. A3-195/90 ' *The Findings of the Committee of Inquiry into Racism and Xenophobia*'; and the Parliamentary Resolutions adopted in Plenary in October 1990, B3-1721/90 and B3-1722/90.

62　For cases where the ECJ has referred to the 1977 Declaration on Fundamental Rights see Case 44/79, *Hauer* [1979] ECR 3727, para. 15; Case 222/84, *Johnston* [1986] ECR 1651, at 1682, para. 18.

reason for different treatment. The ECJ has applied this equality principle to glucose producers' claims to equality with sugar producers.[63] In the *Cousin* case[64] the Court had to deal with a challenge to a Commission Regulation determining the rule of origin of certain cotton yarns. It was shown that the criteria adopted by the Commission differed from its own other, more favourable, regulation applicable to woven yarn. Since the Commission could not show an objective justification for the different treatment, the regulation was held to be discriminatory and consequently was annulled.

Similarly, in a recent case before the European Court of Human Rights the Court held that a Member State had violated Article 14 ECHR by discriminating between people registered as resident and those not so registered and that this discrimination had no legitimate aim under the Convention.[65] The point is that the absence of a specific prohibition on discrimination against gay men and lesbians does not prevent a challenge to Community provisions under the general equality principle.

Furthermore, while the review on general principles of law is confined to *Community provisions* there is no reason why the Community should not impose more progressive standards than those common to all the Member States or contained in international instruments. This the ECJ did in the *Orkem* case where the Court declared that companies have the right not to incriminate themselves in response to questioning by the Commission.[66] In this area the ECJ need not, and should not, follow the approach of the European Court of Human Rights in allowing a margin of appreciation to Member States.[67] It need not because it is not interfering with a Member State's discretion to pass national legislation or adjudicate cases under national law. It should not because once the Community provisions have been adopted it is exclusively for the European Community's Court of Justice to interpret those provisions. While the European Court of Justice may be inspired by fundamental rights it cannot leave the validity of the provision in question to the national court in the same way that the European Court of Human Rights does.[68]

63   Cases 103 & 145/77, *Royal Scholten-Honig Holdings Ltd v. Intervention Board for Agricultural Produce* [1978] ECR 2037.
64   Case 162/82, *Paul Cousin and others* [1983] ECR 1101
65   *Darby case*, judgment of 23 October 1990, Series A, No. 187.
66   Case 374/87, *Orkem v. Commission*, judgment of 18 October 1989.
67   See the section below on discrimination for more detail on the case-law concerning the homosexuals age of consent. For an in depth analysis of the way in which the margin of appreciation doctrine has been applied by the European Court and Commission of Human Rights to the question of the age of consent for homosexuals see Helfer, 1990.
68   As stated at the end of section III.A.1. the entry into force of the European Union Treaty and the duty to respect fundamental rights contained therein should not prevent the European Court of Justice from ensuring compliance with general principles of Community

C. Rights Enforceable Against the State and its Emanations Operating Within the Scope of Community Law

The big difference between this category and the previous one is that where the behaviour of *national authorities* is involved, it is essential to show that the case falls within the scope of Community law and that the Member State is under a Community obligation. Should the case lie outside the scope of Community law the appropriate remedy will merely lie in the national courts or with the European Commission and Court of Human Rights in Strasbourg. It would not be appropriate to enter into a lengthy discussion on when the ECJ will demand that national authorities act in accordance with human rights.[69] Where the issue is connected to national provisions which implement Community provisions, or where one party is relying on a provision of Community law, then national authorities have to apply the law so as that it conforms with fundamental rights. And this application will be controlled by the ECJ.

It would be misleading to speculate as to the level of protection offered by the ECJ. One cannot simply state that the Court offers a maximum standard or a minimum standard inspired by various constitutions from the Member States. Everything depends on the context. When faced with public policy questions touching on cultural or religious matters Member States may be allowed a greater area of discretion than where natural justice procedural rights concerning merger control are involved.[70] According to Jörn Pipkorn, the ECJ's enthusiasm for Community procedural rights stems from its self-interest in ensuring that it does not have to examine in great detail cases which eventually come before it. By demanding high standards from the Commission and national authorities the Court can confine itself to points of Community law and avoid having to scrutinize complex sets of facts.[71]

Let us now examine in greater detail some of the concrete issues we mentioned briefly in setting out the map.

---

law even where they are not common to *all* the constitutional traditions of *all* the Member States.

[69] See generally, Weiler, in Cassese, Clapham, Weiler (eds), *supra* note 6, Vol. II 555-642, esp. 565-615; and Clapham, 1991, 29-62; see also Mancini, 'Robert Schuman Lecture on Community Law', in *Collected Courses of the Academy of European Law* (1990) Vol. I Book 1.

[70] See the *Van Duyn*, *Cinéthèque* cases (*supra*) and compare *Orkem*, *Johnston* (right to a tribunal in administrative matters upheld whereas this is not guaranteed under the ECHR or common constitutional traditions) (*supra*) and see Case C-159/90, *SPUC v. Grogan et al.*, 4 October 1991, *supra* note 33..

[71] 'La protection des droits fondamentaux dans l'ordre juridique de la communauté européenne', exposé lors de la 'Table ronde sur la protection juridique des interêts financiers de la communauté' Cambridge 14 March 1991.

1. Free Movement of Community Workers

Community law grants nationals of Member States the right to enter and seek or take up work in another Member State (Article 48 EEC).[72] Limitations can be imposed by national authorities on grounds of public policy, public security and public health.[73] But these limitations must be *justified*, although Member States are free in principle 'to determine the requirements of public policy in the light of their national needs',[74] such a justification is reviewable by the European Court of Justice. Furthermore the limitations on the fundamental Community freedom must be interpreted strictly and must be no more than is necessary for the protection of those interests in a democratic society.[75] The limitations may not operate so as to impose different conditions on nationals of the Member State concerned when compared to nationals of other Member States seeking, or taking up employment.[76] So, even where repressive measures such as fines or eviction are adopted against a State's own nationals, that State may not *expel* nationals from other States as the measures cannot be considered equal.[77] As

---

72   The position of non-Community workers falls outside the scope of this section. Their rights will be covered by national law or public international law. Even where there is an association agreement such as the EC-Turkey agreement the rights contained therein may not be directly effective and hence outside the scope of Community law and so out-side the sphere of Community human rights protection. See Case 12/86, *Demirel* [1987] ECR 3719, at 3754:

> [T]here is at present no provision of Community law defining the conditions in which Member States must permit the family reunification of Turkish workers lawfully settled in the Community. It follows that the national rules at issue in the main proceedings did not have to implement a provision of Community law. In those circumstances, the Court does not have jurisdiction to determine whether national rules such as those at issue are compatible with the principles enshrined in Article 8 of the European Convention on Human Rights.

On the position of non-nationals see Hoogenboom in Cassese, Clapham, Weiler (eds), *supra* note 6, Vol. II, 351-418. This report also covers the rights of asylum seekers and refugees.

73   Directive 64/221 contains details of the permissible scope of these limitations. Article 3(2) states that previous criminal convictions cannot, in themselves, constitute grounds for taking measures under Article 48(3) EEC. The Annex to the Directive contains a list of the *only* disabilities and diseases which may justify refusal at entry or the refusal of a first residence permit. Article 4(2) states that diseases or disabilities which occur after the first residence permit has been granted are not grounds for refusal of a renewal of the permit or for deportation. See generally Steiner, 1990, 203-209; for the question of whether HIV or AIDS comes within the scope of the Annex see Harris and Haigh (eds), 1990, 112-113. They conclude that these diseases do not come within the scope of the Annex.

74   Case 36/75, *Rutili v. Minister for the Interior* [1975] ECR 1219, at 1231 para. 26.

75   *Rutili*, paras. 27 and 32. See also Case 30/77, *Bouchereau* [1977] ECR 1999, at 2013, where the ECJ added that the notion of public policy implies a threat affecting one of the fundamental interests of society.

76   See Article 10 of Regulation 1612/68 and Joined Cases 115 and 116/81, *Adoui and Cornuaille v. Belgium* [1982] ECR 1665; and Case 249/86, *Commission v. F.R.G. (Re Migrant Workers)* [1989] ECR 1263.

77   See *Bouchereau* (*supra*).

long as nationals are not subjected to the proposed penalty it will remain a breach of Community law when imposed on nationals of other Member States.

2. Acquired Rights for Lesbian or Gay Members of the Worker's Family

Article 10 of Regulation 1612/68 defines the members of a worker's family entitled to the Community right to install themselves with a worker who is a national of a Member State employed in another Member State. The Article covers the worker's spouse, their descendants under 21, descendants who are dependents, dependent relatives in the ascending line of the worker and his or her spouse.

Anyone, whatever their nationality, falling into one of these categories has the right to install themselves with the worker and benefit from various privileges under Regulation 1612/68, Regulation 1251/70 and Directive 68/360.[78]

(a) Does the term 'spouse' include same-sex partners?

In the *Netherlands v. Reed*[79] the European Court of Justice considered whether the term 'spouse' included a cohabitee. Although the Court held that *in the present state of Community law* the term spouse included only marital relationships, it was found that national workers (i.e. Dutch workers) were allowed to reside with their alien cohabitants in *stable relationships*. Therefore the unmarried British couple in this case was allowed to reside in the Netherlands. To have held otherwise would have resulted in discrimination between Dutch workers and other Community workers.[80]

It would seem that where a Member State allows a right to reside to same-sex alien cohabitants of its own nationals, then, same-sex partners of workers from other Member States gain a similar residence right should their partner move to that Member State. Should the above conditions apply, there may not even be an obligation actually to cohabit.[81]

(b) Dependents

As stated above, descendant and ascendant dependents of the worker and his/her spouse are entitled as of right to install themselves with the worker.

---

78 For the proposals by the European Parliament and the Commission to extend the scope of this legislation see Chapter Twelve by Jesserun d'Oliveira.
79 Case 59/85 [1986] ECR 1283.
80 Note the discrimination is not between the cohabitants nor between married couples and non-married couples. For further discussion see also Chapter Fifteen by Emmert.
81 See Case 267/83, *Diatta v. Land Berlin* [1985] ECR 567.

More complicated is the discretionary scope of Article 10(2) of Regulation 1612/68 which states:

> Member States shall facilitate the admission of any member of the family not coming within the provisions of paragraph 1 if dependent on the worker referred to above or living under his roof in the country whence he comes.

It is suggested that same-sex partners are included in this category of persons. Although this paragraph refers to the 'family', the paragraph is not concerned with wives, husbands, children and parents as these are covered by paragraph 10(1) so we can infer that people outside the nuclear family are to be included. The two alternative qualifications are that the person must be *dependent on the worker*, or *living under his or her roof in the country whence he [or she] comes*.[82]

To support this suggestion that Article 10(2) of Regulation 1612/68 should be interpreted so as to include same-sex partners we might briefly examine some of the ECJ's case-law.

The Court's argument in these cases follows a double reasoning.

The first is a functional, utilitarian argument. The Court has held that the Regulation simply

> ... defines more precisely the principle of freedom of movement for workers as formulated in Articles 48 and 49 of the EEC Treaty... [and] must be interpreted in the light of those provisions of the Treaty which call for the adoption of the measures required to bring about ... freedom of movement for workers.[83]

How, we may ask, will a measure ensuring the derivative rights of dependents further that goal? After all, these are not Community workers in themselves. The explanation is obvious. If a worker cannot be joined by his or her dependent, their volition and ability to move within the Community will be seriously compromised. The preamble to the Regulation is explicit:

> Whereas the right of freedom of movement, in order that it may be exercised, by objective standards, in freedom and dignity, requires that... obstacles to the mobility of workers shall be eliminated, in particular as regards the worker's right to be joined by his family...

From the perspective of the lesbians or gay men, the inability of their partners to join them would constitute as big an obstacle to their right of movement in freedom and dignity as would the denial of a more traditional dependent in a traditional family. From the Community perspective such

---

82   Note, where the same-sex partner is a Community national the question as to the applicability of Article 10(2) only arises where the partner is not a worker. Should the EC national partner be a worker he or she would enjoy their own rights under the EEC Treaty. When the partner is a non-EC national then they may wish to rely on Article 10(2).

83   Case 249/86, *Commission v. Germany* [1989] ECR 1263, at para. 8.

denial would compromise the notion whereby, in the language of the Regulation,

> mobility of labour ... must be one of the means by which the worker is guaranteed the possibility of improving his living and working conditions and promoting his social advancement, while helping to satisfy the requirements of the economies of the Member States.

The second line of reasoning is one rooted in human dignity. According to a long line of case-law national authorities are obliged to implement Community provisions in accordance with fundamental human rights.[84] In a recent case, which actually concerned Regulation 1612/68 and the rights of non-Community members of a worker's family, the ECJ stated:

> Regulation 1612/68 must also be interpreted in the light of the requirement of respect for family life set out in Article 8 of the Convention for the Protection of Human Rights and Fundamental Freedoms. That requirement is one of the fundamental rights which, according to the Court's settled case-law, restated in the preamble to the Single European Act, are recognized by Community law.[84a]

Finally, Article 10(3) of Regulation No. 1612/68 must be interpreted in the context of the overall structure and purpose of that regulation. It is apparent from the provisions of the regulation, taken as a whole, that in order to facilitate the movement of members of workers' families the Council took into account, first, the importance for the worker, from a human point of view, of the integration of the worker and his family into the host Member State without any difference in treatment in relation to nationals of that State.[85]

Therefore we see that here the Court emphasizes the non-functional aspect of this right which leads to a generous interpretation of Community provisions which facilitate free movement. Community law demands respect for human rights – in this case respect for private and family life as set out in Article 8 ECHR. The Court also stresses the importance of a worker having his or her family with him or her and characterizes that as 'the human point of view'. Is the gay or lesbian couple any less human in their attachment to their partners, we may ask?

Both the functional and the human dignity dimension of the Court's reasoning mandate the construction of 'dependent' to mean a gay or lesbian partner, the moment one is willing to accept the equivalence of attachment and feeling in homosexual and heterosexual relationships.

---

84   Case 29/69, *Stauder v. City of Ulm* [1969] ECR 419; *Rutili* (*supra*); *Hauer* (*supra*); Case 5/88, *Hubert Wachauf v. F.R.G.* [1989] ECR 2609; Case 265/87, *Hermann Schräder* [1989] ECR 2237; Case 249/86, *Commission v. F.R.G* [1989] ECR 1263.
84a Case 249/86, *Commission v. F.R.G.* [1989] 1263, at 1290, para. 10.
85   Ibid. para. 11.

(c)   Does Article 8 ECHR imply that same-sex partners should enjoy rights under Regulation 1612/68 and indeed in all other discriminatory contexts within the application of Community law?

The case-law of the European Court of Human Rights states that homosexual relations are covered by the protection of private life contained in Article 8.[86] So far the Commission and Court of Human Rights have not held that such relationships fall within the ambit of 'family life'. In *X and Y v. United Kingdom*[87] a British woman was living with an Australian woman and the latter's daughter (conceived by artificial insemination). The Australian woman was refused permission to remain in the United Kingdom as a lesbian cohabitant and she applied together with her daughter to the European Commission of Human Rights. The Commission found 'that a lesbian partnership involves private life within the meaning of Article 8 of the Convention', but the Commission went on to state that lawful deportation could not be regarded as an interference with this provision 'given the State's right to impose immigration controls and limits.'[88] In another case it was held that Article 8 did not grant a right for a lesbian to succeed to council housing from her partner.[89] Most recently, in denying the protection of Article 8 to a Cypriot who had a joint bank account, flat and business together with his partner the Commission reiterated the fact that, in principle, there was no interference with the right to respect for private life; they then added that: 'there has been no "lack of respect" for private life within the meaning of Article 8 paragraph 1 of the Convention.'[90]

But these cases do not really answer our question. They may affirm that individuals cannot rely on Article 8, save in exceptional circumstances, where Member State's immigration controls are legitimately applied to deport illegal aliens. But they do not deny that homosexual couples may be assimilated to heterosexual couples for some purposes. In fact, the case-law of the European Commission of Human Rights allows us to conclude that any legitimate discrimination between homosexual and heterosexual couples will have to be justifiable and proportionate to the aim to be achieved. The discrimination question is discussed in more detail below, suffice it to

---

86   See *Dudgeon* and *Norris* (*supra*).
87   *Application 14753/89*, decision of 27 February 1989; see also the discussion of this case by Jessurun d'Oliveira in Chapter Twelve.
88   Reaffirmed most recently in *X v. United Kingdom*, decision of 10 February 1990. However the Commission continues to leave open the possibility of 'exceptional circumstances' citing their case-law in *Application 10427/83*, decision of 12 May 1986. They were presumably also referring to their remarks in another immigration case where they denied the applicability of Article 8 to a gay couple stating 'it has not been shown that the applicants could not live together elsewhere than in the U.K., or that the link with the U.K. is an essential element of the relationship.' For criticism of this reasoning see the discussion of these cases by Van Dijk in Chapter Six.
89   *Application 11716/85*, decision of 14 May 1986.
90   At para. 1 of 'The Law', *X v. UK*, *Application 16106/90*, decision of 10 February 1990.

say that one cannot extrapolate from the case-law on Article 8 whether same-sex partners may be covered under Regulation 1612/68.

Moreover, it should be remembered, as we noted earlier, that the case-law of the European Commission and Court of Human Rights does not reflect the only legitimate interpretation of the scope of the protection of fundamental rights in Community law. The Council of Europe's Commission and Court of Human Rights only *adjudicate* cases and controversies brought before them, and then only declare a minimum standard taking into account differences across the 27 Member States of the Council of Europe.

Furthermore, these organs are concerned to develop case-law which is abreast of changing standards. Therefore, it may be inappropriate for the 12 of the Community to saddle themselves with the *minimum* standard of the 27. This is especially so in the present context where the European Court of Human Rights has pointed to a lack of a European (of the 27) standard in certain matters related to sexual orientation.[91]

A finding concerning inadmissibility or non-violation at the Strasbourg level does not mean that the Community cannot offer greater protection within its legal order. Theoretically it is even possible that the 12 representatives of the Community Member States in the Committee of Ministers of the Council of Europe could have voted for a violation under Article 32 of the Convention, whereas the non-Community states voted against finding a violation so that 'no violation' was recorded.[92]

It is clear that the Community's Court of Justice may have to go not only beyond the Convention in its search for Community fundamental rights,[93] but it will have to go beyond a preliminary perusal of the Strasbourg case-law and decide how the question raised in Strasbourg really relates to the Community legal order. For instance, most of the Strasbourg case-law concerning claims of discrimination by gay men has related to the criminal law and the age of consent; a finding by the European Commission of Human Rights that discrimination is justified between the

---

91   See the judgments in *Rees*, Series A, No. 106, and *Cossey*, Series A, No. 184, two cases concerning transsexuals, and the judgments in *Handyside*, Series A, No. 24, and *Müller*, Series A, No. 133, cases concerning obscenity; in all these cases the applicants failed through the Court's failure to determine 'common ground' or a European standard. Nevertheless, the Court has now found in favour of a transsexual even though it declined to suggest that it had recognized a new European standard – merely distinguishing the case as relating to different national systems; *B v. France*, judgment of 25 March 1992.

92   It is quite clear that the Committee of Ministers does not really act in a judicial way but the idea that the 12 may form a common front on some questions is not that far-fetched.

93   As it did in the *Hauer* case, (*supra*) para. 19, discussed by Clapham at 49 of *The Human Rights Challenge* Vol. I, and by Weiler in Vol. II of the same series at 590 ff. (*supra* note 6). See also Case 374/87, *Orkem v. Commission* [1989] ECR 3283, judgment of 18 October 1989, where the Court went beyond the rights contained in international instruments and common constitutional traditions.

heterosexual age of consent and the homosexual age of consent cannot be simply transposed to our Community context so that discrimination between heterosexual and homosexual migrant workers is considered lawful under the Convention.

Moreover, much of the Strasbourg case-law turns on the actual facts relating to the victim and may be considered differently should it have to be redecided by the Commission today. For instance, the Commission's 'settled' case-law on discrimination emerges from early decisions such as *Application 5935/72 v. F.R.G.*[94] In this case the applicant had been convicted of several offences against boys under 16. It was argued unsuccessfully that he was discriminated against as female homosexuality was not criminalized. This decision is cited in an early report of the Commission adopted in *Application 7215/75 v. United Kingdom.*[95] This application involved a man convicted and imprisoned for the offence of buggery with men who were 18 years old. Although he was not charged with buggery without consent, the Commission was clear that it had been established that 'there was an element of force in the relationship.'[96] When the question of discrimination was raised under Article 14 the Commission stated that it had already answered this question when dealing with Article 8(2), and it stated there was a reasonable justification for the difference in treatment due to the need to 'protect the rights of others'.

These applications involved homosexual sex with boys under 16 and the use of force respectively, but, the findings of reasonable discrimination are still referred to in Commission decisions on other matters.[97] It is worth noting that the Commission and Court found it unnecessary to determine the discrimination question in the *Dudgeon* case although the separate opinion of Mr Polak, the Dutch member of the Commission, did find that there had been a separate violation of Article 14. Although the United Kingdom Government has cited AIDS as a 'new consideration' which has emerged to justify, on the grounds of the protection of health, discouragement by the criminal law of the procuring of promiscuous homosexual acts, the

94   DR 39, 46.
95   DR 11, 36 (admissibility), DR 19, 66 (report).
96   At para. 137 of the Report of 12 October 1978 pursuant to Article 31 of the Convention. Note also the Commission's reference to the use of force in paragraph 134. The Commission voted unanimously that there had been no violation of Article 8 by virtue of the prosecution, by eight votes to four that the age of consent was not a violation of Article 8, and by nine votes to two with one abstention that the difference in the age of consent for homosexual and heterosexual relations did not constitute discrimination, and unanimously that there had been no violation of Article 10. The Committee of Ministers decided that there had been no violation of the Convention – DH (79) 5 of 12 June 1979.
97   See *Application 10389/83 v. United Kingdom*, decision of 17 July 1986, *Law Society Gazette*, 259, concerning a police raid on a homosexual party at the applicant's home. In this case there was only one person at the party under 21 who was in fact a visitor aged 20 from Italy where 16 is the age of consent for all consensual sexual acts. This guest in fact took no part in the sexual activity.

European Commission of Human Rights did not consider it necessary to address this point.[98] The European Court of Justice is unlikely to be faced with such delicate issues concerning the criminal law and the age of consent. When deciding the rights of Community workers the issues are different and there are good reasons for not blindly incorporating decisions of 'no violation' from the Council of Europe's judicial and political organs.

Returning to the second strand of the Court's rationale for a generous interpretation concerning questions of the free movement of workers and their families, it would seem that the Court's reference to the 'human point of view' and the need to ensure that the worker is not disadvantaged *vis-à-vis* workers in their host state, lead to the conclusion *that same-sex partners should fall within the scope of Article 10(2) of Regulation 1612/68.*

Summarizing, we have seen that in a country where alien same-sex partners are allowed to remain with a national of that state, resident workers from other Member States must equally be allowed to reside with their own same-sex partner (of whatever nationality). This follows from the *Reed* case. Article 10(2) of Regulation 1612/68 in its present form covers dependents and those living under the same roof in the country from wherever the worker comes. The case-law of the ECJ demands that Member States apply articles such as this in conformity with the European Convention on Human Rights and this treaty has been interpreted so that lesbian and gay relationships are considered as 'private life' which is protected under Article 8 ECHR. The fact that no discrimination case has been successful before the Strasbourg Commission of Human Rights does not preclude Article 10(2) of Regulation 1612/68 being interpreted so as to include same-sex partners.

(d) Social security for workers' families

It is worth briefly noting that the definition of a 'member of the family' for the purposes of the social security Regulation 1408/71 is: 'any person defined or recognized as a member of the family or designated as a member of the household by the legislation under which the benefits are provided.' Even where the national legislation demands that the person live under the same roof, the Regulation states that dependency is sufficient to be eligible. Therefore, it would seem that, the definition of a 'family' in this context will depend on a mixture of national and Community law. In this context

---

98   See the full unpublished report of the decision in the application cited in the previous footnote. In that case the applicant's observation states: 'The Government further suggests that interference is justified by seeking to prevent the spread of AIDS, yet the Government's own advertising makes it clear that AIDS is transmitted by a variety of means. It is found to a considerable degree amongst drug addicts and haemophiliacs, yet there are no special legal restrictions on their sexual acts. Concern for the health of the persons at the applicant's party was not one of the police considerations in raiding it.'

the scope of the 'family' can be as broad as national legislatures wish it to be.[99]

(e) A 'rights' approach across the Atlantic in United States and Canada

It is of some interest that the New York Court of Appeals recently decided to interpret the word 'family' in the context of eviction from rent regulated apartments so as to include the survivor of a gay man where one of the couple had died.[100] As the American Civil Liberties Union has pointed out, this decision gave a generic functional definition of the family. So, the 'Court's ruling will benefit not only gay couples, but all people who live in committed family relationships throughout society. For instance, low-income and elderly families, which may not have the financial ability to formalize their relationships because of economic barriers to divorce and adoption, will now be protected by the law.'[101] More generally the Canadian Charter of Rights and Freedoms has been interpreted by the Courts as outlawing unequal treatment on grounds of sexual orientation. So, even where a regulation concerning prison visits expressly referred to 'spouses' the Court held that it was unlawful discrimination to refuse the right to receive visits from his same sex lover.[102] The Court listed the explicitly

---

99   Josephine Steiner has suggested that in this area of Community law reverse discrimina-
      tion is not permitted so that no discrimination against a State's own nationals is al-
      lowed (at 213 of *EEC Law (supra)*). For further discussion see Chapter Fifteen by Em-
      mert.

100   *Brasci v. Stahl Associates Co.* No. 108 NY 6 July 1989. The Justices were prepared to
      formulate a functional rather than formal definition of the family. Note also that five
      States in the United States actually ban discrimination against lesbians and gay men:
      New Jersey, Connecticut, Massachusetts, Hawaii and Wisconsin. In addition there are a
      number of different bans at the State, municipal and county level. See '*A National Sur-
      vey of Anti-Discrimination Laws: A Listing of Legal Protections for Lesbians and Gay
      Men Regarding Employment, Housing, and Pubic Accommodation*' Lambda Legal De-
      fense and Education Fund (1990).

101   *ACLU News*, 7 July 1989. The functions identified by the Court are:
      the exclusivity and longevity of the relationship, the level of emotional and finan-
      cial commitment, the manner in which the parties have conducted their everyday
      lives and held themselves out to society, and the reliance placed upon one another
      for daily family services... These factors are most helpful, although it should be
      emphasized that the presence or absence of one or more of them is not dispositive
      since it is the totality of the relationship as evidenced by the dedication, caring and
      self-sacrifice of the parties which should, in the final analysis, control.
      74 NY2d 201 at 212-3.
      The decision has now been expanded to other forms of renting as well as family benefits
      for teachers. *E. 10th St v. Goldstein* 154 A.D. 2nd 142, 552 N.Y.S. 2sd 257 (1990).
      'Immediate family member' has been interpreted to include lesbian companion of a city
      employee so that she had the right to use her sick leave to care for her partner. *Ross v.
      City of Denver* Housing Officer's Order 4 October 1991.

102   *Versey v. Canada (Correctional Service)* [1989] 44 CRR 364 (FTD), Federal Court of
      Appeal [1990] 109 N.R. 300. Note that the Canadian Human Rights Act 1985 has now
      been interpreted so that the list of prohibited types of discrimination includes 'Sexual

prohibited categories of discrimination under Section 15 of the Charter: race, national or ethnic origin, colour, religion, sex, age or mental or physical disability. The Court then stated that these groups had two important characteristics. First, the status was immutable. It is relatively difficult to change sex or race. Second, these groups had been victimized and stigmatized through history. The Court found that the goal of the visiting programme was the prisoner's reintegration into society and that to exclude same sex partners was unnecessary for any of the reasons given by the prison authorities.

Interestingly, the Court relied on unimplemented recommendations of the Canadian House of Commons Parliamentary Committee made in 1985. So far the European Court of Justice has had little recourse to the debates and recommendations of the European Parliament. But the Parliament's recommendations concerning the illegitimacy of discrimination on grounds of sexual orientation must be relevant when examining evolving European standards in the field.[103]

3. Free Movement of Goods and Services

Unlike Article 48 EEC, the derogation Article relating to the free movement of goods (Article 36 EEC) contains a permissible restriction on grounds of 'public morality'.[104] The ECJ's case-law on the importation of pornography, inflatable dolls and other erotic goods suggests that Member States are given quite a large margin of discretion in this area.[105] But it should be noted that where goods are freely manufactured and marketed in one Member State, that State will not be permitted to prohibit the importation of similar goods on the grounds that they are contrary to public morality. This is so even if the goods are subject to other restrictions in the receiving Member State. In the *Conegate* case[106] inflatable rubber dolls were subject to a ban on transmission by post and a restriction on public display, whilst there was no restriction in the UK on manufacture or marketing. The ECJ therefore held that to restrict the importation of such goods would breach Article 30 EEC. This reasoning applies as much to homosexual pornography as it does to heterosexual pornography.

---

orientation'; *Haig v. Canada (Ministry of Justice)* (Ont. C.A) [1992] OJ No. 09 Action No. 774/91.

103   See 'Resolution on sexual discrimination at the workplace', 13 March 1984, OJ 1984 C 104/46-48.

104   Article 56 EEC which defines the permissible restrictions on services mirrors Article 48 by listing: public policy, public security or public health. The same principles that apply for derogations in the cases of free movement of workers and goods would seem to apply here also.

105   See Case 34/79, *Henn and Darby* [1979] ECR 3795.

106   Case 121/85, *Conegate Ltd v. H.M. Customs and Excise* [1986] ECR 1007.

If a state started to discriminate against homosexual pornography in general, the matter could be considered by the European Commission of Human Rights.[107] It is unlikely that the matter would be reviewable by the ECJ even though it stated in the *Cinéthèque* case that 'it is the duty of this Court to ensure the observance of fundamental rights in the field of Community law'.[108] Arguably, a restriction on homoerotic goods from abroad on the grounds of public morality under Article 36 EEC would fall within the field of Community law, but the Court would probably rely on the remaining part of this paragraph from the same case:

> [the ECJ] has no power to examine the compatibility with the European Convention of national legislation which concerns, as in this case, an area which falls within the jurisdiction of the national legislator.[109]

Even though *Rutili* establishes that the restrictions on Community workers have to be carried out by Member States in accordance with principles found in the European Convention this situation was different because the context involved the 'control of aliens'[110] through Community provisions which would be inapplicable to nationals. Where Member States merely rely on the limitation clauses in Articles 36 and 56, the ECJ has, as mentioned above, also indicated the need to scrutinize actions within these limitations. Additionally, the ECJ will examine the proportionality of the national measures taken.[111] Any discrimination against homosexuals in the national measures should work against a conclusion of proportionality as it contradicts an assumption that the measures were *objectively* justifiable. This does not mean that justifications are not admissible. These will be dealt with in the following section.

4. Equality and Non-Discrimination

Before discussing when the ECJ will have jurisdiction over Member State's actions and their conformity with the general equality principle we might examine some of the justifications for discrimination against homosexuals already put forward in Strasbourg in the context of the European Convention on Human Rights and its application by the European Commission of Human Rights.

---

107 According to Peter Tatchell 'The importation of the educational sex guides, *The Joy of Gay Sex and The Joy of Lesbian Sex*, has been banned by the Customs [in the United Kingdom], though the heterosexual equivalent *The Joy of Sex* can be freely imported.' See Tatchell, 1991, 32.

108 *Supra*, para. 26.

109 Ibid.

110 *Rutili* (*supra*), para. 32.

111 See Case 120/78, *Cassis de Dijon* [1979] ECR 649.

(a) Justifications for discrimination between gay men and lesbians

In *Application 5935/72* the Government of the Federal Republic of Germany
suggested that provisions which punished only homosexual relations for
men and not for women was justified by the need for deterrence and that it
was not necessary to deter female homosexuals for the following reasons:

    a. It is generally admitted that there are comparatively few female homosexuals
       as compared with males.
    b. Experience shows that adult female homosexuals prefer partners of their own
       age.
    c. It is generally admitted that homosexual relationships between an adult and a
       girl under age are very rare
    d. In the rare cases of seduction of a girl by an adult woman experience shows
       that the girl's personal development and the insertion in society are not gen-
       erally affected because female homosexuality does not usually show itself in
       public.

The situation was fundamentally different as regards male homosexuality.

    a. This was much more frequent.
    b. Male homosexuals prefer young partners.
    c. These homosexuals frequently change their partner.
    d. It follows that young men are much more exposed to the risk of homosexual
       relations with adults than girls [are].
    e. On account of the tendency of masculine homosexual couples to show them-
       selves in public, a young man or adolescent is more exposed to social isola-
       tion and conflicts with society.[112]

The Commission concluded that studies carried out in the Federal Republic
of Germany led to:

> convincing conclusions as to the existence of a specific social danger in the case
> of masculine homosexuality. This danger results from the fact that masculine
> homosexuals often constitute a distinct socio-cultural group with a clear tendency
> to proselytize adolescents and that the social isolation in which it involves the
> latter is particularly marked.[112a]

Again it is important to recognize the context in which these decisions were
taken: *the age of consent.* In a way, the Commission had its hands tied.
They could hardly have found unjustified discrimination between the law
regulating homosexual sex and the law covering lesbian sex because they
had already found that criminalizing homosexual sex under 21 was justified – had they made a finding of discrimination the only way for the
Member State to comply with such a finding would be to *criminalize* lesbian relationships under 21. This would hardly be a progressive result from
the Commission of Human Rights!

112   At 53 of the decision (*supra*).
112a At 56 of the decision (*supra*).

But, returning to the reasoning, the reliance on the effects of 'social isolation' may be an acceptable policy consideration but it is not really principled. To what extent 'social isolation' follows from the law is a moot question; but to justify a discriminatory law on the grounds of protecting people from 'social isolation' surely panders to prejudice rather than principle.

(b) Justifications for discrimination between lesbians/gay men and heterosexual couples

On the question of discrimination in the immigration cases discussed above (in the section on acquired rights for members of the worker's family) the Commission adopted the following reasoning:

> the immigration rules in question give priority and better guarantees to traditional established families, rather than other established relationships like a lesbian partnership. The Commission finds no element of discrimination, contrary to Article 14 of the Convention, in such a policy, given the special protection to be afforded to the traditional family.[113]

The Commission was relying on its earlier case-law relating to an application by a lesbian couple claiming discrimination where protection under housing legislation existed for heterosexual couples and not for lesbian couples.[114] The Commission had found such a difference in treatment justified. The Commission assimilated 'the family' with 'heterosexual unmarried couples living together as husband and wife' and found that these relationships were different from 'other stable relationships'. The Commission stated that it considered that 'the family' merits special protection in society and it saw 'no reason why a High Contracting Party should not afford particular assistance to families.' There was therefore, according to the Commission, a reasonable and objective justification.

In another immigration case the European Commission of Human Rights has stated that a legitimate aim may be the 'economic well-being of the country' (Article 8(2)) and the means employed (deportation) were proportionate to this aim.[115] Because many benefits could flow from same-sex partners accumulating rights under Community law this justification could come to play a real role. It is worth remembering that in the context of

---

113   At para. 2 of the unpublished decision in *Application 14753/89*, decision of 27 February 1989.
114   *Application 11716/85*, decision of 14 May 1986.
115   See *Application 12513/86 v. UK*. Cf. *Abdulaziz, Cabales and Balkandali v. United Kingdom*, Series A, No. 94.

Article 10(2) of Regulation 1612/68 the individual may have had to show dependence on the Community worker.[116]

To conclude this section on discrimination we can say that the European Commission and Court of Human Rights do examine the legitimacy and proportionality of differential treatment between homosexual and heterosexual established relationships. Although the Commission and Court have yet to find that an applicant has been unreasonably discriminated against under the Convention, the case-law seems to require that discriminatory treatment against homosexual couples in areas such as immigration and housing has to be justified. Permissible justifications accepted by the European Commission of Human Rights include: 'protecting family based relationships',[117] 'the special protection to be afforded to the traditional family',[118] 'the rights of others',[119] 'the economic well-being of the country'.[120]

Therefore, where the equality principle is applicable under Community law, Member States will have to ensure that discrimination between homosexuals and heterosexuals is proportionate and justifiable.

(c) The Equality Principles as a General Principle of Community Law

The last question to be addressed in this section is: in what circumstances will the European Court of Justice require that Member States apply the equality principle as a general principle of Community law? In the *Klensch*[121] and *Wachauf*[122] cases it has been clearly established that when a Member State acts in implementing a Community policy, the general principles of Community law should apply to these actions. This may be extended to argue that the area of jurisdiction includes those 'subject matters which are *predominantly* within an area which comes under Community jurisdiction, even if incidental Member State action is not always

---

116   Although these partners may qualify for non-contributory State benefits. A solution based on the proposals for non-working Community nationals (students, retired persons, and others who are self-supporting) might be envisaged so that the individual has to show that he or she has insurance and sufficient resources. The cost of some benefits might be borne by the State of origin. Cf. OJ 1989 C 191/2, 3, 5. Of course this would be complicated where the State of origin is a non-Community country. But Parliament, at least, has not ruled out the possibility that some residence rights might be extended to non-Community nationals. See Evans and Jessurun D'Oliveira, 'Nationality and Citizenship', in Cassese, Clapham, Weiler (eds), *supra* note 6, Vol. II, 299-345 at 324.

117   *Application 16106/90, X v. United Kingdom*, decision of 10 February, discussed above.

118   *Application 14753/89 v. United Kingdom*, decision of 27 February 1989, discussed above.

119   *Application 7215/75 v. UK.*

120   *Application 12513/86 v. United Kingdom*, decision of 11 September 1986, discussed above.

121   Joined Cases 201 and 202/85, ECR [1986] 3503.

122   Case 5/88, *Wachauf* [1989] ECR 2609

barred.'[123] For example Member States administering a Community policy, Member State action within an area such as Fisheries or Common Commercial Policy where the Court has held that the Community competence is exclusive, and lastly, Member State action in an area which *could* be pre-empted. Suffice it to say that the case-law of the European Court of Justice has given a special emphasis to the principle of equality whether it be between men and women, between cyclists from different Member States, between sugar producers, between Luxembourgeois dairies or between workers from different Member States who wished to cohabit without getting married. Where there is an inequality between homosexuals and heterosexuals and the situation permeates that area predominantly within Community jurisdiction, the European Court of Justice may have to decide whether it finds this inequality justified and proportionate to the aim to be achieved.

This section has not dealt with the *acquis communautaire* relating to sex discrimination, the directives, the action plan and the prospects for interpretations of the sex discrimination directives so that they would cover discrimination on grounds of sexual orientation.[124] Nor have issues connected with specific Community provisions dealing with the conditions at the workplace been examined.[125] In our view, as explained above, the main utility of these provisions is to demonstrate the competences of the Community to act on gay rights, should the political will be found, rather than to derive direct protection from them.

D. Rights Against Private Actors

From early on in the ECJ's case-law it has been clear that Community law gives rise to enforceable rights and duties for individuals. It is sufficient to refer to the often quoted paragraph from the European Court of Justice's judgment in *Van Gend en Loos*:

> Independently of the legislation of Member States, Community law therefore not only *imposes obligations on individuals* but is also intended to confer upon them rights which become part of their legal heritage.[126]

The first case which should be considered in the present context is *Walrave and Koch v. Association Union Cycliste Internationale,*[127] where the Treaty of Rome's prohibition of discrimination based on nationality was held by

---

123   Weiler in *The Human Rights Challenge, supra* note 6, Vol. II, 602.
124   This is dealt with by Byre in Chapter Seven.
125   These are dealt with by Betten in Chapter Fourteen.
126   *Van Gend en Loos v. Netherlandse Administratie der Belastingen* [1963] ECR 1, at 12
       (emphasis added).
127   [1974] ECR 1405.

the European Court of Justice to extend to the rules of an international cy-
cling organization. The rule in question provided that, for a world champi-
onship race, the pacemaker (motorcyclist) must be of the same nationality
as the stayer (cyclist). The decision was based on the applicability of Articles 7, 48, and 59 of the Treaty of Rome (EEC). To the extent that sport is
an economic activity within Article 2 (EEC) it is subject to Community
law, and when such activity is gainful employment, or remunerated service,
it comes within the protection of the Community freedoms (freedom of
movement of workers, Articles 48-51, and freedom of establishment of services, Articles 59-66). These rules were said to give effect to the general rule
found in Article 7 EEC which prohibits any discrimination on grounds of
nationality in the field of application of the Treaty. The Court then states
in general terms that:

> Articles 7, 48, [and] 59 have in common the prohibition, in their respective
> spheres of application, of any discrimination on grounds of nationality.[128]

The judgment then directly addresses the particular circumstances of the
case at issue and states:

> Prohibition on such discrimination does not only apply to the action of public
> authorities but extends likewise to the rules of any other nature aimed at regulat-
> ing in a collective manner gainful employment and the provision of services.[129]

The Court then continues that any interpretation which permitted private
organizations to construct obstacles to free movement for persons and freedom to provide services would compromise the fundamental objectives of
the Community (as defined in Article 3(c) EEC: the abolition as between
Member States, of obstacles to freedom of movement of persons, services
and capital).

The European Court of Justice adds a further reason why 'associations
and organizations which do not come under public law', are covered by the
prohibitions in question – any solution which limited these prohibitions to
the rules of public authorities would 'risk creating inequality in their application.'[130]

One can easily see two kinds of inequality which would arise from a restrictive interpretation which imposed duties only on public authorities.
First, there would be a certain inequality between workers in the public and
private sectors, and second, there would be inequality between workers in
one Member State and those in another as the sphere which was defined as
belonging to public authorities would vary from state to state.

---

128   At para. 16.
129   At para. 17.
130   At para. 19.

Less than two years later the Court gave its judgment in the *Defrenne II* case.[131] The case raised similar questions to those raised in *Walrave*, but this time we are concerned with the field of equal pay for equal work (Article 119 EEC).

The Court, following the opinion of the Advocate General, opted for a teleological interpretation which recognizes both the importance of fundamental rights in the Community legal order and the need to make Community law effective. The Court stated:

> Article 119 pursues a double aim.
> First, in the light of the different stages of the development of social legislation in the various Member States, the aim of Article 119 is to avoid a situation in which undertakings established in States which have actually implemented the principle of equal pay suffer a competitive disadvantage in intra-Community competition as compared with undertakings established in States which have not yet eliminated discrimination against women workers as regards pay.
> Secondly, this provision forms part of the social objectives of the Community, which is not merely an economic union, but is at the same time intended, by common action, to ensure social progress and seek the constant improvement of the living and working conditions of their peoples, as is emphasized in the Preamble to the Treaty.[132]

These passages are fully cited in order to give an insight into the remarkable dynamics of the Court of Justice's approach to interpretation. The logic of the judgment is supranational. The Court insists on inter-state competition as well as fundamental values for a union which transcends economic integration. Although there are no equivalent Articles which would grant gay men and lesbians directly enforceable anti-discrimination rights against private bodies, the commitment of the Court to these two aims is highly relevant.[133]

Whereas the Court has declared that certain Articles in the Treaty of Rome are enforceable against private bodies the same Court has a mixed jurisprudence as regards those rights contained in directives.

In one line of cases the Court has held that rights in directives, which are clear, precise and unconditional, are enforceable against emanations of the state but are not to be enforceable against private bodies.

---

131   Case 43/75 [1976] ECR 455.
132   Paras. 8-10.
133   The new definition of the objectives of the Community according to the European Union Treaty refers in what would be the new Article 2 EEC to 'a high level of employment and of social protection, the raising of the standard of living and the quality of life, and economic and social cohesion and solidarity among Member States.' For the instruments and methods by which this is to be achieved in the various fields of Community competence see Chapter Eight by Snyder, Somsen and Hoyer.

This line reaches its peak in the *Marshall v. Southampton and S.W. Hampshire Area Health Authority*[134] decision where the Equal Treatment Directive was held only to bind 'organs of the State' when relied on at the national level.

But in other cases such as *Harz*[135] and recently in *Marleasing*[136] the Court has applied rights deriving from directives as between individuals with no regard to the distinction between public or private parties. It is difficult at this stage to predict how this trend will develop.

This, perhaps is the explanation of what has been called 'The von Colson principle'[137] or 'The Interpretive "Solution" to the Horizontal Direct Effect Problem'.[138] In *von Colson*[139] the Court stated:

> [I]n applying the national law and in particular the provisions of a national law specifically introduced in order to implement Directive 76/207, national courts are required to interpret their national law in the light of the wording and the purpose of the Directive in order to achieve the result referred to in the third paragraph of Article 189.[140]

Thus, in *Marleasing* the Court used a similar ruling demanding that national courts interpret national law so as to conform with the wording and text of Directive 68/151/EEC of 9 March 1968 of the Council; but this time there was no mention of national laws specifically introduced to implement the Community law.

Therefore it would seem that in any case which comes before the courts the rights and obligations which can be clearly deduced from directives will be incorporated as interpretative principles into national law, as judges are under a duty to comply with the unimplemented directive.

Given the state of the case-law, a cautionary view would be to say that where someone needs to rely exclusively on rights contained in a directive

---

134   [1986] ECR 723. Briefly, Mrs Marshall had been employed by the authority as a senior dietician, she was dismissed at the age of 62 whereas had she been a man she would have been entitled to continue working until at least 65. She could not rely on the Sex Discrimination Act 1975 as s. 6(4) provided that sex discrimination by employers is not prohibited in relation to death or retirement. She relied on Article 5 of Directive 76/207 as the date for implementation of the Directive had expired and the terms of the article were clear, precise and unconditional. cf. *Becker v. Finanzamt Münster – Innenstadt* [1982] ECR 53.

135   Case 79/83, *Harz* [1984] ECR 1921 (interestingly dealing with sex discrimination).

136   Case 106/89 [1990] ECR I-4135.

137   Arnull, 1987, 383 at 391.

138   Morris and David, 1987, 116. For a discussion of the pros and cons of giving horizontal effect to directly applicable provisions of directives which have not been implemented on time or improperly, see Emmert, *Horizontale Drittwirkung von Richtlinien?*, Europäisches Wirtschafts- und Steuerrecht, 1992, 56-67.

139   Case 14/83, *von Colson and Kamann v. Land Nordrhein-Westfalen* [1984] ECR 1891, and *Harz v. Deutsche Tradex GmbH* [1984] ECR 1921.

140   At para. 26.

and the case is not already before the courts then they can only rely on the directive as against state bodies. This is particularly important in the present context as discrimination against gay men and lesbians is primarily found in the private sector. The main sources of everyday discrimination are landlords, employers, insurance companies, co-workers and so on. Therefore solutions at the Community level should look to avoid this pitfall.

Assuming that a directive was introduced at some time in the future to protect the rights of gay men and lesbians, how could one ensure that it applied in the sectors most concerned? The directive should call on Member States to implement anti-discrimination provisions in the private sphere. Then, as long as the state has properly implemented the directive, no problem arises as gay men and lesbians would be able to rely on the national law in order to gain the appropriate remedy. However, experience shows that directives are often improperly implemented or not implemented on time. In this situation one has to fall back on the directive. In order to avoid the inapplicability of the directive in the private sector one might consider expressly stating that it binds private bodies. Should this not be acceptable, one might have to consider whether it might not be better to proceed by way of a regulation so that private bodies would be bound.

In suggesting that private bodies be bound we are not suggesting that there are no circumstances in which a private body may be allowed to choose not to associate with gay men or lesbians. The test will again be the one used for determining the legitimacy of other types of discrimination: is it justified by a legitimate aim and proportionate to the end to be achieved?

An illustrative example of a case falling on the borderline of discrimination which may be held legitimate was the complaint by the New York Commission of Human Rights against the Ancient Order of Hiberians. This complaint alleged that the private Roman Catholic group which organizes the St Patrick's Day Parade in New York violated the city's civil rights code when they refused to allow the Irish Lesbian and Gay Organization to march with its own banner in the 1991 parade. The case is complicated because the parade is public with political participation rather than private for religious ends. Several commentators have suggested that to force the organizers to allow the Irish Gay and Lesbian Organization to march is akin to suggesting that gay groups would have to allow homophobic gangs to march with them in their own parade. The *New York Times* also suggested that 'Martin Luther King Jr. could not and should not have been forced to include Ku Klux Klan members in his civil rights marches.'[141] But it is

141   'Parading Bigotry', *New York Times*, 25 January 1992, A22, see also 'New York City Seeks to Force Sponsors to Let Gay Irish March in Parade', *New York Times*, 25 January 1992, A1, 'The Parade Seems Set; After That All Bets Off', *New York Times*, 15 March 1992, A34, 'In Other Years Brawls Began After the Parade', *New York Times*, 22 March 1992, A16. The judge of the New York Human Rights Commission saw the

suggested that the analogy is not so evident. There is certainly the same clash of principles; freedom of association versus non-discrimination but in the cases of the gay-bashers or the Ku Klux Klan those groups can hardly claim the right to be treated equally when they advocate just the opposite.

The big difference between private discrimination on grounds of sexual orientation and 'official' discrimination is that private groups or individuals may have religious or sexual interests which justify excluding others. Just as one would not expect the state to insist that all women's clubs admit men on demand so one could foresee that a lesbian group may wish to exclude men or even heterosexual women. Similarly there may be legitimate situations where private associations exclude gays but they will have to show that the exclusion is justifiable. But as is demonstrated throughout this project, it is in the private fields of employment, education, insurance, housing and health care that much of the pervasive discrimination against lesbians and gay men takes place.

IV. The External Dimension

Although the Community now takes into account human rights when questions of the completion on trade of association agreements arise, and although aid from the OECD countries to Eastern and Central Europe is to be distributed by the Commission after consideration of, amongst other things, respect for human rights, it is unlikely that anti-gay or anti-lesbian practices in these countries will jeopardize any such agreements. In the United States the failure of the government to make available suitable life-saving drugs and facilities has been characterized by some groups as a form of genocide.[142] Similarly there has been a challenge under the Canadian Charter of Rights and Freedoms claiming that charging for drugs such as AZT and other AIDS treatment violates the right to life. The plaintiffs alleged that cancer and transplant patients were offered free medical services.[143] Even if one accepts that some countries may be violating the right to life it would be unrealistic to expect automatic Community sanctions against such anti-gay behaviour. Even where human rights provisions are specifically included in Community agreements such as the Lomé IV Convention, breaches of human rights do not mean that obligations can be

---

action of the organizers as unlawful discrimination but found that they were entitled to do this due to the First Amendment to the United States Constitution.

142 See for example the letter by Larry Kramer, the founder of ACT UP (The Aids Coalition to Unleash Power) to *The Economist*, 31 August 1991, 6. On genocide and sexual minorities see H. Fein (ed.), *Genocide Watch* (1992). Suggestions concerning the inclusion of sexual minorities in the genocide Convention have not yet been taken up by the UN expert bodies or by the Member States.

143 *Brown v. British Columbia (Ministry of Health)* [1990] 48 CRR 137.

simply renounced. In the accord establishing the European Bank for Reconstruction and Development human rights are mentioned in the preamble but do not appear in Article 1 which lists the legal requirements necessary for a loan. However, the Resolution of the Council of 28 November 1991, on Human Rights, Democracy and Development reaffirmed that safeguarding human rights is a cornerstone of relations between the Community and other countries. The Resolution also outlines a series of possible measures which the Community and its Member States could take in response to human rights violations. These include confidential and public demarches as well as changes in cooperation programmes. In some cases suspension of cooperation is foreseen.

Moreover, where countries want to join the Community they are more or less obliged to decriminalize homosexuality due to the combined effect of two developments: the 1978 European Council Copenhagen Declaration which demands that new members respect human rights, and second, the interpretation of the Convention by the European Court of Human Rights in the *Dudgeon* and *Norris* cases where it was decided that the minimum standard in Europe demands that homosexual sex between consenting adults be legal where they are both over 21.

In this context two recent applications before the European Commission of Human Rights are relevant. In *Modinos v. Cyprus* the applicant, the president of the 'Liberation Movement of Homosexuals in Cyprus' complained that the maintenance in force in Cyprus of legislation prohibiting male homosexual activity constitutes a continuing interference with his right to respect for private life. The Commission has unanimously concluded that there has been a violation of the Convention.[144] Should the Court find against Cyprus and should Cyprus refuse to change its legislation (the Supreme Court has already upheld it in a similar case[145]) then the Community's declaration that new members have to respect the Convention will be put to the test. Should Cyprus apply to join in such circumstances they could even face a possible veto by the European Parliament. (See Article 237 of the EEC Treaty).

The other case is *X v. United Kingdom* where a Cypriot complained that his removal to Cyprus from the United Kingdom would expose him to persecution by the authorities. The Commission found that the risk of prosecution in the future was not high and that the interference with the applicant's rights under Article 8 was outweighed by 'valid considerations relating to the proper enforcement of immigration controls.'[146] As Community

---

144   *Application 15070/89*, report of the Commission, 3 December 1991, currently pending before the European Court of Human Rights.
145   *Yiannakis Panayiotou Costa v. the Republic*, 8 June 1982.
146   *Application 16106/90*, decision of 10 February 1990 (unpublished) at para. 1 of 'The Law'.

provisions and competence creep into areas such as immigration control, asylum and crime control (Europol is currently being established) the probable treatment of deportees in the country of their destination will have to be considered if the interpretation of Community law is to remain faithful to the minimum standards established under the Convention.

German and Dutch courts have already granted asylum[147] to refugees claiming to be liable to persecution for their sexual orientation in their own country. Recently, an Argentinean was granted refugee status in Canada after he had claimed to have been raped and tortured by the Argentine police.[148] The tribunal in Canada were referred to such European cases. If the Community is not to take a step backwards from the emerging norms in this area it should ensure that claims relating to persecution on grounds of sexual orientation[149] are dealt with by fair and consistent procedures with the necessary opportunities for asylum seekers to have access to legal representation, interpreters and the other guarantees of due process.

V. Strategies for Developing Further Protection

Some tactical and strategic choices may have to be made about what can be gained in the judicial and political fora. The topic has been on the agenda in the United States of America for some time but has not been developed in the European context. In fact lesbian and gay rights activists in the United States are now confronting the question of the effectiveness of civil disobedience as a plan of action. Some American commentators would seek to build on the success and appreciation of Martin Luther King and the Civil Rights movement. Richard Mohr has argued that civil rights legislation in the United States was only placed on the agenda with the catalytic effect of civil disobedience. This disobedience stirred the moral sense of the nation and placed the issue on the legislative agenda. He argues that 'Currently gays are dismissible not only because politically dispossessed but especially and particularly invisible and, in any case, thought to be wimps and pansies'. Therefore, according to Mohr, civil disobedience is triply appropriate as

147 See Chapter Six by Van Dijk and Chapter Eleven by Tanca.
148 'Argentine Homosexual Gets Refugee Status in Canada', *New York Times*, 14 January 1992, A10.
149 The European Parliament's Ford Report 'On Racism and Xenophobia' refers to 'sexual orientation' in its proposed definition of those who should benefit from a future Convention for a common refugee and asylum policy; see also footnote 61.

[i]t would put gays on the national agenda. It would help overcome invisibility and stereotypes ... [and it] would make society aware of what it is unwittingly doing.[150]

A. New Legislation in the Council of Europe and in the Community Legal Order: Processes and Participation

Whether or not this strategy is appropriate at the national level in Europe will be for lesbians and gay men to decide for themselves depending on the particular national context. It should be remembered that the mechanics of the European Community legislative process are very different from the process of federal government in the USA. Chaining oneself to the railings of the Berlaymont in Brussels or the Parliament in Strasbourg would be unlikely to excite much local interest and the perspective of the *fonctionaires* and MEPs would remain little altered. The success of the Agricultural Lobby in using similar tactics derives, we believe, from the importance of their sector as a major Community policy and their political and electoral clout within some critical Member States. In any event it may even be that these civil servants and representatives are already more sensitive to intolerance and discrimination than the average legislator due to their own experiences as atypical migrant workers.

In order to increase the chances of legislative change, pressure will have to be applied at the national level. In this climate the Commission will be able to propose new Community provisions which ease discrimination against lesbians and gay men.

In our view, the most promising avenue would be to insist on equivalence to gender issues which are already widely accepted as legitimate. This strategy would call for a campaign both to include sexual orientation in existing equal treatment provisions on a par with anti-gender discrimination and to include sexual orientation in any new initiative to further the closing of the gender gap such as the recent calls to transform the Sexual Harassment code into binding Community legislation.[151]

In the light of the history of gay rights at the European Community level the most sympathetic branch is likely to be the European Parliament.[152] Even if the legislative powers of the European Parliament are

---

150   Mohr, 1988, 335.
151   See, e.g., the recent call of the Economic and Social Committee to give teeth to the Sexual Harassment Code. *Agence Europe*, 31 October 1991.
152   The Squarcialupi Report (1984) (*Report on sexual discrimination at the workplace*, EP Working Doc. 1-1358/83,13 February 1984) was adopted by the European Parliament together with the following recommendations to the Member States of the Community: abolition of legal proscriptions against consenting relationships between consenting adult homosexuals, introduction of a common age of consent for heterosexuals and homosexuals, banning the keeping of special records on homosexuality by the police,

weak, it may be worth pushing for a Resolution on the topic of lesbian and gay men's rights in order that the contents, as adopted, might be considered firm evidence of a growing European consensus on this matter. In a post-Maastricht environment, the European Parliament's influence will be greater, in some cases even decisive. Apart from the lead this could lend to the European Court of Justice it may be useful in the context of interpretation of the European Convention on Human Rights. In the *Cossey* case the European Court of Human Rights referred to the Resolution of the European Parliament even if they declined to follow the Parliament's recommendations on the rights of transsexuals.[153]

In the later case of *B. v. France* the applicant relied in part on this Resolution and was eventually successful.[153a] The risks of this strategy must also be acknowledged. There is always a tension between working at the judicial level, trying to persuade the Court that a certain right is already embedded in existing norms, and a legislative approach which tries to bring the change through the legislator. Failure at the legislative level may send two negative signals to the Court: First, that the tide of opinion which often influences judicial construction in an area which at times explicitly calls for a reflection of public mores has not in fact changed and hence 'judicial legislation' would be inappropriate; and secondly, the legislative approach, might undermine the claim that the right already exists under existing law.

A proposal for a draft protocol to the European Convention on Human Rights has been prepared by a number of non-governmental organizations and individuals.[154] This proposal need not be examined in detail here as we are primarily concerned with proposals at the Community level. But, for the sake of clarity it is worth making the following point: even if a Protocol came into force which granted an independent right to complain about any discrimination in the law, this would not necessarily add anything to what can currently be claimed *under Community law*. Of course it would send a clear political message to judges at the national and Community level that there was a European consensus that discrimination on grounds of sexual orientation was impermissible, but, this could also be achieved by a Resolution of the European Parliament or a Declaration of the

rejection of the classification of homosexuality as a mental illness, outlawing discrimination in the workplace on the grounds of a person's homosexuality.
153 Judgment of 27 September 1990, Series A, No. 184, see para. 40 of the judgment and footnote 46 of Judge Martens' dissenting opinion.
153a Judgment of 35 March 1992, Series A, No. 232-C.
154 'Study-conference on the possibilities of expanding the European Convention on Human Rights to eliminate discrimination based on sexual orientation', Copenhagen, 26-27 May 1990. The pros and cons of such a protocol together with alternative suggestions can be found in Helfer, 'Lesbian and Gay Rights as Human Rights: Strategies for a United Europe', 32 *Va.J.Int'l.L.* (1991) 157-220.

Commission, Council and Parliament together. Whatever wording the protocol adopted, there would always be the proviso that people can be treated differently where there is an objective and proportional justification. The European Court of Justice of the Community should already examine cases which come before them for unjustifiable discrimination.

Even outside the field of Community law, it is suggested that a protocol which simply included the words 'sexual orientation' in the list of prohibited types of discrimination in Article 14 of the Convention would change nothing and could actually be counterproductive. As we saw above, the European Commission on Human Rights already examines cases of discrimination against homosexuals and lesbians under Article 14. Changing the wording of the Article in this way would open no new vistas for victims of oppression. If such a protocol failed to attract the required number of ratifications by Member States, its failure to enter into force, or its inapplicability, could actually be used as evidence that Member States did not wish the Commission and Court of Human Rights to deal with this sort of case. The possibility of a fruitful development through the jurisprudence of the European Commission and Court of Human Rights would therefore be halted in its tracks. This would be big risk to take in the hope of persuading the European Commission on Human Rights to take a more lenient and considered approach to the claims of unjustified discrimination on grounds of sexual orientation.

The other possibility for an amending protocol would be an autonomous right to protection against discrimination on grounds of sexual orientation. Applicants would not have to show (as they do at present under Article 14 ECHR) that the discrimination related to the enjoyment of another Convention right. Such a proposal is unlikely to be adopted as it would place gay men and lesbians in a better position than other minorities under the Convention. It would also rank discrimination on grounds of sexual orientation above discrimination on grounds of sex. Despite attempts in the Council of Europe, Member States of that organization are still unwilling to allow an autonomous right under the ECHR for women to claim equal pay with men.

As stated above, campaigns for legislative change may achieve more in terms of consciousness-raising, group solidarity and creating an atmosphere in which people can come out. Therefore decisions as to whether to pursue a strategy which focuses on a protocol will have to take into account a plethora of factors extraneous to the concrete normative gains to be made.

What seems to be clear is that, at the Community level, to talk of a Protocol in the Council of Europe is to avoid the issues. The issues are: an asylum policy which takes the plight of persecuted lesbians and gay men seriously, recognition of the problems facing same-sex partners of workers moving around in the single market, discrimination in the workplace, discriminatory life insurance and mortgage requirements, awareness and discussion in the context of the social dialogue, free movement of goods and so on. The Community has the capacity to tackle these and other transnational issues. Taking decisions as closely as possible to Community citizens means that gay men and lesbians should be consulted and considered when Community provisions are drawn up or revised. Those spheres of life which are, or come to be, covered by Community law must take into account the hopes and aspirations of sexual minorities so that provisions do not compound hostility and discrimination by excluding lesbians and gay men from the benefits which other citizens are to be granted in the Community's single market and legal order.

An obvious first step would be for the Community to consult representative groups at an early stage of the legislative process. Such a process has been greatly facilitated by the formation of European confederal networks. Thirty West and East European countries are represented by about one hundred and fifty organizations at the annual European Regional Conference of the International Lesbian and Gay Association. Such consultation should not be confined to issues obviously related to sexuality but should be instituted as a matter of course. Transnational access to children, life insurance regulation and parental leave all raise issues for lesbians and gay men. There is no reason why their perspective should be excluded.

Advocates of the traditional family structure attempt to bolster their case by referring to the necessity of children being exposed to a mother and a father figure. But, if one parent from such a family leaves to take up a lesbian or gay lifestyle with another partner the question arises of the children's and parents' visiting rights. Granting equal visiting rights actually reinforces rather than denigrates family ties and attachment.

Attitudes to paternity leave vary among the governments of the Member States (the Commission's proposal is currently shelved due to opposition in the Council of Ministers). The rationale of paternity leave is to combat discrimination, challenge stereotypes and act in the best interests of the child. With an increasing number of children being born into lesbian relationships (with semen donated through friends, relations of the partner or anonymously) regulatory forms of law will have to adapt to ensure that such children are not deprived of the same sort of sponsored child care that other children benefit from. If the Community is going to penalize these non-traditional forms of family life it will have to explain why. Although voices are often raised claiming that lesbian or gay parents may put a child's development at risk, that children are deprived of experience from which to form their sexual identity, and that the children will be ostracized by society from an early age,[155] this claim has yet to be proved. Although fostering is not legally impossible. In the United States the courts have already examined an enormous amount of empirical evidence and determined in many cases that lesbians may adopt their lesbian partner's child.[156]

In any event, one cannot help wondering if the lesbian or gay dimension is more likely to be overlooked than deliberately excluded. The Commission is to be commended for considering the views of lesbians and gay men and including lesbians as a group of people disproportionately at risk from sexual harassment at the workplace and mentioning gay men and lesbians as also vulnerable to harassment.[157] The challenge is now for the Commission to face the issues which lesbian and gay families present in the context of Community law. They can no longer hide behind the excuse that lesbian and gay rights are not mentioned in the Treaties.[158]

B. Accession by the European Community to the European Convention on Human Rights

It was suggested that this chapter address the issue of accession by the Community to the European Convention on Human Rights and the advantages this would bring for lesbians and gay men. Briefly, it is difficult to foresee any immediate gains for lesbians and gay men should the Community so accede. There could conceivably be a greater permeation of human rights protection into the Community legal order. Accession would obviously be an important and desirable step in reinforcing the protection of human rights in Europe. It has recently been recommended again by the Commission of the Community and now enjoys widespread support.[159]

On the other hand, as we have already seen, the conservative approach of the European Commission of Human Rights and the limited nature of the anti-discrimination protection granted under the Convention could come to unnecessarily cramp the development of Community law in this area. It is suggested that campaigning for accession should not be a priority for lesbian and gay organizations when pursuing their interests at the European level.

---

155   See the examples and their critique in Tasker & Golombok, 1991, 184-187. For details of some of the legislative barriers in the different Member States in this field see the section entitled 'parenthood' in Chapter Three by Waaldijk.
156   Polikoff, 1990, 459-575, and see Marks, 1992, 21.
157   See Commission Recommendation of 27 November 1991 on the protection of the dignity of women and men at work, note 19.
158   The President of the Commission Jacques Delors responding to a question on anti-gay discrimination has stated that all forms of discrimination are contrary to Article 100a EEC. (Response to question by MEP Stephen Hughes, see Jeffery-Poulter, 1991, 249-50.)
159   See SEC(90) 2087, 19 November 1990.

C. Lesbian and Gay Rights in a Community Bill of Rights

There may not even be consensus amongst lesbians and gay men as to the desirability of entrenching specific references to sexuality in legislation. The analogy with ethnicity cannot be taken that far. People clearly do drift in and out of different sexual orientations. For lesbians and gay men to marginalize themselves through pointing to their differences and persecution may not be the most effective way of achieving tolerance and understanding of a preference in public and private life. This may mean challenging society's assumptions about homosexual relations rather than assuming the profile of victims. It is not far-fetched to say that the recent emphasis placed on victimization as a way of arguing for social change has already suffered from a backlash in some contexts.

Should lesbians and gay men come to be seen as privileged in the workplace due to their special constitutionalization, either at the national or international level, the resentment and confusion could be worse than the current distrust and dislike.[160]

Strategies which concentrate on equality risk degenerating into arguments about differences. While the majority of gay men and lesbians remain invisible differences will remain distorted.

By concentrating on difference we highlight the nagging question whether the majority, or the legislature, has a legitimate interest in protecting traditional and established ways of life because that morality is perceived as best serving the interests of all.[161] Choosing an overall equality clause allows opponents to concentrate on the erosion of the tradition of marriage rather than confronting the indignity of dismissal from work for reasons connected to a person's intimate life.

The legal concept of equality, as we have seen, allows for justifiable differences. The discrimination surrounding age of consent laws was held justifiable by reference to protection of children, morals, health and so on. Concentrating on equality ends up highlighting difference – reinforcing and incorporating prejudice. At this point it is hard to separate the prejudice from the legitimate concerns.[162]

---

160   For one vision that homosexuality law in the US is mandating homosexual affirmative action and that gays are restricting heterosexual free speech see Horowitz, 1991, 173-181. Horowitz contends that 'Gay bashing, then, is in some measure a product of the very laws designed to punish it' (178). On the backlash against lesbians and gays men in the United States see 'Gays under Fire', *Newsweek*, 14 September 1992, 35-41.
161   See Posner, 1992, 226-237.
162   See Ellin, 1985, 305; Dworkin, 1977, chapter 10. The European Court of Human Rights will review action by the Contracting Parties to the Convention even where these states rely on the justification that the action is necessary to protect morals based on the stance of the majority. *Case of Open Door and Dublin Well Woman v. Ireland*, Series A, No. 246.

Perhaps the less problematic path is through a return to three concepts which are central to the Universal Declaration of Human Rights (1948) and European Convention on Human Rights and its jurisprudence: dignity, free development of the personality and self-fulfillment.[163] According to the norms contained in the first of these sets of internationally recognized human rights 'national effort and international co-operation' should realize for individuals the rights indispensable for the free development of each individual's personality. This means going beyond striking down those criminal laws which are not necessary in a democratic society; it means creating the conditions in all spheres for self fulfillment and a higher standard of living. The European Community would seem to have already embarked on this track by labelling its sexual harassment Code of Practice 'Protecting the Dignity of Women and Men at Work'. And, as we have mentioned in several places, the European Parliament's Declaration of Fundamental Rights and Freedoms affirms the right to identity in its privacy clause. Simple equality strategies may miss the point. Harassment of lesbians at work by men is not equal to the sexual cajoling and blackmailing which male bosses indulge in – but a way of showing male offence at being classed redundant.

Nevertheless, the symbolic and educational importance of equality strategies should not be underestimated. There has already been an attempt to get lesbians and gay men listed as a protected minority entitled to equal rights in the Community Charter of the Fundamental Social Rights of Workers.[164] Now that separate possibilities exist for decision making in this sphere under the Protocol to the Maastricht Treaty there may be renewed opportunities to address the rights of lesbians and gay men without fear of the British veto. In any event there would seem to be no real reason why discrimination against lesbians and gay men at work should not come to be included in the equality directives or in a new directive.[165]

---

163   See Article 22 of the Universal Declaration on Human Rights: 'Everyone, as a member of society, has the right to social security and is entitled to realization, through national effort and international cooperation and in accordance with the organization and resources of each State, of the economic, social and cultural rights indispensable for his dignity and the free development of his personality.' See also the *Lingens* case Series A, No. 103, para. 41 for a statement by the European Court of Human Rights that freedom of expression is an essential condition 'for each individual's self fulfillment.'

164   This tactic was attempted by the European Parliament when it attempted to amend the Social Charter by introducing an amendment which urged Member States to give priority to 'the rights of all workers to equal protection regardless of their nationality, race, religion, age, sex, sexual preference or legal status.'Although this was passed by a substantial majority of the European Parliament, opposition from Member States in the Council of Ministers meant that the amendment was not adopted in the final version of the Charter.' See Jeffery-Poulter, 1991, 248-250.

165   See the chapters by Byre and Betten in this report. Lammy Betten points to a number of possibilities for a legal basis in this area: Articles 100, 117, 118a and 235.

VI. Concluding Remarks

The weaknesses which surround the protection of the rights of gay men and lesbians under international human rights law need not hinder enhanced protection within the Community legal order. First, there is relatively greater consensus within the Twelve Member States than there is in the international community or even in the 27 Member States of the Council of Europe. Second, within the scope of Community law the ECJ has rejected standards of human rights which merely reflect minimum standards. They have opted for higher standards sometimes going beyond international or *common* constitutional traditions. Third, Community rights operate in such a way that issues can be raised in national courts and tribunals imposing legal obligations on private individuals, associations, employers, insurers, landlords and organs of the state. The potential for a sense of European citizenship through the exercise and enjoyment of these rights is high. These rights may operate horizontally in the private sector as well as vertically against the state and transnationally. They transcend the basic citizen/state dichotomy and promote rights and responsibilities for a multitude of actors throughout the Community's legal order.

The human rights protection offered by the Community legal order has yet to be applied to a claim by gay men or lesbians. But where national provisions extend rights granted to heterosexuals to gay men and lesbians, then Community law will ensure that these rights are extended to Community workers from other Member States. In addition, where Community provisions come to be interpreted and applied in a discriminatory way this will have to be objectively justified.

Many of these acquired rights should perhaps now be specifically declared to *extend* to some of the discrimination now facing gay men and lesbians in the Community legal order. That this has not already occurred can be attributed to inertia at the international level due to opposition in some quarters, to the *invisible* nature of homosexuality and to the lack of organized pressure groups in the past. Much of this has changed. Those who wish to deny gay men and lesbians the rights which other people already enjoy will have to show what justification there is for continuing to discriminate against this minority. If their reasons are connected to traditional notions of the family, religion, culture or morals they now have to show that this type of protection of this cultural heritage is really necessary in a pluralistic democratic society. They will have to show that there is some reason for denying gay men and lesbians rights which others enjoy because they are inherent in human dignity.

The Community has already shown that it can be at the forefront of protecting the rights of gay men and lesbians by taking the small step of mentioning these minorities as specifically threatened at the workplace in its

Code of Practice on the Dignity of Women and Men at Work (the sexual harassment code). Other measures such as a Joint Declaration, a directive on discrimination, initiatives relating to the social dialogue process could similarly involve gay men and lesbians and ensure that the Community remains true to its commitment to European Union entailing 'an ever closer union among the peoples of Europe, where decisions are taken as closely as possible to the citizens.' The European Court of Justice's early commitment to 'the human point of view' should be a reminder that the unity of the peoples of Europe will depend in part on the Community respecting their diversity.

Chapter Three
The Legal Situation in the Member States

by

KEES WAALDIJK[*]

[*] Lecturer, Department of Gay and Lesbian Studies, University of Utrecht, and Department of Public Law, University of Limburg in Maastricht.

Table of Contents

I. Discriminatory Laws and Laws against Discrimination

A. Introduction[1]

Not much is known about the social situation of the 15 million or more[2] homosexual citizens of the European Community. A little more is known about their legal situation, and far less about their economic situation. This and the following two chapters try to give an overview of what is known about the position of lesbians and gay men in the twelve Member States.[3]

On 13 March 1984 the European Parliament observed 'that in the campaign against discrimination of all kinds it is impossible to ignore or passively to accept *de facto* or *de jure* discrimination against homosexuals'. It went on to deplore 'all forms of discrimination based on an individual's sexual tendencies', and to call on the Member States and the EC Commission to take various measures to stop legal and social anti-homosexual discrimination.[4]

This Parliamentary appeal has not led to a complete elimination of anti-homosexual discrimination. In all Member States of the European Community there is still a great deal of social and legal discrimination against lesbians and gay men. However, over the last years several Member

---

1   In this and the next two chapters, the words 'homosexuals' and 'lesbians and gay men' will be used – interchangeably – in a wide sense, referring to anyone who has, or would like to have, sexual contacts and/or affectional relationships with people of the same gender as her or his own, whether or not she or he identifies as being 'lesbian', 'gay' and or/homosexual. The word 'homosexuality' will be used in a similar wide sense.
2   The figure could be as high as that estimated by Peter Tatchell: 32 million (Tatchell, 1992, 12). However, homosexual behaviour is not the same as homosexual preference which is not the same as homosexual identity; all these aspects of homosexuality tend to be underreported in a hostile environment. Due to these and other definition and research difficulties, and because of differences between the notion and practice of homosexuality between different regions and between women and men, it is impossible to give a precise estimate of the number of lesbian and gay citizens in the EC.
    According to J.C. Gonsiorek and J.D. Weinrich research suggests that the incidence of homosexuality in the United States of America ranges between 4% and 17% (1991, 1-12). They quote from a cross-cultural study of same-sex sexual behaviour in men (Sell, 1990). In France 11.6% and in the United Kingdom 7.8% of subjects reported same-sex sexual behaviour since the age of fifteen. In France 10,8% and in the United Kingdom 4,7% reported such behaviour within the last five years. (The percentages for the United States were 11.6 and 6.3.)
3   Information has been included about developments in the twelve Member States since 1980. Some information therefore relates to developments in Greece, Portugal, Spain and the German Democratic Republic that took place before they became part of the EC. Occasionally reference will be made to the small European jurisdictions under the British Crown that are not part of the United Kingdom (the Channel Islands, the Isle of Man, Gibraltar).
4   'Resolution on Sexual Discrimination at the Workplace' (OJ 1984 C 104/46-48), which followed similar texts adopted on 1 October 1981 by the Parliamentary Assembly of the Council of Europe (Resolution 756 and Recommendation 924, both 'on discrimination against homosexuals').

States have abolished some of their discriminatory laws, and have introduced some legal safeguards against anti-homosexual discrimination.[5]

This chapter will describe the changing legal situation of homosexuality in the twelve Member States. I shall assess whether the national laws are in conformity with the criteria formulated in the above mentioned Parliamentary appeal. Each paragraph will mostly deal with one or both of two categories of law: legal discrimination (written and unwritten discriminatory laws) and legal anti-discrimination (written and unwritten laws prohibiting social or legal discrimination). The focus will be on written rules and court cases in which homosexuality is specifically included or excluded. However, some reference will be made to general laws which are themselves worded in a 'neutral' way, but which have been applied in a discriminatory (or anti-discriminatory) way.

Legal developments up to the Summer of 1992 have been taken into account. Efforts to give a complete picture of at least the written laws dealing with homosexuality have not been fully successful for all Member States.[6] As far as case-law and the administrative application of laws are concerned, the picture given by this chapter is even less complete. Whenever possible, reference will be made to original legislative and judicial texts. However, in many instances there will only be references to academic

---

5   Many of these legal developments in the Member States, as well as in countries outside the EC, are documented in 'Iceberg 1991' (see note 7). For overviews, see also Tielman & De Jonge, 1988, Udding & Ramakers, 1991, Tatchell, 1992, and Tielman & Hammelburg, 1993 (in print).

6   An early draft of this chapter was sent for comments to the Ministries of Justice and of Social Affairs in all Member States (except the Netherlands), and to various experts and lesbian and gay organizations in the Member States. I am grateful for having received very useful responses and/or materials from:
    –   Ministry of Justice, Denmark;
    –   Ministry of Social Affairs, Denmark;
    –   Ministry of Justice, Luxembourg;
    –   Ministry of Justice, Portugal, which let a report be drafted specifically for this research: La situation juridique et sociale de l'homosexualité au Portugal (Lisbon, 23 June 1992);
    –   Ministry of Justice, Spain;
    –   Equal Opportunities and General Department, Home Office, United Kingdom;
    –   Criminal Policy Department, Home Office, United Kingdom;
    –   Referat für gleichgeschlechtliche Lebensweisen, Senatsverwaltung für Jugend und Familie, Berlin;
    –   Landesforeningen for bøsser og lesbiske, Denmark;
    –   Gais Pour les Libertés, France;
    –   Bundesverband Homosexualität, Germany;
    –   Gay & Lesbian Equality Network, Ireland;
    –   Riksförbundet för sexuallt likaberättigande, Sweden;
    and from many individuals including: Etienne Bassot (Saarbrücken), Adrianne Dercksen (Utrecht), David Geer (London), Helmut Graupner (Vienna), Aart Hendriks (Leiden), Astrid Mattijssen (Utrecht), Anya Palmer (London), Judith Schuyf (Utrecht), Evert van der Veen (Utrecht), Rob Wintermute (London). Writing this chapter has been made possible by the continuing assistance of Jelle Martens (Maastricht).

publications,[7] to reports in the general and lesbian and gay press,[8] or to information provided by individuals and organizations from several countries.[9] In each paragraph the countries with similar legal situations are grouped together. In each group they are listed in alphabetical order, unless a chronological order seemed more appropriate. If in a particular paragraph some countries are not listed, this means either that I do not have enough information about them or that they do not have the problem discussed.

Part II of this chapter deals with ten different areas in which 'the law' has concerned itself with homosexuality in negative and/or positive ways. Part III contains a summary and recommendations.

B. Equality as Constitutional Principle

There are still no national constitutions in Europe that specifically prohibit discrimination based on sexual orientation.[10] However, many constitutional provisions on non-discrimination or 'equality before the law' are worded in such general terms that 'sexual orientation' may be considered to fall within their scope of protection.[11]

At the start of the eighties the constitutions of nine Member States already contained general equality clauses.[12] In 1983 the Netherlands joined this group of countries, by including a new Article 1 in its revised constitution. This Article now forbids discrimination 'on any ground

---

7   See the literature listed in Annex 1. Many of the examples given are based on the 'Iceberg-project'. This project (initiated by the International Lesbian and Gay Associa- tion, hosted by the Department of Gay and Lesbian Studies of the University of Utrecht, and partly funded by the European Human Rights Foundation) has been documenting examples of legal and social discrimination and of anti-discriminatory measures in the whole of Europe. A first report, *Tip of an iceberg. Anti-lesbian and anti-gay discrimina- tion in Europe 1980 – 1990*, by Kees Waaldijk, is being prepared; the latest draft-ver - sion (dated 16 December 1991) contains most of the examples used in this chapter. Where appropriate, reference will be made to the relevant paragraph of '*Iceberg* 1991', as well as to the source quoted in that draft-report.

8   References to the press are indicated by the word 'press-report'. Of course it was not pos- sible to check the accuracy of each press-report.

9   Therefore, traceable references cannot be given for all the information supplied in this chapter.

10 After the peaceful revolution of 1989 in the German Democratic Republic a new consti- tution was drafted, Article 1 of which provided that nobody 'shall be put at a disadvan - tage because of ... his sexual orientation ...'. Because of the reunification of East and West Germany in 1990, this constitution did not enter into force (see *Bundestag Druck- sache* 11/7197, 9 July 1990, 5-6; see also *Schwule im Recht*, 1992, 309).

11 This is also true for the prohibitions of discrimination contained in the European Con - vention on Human Rights (Article 14) and in the International Covenant on Civil and Political Rights (Article 26), which are binding on all Member States.

12 Belgium (Article 6), France (Article 2), Germany (Article 3), Greece (Article 4), Ireland (Article 40), Italy (Article 3), Luxembourg (Article 11), Portugal (Article 13), Spain (Article 14).

whatsoever'.[13] It has been confirmed in case-law that the words 'any ground whatsoever' do indeed cover sexual orientation.[14] The new 1992 constitution of the German *Land* Brandenburg specifically mentions sexual orientation as one of the forbidden grounds for discrimination.[15]

Although in Denmark the Constitution only prohibits discrimination on the grounds of 'creed or descent', an unwritten principle of equality in other respects has been generally accepted.[16] The United Kingdom has neither a written constitution, nor a general principle prohibiting discrimination.

The significance of constitutional Articles which potentially cover discrimination based on sexual orientation is limited, for three different reasons:

Firstly, in some countries the courts have no[17] or very limited[18] power to review the constitutionality of parliamentary legislation. In those countries courts can not normally determine that a law is discriminatory and therefore unconstitutional and invalid.

Secondly, most constitutions have hardly any 'horizontal effect'.[19] This means that they can only be invoked against the government and against other public authorities (that is: only in a 'vertical' direction). Invoking them against an individual person or against a private organization (that is: in a 'horizontal' direction) is not possible.

And thirdly, 'discrimination' and 'equality' are vague concepts, which leave a wide scope for constitutional interpretation.[20] In general, equality

13   In fact those words have been added during the Parliamentary debate on the revision of the constitution, after criticisms from the Council of State and from the Lower Chamber of Parliament; both bodies thought that the original draft text ('Discrimination on the grounds of religion, belief, political opinion, race or sex shall not be permitted.') should be extended so as to prohibit discrimination against homosexuals as well (see Waaldijk, 1986/1987, 59-60).

14   Amsterdam Court of Appeal, 10 December 1987, 14 *NJCM-bulletin* (1989) 305 at 315.

15   Article 12 (Gesetz- und Verordnungsblatt für das Land Brandenburg, 1992, No. 18).

16   Article 70 (see Steenbeek, 1988, 106).

17   As is the case in Luxembourg (see Thill, 1988, 431-432) and in the Netherlands (Article 120 of the Constitution).

18   For example in Belgium (see Koopmans, 1992, 41), Denmark (see Steenbeek, 1988, 98) and France (see Koopmans 1986, 72-78).

19   See for Germany, for example, *Schwule im Recht*, 1992, 314.
      An exception is the Portuguese Constitution: according to Article 18, the constitutional rights are also binding on private entities. A report from the Ministry of Justice of Portugal concludes from this (in combination with the constitutional prohibition of all discrimination in Article 13) that discrimination of homosexuals will lead to civil and/or criminal responsibility (*La situation juridique et sociale de l'homosexualité au Portugal*, Lisbon, 23 June 1992, paragraphs 7, 12 and 19 to 21).
      Some horizontal effect is also attributed to (the anti-discrimination provision of) the Dutch Constitution (see Mattijssen, 1992, 14-15).

20   Article 40 of the Irish Constitution makes the point explicitly that: 'All citizens shall, as human persons, be held equal before the law. This shall not be held to mean that the State shall not in its enactments have due regard to differences of capacity, physical or moral, and of social function.'

clauses are interpreted as only prohibiting distinctions which are not based on an acceptable ('reasonable and objective') justification.[21] The result is that a court may well be led by its own moral objections against homosexuality to conclude that certain distinctions based on sexual orientation are 'reasonably and objectively justified'.[22]

For these reasons, legal discrimination is more likely to be ended through measures taken by national legislatures (or through the use of the international law of human rights), than through constitutional litigation in national courts. And as a legal instrument to fight social discrimination, a general constitutional equality clause will be far less effective than specific anti-discrimination legislation.

C. Anti-Discrimination Legislation

Most Member States have specific legislation prohibiting social discrimination based on race or sex. Specific prohibitions on discrimination based on sexual orientation are still rare and are found only in France, Denmark, Ireland and the Netherlands.

The French Law of 25 July 1985 inserted the words 'sex', 'family situation' and '*mœurs*' (which may be translated as morals/habits/lifestyle including sexual orientation) into most of the anti-discrimination provisions of the Penal Code[23] and the Code of Criminal Procedure.[24] The Laws of 17 January 1986 and 12 July 1990 amended the Code of Labour Law so as to cover discrimination on the basis of *mœurs*.[25]

---

21   For such an interpretation of the constitution in:
      Belgium, see Delpérée, 1980, 190-192;
      France, see note 22;
      Germany, see Koopmans, 1986, 65-66; *Schwule im Recht*, 1992, 308-309; and Malt, 1991, 87-88;
      Ireland, see Casey, 1987, 348;
      the Netherlands, see Waaldijk, 1992a, 66-70.
      The European Court of Human Rights (for example in its judgment of 23 July 1968 in the *Belgian linguistics* case, Series A, No. 6, para. 10) and the United Nations Human Rights Committee (opinion of 9 April 1987 in the case of *Broeks v. the Netherlands*, in *NJCM-bulletin* (1987) 377-391) have given similar interpretations to the anti-discrimination provisions in human rights treaties.
22   The French Constitutional Council, for example, held in 1980 that the (then still applicable) different age limits for heterosexual sex and for lesbian and gay sex did not violate the constitutional principle of equality before the criminal law, because that principle was no bar to 'differentiations between acts of a different nature' (decision of 19 December 1980, D.1981 – IR – 358; see Boutet, 1988, 31).
23   Articles 187-1, 187-2, 416 and 416-1.
24   Article 2-6.
25   Articles L.122-35 and L.122-45 respectively (see *Juris classeur périodique*, 1991, 21724). The Law of 12 July 1990 also added the words 'state of health' and 'handicap' in most of the existing anti-discrimination provisions.

In Denmark on 1 July 1987 'sexual orientation' was inserted in the Law 289 of 9 June 1971 (which forbids discrimination on the grounds of race etc.) and in an anti-discrimination provision of the Penal Code.[26]

In Ireland the 'Prohibition of Incitement to Hatred Act 1989' makes it a criminal offence to incite to hatred on the basis of sexual orientation.[27]

The Dutch Law of 14 November 1991[28] amended most of the anti-discrimination provisions of the Penal Code so as to cover discrimination on the basis of 'heterosexual or homosexual orientation'.[29]

In Belgium a proposal for an anti-discrimination law has been before Parliament since 1985.[30] In the Netherlands[31] a proposal for further anti-discrimination legislation has been introduced. Proposals for anti-discrimination legislation in Ireland[32] and the United Kingdom[33] have been defeated.

---

26 Article 266b.
27 Acts of the Oireachtas, 1989, No. 19; See *Equality Now,* 1990, iii.
28 *Staatsblad,* 1991, No. 623. The Law, which resulted from proposal 20239 of 1987, came into force on 1 February 1992. See Haveman & Moerings, 1992, 53-58.
29 Articles 137c, 137d, 137e, 137f and 429quater; Article 90quater defines discrimination as 'unjustified distinctions' which have a negative effect on the exercise of human rights in the area of politics, economics, culture or social life.
30 Proposal No. 1219/1 of 23 May 1985, reintroduced on 29 March 1988 under No. 339/1. This proposal has not been debated yet.
31 Since 1981, several proposals for a separate anti-discrimination law have been presented (and withdrawn) in the Netherlands. The last in this series is the proposal for a 'General Equal Treatment Act' containing private and administrative law prohibitions of discrimination that are more specific than the criminal law provisions of 1992. The proposed law would also establish an 'Equal Treatment Commission', which would give non-binding judgments on cases of suspected illegal discrimination, and which would have the power to take such cases to court (proposal 22014, introduced in 1991, not expected to enter into force before 1994; see Mattijssen, 1992, 29-35; and see Hoogma, 1992 and Waaldijk, 1986/87, 60-64 for history of the earlier drafts).
32 In March 1992 a proposal 'Equal Status Bill' (which was introduced by the opposition in 1990, and which would outlaw discrimination on various grounds including sexual orientation) was narrowly defeated in the Irish Parliament (see *Resource material on lesbian/gay law reform,* 1992, item 4.1a). In 1989 the Irish Council for Civil Liberties had published proposals for legislation against discrimination on account of 'sexual orientation, gender, family status, health disability' etc. (see *Equality Now,* 1990, 54-60).
33 In the United Kingdom in 1983, a private member's bill on Sex Equality, which would have outlawed employment discrimination based on homosexuality, was rejected in parliament (see Jeffery-Poulter, 1991, 167). In 1990 a survey among Members of Parliament (held for the *Guardian* newspaper and the television series *Out On Tuesday*) shows that 45% of them would (and 47% would not) support the introduction of legislation to protect homosexuals against discrimination in employment and in the provision of services (press-report: *Gay Times*, April 1990, 8). According to a letter of 21 February 1992 from the Home Office to me, the British government holds the view that while it is opposed to unfair treatment of any minority, legislation to outlaw discrimination against homosexuals would not command the degree of general public assent necessary for it to be acceptable and effective given that lesbian and gay sexuality is an issue on which widely different views are sincerely held.

The existing and proposed anti-discrimination laws mentioned above cover three different forms of discrimination:
-   employment discrimination (to be discussed in paragraph II.D); this is covered by the French and Dutch laws and proposals and by the Belgian proposal;
-   discrimination in relation to goods and services (to be discussed in paragraph II.E, II.F.1 and II.I); this is covered by the French, Danish and Dutch laws and by the French, Dutch and Belgian proposals;
-   verbal discrimination (to be discussed in paragraph II.H.2.); this is covered by the Danish, Dutch and Irish laws and by the Belgian proposal.

The Dutch and Belgian proposals explicitly also cover *indirect discrimination*. This does not mean, however, that other existing laws only cover direct discrimination. In particular it may be argued that discrimination against unmarried couples and discrimination because of an individual's actual or perceived HIV antibody status amounts to indirect discrimination on the ground of sexual orientation.

It goes beyond the scope of this chapter to assess the impact and effectiveness of the various pieces of anti-discrimination legislation.

D. Repeal of Discriminatory Laws

The introduction of anti-discrimination legislation has not been the only legislative development concerning homosexuality in the Member States. In recent years several countries have repealed some of their anti-homosexual laws, notably by:
-   decriminalizing homosexual sex between adults,[34]
-   equalizing the minimum ages for homosexual and heterosexual sex,[35]
-   repealing specific bans on homosexuality,[36]
-   extending the availability of some of the legal benefits of marriage to unmarried couples of the same sex.[37]

Similar moves towards greater equality have been witnessed in many other countries of Europe. The overall picture is one of a slow but progressive implementation of the principle of non-discrimination in relation to homosexuality.[38] Over the last decades no anti-discrimination law covering

---

34   Scotland in 1980, Northern Ireland in 1982, Guernsey in 1983, Jersey in 1990, Isle of Man in 1992 (see paragraph II.A.1).
35   France in 1982, Belgium in 1985, Greece in 1987, the German Democratic Republic in 1989, Luxembourg in 1992 (see paragraph II.A.2).
36   France in 1980 (see paragraph II.A.3), Spain in 1984 (see paragraph II.A.4).
37   See paragraph II.B.
38   See the *Memorandum on Recent Developments in Law Affecting the Human Rights of Homosexual Women and Men*, submitted by the International Humanist and Ethical Union to the 64th meeting of non-governmental organizations holding consultative status with the Council of Europe, Strasbourg, 28 September 1989.

sexual orientation has been repealed, and only very few new anti-homosexual laws have been introduced.[39] To illustrate the ongoing character of this process, all major legislative changes since 1980 are mentioned in this chapter.

II. Law and Homosexuality in Ten Different Areas

A. Expressions of Sexuality and Affection

In 1984 the European Parliament urged Member States to:
- abolish any laws which make homosexual acts between consenting adults liable to punishment,
- apply the same age of consent as for heterosexual acts.[40]

Unequal minimum ages for heterosexual and homosexual sex are the most common form of anti-homosexual discrimination in criminal law (paragraph 2 below).[41] Lesbian and gay sex between adults has not only been the subject of total prohibitions (paragraph 1) but also of various other restrictions (paragraphs 3 and 4).

---

39 The notable exception to the rule being Section 28 of the British 'Local Government Act 1988', to be discussed in paragraph II.G.1. The general trend and this exception have led the 67th meeting of non-governmental organizations holding consultative status with the Council of Europe and interested in Human Rights (Strasbourg, 2 October 1990), on the basis of the Memorandum mentioned in the previous note, to adopt a 'Motion on the Legal Situation of Homosexuality', calling on the Member States 'to repeal all laws which discriminate against homosexuality' and 'to refrain from introducing new dis-criminatory laws' (Summary report H/ONG (90/3) Strasbourg 19 November 1990, 4 and 12).

40 'Resolution on Sexual Discrimination at the Workplace', adopted on 13 March 1984 (OJ 1984 C 104/46-48), following Recommendation 924 of the Parliamentary Assembly of the Council of Europe, adopted on 1 October 1981.
     At the start of the eighties Denmark, Italy, Netherlands, Portugal and Spain had already fulfilled both criteria – for gay sex and for lesbian sex.
     As far as lesbian sex is concerned, the Federal Republic of Germany, Greece, Ireland and the United Kingdom then also fulfilled both criteria. Belgium, France, Luxembourg and the German Democratic Republic, however, had a higher age limit for lesbian sex than for heterosexual sex.
     As far as gay sex is concerned, Belgium, France, both Germanies, Greece and Luxem-bourg only fulfilled the first criterion – they still had a higher age limit for gay sex than for hetero sex. In the United Kingdom gay sex between consenting men was only lawful in England and Wales, but not from the same age as heterosexual sex. In the other parts of the United Kingdom (Scotland and Northern Ireland) as well as in the Channel Is-lands, the Isle of Man, Gibraltar and in Ireland all gay sex was illegal.

41 See paragraph 2.3 of *Iceberg* 1991.

1. Total Prohibitions

In all Member States except one – Ireland[42] – the total prohibition of gay sex has been abolished. The abolition in Northern Ireland in 1982[43] followed the judgment of the European Court of Human Rights in the *Dudgeon* case.[44] The same laws of 1861 and 1885 that had been held, in this judgment, to violate the European Convention on Human Rights, are still in force in the Republic of Ireland.[45] They have been challenged by David *Norris*. In his case, the Irish Supreme Court found the laws to be consistent with the Irish constitution.[46] The case was then taken to Strasbourg, where the European Court of Human Rights applying the same reasoning that it had applied in the *Dudgeon* case, concluded that Ireland was in breach of the European Convention of Human Rights.[47]

Thus far, Ireland has not abolished its total prohibition on gay sex. In 1989 the Irish Law Reform Commission recommended legalizing gay sex, and introducing equal ages of consent for heterosexual, lesbian and gay sex.[48] The government first announced that it would introduce a legislative

42   The only other jurisdiction within the EC where gay sex is still always a crime is Gibraltar.

43   In the other two parts of the United Kingdom the total prohibitions of gay sex had been abolished before: in England and Wales by section 1 of the 'Sexual Offences Act 1967' and in Scotland by Section 80 of the 'Criminal Justice (Scotland) Act 1980'.
     In three of the Channel Islands (Guernsey, Alderney and Sark) the total prohibition of gay sex was abolished by Section 1 of the 'Sexual Offences (Bailiwick of Guernsey) Law 1983'. The duration of this law was made indefinite by the 'Sexual Offences (Bailiwick of Guernsey) Law 1983 (Continuation) Ordinance 1986'.
     On Jersey, the fourth Channel Island, the total prohibition of gay sex was abolished by Article 1 of the 'Sexual Offences (Jersey) Law 1990'.
     The total prohibition of gay sex on the Isle of Man was abolished by the 'Sexual Offences Act 1992' of 7 July 1992.
     In Gibraltar it was abolished in December 1992.

44   Judgment of 22 October 1981, Series A, No. 45.

45   Section 61 of the 'Offences against the Person Act 1861', dealing with ' *the abominable crime of buggery*' (that is: anal intercourse – maximum penalty life imprisonment) and Section 11 of the 'Criminal Law Amendment Act 1885', dealing with '*any act of gross indecency with another male person*' (that is: any other form of gay sex – maximum penalty two years imprisonment).

46   In its judgment of 22 April 1983 it considered that no right of privacy covering consensual homosexual conduct could be derived from 'the Christian and democratic nature of the Irish State' (as quoted by the European Court of Human Rights, see the following note).

47   *Norris* case, 26 October 1988, Series A, No. 142.

48   Followed in 1990 by the Irish Council for Civil Liberties (see *Equality Now*, 1990, iii; press-reports: *Gay Community News*, October 1990; *Gay Times*, November 1990). An opinion poll (held in 1990 by Irish Marketing Surveys for the *Sunday Independent*) suggested that 48% of the population thinks that the law governing homosexuality should not be changed, and that 30% thinks that it should be changed. In two similar polls (held in 1991 by Irish Marketing Surveys for *Family Solidarity* and by Lansdowne Market Research for the *Sunday Press*) the figures against change were 49% and 42%, and the figures in favour of law reform were 34% and 39% (see *Resource material on lesbian/gay law reform* 1992, items 8.1, 8.2 and 8.3).

proposal in 1991,[49] then in 1992,[50] and recently that such a proposal would not reach Parliament before 1993.[51]

All gay sex is therefore still illegal in Ireland. However, since at least 1974 there have not been any prosecutions, except where minors have been involved or where the acts were committed in public or without consent.[52]

2. Age Limits

The criminal laws of all Member States make it a criminal offence to have sex with persons under certain ages.[53] In four Member States there is not (yet) an equal minimum age for heterosexual, lesbian and gay sex. In the other eight Member States, as well as in the eastern part of Germany (the former GDR), equal minimum ages for heterosexual, lesbian and gay sex now apply.

---

49   Statement by the Minister of Justice, *Seanad Éireann*, Parliamentary Debates, 12 December 1990.

50   Statement by the Ambassador of Ireland on 15 May 1992 at the meeting of the Committee of Minister's Deputies on Human Rights of the Council of Europe (quoted in a letter of 9 July 1992 from the Gay & Lesbian Equality Network in Dublin to the Secretary-General of the European Commission of Human Rights in Strasbourg).

51   Statement by the Prime Minister, *Dáil Éireann*, Parliamentary Debates, 3 June 1992.

52   See judgment in *Norris* case, Series A, No. 42, para. 19-20. The Court ruled that although David Norris had not been prosecuted, he was still a 'victim' of the laws, because these 'may be applied again (...) if for example there is a change of policy' (para. 33).

53   It should be noted that in several countries higher age limits apply:
- if the older person is responsible for the upbringing, education or care of the youngster;
- if the older person misuses a position of authority;
- in case of deception;
- in case of 'seduction'; or
- in case of prostitution.

Where the general age limits are the same for heterosexual, lesbian and gay sex, these higher age limits are also equal – with the exception of the Greek age limit of 17 for 'seduction' leading to gay sex (see below).

(a) Overview

The following *equal* age limits are in force in the EC:

- 16 in Belgium, [54]
- 16 in Italy, [55]
- 16 in Luxembourg, [56]
- 16 in the Netherlands, [57]
- 16 in Portugal, [58]
- 15 in Denmark, [59]
- 15 in France, [60]
- 14 in eastern Germany, [61]
- 12 in Spain. [62]

---

[54] Article 372 of the Penal Code.
Until 1985 Article 372bis provided for a higher minimum age of 18 for lesbian and gay sex; this Article was abolished by the Law of 18 June 1985.

[55] Article 530 of the Penal Code.
A lower minimum age of 14 applies to sex with a young person who has been 'corrupted' before (Article 519).

[56] Article 372 of the Penal Code.
Until 1992, Article 372 set the age limit for heterosexual sex at 14, and Article 372bis made it an offence for someone over 18 to have lesbian or gay sex with someone under 18. Article 372 was changed and Article 372bis abolished by the Law of 10 August 1992 (*Receuil de Législation*, 25 September 1992, A-No. 70, 2195-2202).

[57] Articles 244, 245 and 247 of the Penal Code. Until 1991, a man who had 'sexual intercourse' with a girl between the ages of 12 and 16, could only be prosecuted on the basis of a formal complaint. Such a formal complaint was not required for the prosecution of a woman who had sex with a boy or girl under 16, nor for the prosecution of a man who had sex with a boy under that age. In 1991 the complaint-requirement was laid down for the prosecution of any person who has sex with someone between 12 and 16; valid complaints can be made by the youngster involved, by his or her legal representative (normally either parent), or by the Child Welfare Council (see Articles 245 and 247 of the Penal Code, as amended by the Law of 9 October 1991, *Staatsblad* 519).

[58] Article 206 of the Penal Code. According to Article 211 a person who has sex with a girl or a boy over the age of 12 can only be prosecuted on the basis of a formal complaint by the youngster involved or by his or her parent or custodian.

[59] Article 222 of the Penal Code (Tatchell, 1992, 106).

[60] Paragraph 1 of Article 331 of the Penal Code.
Until 1982 paragraph 2 of that Article provided a higher minimum age of 18 for lesbian and gay sex; this paragraph was abolished by the Law of 4 August 1982, No. 82-683 (Boutet, 1988, 32).
In 1991 an amendment to reintroduce a minimum age of 18 for gay sex was passed by the Senate but defeated by the National Assembly (see Udding & Ramakers, 1991).

[61] Article 148 of the Penal Code of the former German Democratic Republic (this Article temporarily remained in force on the former GDR's territory when on 3 October 1990 it became part of the Federal Republic of Germany; see *Schwule im Recht*, 1992, 200-201). Until 1989 Article 151 of the Penal Code provided a higher minimum age of 18 for lesbian and gay sex; this Article was abolished (*Gesetzblatt der DDR Teil 1*, No. 29, 28 December 1988) after a decision of the East German Supreme Court (*Oberste Gericht*, 11 August 1987, *Neue Justiz* 1987, No. 11, 467) ruling that the higher age for gay and lesbian sex should not be enforced in cases where the rights and interests of other citizens and society had hardly been affected and where the accused was hardly to blame (Thinius, 1990, 149-160).

[62] Article 429 of the Penal Code.

And the following *unequal* age limits apply in the EC:[63]

- 17 for gay sex by seduction in Greece,[64]
  15 for other gay sex, and for lesbian and heterosexual sex in Greece,[65]
- 18 for gay sex in western Germany,[66]
  14 for lesbian and heterosexual sex in western Germany,[67]
- 21 for gay sex in the United Kingdom,[68]
  17 for lesbian and heterosexual sex in Northern Ireland,[69]
  16 for lesbian and heterosexual sex in Great Britain,[70]
- total prohibition for gay sex in Ireland,[71]
  17 for heterosexual intercourse with a girl in Ireland,
  15 for other heterosexual and for lesbian sex in Ireland.

In western Germany homosexual sex with someone under the higher age limit is only a criminal offence for persons *over* that age and in Greece 'seduction' of a man under 17 is only an offence for a man over 18. In the United Kingdom, however, gay sex with someone under the higher age limit is also a criminal offence for persons *under* that age.[72]

In short: in addition to Ireland three Member States have not yet acted upon the Resolution of the European Parliament calling for the abolition of anti-homosexual discrimination in criminal law. In no Member State is the age of consent for lesbian sex higher than for heterosexual sex. Two gay lovers, one of them almost 17 and the other 19, travelling throughout the EC, might well find themselves breaking the law in Ireland and in the United Kingdom, and discover that the older one is committing criminal offences in the western part of Germany and is being accused of 'seduction' in Greece.

---

63   See also note 53.
64   Article 347 of the Penal Code makes it a criminal offence for a man over 18 to 'seduce' a man under 17 to have gay sex.
65   Article 339 of the Penal Code.
66   Article 175 of the Penal Code makes it an offence for a man over the age of 18 to have sex with a man under that age (maximum penalty five years imprisonment). This Article temporarily remained in force in the western part of Germany when on 3 October 1990 the territory of the former German Democratic Republic became part of the Federal Republic of Germany (see *Schwule im Recht,* 1992, 200-201).
67   Article 176 of the Penal Code. According to Article 182 it is also an offence for a man to 'seduce' a girl under 16 to have sexual intercourse (*Beischlaf*) with him – but only if the man does not marry the girl.
68   See section 80 of the 'Criminal Justice (Scotland) Act 1980', the 'Homosexual Offences (Northern Ireland) Order 1982', and for England and Wales Sections 1 and 3 of the 'Sexual Offences Act 1967' (maximum penalty five years imprisonment; and two years for offenders under 21). According to Section 8 of the 1967 Act, prosecutions in England and Wales can only be brought with permission of the Director of Public Prosecutions (see Crane, 1982, 8 and 24).
69   See Crane, 1982, 8 and 15.
70   See section 14 of the 'Sexual Offences Act 1956' for England and Wales.
71   See paragraph II.A.1 above.
72   See paragraphs II.A.3 and II.A.4 for further restrictions.

(b) Enforcement of unequal limits

Although it is sometimes argued that laws which create higher age limits for homosexual sex are 'dead laws' there is evidence, in recent years, of their actual enforcement:

- in western Germany, in the period 1985 to 1987 the average annual number of convictions on the basis of Article 175 was 119; in 1985 52 men were given prison sentences;[73]
- in England and Wales, in 1989, 31 men over the age of 21 were imprisoned for consenting sex with a man between the ages of 16 and 21; greater numbers will have been convicted or prosecuted;[74]
- in 1988 the High Court in Edinburgh sentenced a 36 year-old man to five years imprisonment, for having had sex with two 17 year-old men.[75]

In many more cases decisions will have been taken not to prosecute. Whether there are official policies in Greece, western Germany and the United Kingdom on the selective or non-prosecution of homosexual sex between people over the minimum age for heterosexual sex, is unclear. In 1991 it was reported in the press that the Lord Advocate (a Minister of Justice for Scotland) was planning to give instructions not to prosecute in cases of consensual sex between men over 16. However, such an announcement has not been made.[76]

The very existence of unequal age limits can be seen as a form of discrimination, which is aggravated by the great uncertainty over the likelihood of prosecution. The threat of possible prosecutions and punishment cannot fail to have a negative impact on the happiness and security of the (younger and older) individuals involved. For many of them it will be difficult and sometimes even dangerous to be open about their love life.

In addition, legal inequality as such is likely to reinforce ideas that homosexuality is a less acceptable form of love than heterosexuality (whatever the ages of the lovers concerned). More specifically, the existence of higher age limits for homosexual sex may help to reinforce the idea that homosexuality is contagious, that people (in particular, the young) can be 'made' lesbian or gay.

Finally, the fact that the criminal law discriminates against homosexuality, may operate as a justification for the perpetuating of other forms of discrimination by public authorities and by private organizations and individuals.

---

73 See Dworek & Kühn, 1989, 59, and Dose, 1990, 131.
74 Their prison sentences were sometimes as long as for rape, and often twice as long as the gaol terms for 'unlawful sexual intercourse' with a girl between the ages of 13 and 16 (see Tatchell, 1992, 85 and 90).
75 Press-report: *Gay Times*, May 1990, 17.
76 Press-report: *ILGA Bulletin*, 1991, No. 3, 27-28; No. 5, 26.

In the case of actual prosecutions or convictions the consequences for the individuals concerned are often dramatic: break up of friendship and family relationships, loss of housing and employment, and great difficulties in finding new jobs – both in their own country and abroad (even in countries where separate homosexual offences no longer exist).

(c) Challenges and proposals for change

Several attempts by British gay men to challenge the lawfulness of differential legal minimum ages have failed at the European Commission of Human Rights.[77] In 1981 the Criminal Law Revision Committee recommended lowering the age of consent for gay sex from 21 to 18, but considered it 'wholly unacceptable to public opinion' to bring it down to 16.' An opinion poll suggested that 74% of the population think that the minimum age limit for sex should be the same for everyone, regardless of gender or sexual orientation.[78] In Parliament the main opposition parties are committed to equalizing the age limits for heterosexual, lesbian and gay sex.

In Germany the equalization of the age limits is more likely in the near future. Upon the reunification of the two Germanies in 1990 it was agreed that, for the time being, the German Democratic Republic's laws on sex with young people (equal age) would remain in force in the eastern part of the country, and the corresponding laws of the Federal Republic of Germany (unequal ages) would remain in force in the western part. The government has announced plans to replace both sets of laws with a general minimum age of 14, plus an age limit of 16 in cases where a person over 18 has abused the immaturity or inexperience of the younger person in order to have sex.[79]

3. Public Indecency

In most countries 'public indecency' is a criminal offence, whether it consists of heterosexual or homosexual behaviour.[80] Nevertheless, reports from several Member States suggest that – neutrally worded – laws against 'public indecency' are more often used against homosexual acts in 'public'

---

77   See Chapter Six by Van Dijk.
78   Poll held in 1992 by Harris for the Stonewall Group and the Tory Campaign for Homo-sexual Equality (press-report: *Gay Times*, April 1992, 7).
79   See *Referentenentwurf eines ... Strafrechtsänderungsgesetzes – §§ 175, 182 StGB*, Ministry of Justice, Bonn, 21 October 1991; and also *Schwule im Recht*, 1992, 198-202.
80   In France the second paragraph of Article 330 of the Penal Code provided for an extra high maximum penalty for 'public indecency' consisting of 'an act against nature with a person of the same sex'. This paragraph was abolished by the Law of 23 December 1980, No. 80-1041 (see Boutet, 1988, 30).

places, than against heterosexual acts in such places.[81] For example: In 1981 in Sicily, two women were arrested after kissing each other in a park; they were found guilty of 'public indecency' and sentenced to seven months imprisonment.[82] In 1984 in London, two men were arrested after cuddling, kissing and fondling each other at a bus stop; they were found guilty of the offence of 'insulting behaviour'.[83]

In the United Kingdom the law specifically provides that gay sex can only be legal, if it takes place 'in private'. In deciding whether sex took place 'in private', the court may look at all the surrounding circumstances. However, according to the relevant laws, a male homosexual act is never done 'in private' when more than two persons take part or are present, or when it takes place in a public toilet. Police frequently hide in or near public toilets, to 'catch' gay men having sex in there.[84] Convictions for sex in a 'public' place where in fact no one else was present account for a large proportion of the total number of men who in the United Kingdom are convicted each year of homosexual offences having, in practice, no heterosexual equivalent.[85]

4. Other Legal Restrictions on Sex

Apart from public indecency laws, total prohibitions and discriminatory age limits, some countries have other partial legal bans on lesbian or gay sex.

---

81   See *Iceberg* 1991, paragraphs 2.4 and 2.6.
82   Press-reports: *Sek*, November 1981, 20, *Bolletino del CLI*, January 1983, 7.
83   On appeal their conviction was upheld by the High Court, which held that 'homosexual conduct in a public street ... may well be regarded by another person, particularly by a young woman, as conduct which insults her by suggesting that she is somebody who would find such conduct in public acceptable herself' (*Masterson v. Holden*, Queen's Bench Division, 18 April 1986, *1 Weekly Law Reports* 1986, 1017-1024).
     However, in 1988, in a trial of two men who had beaten up a gay man they had seen kissing his lover on the street, the judge reminded the jury that in Britain it is not illegal for two men to walk hand in hand and to kiss in the streets (press-report: *De Gay Krant*, November 1988, 10).
84   See Crane, 1982, 49, and Hurwitt & Thornton 1989, 219. In a letter from the Home Office, sent to me on 2 June 1992, it is claimed 'that the police, whilst not relishing such operations, see them as occasionally necessary to respond to public complaints when people are effectively barred from using public lavatories because homosexuals are using them as centres for sexual activity'.
85   Tatchell estimates that in 1989 around 2700 men were convicted for consensual offences between men over the age of 16. Around half of this number consists of convictions for 'indecency', which, according to Tatchell, mostly is 'gay sex in non-private places' (with another 500 men being convicted for homosexual indecency as defined by bye-laws, public order legislation and common law). The annual number of convictions for homosexual 'indecency' more than doubled between 1985 and 1989. See Tatchell, 1992, 88-90.

In Greece, it is a criminal offence to have gay sex with the intention of earning money.[86] Under a law passed in 1981 for the 'protection of public health', the police are empowered to require gay men to be forcibly tested for sexually transmitted diseases; there are reports that this law is used to harass homosexuals.[87]

In the United Kingdom, homosexual prostitution as such is not forbidden. However, it is a criminal offence for a man to 'procure' another man to have sex with a third man, and for a man or a woman to live on the earnings of male prostitutes.[88]

For a woman or man who belongs to the armed forces of the United Kingdom it is unlawful to have lesbian or gay sex with anyone, on or off duty, because this counts as *'disgraceful conduct of a cruel, indecent, or unnatural kind'*.[89] The European Commission of Human Rights found these prohibitions on consensual sex to be justified as 'necessary for the prevention of disorder' in the sense of Article 8 of the European Convention on Human Rights.[90]

On United Kingdom merchant ships it is illegal for a member of the crew of such a ship to have gay sex with another crew member.[91]

The conclusion from paragraph II.A can be that in a few Member States, in particular the United Kingdom, many people are actually convicted for homosexual offences that, in practice, have no heterosexual equivalent.[92]

---

86   Article 347 of the Penal Code.
87   See Udding & Ramakers, 1991.
88   Sections 4 and 5 of the 'Sexual Offences Act 1967' and section 80 of the 'Criminal Justice (Scotland) Act 1980' (see Crane, 1982, 26-29). In 1989 in England and Wales 346 men were convicted for 'procuring' (see Tatchell, 1992, 89).
89   Which is forbidden by the Army Act 1955, the Air Force Act 1955 and the Naval Discipline Act 1957 (in theory this could also apply to heterosexual sex, but in practice only gay sex has been punished). In May 1991 a Parliamentary Commission has recommended that 'homosexual activity of a kind that is legal in civilian law should not constitute an offence under Service law'. In June 1992 the government announced that it would implement this recommendation – first in practice and as soon as possible also by introducing legislation (information provided by the Stonewall Group, August 1992). Until 1984 it was illegal in Spain for people in the armed forces to 'commit dishonourable acts with individuals of the same sex' (Article 352 of the Military Penal Code); now gay and lesbian (and heterosexual) sex is only prohibited during military duty or inside military barracks (Elsen, 1987; press-report: *Mundo Gay*, January 1985, 3-5).
90   *B. v. the United Kingdom*, 9237/81.
91   Section 2 of the 'Sexual Offences Act 1967' and section 80 of the 'Criminal Justice (Scotland) Act 1980' (see Crane, 1982, 184).
92   Tatchell estimates that in 1989 around 2700 men were convicted for consensual offences between men over the age of 16; around 40 of them were given prison sentences. 'Hardly any of these men would have been arrested if their partner had been a woman.' (Tatchell, 1992, 88).

B. Partnership

1. The Exclusion from Marriage

In all Member States marriage is a form of legally registered partnership between one woman and one man.[93] This heterosexual character of marriage is not always spelled out in legislation. For example, the French and Dutch civil codes are silent on this point. The courts, however, are in no doubt.[94]

The right to marry is guaranteed in several constitutions and human rights treaties.[95] This fundamental right of 'men and women' has been interpreted as covering only heterosexual marriage. The European Court of Human Rights reached that conclusion in two cases where a British transsexual had claimed the right to marry someone of his/her 'first' sex.[96] A Catalonian court ruled, in a case of two gay men who wanted to marry, that it goes without saying that a marriage between a man and a woman had been intended by the legislature.[97]

The heterosexual exclusivity of marriage as such may be considered to be discriminatory. More importantly, the unavailability to same-sex couples of the many legal benefits consequent upon marriage can be said to amount to discrimination.[98] In spite of some recent developments[99] this type of legal discrimination can still be found in all Member States.

Traditionally, marital status has been used as a determining criterion in many branches of law, including:
- family law,[100]
- property and inheritance law,[101]

---

93 Article 1628(e) of the Portuguese Civil Code specifically provides that 'marriage between two people of the same sex' is 'legally non-existent'.

94 The French *Cour de Cassation* already in a judgment of 6 April 1903 considered gender difference to be one of the conditions for the validity of marriage (D-1904-1-397, S 1904-1-223, see Boutet, 1988, 91-92). Recently the Dutch supreme court (*Hoge Raad*, 19 October 1990, *Nederlandse Jurisprudentie*, 1992, No. 129) reached the same conclusion in a case of two women who wanted to marry each other.

95 For example in Article 6 of the German Constitution, in Article 32 of the Spanish constitution, in Article 12 of the European Convention on Human Rights, and in Article 23 of the International Covenant on Civil and Political Rights.

96 *Rees* case, 17 October 1986, Series A, No. 106, para. 49; *Cossey* case, 27 September 1990, Series A, No. 184, para. 46.

97 Press-reports: *De Gay Krant*, November 1987, 19, and *Lambda*, September 1987, 48 (see *Iceberg* 1991, paragraph 3.1). For German case-law, see *Schwule im Recht*, 1992, 57-59.

98 See *Schwule im Recht*, 1992, 55-57, and Waaldijk, 1992a.

99 These will be discussed in the paragraphs II.B.2, II.B.3, II.B.4 and II.C.

100 For example: mutual maintenance liability during and after marriage; different forms of parenthood (see paragraph II.C).

101 For example: simple possibilities to have common property; automatic mutual rights of inheritance without claims of the parent of the deceased partner (see paragraph II.B.3).

- immigration and nationality law,[102]
- tax law,[103]
- social security and pension law.[104]

In addition to that, many employers and other private organizations have always differentiated between their married and their unmarried employees and clients. And finally, often marriage is seen as an important symbol of social and religious status.[105]

Not surprisingly therefore, some same-sex couples have gone to court claiming that their exclusion from marriage is a violation of their human rights. In 1987 two gay men in Catalonia lost their case, but won the support of a majority of public opinion in their town, and also of the attorney-general of Catalonia who thought that, given the principle of non-discrimination, 'people of the same sex have the right to be recognized as a couple'.[106] In 1988 and 1989 two similar cases were started in the Netherlands. In these cases the Amsterdam District Court refused to rule on whether the applicants' human rights were violated, on the grounds that it was up to the parliamentary legislature to remedy any discrimination which might exist.[107] These cases attracted a great deal of publicity and good will, although part of the lesbian and gay movement was critical of these efforts to 'imitate heterosexism'. Having lost their case at three different stages one of the couples appealed to the Supreme Court. The Supreme Court relied on the decision of the European Court of Human Rights in the *Rees* case (see above), and ruled that the exclusion of same-sex couples from marriage was not unjustified (and therefore not discriminatory), because one of the legal consequences of marriage was that the spouse of a woman giving birth was legally considered to be the father of her child. However, in an aside which has since been interpreted as a clear signal towards the legislature, the supreme court referred to the 'possibility' that there might be insufficient justification for the fact that specific other consequences of marriage are unavailable in law for same-sex couples in a lasting relationship.[108]

---

102   Rights to a residence permit for a foreign partner; possibilities to acquire the nationality of your partner (see paragraph II.B.4).
103   For example: calculation of income tax (sometimes disadvantageous to the married couple); no or lower taxation over property transfer and inheritance (see paragraph II.B.3).
104   For example: calculation of premiums and benefits; widows' pension schemes (see paragraph II.B.3).
105   See Waaldijk, 1992b.
106   Press-reports: *De Gay Krant*, November 1987, 19, and *Lambda*, September 1987, 48 (see *Iceberg* 1991, paragraph 3.1).
107   *Rechtbank* Amsterdam, 13 February 1990, *NJCM-bulletin*, 1990, 456-460.
108   *Hoge Raad*, 19 October 1990, *Nederlandse Jurisprudentie*, 1992, No. 129 (see Waaldijk, 1991).

One may safely conclude that for the foreseeable future no Member State will allow same-sex couples to marry.[109] That does not mean that no action will be taken to combat discrimination that occurs as a result of the non-availability of the legal benefits that flow from marriage. In fact, marriage-related anti-homosexual discrimination is already being reduced in several Member States.

2. Equal Rights Outside Marriage

The efforts of the European lesbian/gay movements (often parallel to the efforts of the women's movement and various pressure groups) have been mostly concentrated upon the specific legal consequences of marriage, rather than upon acquiring admission to the traditional institution of marriage itself. Three routes for reducing marriage-related anti-homosexual discrimination have been chosen:

(a)   recognition of cohabitation;

(b)   individualization;

(c)   registered partnership.

The first route has had most success in the Netherlands, the third route has so far only been successful in Denmark.

(a) Recognition of cohabitation

Over the last decades there has been a political and legal trend towards extending certain marriage benefits to couples living in unmarried co-habitation.

In Germany unmarried cohabitation has been recognized for various legal purposes, sometimes as *eheähnliche Gemeinschaft* (which only applies to heterosexual cohabitation – as is the case in social security law), and sometimes as *nichteheliche Lebensgemeinschaft* (which also covers homosexual cohabitation – which is mainly relevant in the relationship between the partners themselves).[110] Cohabitation has not been recognized for the purposes of calculating income tax according to the system of *Splitting*, which favours married couples by splitting their joint income in two.[111]

In France the legislature and the courts have gradually extended some of the legal consequences of marriage to unmarried heterosexual couples living together. On the ground that a relationship of two women or two men

---

109   Although two different opinion polls held in the Netherlands suggested that around 50% of the population is in favour of opening marriage to homosexuals (*Inter/View*, press-report: *De Gay Krant*, 17 November 1990, 6; *Nipo*, press-report: *De Gay Krant*,10 August 1991, 5; see Waaldijk, 1992a, 85).

110   See *Schwule im Recht*, 1992, 62-75.

111   Idem, 78.

living together does not resemble marriage, the same legal consequences
have been mostly denied to homosexual couples.[112] The most celebrated
example of this is that of the case of Nadia and Annie. Nadia together with
her three children and Annie had been living together since 1980. Annie was
covered by social security insurance. Nadia, out of work, wanted to benefit
from the same social security benefits that would be available (for herself
and her children) if Annie had been a man. In fact, Article 13 of the relevant law provides that such benefits are available 'to the person who lives
in a marriage-like manner with the person insured'. Nevertheless, Nadia
was denied these benefits. The two women took their case to court, lost at
first instance and on appeal. On a final appeal the *Cour de Cassation* ruled
that the phrase 'in a marriage-like manner' in Article 13 only refers to people who have decided to live together without marrying each other first, and
that therefore it can only be applied to couples consisting of a man and a
woman.[113]

However, there are some positive developments for same-sex couples
too. In 1988 the public notaries of France, at their annual conference, spoke
out in favour of the same rights for homosexual and heterosexual couples
living together.[114] Since 1989 not only breadwinners in heterosexual couples, but also those in homosexual couples are exempted from compulsory
military service.[115]

In Italy unmarried couples do not have the same rights as married couples, according to the constitutional court in June 1989 (however, the court
invited parliament to legally recognize forms of cohabitation).[116]

In the Netherlands hardly any distinction is made in law between
heterosexual and homosexual cohabitation. And in an increasing number of
areas (including rent protection, income tax, social security) the law does
not distinguish any more between marriage and unmarried cohabitation
(mostly defined as permanently having a joint household).[117]

In Portugal unmarried cohabitation is recognized for some purposes by
the Civil Code and in case-law. This recognition does not extend to homosexual cohabitation.[118]

112 An opinion poll held by *Ipsos/GPH/Collectif Cuc* in May 1991 suggests that 35% of the
     French population think that homosexual couples living together should have the same
     rights and duties as other couples living together, and that 53% is against that idea
     (press-report: *Gai Pied Hebdo*, 21 May 1991, 10).
113 Judgment of 11 July 1989, *Bulletin Civil des arrêts de la Cour de Cassation*, 1989, V,
     No. 515, 312; press-reports: *Gai Pied Hebdo*, 1983, No. 68, 16; 1985, No. 197, 6; 1989,
     No. 375, 11-12.
114 Press-report: *Gai Pied Hebdo*, 1988, No. 324, 12.
115 Press-report: *De Gay Krant*, 29 July 1989, 31.
116 Press-report: *Babilonia*, October 1989, 7.
117 See Martens & Van Straaten, 1992 and Westerveld, 1992.
118 This is the conclusion of the report from the Ministry of Justice *La situation juridique et
     social de l'homosexualité au Portugal* of 23 June 1992 (paragraphs 27-38). However, in

In Spain there is also a trend towards extending some of the legal effects of marriage to same-sex couples. In 1987 a Spanish court acquitted a man who had been hiding his (male) lover who had escaped from prison. Hiding someone who has escaped is a criminal offence, unless it is your spouse or a member of your family, but the judge was of the opinion that the exception should also cover homosexual lovers.[119]

In Belgium and the Netherlands legislative proposals have been introduced in parliament to make it unlawful for most employers and other private individuals and organizations to discriminate on the basis of 'civil status', that is: married or unmarried status.[120]

One of the main problems in recognizing cohabitation concerns the question of proof. How can it be established that person A is indeed the domestic partner of person B? In the case of marriage, this problem does not exist because of the public register of marriages. In the case of cohabitation sending inspectors to the couple's home both creates a great administrative burden and constitutes a deep intrusion into privacy.[121] Different solutions have been tried in different countries:

French couples living together can obtain a *certificat de concubinage* from their local authority. With this certificate they can prove that they are living-together to their landlord, employer, etc. Most local authorities refuse to issue a certificate to lesbian and gay couples. However, a few lesbian and gay couples (including Nadia and Annie, see above) have managed to obtain such a certificate.[122]

Unmarried couples in Italy can register with a public notary (or, since 1989, with the local authority) as 'living together'. Such registration has some advantages (including medical help and transfer of pension), but is normally not recognized by employers. Income tax benefits and family allowances are only available to married couples.[123]

In the Netherlands *cohabitation contracts* (drawn up by public notaries) can be used by unmarried partners to regulate property rights and other mutual obligations. Such a contract has no automatic effect on third parties,

paragraph 38 it adds that no case is known in which this problem has been put before the courts.

119 Press-report: *De Gay Krant*, November 1987, 19.
120 Because of the legal impossibility for same-sex couples to marry, discrimination against unmarried couples can also be classified as indirect discrimination on the basis of sexual orientation.
121 This dual problem is the starting point of the report on partnership, produced by the Dutch government's Advisory Commission for Legislation (*Advies Leefvormen*, by the *Toetsingscommissie voor wetgevingsprojecten*, Ministerie van Justitie, Den Haag 1992; see Waaldijk, 1992b, 87-88, and Waaldijk, 1992c).
122 Press-reports: *Gai Pied Hebdo*, 1986, No. 254, 7; 1989, No. 378, 14; 1990, No. 409, 10.
123 Press-reports: *Gai Pied Hebdo*, 1986, No. 243, 30; *Gay Times*, September 1989, 22; *Babilonia*, October 1989, 7.

although some employers (including the state itself) do award some (or even all) 'spousal' benefits to those who have entered into one.[124]

There are also two more radical solutions to the problem of proof of partnership: 'individualization' and the introduction of 'registered partnership'.

(b) Individualization

The object of 'individualization' is to remove the legal consequences that flow from married status or from co-habitation so that rights and duties are given to individuals, irrespective of whether they have partners or not. This technique would work in many areas of law (notably with regard to tax, social security, pensions and property). In areas like immigration, nationality, co-parenting and inheritance, however, it would be difficult or even impossible to take away all the consequences of (married and unmarried) partnership.

In the Netherlands some social security benefits have been 'individualized' for people who are born after 1972. For them the level of their benefit will normally not be influenced by the fact that they are married to, or living together with a partner. In many other respects the laws of the Netherlands (and of many other Member States) still distinguish between people with a partner and people who do not live with a partner.[125]

(c) Registered partnership

The third route chosen to overcome marriage-related anti-homosexual discrimination, has been a call for the introduction – alongside heterosexual marriage – of another form of legally registered partnership.

In Denmark this has led to the adoption in 1989 of the 'Law on registered partnership', which makes it possible for same-sex couples to enter into 'registered partnership'. This can be done at the town hall offices, but (unlike marriage) not in churches. Another difference with marriage is, that 'registered partnership' can only be entered into, if at least one of the partners is domiciled in Denmark and of Danish nationality. Within Denmark 'registered partnership' has most of the legal effects of marriage (especially in the fields of maintenance, property, inheritance, immigration, tax and social security), although there are a number of exceptions, including: joint custody over children, adoption, and some widows' pensions.[126] During the

---

124   See Martens & Van Straaten, 1992, 125-132.
125   See Westerveld, 1992 and Waaldijk, 1992c.
126   The law came into force on 1 October 1989; see Emborg, 1989, Elmer & Lund Larsen, 1990, and *Schwule im Recht,* 1992, 60. A Gallup poll held in November 1989 suggested

first two years and three months 492 lesbian and 809 gay partnerships were registered.[127]

In 1990 a member of the French Senate proposed the introduction of a 'contract of civil partnership', which would be similar in effect to the Danish registered partnership, but which would also be open to heterosexual couples. A year later another proposal for a law on partnership was introduced in the *Assemblée Nationale*.[128]

In 1990 in the Netherlands, after the publicity concerning the Supreme Court's ruling on lesbian marriage,[129] most political parties have declared themselves in favour of introducing some form of registered partnership for homosexual and heterosexual couples, which has resulted in the Minister of Justice asking the advice of the government's Advisory Commission for Legislation. In 1992 this Commission recommended the introduction of *two forms of registered partnership* – parallel to marriage as it exists. Both forms would be open to couples of the same sex and to couples of the opposite sex (including partners who cannot marry because of a close family link).[130]

Since 1991 several Dutch local authorities have started offering semi-official registration of lesbian and gay partnerships. As long as there is no parliamentary legislation on this subject, these registrations will have symbolic, but no legal significance (although employers, insurance companies, etc., could choose to recognize these local registers as proof of cohabitation).[131]

that 64% of the population thought that registered partnerships should be a possibility for same-sex couples (*Berlingske Tidende*, 26 November 1989).

127 Figures provided by the *Landesforeningen for bøsser og lesbiske*. The comparatively low number of lesbian registrations might be explained by the fact that the law does not provide for joint legal parenthood for the partners.

128 '*Contrat d'union civile*' (see press-reports: *Gai Pied Hebdo*, 24 May 1990, 14, and 21 May 1991, 10). An opinion poll held by *Ipsos/GPH/Collectif Cuc* in May 1991 suggests that 72% of the population is in favour of the introduction of such a partnership law, and that 23% is against (*Gai Pied Hebdo*, 21 May 1991, 9).

129 See note 108.

130 The other form of registration would have the same legal consequences as marriage (including property and pension rights, inheritance, divorce and maintenance). However, the Commission considered it too early to propose creating legal parenthood for same-sex couples. It therefore suggested that for the time being the marriage-related forms of legal parenthood (including parental authority and adoption) should only be extended to registered partners of the opposite sex who could also have chosen to marry each other. The other form of registration would have less consequences; it would replace existing criteria like 'non-marital cohabitation' in tax law and in most parts of social security law. People living together would be free to choose not to register their partnership. In that case most laws would consider them as single individuals. (*Advies Leefvormen*, Den Haag: Toetsingscommissie voor wetgevingsprojecten, Ministerie van Justitie, 1992; see Waaldijk, 1992b, 87-88, and Waaldijk, 1992c).

131 See Waaldijk, 1992a, 85-86.

3. On the Death of a Partner

Apart from issues of parenthood and secondary conditions of employ-ment,[132] the heterosexual exclusivity of marriage and its legal consequences is particularly disadvantageous to same-sex couples if one of them is from another country (see paragraph 4 below) or after the death of one of the partners. The disadvantages of the second group (in the areas of inheritance, death duties, accident compensation, pensions, and rent protection) can be great and *cumulative*.[133]

Whereas married partners would *automatically inherit* from each other, unmarried partners will first have to make a will. But even then, the surviv-ing partner can be confronted with legal claims from the family of the de-ceased.[134]

In several countries the tax to be paid on inheritance (*death duties*) would be higher in the case of a will leaving property to an unmarried lover, than in case of (automatic) inheritance by the married partner.[135] In the Netherlands these tariff differences have been greatly reduced for couples (with a cohabitation contract) who have been living together for a few years.[136] In Denmark in 1986, these tariff differences were completely abol-ished for homosexual couples. In 1989, with the introduction of 'registered partnership', this specific provision became irrelevant: since that year Dan-ish inheritance law and inheritance tax law has treated homosexual regis-tered partners in exactly the same way as heterosexual married partners.

If a married person dies as a result of an accident that was somebody's fault, his widow or her widower can often claim *compensation*. No such right to compensation exists for lesbian and gay partners in Germany,[137]

---

132   See paragraphs II.C and II.D respectively.
133   An opinion poll (held in 1992 by Harris for the Stonewall Group and the Tory Cam-paign for Homosexual Equality) suggested that 70% of the British population agrees that when one partner dies in a gay or lesbian relationship the surviving partner should have the same rights as the surviving partner in a heterosexual relationship (press-report: *Gay Times*, April 1992, 7).
134   In, for example, the Netherlands, parents (if still alive) would normally be entitled to claim half of the property left by their deceased child, irrespective of any testament (Articles 960 and 962 of Book 4 of the Civil Code; see Martens & Van Straaten 1992, 132-137). Similar rules apply in Germany (Articles 2303-2310 of the Civil Code; see *Schwule im Recht*, 1992, 145-146).
      And a French example: A man had made bequests in his testament to three gay friends. After his death the bequests were contested in court by his family. The court ruled that these are indeed void (Article 1133 of the Civil Code), because they had to be regarded as a remunerations for 'immoral relations' (*Tribunal de Grand Instance de Paris*, 28 June 1985; see Boutet, 1988, 102; press-report: *Gai Pied Hebdo*, 1986, No. 215, 34).
135   See for example *Schwule im Recht*, 1992, 157.
136   See Martens & Van Straaten 1992, 138.
137   Article 844 of the Civil Code (see *Schwule im Recht*, 1992, 71).

Portugal[138] and the United Kingdom.[139] In Belgium a man found his claim for damages after the death of his gay lover rejected in court on the ground that 'an immoral situation or relationship can never be the basis of damages'.[140]

Pension schemes for widows and widowers seldom provide for a pension to be paid to the surviving lesbian or gay partner.[141] In Denmark the 'Law on registered partnership' of 1989 covers pension rights that are provided or guaranteed by law, but widow's pensions as provided by Law 102 of 14 March 1941 are still only available after marriage – and not after 'registered partnership'. The 1989 law does not cover pensions provided by private contract either, although some private pension funds have decided to treat registered partnership in the same way as marriage.[142] In the United Kingdom, state pension schemes only provide pensions to wives who survive their husbands; unmarried partners are not provided with pensions. Under private pension schemes, however, employees can nominate someone (for example a lesbian or gay partner) who would receive a pension after their death.[143] In the Netherlands only a few private pension-funds have introduced pensions for the unmarried surviving partner; all other collective pension-funds – including those created by law for public employees – only pay a pension to the surviving spouse of a married employee, although unmarried employees have to pay the same pension contribution as their married colleagues.[144] For individuals, banks and insurance companies would normally be prepared to create a pension-contract from which an unmarried surviving partner would benefit. Under the proposed Dutch 'General Equal Treatment Law' it will be unlawful for private pension funds to discriminate on the basis of sex or sexual orientation, but it will remain legal for them to distinguish between married and unmarried partners.[145]

A surviving lesbian or gay partner will frequently also encounter difficulties in obtaining rights of succession to *rented accommodation* even though she or he may have been living in the accommodation prior to the partner's death. In the United Kingdom the Housing Act 1980 only provides for such a right of succession for married couples, for certain members of

138 See paragraphs 37 and 38 of the report from the Ministry of Justice, *La situation juridique et social de l'homosexualité au Portugal*, of 23 June 1992.
139 Fatal Accidents Act 1976 (the Law Commission is presently reviewing the position of same-sex partners under this law).
140 Court of Dendermonde (see *Iceberg* 1991, paragraph 3.2).
141 In Germany no pensions are available for surviving lesbian and gay partners (see *Schwule im Recht*, 1992, 72).
142 See Emborg, 1989, and Elmer & Lund Larsen, 1990.
143 Press-report: *Capital Gay*, 24 March 1989, 12.
144 See Martens & Van Straaten, 1992, 128, and Waaldijk, 1992a, 79-80.
145 Due to the exception in Article 5(6) of proposal 22014, introduced in 1991 (see paragraphs I.C).

the tenant's family and for cohabiting couples of the opposite sex;[146] this exclusion of same-sex couples was accepted by the European Commission of Human Rights.[147] In France a court ruled that even 'if the existence of stable homosexual couples constitutes a social fact, such a situation cannot be held to create rights', and it therefore refused in a homosexual case to apply the law that provides that after the death of a tenant his or her 'known concubine' (unmarried partner) could continue the tenancy.[148] By contrast, Dutch[149] and German[150] law do offer rent protection to the surviving lesbian or gay partner.

4. Foreign Partners

In only a few countries (including Denmark and the Netherlands) can a foreign lesbian or gay partner be allowed to enter the country or to stay there on the basis of her or his relationship with a citizen of that country.

In Denmark a residence permit will be issued to a foreigner who cohabits at a shared residence, either in marriage or in regular cohabitation of prolonged duration, with a person permanently resident in Denmark. For both same-sex and opposite sex 'cohabitation of prolonged duration', a period of up to two years is normally required. This requirement does not apply to married couples, nor to registered partnerships.[151]

In the Netherlands a partner-dependent residence permit is available to the unmarried partner of a Dutch national (or of a recognized refugee, a favoured EC-citizen, or a person holding an establishment permit). The main requirements are that the partners must have been living together for a prolonged period (normally at least six months) in suitable housing, and that the Dutch partner guarantees the costs of living (and of possibly travelling back) of the foreigner; in practice this means that the Dutch partner must have an income above the social security minimum.[152]

---

146 See Crane, 1982, 142.
     The situation in Portugal is the same (see paragraph 35 of the report from the Ministry of Justice, *La situation juridique et social de l'homosexualité au Portugal*, of 23 June 1992).
147 *Mary X v. United Kingdom*, 11716/85.
148 Paris, 27 May 1986, D.1986.IR.436 (see Boutet, 1988, 97-103).
149 Article 1623i of the Civil Code.
150 See *Schwule im Recht*, 1992, 65.
151 Article 9(1) of the Aliens Act (see Frowein & Stein, 1987, 249; Wong, 1988, 4; and Elmer & Lund Larsen, 1990). As indicated in paragraph 2.c above, a 'registered partnership' is available if at least one of the partners is domiciled in Denmark and of Danish nationality.
152 See Bos, Pot & Willems, 1992, 180-181. In two cases lower courts have held that it is unlawful discrimination to apply the housing or financial requirements (which do not apply to married couples) in the case of same-sex couples, because they are unable to marry (*President Rechtbank* Amsterdam, 13 September 1984, *Kort Geding* 1984, No.

In Germany it may be possible for a foreign same-sex partner to obtain a residence permit. According to the new Aliens Law of 1991 such a permit should be given to 'other family relatives' if it is 'necessary to avoid extraordinary hardship'.[153]

According to the Immigration Rules of the United Kingdom, heterosexual partners can enter or stay when they are married to a UK citizen and immigration officials have found the marriage to be 'genuine'. There is also a provision for heterosexual couples 'living in permanent association'. According to the government it would be too difficult for immigration officials to assess the stability of lesbian or gay relationships.[154] A complaint about this exclusion of homosexual partners was declared inadmissible by the European Commission of Human Rights.[155]

In Belgium, France, Ireland, Luxembourg and Portugal it is only possible for married foreign partners to obtain a partner-dependent residence permit.[156]

In all Member States it is possible for foreigners, under certain conditions, to acquire the country's *citizenship* (nationality). If the foreigner is married to a national of that country, fewer or less onerous conditions apply. In most Member States similar facilities for lesbian and gay partners do not exist.[157] The Dutch Nationality Act, however, contains some recognition for lesbian, gay and other non-marital relationships. One of the general conditions for acquiring Dutch nationality is that the foreigner must have been living in the Netherlands for at least five years. This condition does not apply if the foreigner has been married to a Dutch national for at least three years. It is irrelevant where the married couple lived during those three years. A foreigner who has been living in a permanent non-marital (heterosexual or homosexual) relationship with a Dutch national for at least three years, can acquire Dutch nationality if he or she has been living *in the Netherlands* for at least three years.[158]

280, see Waaldijk, 1992a, 92; *President Rechtbank* Groningen, 14 March 1990, No. 90/53, see Bos, Pot & Willems, 1992, 181).

153 Articles 12, 22 and 23 of the *Ausländergesetz*, which came into force on 1 January 1991. According to *Schwule im Recht*, (1992, 199-120) it should be possible to include lesbian and gay partners in the term *sonstige Familienangehörige*, and to argue that – given the unavailability of marriage – the refusal of a permit would cause great hardship.

154 See Crane, 1982, 149-150.

155 *X v. the United Kingdom*, 12513/86.

156 See Frowein & Stein, 1987, 349-356, 461-462, 624-625, 849, 1048 and 1275.

157 For example in Belgium, France, Germany, Italy, Spain and the United Kingdom (see De Groot, 1988, 274-279).

158 Article 8 of the *Rijkswet op het Nederlanderschap* (*Staatsblad*, 1984, No. 628), which came into force on 1 January 1985 (see De Groot, 1988, 280).

C. Parenthood

1. After Divorce

In 1981 the Parliamentary Assembly of the Council of Europe recommended that the Committee of Ministers call on the governments of the Member States 'to ensure that custody, visiting rights and accommodation of children by their parents should not be restricted on the sole grounds of the homosexual tendencies of one of them'.[159] In doing so, the Assembly only addressed one of the forms of possible homosexual parenthood: the situation of a separating or divorced opposite-sex couple with one or more children, where either the mother is lesbian or the father is gay. Other forms (children born in lesbian couples; fostering; adoption) will be discussed in the following paragraphs.

Cases in which courts, at or after the divorce of a married couple, decided to deny custody, visiting rights or accommodation of children to a mother because she was lesbian, or to a father because he was gay, have been reported in most Member States.[160] However, cases have also been reported in some Member States in which the court did not accept a parent's homosexual orientation as a valid reason to deny custody or visiting rights.[161]

2. Children Born in Lesbian Couples

When a child is born in a heterosexual couple, then legal parenthood over the child will be shared between the mother and her partner – even if he is not the biological father. If the man is married to the mother, he will normally be deemed to be the father. If he is not married to her, he will normally be able to acknowledge the child as his own. Neither of these options

159 Recommendation 924, adopted on 1 October 1981.
160 Paragraph 4.4 of *Iceberg* 1991 contains examples from:
      Belgium (press-reports: *De Gay Krant*, April 1985, 17; and January 1989, 26; *Lesbia*, December 1989, 18);
      France (press-report: *Gai Pied Hebdo*, 28 May 1983, 21);
      Germany (see *Bundestag Drucksache* 11/7197, 9 July 1990, 11; and *Schwule im Recht*, 1992, 89; press-report: *De Gay Krant*, August 1988, 16),
      Ireland (see *Equality Now* 1990, 33);
      Spain (press-report: *Lambda Nachrichten*, 1988, No. 1, 54);
      United Kingdom (see Crane, 1982, 122-128, and Durell 1983, 9-10; press-report: *Lesbian Information Service*, September 1988, 2).
161 For examples from Germany, see *Schwule im Recht*, 1992, 89.
      Paragraph 4.4 of *Iceberg* 1991 contains examples from:
      Belgium (Court of Appeal Gent, 10 December 1982, *Rechtskundig Weekblad* 1984-85, 2134-2137; press-report: *De Gay Krant*, May 1985, 14);
      France (press-reports: *Gai Pied Hebdo*, 28 May 1983, 21, and 1988, No. 311, 17; *Lesbia*, May 1988, 4);
      United Kingdom (press-report: *Gay Times*, December 1990, 8).

is open to the lesbian partner of a woman who has given birth. Marriage between two women is impossible,[162] and only a man can acknowledge children as his own. In 1991 a Dutch court ruled that the human rights of lesbians are not violated by the law which excludes women from the right to acknowledge another woman's child.[163] In Denmark, the exception contained in Article 4(3) of the 'Law on Registered Partnership' of 1989 means that a child born during a registered lesbian partnership will not have the partner of her mother as co-parent.[164]

This means that no *legal* parenthood-relationship can be established between a child and the lesbian partner of its mother – even if the two women jointly take factual and financial responsibility for the upbringing of the child.[165] Therefore, the child will have neither a legal claim to maintenance by the partner, nor the right to inherit from her or to acquire her nationality. And the partner will have no formal say in decisions over the upbringing of the child. The inheritance problem can be partly remedied by the partner making a will.[166] In the Netherlands two women who realized that full legal parenthood would not be possible, tried to obtain at least joint parental authority over their children. The Supreme Court rejected their application on the ground that only one of them legally counted as 'parent'.[167] They applied to the European Commission of Human Rights, which declared there application inadmissible.[168]

To establish a *factual* parenthood-relationship between a child and the lesbian partner of its mother is not impossible in the Member States. However, in several countries obstacles may exist preventing lesbians from becoming pregnant: many doctors, clinics and insurers refuse *artificial insemination* to unmarried, single and/or lesbian women.[169] In the United Kingdom an effort to make artificial insemination illegal for lesbians[170] failed. In spite of various advisory bodies in France recommending the prohibition

---

162 See paragraph II.B.1 above.
163 Court of Appeal, Leeuwarden, 22 January 1992, No. 171/1991 (*Nieuwsbrief Homosexualiteit en Recht*, No. 2, October 1992) about Article 221 of Book 1 of the Civil Code.
164 See Elmer & Larsen, 1990.
165 See Van Vliet, 1992, 102-103, and *Schwule im Recht*, 1992, 99.
166 But then similar complications can arise as have been described in paragraph II.B.3.
167 *Hoge Raad*, 24 February 1989, *Nederlandse Jurisprudentie*, 1989, No. 741.
168 Decision of 19 May 1992, *Kerkhoven, Hinke and Hinke v. the Netherlands*, 15666/89 (the Commission considered 'that, as regards parental authority over a child, a homosexual couple cannot be equated to a man and a woman living together').
169 See Enkelaar & Rood-de Boer, 1986, 141; Hendriks & Markestein, 1992, 206-208; *Schwule im Recht*, 1992, 97; and *Iceberg* 1991, paragraph 4.3. It would appear, that in Denmark, France and the Netherlands the refusal of artificial insemination to lesbians is covered by the text of the anti-discrimination laws to be discussed in paragraph II.E. The Danish 'Law on registered partnership' of 1989 does not give lesbians a right to have artificial insemination.
170 By amending the Human Fertilization and Embryology Bill in 1990 (press-report: *Gay Times*, June 1990, 6).

of the provision to homosexuals of medically assisted procreation, no legislation to that effect has been adopted so far.[171]

3. Adoption and Fostering

In no Member State may a lesbian or gay couple adopt children. In Denmark the possibility of adoption by registered partners is specifically excluded by Article 4(1) of the 'Law on registered partnership' of 1989.

In Ireland[172] and the Netherlands[173] only married couples may adopt a child. In most other countries adoption is not only possible for a married couple, but also for a single person. In practice, however, single-parent-adoption is very rare in these countries, especially adoption by a lesbian or by a gay man.[174]

Fostering by lesbian or gay couples or individuals is not legally impossible. In the United Kingdom decisions concerning the placing of children with lesbian or gay foster-parents will depend on the social services department of the local authority concerned.[175] In Germany the authorities (*Jugendämter*) are very restrictive in placing children with such couples.[176] In the Netherlands children are more often fostered by lesbians and gay men.

D. Employment

In 1981 the Parliamentary Assembly of the Council of Europe recommended that the Committee of Ministers should 'call on the governments of the Member States to assure equality of treatment, no more no less, for homosexuals with regard to employment, pay and job security, particularly

171 Press-report: *Gai Pied Hebdo*, 1986, No. 249/250.
172 Adoption Act 1952 (see *Equality Now* 1990, 33).
173 Article 227 of Book 1 of the Civil Code.
174 See *Iceberg* 1991, paragraph 4.2; and for:
    Belgium, see Article 346 of the Civil Code (press-report: *De Gay Krant*, 2 November 1991, 5);
    Denmark, see the Adoption Act of 1972, and Emborg 1989;
    France, see Article 343/1 of the Civil Code, and Boutet, 1988, 119 (press-report: *Gai Pied Hebdo*, 1986, No. 215, 34);
    Germany, see Article 1741 of the Civil Code (*Schwule im Recht*, 1992, 93, and *Bundestag Drucksache* 11/7194, 11);
    Spain, see Article 175/4 of the Civil Code;
    United Kingdom, see the Adoption Act 1976 (here most adoption agencies do not accept single people as adoptive parents, but 'private' adoptions – not via an adoption agency – are possible after notification of the local authority, which will 'investigate the suitability of the applicant', see Crane, 1982, 145).
175 See Crane, 1982, 145.
176 See *Schwule im Recht*, 1992, 91-92.

in the public sector'.[177] Three years later, the European Parliament called on the EC Commission 'to renew its efforts with regard to dismissals to ensure that ... individuals are not unfairly treated for reasons relating to their private life' and 'to submit proposals to ensure that no cases arise in the Member States of discrimination against homosexuals with regard to employment and working conditions'.[178]

Throughout the eighties, cases of anti-homosexual employment discrimination have been reported from almost all Member States, including those countries where some forms of discrimination have been declared unlawful in judicial decisions and in anti-discrimination legislation.[179] No Member State therefore offers full legal protection against employment discrimination based on sexual orientation. In most countries dismissal is still only covered by the general vague laws against 'unfair dismissal'.[180]

Below, I shall first deal with anti-discrimination legislation relevant to both the private and the public sector. I will then discuss the situation in the private sector in general, and in religious employment in particular. Finally the situation in the public sector, and specifically in military employment will be discussed.

In paragraph II.B.3 we have already seen that in general the surviving partners of lesbian and gay employees do not receive pensions, although these employees almost always will have paid the same premiums as their married colleagues. This means that there is *unequal pay*: many homosexuals get less pay than their heterosexual colleagues get for the same work.

1. Anti-Discrimination Legislation

Only two Member States have introduced legislation specifically prohibiting anti-homosexual discrimination in the field of employment. France has been the first to do so, recently followed by the Netherlands.[181]

In France it is unlawful for an employer to dismiss or not-employ someone because of his or her *mœurs*.[182] And the internal regulations of an enterprise may not contain disadvantages for employees because of their *mœurs*.[183] The word *mœurs* covers sexual orientation.[184]

---

177 Recommendation 924, adopted on 1 October 1981.
178 'Resolution on Sexual Discrimination at the Workplace', adopted on 13 March 1984 (OJ 1984 C 104/46-48).
179 See *Iceberg* 1991, chapter 5.
180 See for example Malt 1991, 64-67, and *Schwule im Recht,* 1992, 24-30.
181 See paragraph I.C.
182 Article 416(3) of the Penal Code, as amended by the Law of 25 July 1985. Employment discrimination on the basis of *mœurs* is also prohibited by Article L.122-45 of the Code of Labour Law, as amended by the Law of 12 July 1990 (see *Juris classeur périodique,* 1991, 21724).
183 Article L.122-35 of the Code of Labour Law, as amended by Law of 17 January 1986.
184 See paragraph I.C.

In the Netherlands it is a criminal offence 'in the performance of a public office, a profession or a business'[185] to 'discriminate' against persons on account of 'their heterosexual or homosexual orientation'.[186] The term 'to discriminate' is meant to refer to unjustified distinctions which have a negative effect on the exercise of human rights in the area of politics, economics, culture or social life.[187] It therefore covers employment discrimination.

The Dutch Parliament is presently considering a proposal for a 'General equal treatment law', containing more specific (private and administrative law) prohibitions of anti-homosexual discrimination.[188] Article 5 of this law would make it unlawful for employers to make direct or indirect distinctions based on '... heterosexual or homosexual orientation, or civil status'. Article 6 contains a similar prohibition relating to the (self-employed) professions.

In the other Member States no legislation against anti-homosexual employment discrimination is in force.[189] An anti-discrimination law proposed in Belgium in 1985 would make it a criminal offence for employers 'to distinguish, directly or indirectly, on the ground of sex, sexual and relational behaviour or preference, civil status, or family situation'.[190] In Portugal anti-homosexual discrimination by private and public employers would probably be considered to be against the Constitution.[191]

2. Private Sector Employment

(a) General case-law

When there is no specific anti-discrimination legislation, the courts will be left to decide whether certain forms of discrimination should be considered legal.[192] Several courts have ruled anti-homosexual discrimination to be permissible:

---

185 This means that non-profit employers (schools, hospitals, etc.) are not covered by this law (see paragraph II.D.2.b).
186 Article 429quater of the Penal Code, as amended per 1 February 1992 by the Law of 14 November 1991, *Staatsblad* 623.
187 Article 90quater of the Penal Code, as amended by the Law of 14 November 1991, *Staatsblad* 623.
188 Proposal 22014, introduced in 1991, not expected to enter into force before 1994.
189 The Danish anti-discrimination laws (into which the words 'sexual orientation' were inserted in 1987; see paragraph I.C) do not cover employment. The 'Law on registered partnership' of 1989 does not make it illegal for employers to discriminate between married employees and employees who have registered their partnership (see paragraph II.B.2.c and II.B.3).
190 Article 1 of proposal No. 1219/1, reintroduced on 29 March 1988, No. 339/1.
191 Article 13 (which has both vertical and horizontal effect) outlaws all discrimination, including that based on someone's 'social condition' (see note 19).
192 For a discussion of German case-law, see Malt 1991, 42-63, and for a discussion of Dutch case-law, see Mattijssen 1992, 19-23.

In 1983 (before the introduction of anti-discrimination legislation) a French airline steward tried to claim the same financial benefits (cheap flights etc.) for his male partner as were available for married and unmarried heterosexual couples. The company rejected his request. The employment tribunal ruled in favour of the steward, considering that to refuse to recognize homosexuality, would be a denial of the right to be different and could be discriminatory.[193] On appeal the decision was overturned on the grounds that 'homosexuality, even if it is no longer a criminal offence, can nevertheless not generate rights' and that the steward and his partner could not be regarded as 'concubines'.[194] On 11 July 1989 this decision was confirmed by the *Cour de Cassation* which argued that only couples which had decided not to marry could be regarded as 'concubines' under the relevant regulation of the airline company.[195]

In the United Kingdom the courts have repeatedly accepted the dismissal of some employees on the ground of homosexuality. Two examples:

After the authorities of a college had read a newspaper report about the court case in which one of their lecturers had pleaded guilty to sex with another adult man in a locked cubicle of a public toilet, they dismissed him on the grounds that he had shown 'lack of control', and that therefore his students might be at risk, and that he might be vulnerable to approaches from his students. The Employment Appeal Tribunal, recognising that the question whether the lecturer is a 'risk' to his students was a 'highly controversial subject', concluded that the college was 'not making an error of law' if they concluded that there was a 'risk'.[196]

A maintenance man working at a youth camp reported to the police that he had been robbed in a gay bar. The police then informed his employers about his homosexual orientation. They responded by dismissing the man, writing to him that the reason was 'that information was received that you indulge in homosexuality. At a camp accommodating large numbers of schoolchildren and teenagers it is totally unsuitable to employ any person with such tendencies.' His employers accepted that he never had a homosexual relationship with any resident of the camp. The dismissal was accepted as 'fair' by the Glasgow Industrial Tribunal. The Employment Appeal Tribunal later considered it proper for the first tribunal to take account of the fact that many employers 'would take the view that the employment of homosexuals should be restricted, particularly when required to work in

193 *Conseil des Prud'hommes*, 14 November 1984.
194 Court of Appeal of Paris, 11 October 1985, D.1986.J.380.
195 *Bulletin Civil des arrêts de la Cour de Cassation*, 1989, V, No. 514, 311.
196 *Wiseman v. Salford CC* [1981] *IRLR* 202 (see Crane, 1982, 106-107, and Daly, 1983, 38-40).

proximity and in contact with children', although 'whether that view is scientifically sound may be open to question'.[197]

But there have also been cases with a positive outcome for the discriminated employee:

In 1980 the Employment Tribunal of Barcelona ruled that the dismissal of a bartender who had been fired because he was gay, was 'unfair'.[198]

On 14 February 1989 an Italian court found in favour of a man who had sued his employer for discrimination, after the employer (a bank) had suspended the man for five days without wages, as a disciplinary measure for his activities as a gay activist which were deemed damaging to the bank's image.[199]

(b) Religious institutions

Within the private sector, religious employment forms a particular field. Given the religious history of many anti-homosexual ideas, it is not surprising that employment by churches and by religious schools, hospitals and other institutions is an area where discrimination against lesbians and gay men frequently occurs – and where it is often accepted by law.[200]

In both the Belgian and the Dutch proposed anti-discrimination laws (see above) exceptions have been included for religious employment.[201] In fact, the main reason why the Netherlands are taking so long in considering and discussing different proposals for anti-discrimination legislation, is the intense political disagreement about the degree to which christian schools, hospitals, children's homes, nursing homes, etc. should be brought under the legal prohibition of discrimination based on sexual orientation or civil status.[202]

Article 2 of the Belgian proposal exempts 'the internal organization and the practice of a religion or belief' from the prohibition of discrimination contained in Article 1. This exemption seems not to cover Christian schools, hospitals, etc.[203]

197 *Saunders v. Scottish National Camps Association Ltd.*, [1980] *IRLR* 174. This decision
      was confirmed by the Court of Session in Edinburgh, [1981] *IRLR* 277.
198 Press-report: *Lambda*, April 1980, 2.
199 Press-report: *Babilonia*, April 1989, 52-53.
200 See for example Malt, 1992, 42-56, and *Schwule im Recht*, 1992, 43-50.
201 Dutch non-profit organizations (whether religious or not) will hardly be affected by the
      new text of discrimination-prohibition in Article 429quater of the Penal Code, because
      they are not a 'public office' and normally neither a 'profession' nor a 'business' (see
      paragraph 1 above).
202 See Hoogma, 1992.
203 See paragraph 1 above.

Article 3 of the Dutch draft 'General Equal Treatment Law'[204] provides that the internal affairs of churches (such as the appointment of clergy) are completely exempted from the prohibition of discrimination. In Article 5(2) there are two vaguely worded exceptions to the rule against discrimination: Private schools (which are mostly Christian schools) will be free 'to set requirements for the fulfilment of a job, if these requirements are necessary, given the school's objective, for the realization of its principles'. Other institutions founded on religious or philosophical principles will be free 'to set requirements which, given the institution's objective, are necessary for the fulfilment of a job'. However, none of these requirements may lead to discrimination 'based on the sole fact of ... heterosexual or homosexual orientation or civil status'. The wording of these exceptions has been heavily criticized.[205] Eventually it will be up to the courts to decide which requirements they consider as 'necessary', and how to differentiate between the notion of discrimination 'based on homosexual orientation' and that of discrimination 'based on *the sole fact of* homosexual orientation'.

Under the present law, Dutch courts have accepted as permissible discrimination the non-renewal of an employment-contract of two homosexual teachers at Christian schools. In both cases it was fairly evident that the decision not to renew the contract had been based on the apparent homosexuality of the teacher. In the first case, concerning an openly lesbian teacher at a Catholic school, the court simply ruled that there was no legal obligation for the school to give formal reasons for its decisions.[206] In the second case, concerning a teacher contracted by the Catholic Church to give some religious instruction classes at a school run by the City of Maastricht, the court considered the claim of discrimination irrelevant, because the original contract only lasted for one year.[207]

In France in 1988, a gay man was dismissed from his job as a verger, after the church had found out about his homosexuality. The verger took his case to the employment tribunal, which ruled that the dismissal lacked a 'real and serious reason', and therefore ordered the church to pay compensation to the verger.[208] This decision was later overturned by the Court of Appeal, which considered that a verger in a Catholic Church is required by his contract of employment to carry out his duties with an attitude which is not only externally but also internally compatible with that religion, that homosexuality has always been condemned by the Catholic Church, and that therefore the verger's 'homosexual characteristics' are violations of his

---

204 See paragraph 1 above.
205 See Mattijssen, 1992, 31-33.
206 *President Rechtbank* Den Bosch, 16 July 1982, *NJCM-bulletin*, 1982, 334-344.
207 *Rechtbank Maastricht*, 21 May 1987 (unpublished, see Mattijssen 1992, 21-22).
208 *Conseil des Prud'hommes* Paris, 6 December 1988 (No. 14656/87).

contractual obligations.[209] The *Cour de Cassation* overturned the decision
of the Court of Appeal. It held that the Code of Labour Law[210] makes it
unlawful for an employer to dismiss an employee *on the sole ground* of his
or her orientation,[211] but that it would be lawful to dismiss an employee
because of behaviour 'that, given the character of his functions and the
proper purpose of the organization, had created evident unrest within that
organization'.[212] The Court concluded that the Court of Appeal had broken
the law by only considering the *mœurs* of the verger, without establishing
whether his behaviour had created evident unrest.[213]

3. Public sector employment

In general, anti-homosexual discrimination in public employment is more
often prohibited than such discrimination in the private sector. However,
employment in the military (and in other 'sensitive' areas, like the intelligence and diplomatic services) is often exempted from prohibitions on discrimination.

(a) The civil service

Anti-homosexual discrimination in employment by government and other
public authorities can be considered generally illegal in at least three
Member States:

In France and the Netherlands laws against employment discrimination
do not exempt employment in the public sector.[214]

In Denmark, it follows from the principle of equal treatment[215] that in
the public sector homosexuality is not a valid reason for refusing employment. This was confirmed by the Minister of Justice in 1989.[216]

In some other countries anti-homosexual discrimination by public employers is prohibited administratively:

---

209   Paris, 30 March 1990, *Répertoire Général*: 33968/89.
210   Articles L.122-35 and L.122-45 (see paragraph 1 above).
211   '*pour le seul motif tiré de ses mœurs*'.
212   '*qui, compte tenu de la nature de ses fonctions et de la finalité propre de l'entreprise, a
      créé un trouble caractérisé au sein de cette dernière*'.
213   Judgment of 17 April 1991, *Juris classeur périodique*, 1991, 21724.
214   See paragraph 1 above. Article 1 of the Dutch Constitution is directly applicable in ad-
      ministrative cases (see paragraph I.B). In addition Article 3 of the Constitution provides
      that all Dutch citizens are equally eligible for appointment to the public service. (See
      also the 1982 judgment of the Supreme Public Employment Tribunal, to be discussed in
      paragraph b below.)
      The equality provisions of the Constitutions of other countries may also be directly ap-
      plicable to discrimination in public employment.
215   See paragraph I.B.
216   See *Iceberg* 1991, paragraph 5.1 (press-report: *Pan*, 1989, No. 2, 3).

According to Irish ministerial guidelines it is illegal in the civil service to discriminate on the basis of sexual orientation.[217]

In the United Kingdom various local authorities have adopted equal opportunities policies, covering 'sexual orientation'.[218] In 1988 the Cabinet Office sent out a reminder to all national government departments, that in the Civil Service 'discrimination on the grounds of sexual orientation is not tolerated and any harassment from such a cause will be considered an offence under the disciplinary rules'.[219] Until 1991 known lesbians and gay men were not covered by this equal opportunities policy where their work involved access to highly classified information (including senior positions in the Civil Service and diplomatic positions).[220] This bar has now been lifted.[221]

In Belgium, the question of whether it was lawful to subject public employees to a disadvantage on account of their homosexuality was raised without being answered in the celebrated case of Eliane Morissens. In 1980 Ms Morissens, assistant headmistress at a technical college, had appeared in a television programme, talking about being a lesbian and the way in which this has been a handicap to her career.[222] She was then dismissed by her employer, the provincial authorities, on the grounds that she had

217 Department of Finance, Circular 12/88, 22 June 1988 (see *Resource material on lesbian/gay law reform* 1991, item 3.4, and *Iceberg* 1991, paragraph 5.1).
218 See *Iceberg* 1991, paragraph 5.1 (press-reports: *Gay Times*, November 1984, 18; December 1984, 10)
219 Press-report: *Gay Times*, June 1988.
220 In one case, a man who had been working as a data processor at GCHQ (the UK Government's intelligence gathering centre in Cheltenham) aware of the security requirements decided to tell his boss when he discovered he was gay. His employers responded by removing his security clearance, and suspending him while trying to find work for him which does not involve secret information. The man took his case to the High Court, which ruled in 1988 that – because national security was involved – it could not decide whether the removal of his security clearance had been reasonable. The court praised the man's courage and honesty (press-report: *Gay Times*, August 1988). See also the comparable case of a German military intelligence worker (discussed in paragraph b below, note 234).
221 On 23 July 1991, in answer to a parliamentary question, the Prime Minister stated that in the light of changing social attitudes towards homosexuality and the greater willingness of homosexuals to be more open about their relationships, the Government had concluded that there should be no posts involving access to highly classified information for which homosexuality would represent an automatic bar to security clearance (letter from the Home Office, sent to me on 2 June 1992).
     However, at the same time a Foreign Office circular was sent out which made it clear that if anyone at the time they applied to the Foreign Office had lied about their sexual orientation (when restrictions were still in force), this fact would be taken into account when considering future clearance.
222 She had said: 'I was preparing to become responsible for a very large school that was attended by 1000 girls and 200 boys. It was said – but unfortunately not put into writing – that it was unthinkable that a homosexual woman should be the Head of a school attended by girls – that's funny! ... At present, the school is run by two men; I don't know if the danger is not even greater...' (press-report: *IGA-bulletin*, 1982, No. 2, 2-3).

'deliberately challenged the Provincial authorities by arguing that her homosexuality had been an obstacle to her being appointed as a headmistress'
and that she had 'insinuated that it was just as dangerous to have entrusted
the headship to two men, thus challenging the integrity and moral sense of
her immediate superiors'. Ms Morissens appealed to the Council of State,
which ruled that civil servants should not make unjustified criticisms of
their superiors, and that the punishment (the dismissal) was 'not wholly
disproportionate to the acts in question'.[223] The European Commission of
Human Rights declared an application brought by Ms Morissens to be
inadmissible.[224]

(b) The armed forces

In most Member States lesbians and gay men are not always allowed to
serve in the armed forces.[225] In a few of these countries homosexuals are
almost completely banned from the armed forces:

In Greece homosexuals are not allowed to serve in the Navy.[226]

In Italy, homosexuality is included among those 'deficiencies and ill-
nesses which are ground for unfitness for military service'. In this way,
'sexual inverts' are prevented from carrying out military service.[227]

In the United Kingdom, where all lesbian and gay sex still is illegal for
members of the armed forces,[228] lesbians and gay men are not accepted in
the armed forces. Most people who are found breaking the prohibition on
lesbian and gay sex are discharged administratively, without being brought
before a court martial. In the period 1987 – 1989 196 men and women were
administratively discharged because of their homosexuality.[229]

In other countries the anti-homosexual bans of the armed forces are less
wide:

In Ireland, Portugal and Spain the military laws provide for vague
clauses which are sometimes relied upon to discharge openly homosexual
members of the forces for:
- behaving 'in a scandalous manner, unbecoming the character of an
  officer'[230] or 'to the prejudice of good order and discipline',[231]

---

223   Decision of 27 June 1984 (press-report: *ILGA-bulletin*, 1988, No. 4, 15-16).
224   Decision of 3 May 1988, case 11389/85.
225   See *Iceberg* 1991, paragraph 5.4.
226   Press-report: *Gai Pied Hebdo*, 1983, No. 70, 13.
227   Law 1008 of 2 September 1985 (see Elsen, 1987; press-reports: *Unità*, 23 December
      1987; *ILGA-Bulletin*, 1988, No. 3).
228   See paragraph II.A.4, especially note 90.
229   See Crane, 1982, 184; and Elsen, 1990.
230   Article 139 of the Irish 'Defence Act 1954' (see Elsen, 1987).
231   Article 168 of the same act.

- 'offensive acts either against good conduct or seriously affecting their dignity',[232] or
- 'incapability to follow the regimen of service life'.[233]

In the Federal Republic of Germany homosexuals are allowed to serve in the military,[234] but they are not appointed to senior or educational positions. The exclusion of homosexuals from senior positions was approved in several judgments of the Supreme Administrative Court.[235] In 1990 the same court rejected the case of an army lieutenant who had been refused an appointment as instructor on the ground that his homosexuality made him unsuitable for an educational job. The court ruled the refusal to appoint and the reasons for it to be legal, considering that although tolerance of homosexuality may have increased in society, it was far from certain that such tolerance could be expected from the young soldiers the instructor would be training.[236]

Only in a few Member States is anti-homosexual discrimination in military employment considered unlawful:

In France dismissal of military personnel because of their being openly homosexual is covered by the general prohibition of discrimination in employment.[237]

The Dutch Supreme Public Employment Tribunal has ruled in the case of a gay man who had been discharged from the military on the ground of 'unsuitability because of illness', that this could not be concluded from 'the sole fact of homosexual inclination'. In fact, the military authorities had

232 Article 22(2) of the Portuguese 'Law on military service' (see Elsen, 1987).
233 Regulation of the Spanish Council of Ministers of 21 March 1986 (see Elsen, 1987, and *Iceberg* 1991, paragraph 5.4; press-report: *Mundo Gay* April 1986, 3-5).
234 See *Schwule im Recht,* 1992, 101-107. In 1986 the security clearance was withdrawn from a gay man working at the Air Force intelligence gathering centre; he was moved to another job in the Air Force. As reason for the decision he was told that 'in view of his sexual behaviour' there was no guarantee that secret information is safe with him, and that because of his homosexuality blackmail could not be ruled out. The man appealed against this decision. The military court found in his favour, arguing that the man's homosexuality as such could not be considered a security-risk, especially because he had not concealed his homosexuality, and was living in a steady relationship with one partner (*Truppendienstgericht Süd, 4. Kammer*, Karlsruhe, 17 August 1987, S 4 – BLa 1/87).
     See also the comparable – but with a different result– case of a British civil servant working with secret information at GCHQ (discussed in paragraph a above, note 220).
235 *Bundesverwaltungsgericht*, Judgments of 16 December 1976 and 25 October 1979 (see *Bundestag Drucksache* 11/7197, 14, and Elsen, 1987).
236 *Bundesverwaltungsgericht*, 8 November 1990, 1 WB 61/90.
237 See paragraph 1 above. This was confirmed by Magistrate General Ors, speaking at the Xth Congress of the International Society for Military Law and Law of War, Garmisch-Partenkirchen, 2-7 October 1985 (see Elsen 1987).

relied heavily on the man's homosexuality in concluding that he was 'ill' and therefore unsuitable for continued military employment.[238]

E. Goods and Services

Compared to the field of employment, anti-homosexual discrimination in the provision of goods and services has attracted little attention from the European Parliament. However, in 1984 the Parliament did call on the EC Commission 'to identify ... any discrimination against homosexuals with regard to ... housing and other social problems'.[239]

1. Anti-Discrimination Legislation

Three Member States have enacted legislation specifically prohibiting discrimination on the basis of sexual orientation in the field of goods and services:[240]

In Denmark it is a criminal offence 'to refuse, in business or public utility activity, to serve someone on the same conditions as others on account of his or her ... sexual orientation', and also to refuse – on such a ground – 'to admit someone on the same conditions as others to a place, a performance, an exhibition, a meeting or something similar, which is open to the public'.[241]

In France it is a criminal offence to refuse goods or a service to someone because of his or her *mœurs*, or to make the exercise of any economic activity more difficult for someone because of the same reason.[242] The word *mœurs* covers sexual orientation.[243]

In the Netherlands it is a criminal offence 'in the performance of a public office, a profession or a business' to 'discriminate' against persons on account of 'their sex or their heterosexual or homosexual orientation'.[244]

---

238 *Centrale Raad van Beroep*, 17 June 1982, *Militair Rechterlijk Tijdschrift*, 1982, 300-304 (see Mattijssen 1992, 20-21).
239 'Resolution on Sexual Discrimination at the Workplace', adopted on 13 March 1984 (OJ 1984 C 104/46-48).
240 See paragraph I.C. Many gay men have been refused health care and insurance services because of (being suspected of) being HIV-positive or having AIDS (see for example the Dutch situation as described by Hendriks & Markestein 1992, 197-199 and 204-206). In the domestic law of the Member States it is not clear whether such refusals are legal. Some of these refusals could be classified as indirect discrimination on the basis of sex-ual orientation.
241 Article 1 of Law 289 of 9 June 1971, as amended per 1 July 1987.
242 Articles 416(1) and 416-1(1) of the Penal Code, as amended by the Law of 25 July 1985.
243 See paragraph I.C.
244 Article 429quater of the Penal Code, as amended per 1 February 1992 by the Law of 14 November 1991, *Staatsblad 623*.

The term 'to discriminate' is meant to refer to unjustified distinctions which have a negative effect on the exercise of human rights in the area of politics, economics, culture or social life.[245] The draft 'General Equal Treatment Law' contains a less vague prohibition on discrimination in the provision of goods and services: Article 7 makes it illegal to distinguish on the basis of sexual orientation, civil status, etc., if goods or services are either provided by a public authority, or if they are provided in public by private individuals or organizations. Unlike the provisions of the Penal Code, Article 7 also applies to discrimination by non-profit organizations in the fields of housing, welfare, health care, culture and education. However, according to the same Article, private schools (which are mostly Christian schools) are free to set admission requirements 'if these requirements are necessary, given the school's objective, for the realization of its principles', provided that these requirements do not lead to discrimination 'based on the sole fact of ... heterosexual or homosexual orientation or civil status'.[246]

The Belgian draft anti-discrimination law of 1985 also covers discrimination in relation to goods and services.[247]

2. Housing

Throughout the EC married (and unmarried) opposite-sex couples enjoy a number of advantages over same-sex couples with respect to renting and owning accommodation. The announcement by the City Council of Bologna, that it planned to offer public housing to homosexual couples led to fierce protests from the Catholic Church.[248]

In Germany it is lawful for a landlord to refuse to accept same-sex couples as tenants. However, a landlord is not allowed to terminate a tenancy contract on the ground that a partner of the same sex has moved in to live with the tenant.[249]

However, a German court has also accepted the claim from tenants of a block of flats, that the presence of a gay group in one of the flats was a reason to lower their rents. The court agreed that the value of their flats had gone down, because they were now in danger of being seen as homosexuals themselves. The court ordered the owner of the building to reduce the rent for all tenants who were not gay.[250]

---

245 Article 90quater of the Penal Code, as amended by the same law.
246 Proposal 22014, introduced in 1991, not expected to come into force before 1994.
247 See paragraph I.C.
248 Press-report: *Guardian*, 29 January 1992.
249 *Entscheidungen des Bundesgerichtshof in Zivilsachen*, 92, 213; see *Schwule im Recht*, 1992, 63. See also paragraph II.B.3 (above) for rent protection available to lesbian or gay partners when one of the couple dies (a protection that is absent in France and the United Kingdom).
250 *Amtsgericht* Hamburg, 26 September 1985, *Neue Juristische Wochenschrift*, 1986, 1114 (see *Bundestag Drucksache* 11/7197, 9 July 1990, 9; press-report: *Gay Times*, March 1986, 23).

In Germany public housing in general is only available to families and married couples on a low income.[251] This means that unmarried hetero-sexuals and lesbians and gay men (whether they live alone, in couples or with children) are dependent on the private housing market. In 1989 a legislative proposal from the Green Party to make public housing also available to other households than families and married couples, failed to get a majority in the Housing Committee of the Federal Parliament.[252]

3. Condoms

One particular product that is of increasing importance to many gay men — condoms — has been subjected to various legal bans. In Ireland condoms can only lawfully be sold to people over 18 years by dispensing chemists and officially registered family planning clinics. Sales by other shops or by vending machines are illegal. In Belgium and Italy the sale of condoms was legalized at the end of the eighties as a direct result of government re-sponses to AIDS.[253]

F. Association

The opportunities for lesbians and gay men to meet or to organize (either for political or recreational purposes) have been reduced in many countries by different legal restrictions. However, in a few countries the law has also strengthened the legal position of lesbian and gay organizations.

1. Lesbian and Gay Organizations

Lesbian and gay organizations in several Member States have had difficul-ties in obtaining legal recognition.[254] In 1981, for example, a German court gave the following reasons for refusing to register a gay association on the register of associations: the aim of the association is 'against public morals and therefore does not deserve the protection of the legal order'; ho-mosexuality is a 'deviation from the sexual function', 'condemned to infer-tility' and 'against human nature'.[255] In the same year German tax author-ities refused charitable status (*Gemeinnützigkeit*, which is necessary for tax relief) to two homosexual organizations, on the grounds that their aims go

---

251 *Zweites Wohnungsbaugesetz* (the Second Housing Law).
252 *Bundestag Drucksache* 11/1955, 7 March 1988, 4, and 11/7197, 9 July 1990, 9 (see also the report of 5 December 1989 from the Federal German Housing Department on housing problems of unmarried people, 12-16).
253 See *Iceberg* 1991, paragraph 7.5.
254 See *Iceberg* 1991, paragraph 8.1.
255 *Amtsgericht* Ingolstadt, *Kritische Justiz*, 1981, 82 (see *Recht schwul*, 1982, 174-175).

against the moral opinions of the majority of the population.[256] In 1987 another German court refused to register an association because it used the word *schwul* (gay) in its name; this refusal was overturned on appeal.[257]

The legality of granting subsidies to lesbian and gay organizations has been called into question in a few countries. In 1988 the Minister of the Interior of the German *Land* Bavaria, forbade the City of Nürnberg to subsidize such organizations, because the majority of the population would reject their aims as scandalous.[258] In Great Britain, Section 28 of the Local Government Act 1988 (which makes it unlawful for local authorities to '*promote homosexuality*') has been used by some local authorities as a reason to refuse subsidies to lesbian and gay organizations.[259]

In France, on the other hand, lesbian and gay organizations have been supported by the anti-discrimination legislation of 1985.[260] It now is a criminal offence to refuse goods or a service to an organization (or to members of it) because of the *mœurs* of its members,[261] or to make the exercise of any economic activity more difficult for any corporate person because of the *mœurs* of its members.[262] And for organizations whose official aim is to combat discrimination based on *mœurs* it is now possible to play a formal role as a civil party in enforcing the various anti-discrimination provisions.[263] In the Dutch proposal for a 'General Equal Treatment Law' lesbian and gay organizations are also given competence to take cases of suspected discrimination to court.[264]

2. Bars, Discos, Saunas

Reports about police raids on lesbian and gay bars and discos are numerous.[265] Normally, the official reason given for such a raid is that breaches

---

256 *Recht schwul*, 1982, 167-168. Such refusals are now considered unlawful (see *Schwule im Recht,* 1992, 160-163).

257 *Amtsgericht Freudenstadt*, 15 July 1987 (I GR 1142/87), and on appeal: *Landgericht Rottweil* (1 T 218/87); see *Schwule im Recht,* 1992, 158.

258 Press-report: *De Gay Krant*, July 1988, 9.

259 See Thomas & Costigan 1990, 4 and 22 (see also paragraph II.G.1 below).

260 See paragraph I.C.

261 Article 416(2) of the Penal Code, as amended by the Law of 25 July 1985.

262 Articles 187-2(2) and 416-1(2) (idem).

263 Article 2-6 of the Code of Criminal Procedure (idem).

264 Article 10 of proposal 22014, introduced in 1991 (see paragraph I.C). The courts had already given this competence to the Dutch Society for the Integration of Homosexuality COC (*President Rechtbank* Utrecht, 5 March 1987, *NJCM-bulletin*, 1989, 305 at 306).

265 Paragraph 8.2 of *Iceberg* 1991 contains examples from:
Belgium (press-reports: *De Gay Krant*, 9 September 1989, 5, and 16 June 1990, 7)
France (press-reports: *Gai Pied Hebdo*, 1984, No. 103; 14 April 1984, 5-6; 1985, No. 170; and 3 May 1990, 16);
Greece (press-report: *Gai Pied Hebdo*, 1984, No. 146, 7);
Spain (press-reports: *Mundo Gay*, January 1985, 4; *ILGA-bulletin*, 1989, No. 4, 18; *De Gay Krant*, 23 September 1989, 9); and the

of licensing laws or of the laws on drugs are suspected. However, the frequency of such raids, suggests that these laws are more severely enforced against lesbian and gay establishments, than against their heterosexual equivalents.

Police raids on saunas frequented by gay men, have also been reported many times.[266] Sometimes, such raids have led to prosecutions (and convictions) based on the laws against prostitution – even when none of the sex that took place in the sauna was between a prostitute and his client.[267]

3. Cruising Areas

Another way of meeting, popular among some gay men, is 'cruising' in public places (parks, beaches, in and around public toilets, stations, outside gay bars).

In the United Kingdom this can be illegal. In England and Wales it is a criminal offence 'for a man persistently to solicit or importune in a public place for immoral purposes'.[268] The term 'persistently' is interpreted as meaning: more than once. To 'solicit or importune' covers any words or gestures used in cruising and chatting-up. The term 'public place' not only covers streets and parks, but also pubs, discos and public toilets. Courts have interpreted the term 'immoral purposes' as covering any sex between

United Kingdom (see Crane, 1982, 31-33, and the Third Annual Report of GALOP, the Gay London Police Monitoring Groups, 1986-1987, 15; press-reports: *Gay Times*, November 1987, and November 1990, 7).

266   Paragraph 8.3 of *Iceberg* 1991 contains examples from: Belgium (see below), France (press-reports: *Gai Pied Hebdo*, 1986, Nos. 186, 208, 215 and 216) and the United Kingdom (see Crane, 1982, 35).

267   For example, two men in Wales who ran a sauna for gay men, were prosecuted in 1983 on the charge that they allowed gay sex to take place in the sauna. After admitting to 'keeping a brothel' (and to possessing 'obscene videos') they were each sentenced to paying a fine of £ 480. Because of this sentence they were later refused a license for running a restaurant they had bought (press-report: *Gay Times*, November 1983, 13).
A similar case started in Belgium in 1984, when the owners of two gay saunas were prosecuted for the 'exploitation of a house of debauchery' (Article 380bis/2 of the Penal Code; see De Wit 1987, 253-257). The public prosecutor claimed that the term 'debauchery' meant 'indecency', and that 'indecency' covered gay sex. On 29 May 1985 they were acquitted by the Criminal Court of Brussels, which ruled that 'debauchery' only meant 'prostitution'. On 11 December 1985, after an appeal by the public prosecutor, they were found guilty (and sentenced) by the Brussels Court of Appeal, which considered 'homosexuality' to be covered by the term 'debauchery'. After an appeal to the *Cour de Cassation* (which on 7 May 1986 quashed the conviction on minor technical points), the case was referred to the Liège Court of Appeal, which acquited the men, ruling that although 'debauchery' meant more than only 'prostitution' (also 'promiscuity' for example), in defining the term one should not discriminate against homosexuality (23 April 1987, *Journal des Procès*, 1 May 1987, 106).

268   Section 32 of the Sexual Offences Act 1956. In Northern Ireland 'soliciting' and 'importuning' is also prohibited (section 1 of the Vagrancy Act 1898 (see Crane, 1982, 17). In Scotland, cruising (as any homosexual conduct in public) can be interpreted by the courts as the common law offence of 'shameless indecency' (see Crane, 1982, 17).

men, even if the sex would be lawful because it would take place in private between two consenting men over the age of 21. However, some juries have taken the view that picking up another man for sex is not 'immoral'.[269] Repeatedly police act as *agents provocateurs* by standing around gay bars or public toilets, often dressed attractively, making it obvious that they are looking for sexual contacts. When they are approached by a gay man, they will charge him with 'importuning'.[270] This practice is against Home Office guide-lines.[271] However, in court it will be no defence for the accused that the charge is the result of police acting as *agents provocateurs*.[272] In 1989 a total of 462 men were convicted for 'soliciting'.[273]

Also in countries where 'cruising' as such is not a criminal offence, police have been reported to 'invade' cruising areas, making identity checks and sometimes arrests.[274]

G. Information

The freedom of expression of lesbians and gay men, and in particular their freedom *'to receive and impart information and ideas without interference by public authority and regardless of frontiers'*,[275] has been restricted in various 'legal' ways. Information (books, periodicals, films, etc.) about homosexuality has been subjected to various legal restraints – mainly on one of two grounds: that the information is too 'positive', or that it is 'indecent'.

Of course it is not always easy to distinguish between these two grounds, especially in the case of films and other art forms.[276]

269   See Crane, 1982, 15-17, and Hurwitt & Thornton, 1989, 217-218.
270   See Hurwitt & Thornton, 1989, 220.
271   According to the letter from the Home Office, sent to me on 2 June 1992, the 'Home Office guidance for police forces ... states that no member of a police force should counsel, incite or procure the commission of a crime, and all chief officers are aware of the need for care to avoid plain-clothes officers putting themselves in situations where accusations could be made that they have acted as *agents provocateurs'*.
272   See Crane, 1982, 15-17; and Hurwitt & Thornton, 1989, 217-220.
273   See Tatchell, 1992, 89.
274   Paragraph 8.4 of *Iceberg* 1991 contains examples from Greece (press-reports: *Sek*, August 1981, 15, and October 1982, 20; *Gai Pied Hebdo*, 1984, No. 146, 7; *IGA-bulletin*, 1984, No. 1, 20) and France (press-reports: *Sek* December 1981, 13, March 1982, 10, and September 1985, 9; *Gai Pied Hebdo*, 29 October 1983, 6, and 1989, No. 368, 8-9).
275   Article 10 of the European Convention on Human Rights.
276   See paragraph 9.6 of *Iceberg* 1991. Films with homosexual themes have been stopped by censor boards (*Nighthawks* in Greece in 1980, press-report: *Sek*, May 1980, 20; *Taxi zum Klo* in Italy in 1983, press-report: *Babilonia*, November 1983, 31), or were scrapped (after pressure from the mayor) from the programme of a filmfestival (*Lisboa 86*, press-report: *Gai Pied Hebdo*, 1986, No. 249/250, 13). In Italy a lesbian and gay filmfestival was stopped by the local mayor (press-report: *Haagsche Courant*, 14 August 1985). Paintings have been seized by the police at an exhibition held at a gay centre in France (press-report: *Gai Pied Hebdo*, 3 December 1983, 8).

1. Information Considered Too 'Positive'

With the ostensible aim of protecting young people from 'positive information' about homosexuality the United Kingdom parliament prohibited local
authorities in Scotland, England and Wales from 'promoting homosexuality'. Section 28 of the Local Government Act 1988 provides that local
authorities shall not 'intentionally promote homosexuality or publish material with the intention of promoting homosexuality' and shall not 'promote
the teaching in any maintained school of the acceptability of homosexuality as a pretended family relationship'.[277] There has been much discussion about the actual meaning of these two vague phrases. Several commentators have suggested that their legal effect is probably rather limited.[278] However, there have been a few cases in which local authorities
have refused subsidies or services, because of Section 28.[279] Since Section
28 only regulates the behaviour of local authorities, it has no direct relevance for schools and teachers. However, it may serve as an encouragement
for school authorities to stop their teachers from providing their pupils with
'positive' information about homosexuality.[280]

   Even where there is no specific law against the 'promotion of homosexuality' administrative authorities may well take decisions aimed at preventing young people receiving 'positive' information about homosexuality.[281]

   For example, in 1984 the Italian Minister of Education issued a circular
forbidding schools to invite homosexuals and prostitutes, after a school had
invited a few homosexuals and prostitutes to come and talk to students
about their experiences.[282]

---

277   See paragraph 9.4 of *Iceberg* 1991.
      Section 38 of the 'Sexual Offences Act 1992' of the Isle of Man introduced the same
      prohibitions for public bodies. Unlike its British equivalent, Section 38 in subsection 5
      provides that 'none of the following ... shall of itself amount to the promotion of homo -
      sexuality –
      (a)   incidental references to homosexuality;
      (b)   discussion of issues relating to homosexuality;
      (c)   use of material for educational or recreational purposes which is created by homo -
      sexuals, portrays homosexuals or includes references to homosexuality'.
278   See Colvin, 1989, 14, and Thomas & Costigan, 1990, 18.
279   See Thomas & Costigan, 1990, 4 and 22.
280   See Colvin, 1989, 44 and 52. An example: in 1988 a teacher was dismissed from his
      job at a secondary school, on the ground that he had 'promoted homosexuality' by deal-
      ing with the issue of homosexuality in sex education classes. The teacher, who was not
      gay, took his case to court. The Industrial Tribunal ruled that his dismissal had been
      unfair, and that the education authorities had been guided by prejudice. The teacher was
      awarded compensation of £ 12,500 (but did not get his job back). The education au-
      thority appealed against the decision. The Employment Appeal Tribunal overturned the
      decision, on the ground that the Industrial Tribunal had used the wrong 'test of reason -
      ableness' in judging the fairness of the dismissal; the teacher lost the compensation
      (press-reports: *Gay Times*, April 1990, 7; August 1990, 5).
281   See paragraphs 9.2 and 9.4 of *Iceberg* 1991.
282   Press-report: *De Gay Krant*, March 1984, 16.

In 1990 in Ireland, the Censorship of Publications Board banned the import and sale of the Danish book *Jennie Lives With Eric and Martin* (telling the story of a girl living with her father and his lover).[283]

In 1985, Belgian police seized two lesbian/gay books (*Ook zo* and *Een ander strand*) on display in a youth centre during an information market on homosexuality. The legal basis for the seizure seems to be Article 380quater of the Penal Code, which forbids the incitement of 'debauchery'.[284]

2. Information Considered 'Indecent'

Bookshops stocking lesbian and gay books and magazines have been subjected to raids and seizures. In 1984, Belgian police seized almost the complete stock of gay books and magazines in a bookshop in Brussels (on the basis of Article 380quater of the Penal Code, see above).[285]

In April 1984 Customs officers raided the London bookshop *Gay's The Word*, questioned the staff and seized many books[286] (all imported from the USA). Later that year, nine directors and workers of the bookshop were charged with the criminal offence of conspiracy to import indecent and obscene books. In the meantime, Customs seized five gay books on their way to the Edinburgh lesbian and gay bookshop *Lavender Menace*. After many delays, in 1986 the Customs authorities decided to drop all criminal charges against the people of the London bookshop, returning most of the contentious books to the bookshop. Only 19 books were still considered to be 'indecent' or 'obscene', and therefore sent back to the USA. In order to challenge the opinion of the Customs authorities, the bookshop decided to import some of these 19 titles again, this time from the Netherlands.[287] Customs officials seized the books (on the basis of section 42 of the Customs Consolidation Act 1876, which forbids the importation of obscene

---

283 Press-report: *Gay Times*, October 1990, 5.
284 Press-report: *De Gay Krant*, July 1985, 22. That same year, when gay organizations were distributing a leaflet about an information market on homosexuality at the entrance of a school, some members of a right wing party intervened by grabbing the leaflets and beating the distributors. One of the attackers, who admitted using violence, was prosecuted. On 17 September 1987 the Criminal Court of Antwerp acquitted him, considering his actions justifiable, arguing that 'although homosexuality in the last decennia has been accepted as a lifestyle by many people, there still is a large majority in our country who is disgusted by this lifestyle and takes a defensive position, especially with regard to youngsters'. On 4 October 1989 the acquittal was overruled by the Antwerp Court of Appeal, which sentenced the attacker to pay a fine of 3,000 Belgian francs, to pay all costs of the trial, and to pay damages of 1 franc to one of the gay men that he attacked (press-report: *ILGA-bulletin* 1989, No. 5/6, 26).
285 Press-reports: *Gai Pied Hebdo*, 1984, No. 146, 7, and No. 147, 5; *De Gay Krant*, January 1985, 37.
286 According to a letter from the Home Office, sent to me on 2 June 1992, '198 books (22 titles) were seized'.
287 Press-reports: *Gay Times*, December 1984, 21; *ILGA-bulletin*, 1986, No. 3, 6-7.

articles). The bookshop claimed that the books were 'for the public good' (in the sense of section 4 of the Obscene Publications Act 1959, which exempts British publications which are 'in the interests of science, literature, art or learning or of other objects of general concern'), arguing that Articles 30 and 36 of the EEC-Treaty require that the same rules should be applied to imported publications. This argument was rejected by the Court of Appeal.[288]

The publishers of several gay magazines have been prosecuted for publishing 'indecent' material. Such prosecutions have led to convictions and sentences in Spain[289] and in Greece.[290]

In 1987 the French Minister of the Interior threatened to use the 'Law on Publications Aimed at the Young'[291] against several gay magazines. Article 14 of this law gives the Minister power to put restrictions on 'publications of any kind which, because of their licentious or pornographic character or because of the place given to crime and violence, present a danger to the young'. After protests the Minister dropped his threat.[292]

In 1984 the publisher of a French gay magazine was convicted of breaking Article 284 of the Penal Code (drawing attention to an 'occasion of debauchery') by publishing homosexual personal advertisements.[293] A similar case in Belgium did not lead to a conviction, but to acquittal of the publishers, who had been prosecuted for facilitating 'debauchery' (Article 380quater of the Penal Code) by publishing personal adverts.[294]

H. Hate Crimes

1. Physical Violence

In 1981 the Parliamentary Assembly of the Council of Europe recommended that the Committee of Ministers should 'call on the governments of

---

288   Judgment of 14 December 1988, *Noncyp Ltd. v Bow Street Magistrates' Court and Another*, [1989] 1 CMLR 634.
289   Press-report: *De Gay Krant*, October 1982, 11.
290   Press-reports: *IGA-bulletin*, 1984, No. 1, 20-21; No. 3, 5-6; No. 4, 31-33.
      On 8 November 1991 the editor of the magazine *AMPHI* was sentenced to 5 months imprisonment plus a fine of 50,000 drachmas, after the court had found the magazine's use of the word '*lesbians*' for lesbians a violation of the provisions in the Penal Code against publications that are 'indecent' and 'offensive for the public feeling' (information from the Greek organization AKOE-AMPHI and from the International Lesbian and Gay Association).
291   Law No. 49-956 of 16 July 1949, as amended by Law No. 67-17 of 4 January 1967 (JO, 6 January 1967).
292   Press-report: *Gai Pied Hebdo*, 1987, No. 263, 6-18.
293   *17e chambre corretionnelle du tribunal de Paris*, 21 December 1988 (press-report: *Gai Pied Hebdo*, 1989, No. 352, 11).
294   Criminal Tribunal of Brussels, 31 May 1989 (press-report: *Gai Pied Hebdo*, 1989, No. 376, 2).

the Member States to ask prison and other public authorities to be vigilant against the risk of rape, violence and sexual offences in prisons.'[295] Many incidents of anti-homosexual violence have been reported from most Member States (and not only from within prisons). Only in a small number of cases were the attackers brought before a court.[296] With the exception of marital rape, physical violence against persons has always been a criminal offence.[297] Not surprisingly, there have been no calls for new laws specifically criminalizing anti-lesbian and anti-gay violence.[298]

2. Verbal Violence

Verbal attacks generally do not count as crime. However, in Denmark, Ireland and the Netherlands some forms of verbal abuse against lesbians and gay men have been made into criminal offences:[299]

In Denmark it is now illegal 'to utter publicly or deliberately, for the dissemination in a wider circle, a statement or another remark, by which a group of people are threatened, derided or humiliated on account of their ... sexual orientation'.[300]

The Irish 'Prohibition of Incitement to Hatred Act 1989' makes it a criminal offence to incite hatred on the basis of sexual orientation.[301]

In the Netherlands it is a crime to 'incite to hatred or discrimination against persons or to violence against the bodies or goods of persons on

295 Recommendation 924, adopted on 1 October 1981.
296 See *Schwule im Recht*, 1992, 236.
297 In some countries the definition of rape has been extended so as to cover homosexual rape, for example in France in 1980 (press-report: *Gai Pied Hebdo*, 22 December 1989, 32) and in the Netherlands in 1992 (Article 242 of the Penal Code, as amended by the Law of 9 October 1991, *Staatsblad* 519).
298 Nor has the possibility of introducing extra high maximum penalties for anti-homosexual violence emerged as an issue within the European lesbian and gay movements.
299 The proposed anti-discrimination law in Belgium would make it a criminal offence 'to incite to discrimination, hate or violence against a person, a group or members of a group' on the ground of 'sex, sexual and relational behaviour or preference, civil status, or family situation'. To insult a group or members of a group on these grounds in commercial advertising would also become a criminal offence (Article 3 of proposal 1219/1, introduced on 23 May 1985, and reintroduced on 29 March 1988 as No. 339/1).
300 Article 266b of the Penal Code, as amended in 1987. This law has been tested in the case of a woman who, in a public letter to the editor of a newspaper, had written: 'For how long may a thief be called a criminal? Is a homosexual not a thief? Does he not steal his neighbour's honour, and maybe his life, by exploiting him and perhaps infecting him with AIDS? ... Homosex is the most foul form of fornication.' In the court of first instance she was acquitted (Skjern, 16 January 1990). An appeal by the public prosecutor was dismissed by the Court of Appeal (*Vestre Landsret, 7. afdeling*, 29 March 1990). However, three of the six judges on that Court found that 'regard for the protection of homosexuals against insulting and degrading statements of the kind mentioned weighs heavier than regard for the principal that such statements should be capable of being freely made in an open, public discussion'.
301 See *Equality Now*, 1990, iii.

account of their ... heterosexual or homosexual orientation' and also to 'insult' a group of persons on that ground.[302]

In the absence of specific laws against anti-homosexual incitement, in some countries general laws might be used. Article 130 of the German Penal Code, for example, speaks of incitement to hate, violence or discrimination (and of other verbal abuse) 'against parts of the population'.[303]

In France[304] and the Netherlands[305] the general civil laws against insults have been invoked – with limited success – in cases where preachers had made negative remarks about homosexuality.

I. Official Oppression

For most of the legal discrimination described above, the word 'oppression' may sound too big. However, due to the many forms of legal discrimination, and due to the absence of comprehensive legal protection against discrimination, many lesbians and gay men in the EC cannot exercise their civil, political, economic, social and cultural human rights as freely as heterosexual women and men can.

Not all anti-homosexual laws are enforced, but each year many hundreds of citizens are prosecuted for homosexual offences that have no

---

302   Articles 137c and 137d of the Penal Code, as amended per 1 February 1992 by the Law of 14 November 1991, *Staatsblad* 623 (see paragraph I.C).

303   According to the German Embassy in London 'homosexuality' is covered by the words 'other features' (letter of 26 February 1990); see also *Schwule im Recht,* 1992, 235.

304   In 1982 homosexuals sued the Bishop of Strasbourg who had declared that he 'respects homosexuals as sick people'. The Court of Appeal dismissed the case, arguing that the remark was only general, and that no one in particular was insulted. Furthermore, it considered that the angry reactions following the Bishop's remarks had damaged his reputation. It therefore ordered the homosexual organization involved to pay damages of 20.000 French francs to the Bishop (Colmar, 27 June 1983, D.1983.J.550 (see Boutet, 1988, 50; press-reports: *De Gay Krant*, April 1983, 25, and August 1983, 21).

305   The Archbishop of Utrecht, in a radio interview in 1987, had expressed understanding for landlords who refused to rent out accommodation to homosexuals, and had also said that homosexual acts were 'an evil' and a 'threat to society'. The Dutch Society for Integration of Homosexuality COC responded by suing the archbishop. In the end, the Court of Appeal of Amsterdam dismissed the case, on the ground that it was not unlawful to explain, in moderate language, the position of the catholic church on homosexuality (*Gerechtshof Amsterdam*, 10 December 1987, *NJCM-bulletin*, 1989, 305-317).

Around the same time a gay man successfully sued two fundamentalists, who had distributed a magazine in which they claimed that homosexuality had now 'been crowned by death' by the 'result of sin: AIDS!', and that AIDS was a 'result of homosexuality' that 'irrevocably' led to death. The Court of Appeal of Arnhem ruled that the freedom of expression did not give the evangelists the right to insult homosexuals by claiming that homosexuality always caused AIDS and that AIDS always caused death (*Gerechtshof* Arnhem, 9 February 1988, *NJCM-bulletin*, 1989, 317-323). This decision was confirmed by the Supreme Court (*Hoge Raad* 2 February 1990, *Nederlandse Jurisprudentie*, 1991, 289.

heterosexual equivalent,[306] thousands of parents are denied full parental responsibility for the children they are bringing up,[307] and many thousands of lesbian and gay couples are denied various financial benefits that are available to married and unmarried heterosexual couples.[308] In addition, the police and other authorities frequently apply laws which are in themselves 'neutral' in a discriminatory way. It was for precisely that reason, that in 1984 the European Parliament urged the Member States 'to ban the keeping of special records on homosexuals by the police or any other authority'.[309]

Nevertheless, throughout the eighties cases of police registration of homosexuals have been reported.[310] In Germany these are called *Rosa Listen*,[311] and in the United Kingdom *trawls*.[312] There are also similar reports from Denmark,[313] Greece,[314] Ireland[315] and Italy.[316] In France this type of registration has been prohibited by the Minister of the Interior in 1981. Furthermore, since the anti-discrimination law of 1985 it is a criminal offence for public officials to knowingly refuse someone the benefit of a legal right because of his or her *mœurs*, or to make any economic activity more difficult for someone because of the same reason.[317] Whether such a law can effectively prevent all official oppression, can be doubted. However, it can be seen as powerful (and symbolically important) support for the notion that *equality before the law* should cover lesbians and gay men too.

---

306 See paragraphs II.A and II.F.3.
307 See paragraph II.C.
308 See paragraph II.B.
309 'Resolution on Sexual Discrimination at the Workplace', adopted on 13 March 1984 (OJ 1984 C 104/46-48), following Recommendation 924 of the Parliamentary Assembly of the Council of Europe, adopted on 1 October 1981.
310 See paragraph 12.1 of *Iceberg* 1991.
311 Although not allowed under German law, every now and again examples of *Rosa Listen* kept by police forces appear (see *Schwule im Recht*, 1992, 289). In reply to parliamentary questions (*Bundestag Drucksache* 11/4299), the German government has admitted that the secret services and the federal police (*Bundeskriminalamt*) keep extensive files with data on homosexuals (see *Bundestag Drucksache* 11/7197, 9 July 1990, 13).
312 See Crane, 1982, 53-55, and Galloway, 1983, 114-116; press-reports: *Gay Times*, November 1990, 5, December 1990, 7.
313 Press-reports: *Sek*, June 1980, 15; *Pan*, 1980, No. 5/6, 30.
314 Press-report: *Gai Pied Hebdo*, 1984, No. 146, 7.
315 See *Out for Ourselves* 1986, 192-194.
316 Press-reports: *Babilonia*, June 1984, 31; *ILGA-bulletin*, 1984, No. 5, 21.
317 Article 187-1 and 187-2 of the Penal Code, as amended by the Law of 25 July 1985 (the word *mœurs* includes sexual orientation; see paragraph I.C). In Denmark and the Netherlands this type of discrimination would be prohibited by the anti-discrimination provisions discussed in paragraph II.E.1.

J. Asylum

In many countries in and outside Europe lesbians and gay men suffer from rather more – official and unofficial – oppression than is the case in most Member States of the EC. It is therefore not surprising that women and men seek refuge and asylum in one of the Member States, because of the severe anti-homosexual discrimination they fear in their home country (outside or inside the EC). So far, the laws of the Member States have only recognized faraway anti-homosexual oppression in a very limited way.[318] However, some advances have been made:

In Denmark persecution for reasons of sexual orientation is not considered to amount to 'persecution' in the sense of the Geneva Convention on Refugees. However, a homosexual asylum seeker may be permitted to remain in Denmark when 'for reasons similar to those listed in the Geneva Convention or for other weighty reasons, (he) ought not to be required to return to his home country'; homosexual asylum seekers may also be permitted to stay for 'exceptional reasons'.[319]

In the Netherlands it is possible to be granted refugee-status on the ground of justified fear for anti-homosexual 'persecution',[320] but as yet no asylum has been granted on this ground.[321] However, in some cases eventually so-called 'C-status' has been given to homosexual asylum seekers,

---

318   In 1989 a gay man from Turkish Northern Cyprus (where all gay sex is forbidden) asked asylum in the United Kingdom, claiming that if he lived with a male friend in Cyprus he would be shunned and made fun of and would risk being sent to prison. The British Government decided not to grant asylum, arguing that the risk of prosecution was small, that the man could reduce this risk by not openly behaving 'in a homosexual manner', and that the consequences of a possible prosecution (a few months in prison) would be 'not particularly dire'. The man appealed, but lost his case in the High Court, which agreed with the government that an arrest for a private homosexual act between consenting adults would not amount to 'persecution', and that the government 'was entitled to recognize that the risk of prosecution would be avoided by self restraint' (press-report: *The Pink Paper*, 5 August 1989, 1).

319   Articles 7 and 9 of the Aliens Law (see Wong, 1988, 2).

320   Following a resolution adopted in the Dutch Parliament on 28 January 1980 (*Kamerstukken II*, 1979/80, 15649, Nos. 16 and 20) the courts have accepted the principle that persecution on the basis of sexual orientation can amount to persecution on the basis of 'membership of a particular social group' (*Afdeling Rechtspraak, Raad van State*, 13 August 1981, No. A-2.1113 (1980); see Bos, Pot & Willems 1992, 166 and 176).

321   In all known cases so far, the immigration authorities (and the court) have found that the feared (discriminatory) treatment in the home country did not amount to 'persecution'. See Bos, Pot & Willems 1992, 176-179, for such decisions involving refugees from Poland (1981), from Austria (1987) from England (1989 and 1990). There are also examples involving refugees from Chile (*Afdeling Rechtspraak, Raad van State*, 28 July 1983, *Gids Vreemdelingenrecht No. D12-85*), from Portugal (press-report: *De Gay Krant*, October 1987, 5; see *Iceberg* 1991, paragraph 12.3), from Lebanon (*President Rechtbank* Amsterdam, 31 August 1989, No. KG 89/1646V) and from Romania (see *President Rechtbank* Den Haag, 24 April 1992, No. 91/5/02272).

allowing them to stay in the Netherlands for urgent humanitarian reasons.[322]

According to Article 16 of the German Constitution anyone persecuted for political reasons has a right to asylum. In 1988 the Supreme Administrative Court ruled that the persecution of homosexuals can amount to political persecution. However, the court also ruled that more is needed than just the prosecution for homosexual acts: there should be a danger of heavy corporal or capital punishment, and such punishment should affect the persons involved in their 'homosexual disposition as a personal trait' in the same way as political dissidents are affected.[323] In cases of lesser persecution, it may be possible for the asylum seeker to qualify for a *Duldung*, which can be given if he or she is in a concrete danger of being tortured or of being sentenced to death, or in considerable danger of body, life or liberty.[324] In 1989 the *Land* of Berlin decided that asylum seekers who have reason to fear persecution on the grounds of their homosexuality, would be allowed to stay in Berlin.[325]

III. Conclusions

A. Summary

In 1992 the law in all Member States of the EC still contains at least some legal discrimination and still accepts various forms of social discrimination. This is in contradiction with international human rights, with the constitutional principles of almost all Member States, and with the expressed condemnation by the European Parliament of 'all forms of discrimination based on an individual's sexual tendencies'. However, a growing number of Member States have enacted anti-discrimination legislation, and have worked towards the repeal of existing anti-homosexual laws.

Paragraph II.A

In a few countries homosexuals are criminalized for *sexual offences* that, in practice, have no heterosexual equivalent. However, of the three countries with unequal age limits for heterosexual and lesbian and gay sex, two are moving towards equalization – one rather slowly and the other (half) country a little faster. At the same time the only country which still has a total

---

322   See Bos, Pot & Willems, 1992, 165, 177 and 179-180.
323   *Bundesverwaltungsgericht*, 15 March 1988, *Entscheidungen des Bundesverwaltungsgericht* 79, 143. The case involved a gay refugee from Iran; given the criteria of the court, it is unclear whether homosexual refugees from other countries could also qualify as political refugees (see *Schwule im Recht,* 1992, 114-116).
324   Article 53 of the *Ausländergesetz* of 1991 (see *Schwule im Recht,* 1992, 116).
325   Press-report: *De Gay Krant,* 26 August 1989, 16 (about the competence of each *Land* in this respect, see *Schwule im Recht,* 1992, 116).

prohibition on gay sex on the statute book is slowly moving towards decriminalization in a way that will probably also establish equal age limits.

Paragraphs II.B and II.C

In a growing number of Member States some discriminatory consequences of the heterosexual exclusivity of marriage are being mitigated by the granting of certain rights and duties to unmarried *couples* that are living together or that have registered as partners. However, many benefits are still only available to married couples, or only to married and unmarried heterosexual couples. The cumulative effect of the exclusion of same-sex couples from numerous marital rights is especially disadvantageous after the death of one of the partners, when one of the partners is from another country, with regard to parental rights, and with regard to pensions and secondary conditions of employment. In several Member States discussions are going on as to the best way of granting rights and duties to unmarried couples. Although more and more lesbian and gay couples have taken responsibility for the upbringing of children, in no Member State can they acquire full legal responsibility as co-parents.

Paragraph II.D

The law of most Member States accepts various forms of discrimination against lesbians and gay men in the field of *employment*. However, both with regard to private and public employment, the legal principle that lesbians and gay men should not be discriminated against, seems to be developing fast in legislation, in case-law, and in administrative guidelines. Such developments are less prominent in two sectors where homosexuality has traditionally been considered as problematic: religious institutions on the one hand, and the military and intelligence services on the other. But here too, the beginning of a consensus between different Member States can be discerned: new legislation and case-law states that religious institutions should not be completely free to discriminate against individuals because of their homosexual orientation; and most jurisdictions now seem to agree that total bans on homosexuals serving in the armed forces or in the intelligence services are not in order.

Paragraphs II.E, II.F and II.G

Anti-homosexual discrimination in the provision of *goods and services* has been outlawed in three Member States. Whether or not such discrimination is or would be regarded as lawful in the other Member States, is difficult to say. Three problem areas are: housing and rent protection (same-sex couples are often worse off than married couples), visiting lesbian/gay bars etc. (where the patrons can be confronted with police raids), and lesbian/gay books, periodicals and films (which may be seized or stopped at the border or elsewhere). Legal difficulties around lesbian/gay *information* and bars etc. are only very rarely a consequence of specific anti-homosexual laws.

Mostly these problems are caused by the unpredictable and sometimes discriminatory enforcement of various laws on indecency, obscenity, drugs, licensing, etc. The cumulative effect of such law enforcement can be that it becomes very difficult to set up or run a lesbian/gay magazine, business, social group or political *organization*. In a few Member States anti-discrimination laws offer some protection to lesbian and gay organizations.

Paragraphs II.H, II.I and II.J

Throughout the EC most people would consider *violence* against homosexuals unacceptable. In most Member States, however, the law seems unable to protect lesbians and gay men against physical violence and the excesses of police repression. In some countries verbal anti-homosexual violence has been prohibited. Only in a few Member States – and here only in a very limited way – has the law recognized the persecution of homosexuals abroad as a ground for *asylum*.

As well as numerous legal differences, there are great similarities between the Member States too. In particular: in almost all Member States there are clear developments towards greater equality in the law and towards better legal protection against social discrimination. At the same time the laws of all member states still contain significant inequalities between homosexuality and heterosexuality.

B. Recommendations

As is to be expected in a first comparative study of a particular area of law in the twelve Member States, the main recommendations are concerned with the need for (further) research.

To develop a better picture of the actual legal situation in the Member States, *comparative research* is needed on the following issues:

- the impact and effectiveness of the various laws that have been introduced to stop anti-homosexual discrimination;
- the degree of protection against anti-homosexual discrimination offered by general public and private law;
- the inclusion or exclusion of same-sex couples in the increasing number of domestic laws that recognize forms of partnership other than marriage;
- the developments (in legislation, case-law, administrative guidelines and collective agreements) relating to the (un-)lawfulness of anti-homosexual discrimination in different sectors of employment;
- the possibilities for lesbians and gay men in the different Member States to actually enjoy their human rights and fundamental freedoms

(in particular their rights to form organizations and set up businesses,
and to receive and impart information);
— the laws, policies and practices relating to the offering of asylum to
    people who have fled from their countries because of the anti-homosex-
    ual oppression they fear there.

To assess the way in which differences between national laws have an *impact on the Single European Market*, it will be necessary to investigate:

— how the free movement of persons within the EC is hindered by (old)
    convictions for (old) homosexual offences that have no or had no
    heterosexual equivalents;
— how the free movement of persons within the EC is hindered by the very
    disparate ways in which laws in different Member States recognize
    same-sex partnerships (and same-sex co-parenting);
— how the free movement of (homosexual) goods (especially books,
    magazines and videos) within the EC is hindered by the very disparate
    laws on decency and obscenity in the different Member States.

However, at this stage it is already possible to suggest several *measures* by
which the *institutions of the EC* could contribute to the improvement of the
legal situation of lesbians and gay men. They could do this by:

— explicitly including sexual orientation in its various legal texts on dis-
    crimination;
— preparing directives that require the prohibition of non-recruitment, non-
    promotion and dismissal on the basis of sexual orientation;
— preparing directives that guarantee equal pay – including pension enti-
    tlements and other benefits for the employee's partner of either gender –
    for equal work;
— ensuring that in the single european market there will be no anti-homo-
    sexual discrimination in the provision of goods and services;
— monitoring any serious violation of the human rights and fundamental
    freedoms of lesbians and gay men in the Member States (in particular
    their rights to express love emotionally and physically, to take respon-
    sibility for the children they are bringing up, to form organizations and
    set up businesses, to receive and impart information, and to be protected
    against violence);
— enabling and encouraging the Member States to continue (or to start) to
    offer asylum to people who have fled from their countries because of the
    anti-homosexual oppression they fear there.

Chapter Four
The Social Situation in the Member States

by

EVERT VAN DER VEEN and ADRIANNE DERCKSEN[*]

[*]   Formerly researchers in the Department of Gay and Lesbian Studies, University of Utrecht.

Table of Contents

I. Introduction

A. Social Situations in the Member States: Different, Changing, and Relatively Unknown

The social situation of lesbian and gay citizens of the European Community is still far from optimal, despite the ongoing (and sometimes successful) efforts of lesbian and gay organizations to change it. In this chapter we will describe the social discrimination faced by lesbians and gay men within the Member States.

Because there have been very few social scientific studies of the social situation of homosexuality in most Member States, and because the scope of this project did not allow for the collection, translation and comparison of the results of all those studies, we do not claim to give a full picture of the social situation throughout the EC. This chapter should be seen as a first effort to give a general overview of social discrimination on the grounds of homosexuality. Some of this discrimination can be seen in all Member States, whereas other issues have so far only come to light in a few countries.

The findings in this chapter are partly based on academic studies carried out by others,[1] partly on our own research for the Dutch organization *Centrum Anti-discriminatie Homoseksualiteit (CAdH)* which has been monitoring the social situation of lesbians and gay men in the Netherlands,[2] partly on reports in the general and lesbian/gay press, and partly on information

---

[1] See the literature listed in Annex 1. Many of the examples given are based on the 'Iceberg-project'. This project (initiated by the International Lesbian and Gay Association, hosted by the Department of Gay and Lesbian Studies of the University of Utrecht, and partly funded by the European Human Rights Foundation) has been documenting examples of legal and social discrimination and of anti-discriminatory measures in the whole of Europe. A first report, *Tip of an iceberg. Anti-lesbian and anti-gay discrimination in Europe 1980 – 1990*, by Kees Waaldijk, is being prepared; the latest draft-version (dated 16 December 1991) contains most of the examples used in this chapter. Where appropriate, reference will be made to the relevant paragraph of '*Iceberg 1991*', as well as to the sources quoted in that draft-report.

[2] CAdH has been operating from 1988 until the end of 1991 and has been funded by the Dutch Ministry of Welfare, Health and Culture. The documentation and research activities of CAdH have been hosted by the Department of Gay and Lesbian Studies of the University of Utrecht. Because many examples in this chapter are based on the first CAdH-report (Van der Veen and Dercksen 1990), and because anti-homosexual discrimination in the Netherlands has been the subject of more academic studies than in any other country, this chapter may give the false impression that lesbians and gay men are worse off in the Netherlands than in other Member States. This does not, of course, reflect the actual situation. More research is necessary to complete an overview of the social situation of lesbians and gay men in all EC Member States.

provided by individuals and organizations from the lesbian and gay community in several countries.[3]

The problems described in this chapter occur in every Member State. However, between the countries there are differences in the general tolerance and acceptance of homosexuality. Opinion polls give some insight into the attitude towards homosexuality in the Member States.[4] In several countries opinion polls show a slight shift towards acceptance. There is a growing recognition of the rights of lesbians and gay men. Partly because of this perceived shift, countries cannot easily be classified as tolerant, intolerant, or hostile.[5] Reality is far more complex than such a classification would

---

3   This last category means that references cannot be given for all examples cited in this chapter.

4   There is no complete inventory of opinion poll findings concerning attitudes towards homosexuality (although a number of them are listed in paragraph 10.3 of *Iceberg* 1991). Some of the results give the impression of a growing general acceptance of homosexuality in some member states:
In *Spain* a poll held in 1987 by the State Institute for Sociological Research suggested that 16% of the population considered homosexual relations to be socially acceptable behaviour, whereas 50% condemned such relations (*De Volkskrant*, 10 October 1988). However a 1985 poll, held for the Asociácion Gai de Madrid and published by the national Association for Human Rights in Madrid, suggested that two thirds of the Spanish population agreed that homosexuality should be recognized as a fundamental human right, whereas 23% objected (*Mundo Gay*, September 1985, 8, 13-19; *De Gay Krant*, November 1985, 6).
In *France* a poll held in 1987 by Sofres for *Le Nouvel Observateur* suggested that 36% of the population considers homosexuality 'an acceptable way to live one's sexuality'; in similar polls the figure had been 29% in 1981 and 41% in 1984 (*Gai Pied Hebdo* 1987, No. 298, 9).
In *Italy* a poll held in 1989 by the Institute of Economic, Political and Social Studies suggested that 50% of the population believe that society should defend the rights of homosexuals and that society should guarantee them the same dignity as other citizens, whereas 10% considered homosexuality to be a disease and 2% a perversion (*Gai Pied Hebdo* 1989, No. 370, 14). A poll held six years before (by the Institute Demoskoea) suggested that 24% of the population considered homosexuality as a normal expression of sexuality, whereas 42% considered it to be a serious mental problem and 17% saw it as a vice (*Gai Pied Hebdo* 1983, No. 84, 15).
In the *United Kingdom* a poll held in 1991 by Gallup suggested that 53% of the population over 18 considered homosexuality to be an acceptable alternative lifestyle; in a similar poll in 1986 this figure had been 44% (*Capital Gay*, 18 October 1991, 3). In 1992 a poll held by Harris for the Stonewall Group and the Tory Campaign for Homosexual Equality suggested that 71% of the population believe that lesbians and gay men should have the same rights under the law as everyone else (*Gay Times*, April 1992, 7).
In *Denmark* a 1990 poll held by Institute Sensor suggested that 63% of the population finds sex between women acceptable (and 29% find it unacceptable) (data provided in a letter of 2 March 1992 from the *Landsforeningen for bosser og lesbiske* to the Iceberg-project.)
In the *Netherlands* a 1990 poll suggested that 95% of the population believe that one should let homosexuals be as free as possible to live in their own way (*Sociaal en Cultureel Rapport 1992*, Rijkswijk: Sociaal en Cultureel Planbureau, 1992, 465).

5   For an assessment of the general level of acceptance of homosexuality in all European countries, see: Tielman and De Jonge, 1988, 185-187, 225-242; Tatchell, 1992, 79-139; Tielman and Hammelburg, 1993 (in print).

suggest. As will be seen in this chapter, the situations differ from region to region, from person to person, from social area to social area.

The rest of this introduction will be devoted to a brief discussion of the phenomenon of anti-lesbian and anti-gay social discrimination, and of its causes, mechanisms and consequences. The introduction is followed by Part II, dealing with the problems relating to major areas and aspects of the social situation of lesbians and gay men.[6] We will conclude with Part III which contains a summary and recommendations.

B. Social Discrimination against Lesbians and Gay Men: Causes, Mechanisms and Consequences

Social discrimination creates barriers for lesbians and gay men to the achievement of social well-being and economic progress. It also limits their opportunity to participate fully in social life. Social discrimination finds its origins in negative views of homosexuality. These negative views are deep rooted in religious and 'scientific' ideas in society. Although mainstream opinion is changing more and more towards accepting homosexuality as one of the many variations of human nature, negative conceptions of homosexuality as a sin (Judaeo-Christian origin), a shame (Islam), disease (medicine) or abnormality (psychiatry and the social sciences) still persist and are used to reinforce and justify discriminatory behaviour, whether conscious or unconscious. These negative views are reflected in legislation through which homosexuality is criminalized and marginalized.

1. Homosexuality as a Sin

The arguments most commonly used to justify discrimination against lesbians and gay men are religious in origin. In the past people persecuted for their sexual orientation were known as 'sodomites' and 'witches'. Such persecution has been banned since the 18th century, but religious conceptions of homosexuality as a sin are still used to justify unequal treatment. The

6   Roughly following the structure of Part II of Chapter Three by Waaldijk, ten aspects
     and areas will be dealt with:
     A. expressions of affection and sexuality – and reactions of violence,
     B. partnership,
     C. parents and children,
     D. employment,
     E. education,
     F. health care,
     G. housing and recreation,
     H. religion,
     I. association,
     J. information and culture.

religious conviction that homosexual behaviour is a sin and that homosexuals should refrain from homosexual acts is invoked to justify discrimination against lesbians and gay men by religious groups and organizations.[7]

2. Homosexuality as a Disease or Abnormality

The belief that homosexuality is a disease is not only a deeply rooted conviction, but was until recently officially accepted. Homosexuality was listed as a disease in all the major classifications.[8] This view of homosexuality can be traced to the mid-19th century. With the increased medicalisation of society and the idea that same sex acts were 'sinful' gave way to the notion that sexual behaviour follows from sexual identity. Same-sex love was no longer seen simply as an act, a sinful act which anyone was capable of, but rather came to be seen as a psychiatric deformation afflicting certain people only, who needed to be cured. This view was based on studies of homosexual patients in psychiatric care. In the late 19th century and the beginning of this century, the study of physical appearance of homosexual patients gave further support for the conviction that homosexuality is both a physical and a psychiatric condition. On top of that, biased studies of group behaviour further acknowledged the conception of homosexuality as a deviation.[9]

With the medicalisation of homosexuality, homosexual men and women were further stigmatised, to such an extent that many societies found it appropriate to legalise this stigma. Some people feared openness about homosexuality on the assumption that homosexuality was contagious. Open homosexuals would cause others, especially children, to become homosexual. Although this idea is still widespread in Europe, there is no evidence that homosexuality can be acquired in this way.

It was not until the late 1950s that large scale studies of non-patient homosexuals proved that homosexuality was not limited to patients and that lesbians and gay men were as capable as heterosexuals of leading a normal life.[10] Gradually the idea began to take hold that homosexuality is a simple variation of affection and sexuality. However, many people still see homosexuality as a mental disease or a biological deviation. Many

---

7   Van der Veen and Dercksen, 1990. See paragraph II.H for examples.
8   The International Classification of Diseases (ICD) of the World Health Organization (WHO) and the Diagnostic Statistical Manual (DSM) of the American Psychological Association (APA) both mentioned homosexuality as a disease. Both organizationss have deleted it in their most recent update (ICD IV, DSM III+).
9   See Hekma, 1987.
10   See for example Evelyn Hooker's study of non-patient homosexuals in which psychiatric experts were unable to tell from the results of the Rorschach tests which were the homo - sexuals and which were the heterosexuals, leading Hooker to conclude that

politicians and religious leaders nowadays use the illness model to justify their negative views on homosexuality.

3. Homosexuality as a Crime

Negative views of homosexual behaviour have been and are reflected in many laws and regulations. The social effects of such criminalization are far reaching.

Firstly, homosexuals are forced into illegality. Criminalization of homosexuality does not prevent or even diminish the incidence of homosexual behaviour, it merely criminalizes the people who behave that way. Insofar as they were intended to prevent unwanted behaviour, nearly all such laws have failed.[11] For example, a recent survey of 1,000 gay and bisexual men found that despite the United Kingdom law forbidding young men to have sex with another man until they are 21, 90% had already had sex with a man by the time they were 21.[12]

Secondly, homosexuality becomes largely invisible for the general public: if one does not have personal knowledge of homosexual lifestyles e.g. by knowing homosexuals who are open about their sexuality (and many lesbians and gay men are not eager to be open about it), the major impression one gets of homosexuality is one of perversion and crime. The media reinforces this negative image by reporting almost exclusively when something bad happens. Where the perpetrator is of the same sex as the victim, we hear of 'homosexual rape', 'homosexual abuse' and 'homosexual murder' – even where the perpretrator actually identifies as heterosexual. Yet we never hear of 'heterosexual rape' 'heterosexual abuse' or 'heterosexual murder'. We see homosexuality connected to extortion, dishonourable discharge, violence and perversion. Because of negative images of homosexual lifestyles, homosexuality is often, therefore, associated with criminality.[13]

4. The Consequences: Invisibility and Marginalization

These negative views of homosexuality have serious social consequences.

Firstly, as a result of the stigmatization of homosexuality it is considered appropriate to censor positive information on homosexuality. As a consequence, homosexuality becomes mostly invisible, and where it is reported it is usually portrayed negatively.

'homosexuality as a clinical entity does not exist' (Hooker, 1957). For an overview of the shift in medical and psychiatric models, see Bayer, 1981.
11   Lautmann, 1977; Van der Veen, 1992.
12   The Sigma project.
13   Lautmann, 1977; Armitage, Dickey & Sharples, 1987.

Secondly, the quality of life of lesbians and gay men is affected by these views. Many experience discrimination in the form of exclusion or open hostility. Due to the stigma they face, most lesbians and gay men tend not to be open about their sexual orientation and lifestyle. This in turn contributes to the invisibility of homosexuality, which helps to keep the process of denial and ignorance alive. The people most affected by this silence are those who are uncertain about their sexual orientation. Because nearly everyone is raised in a heterosexual world, positive role models for homosexual lifestyles are hard to find. It is not surprising, therefore, that the rate of suicide among young lesbians and gay men is significantly higher than that of their heterosexual peers.[14]

II. Different Areas and Aspects of the Social Situation of Homosexuality

A. Expressions of Affection and Sexuality – and Reactions of Violence

The repression of lesbian and gay sexuality is probably one of the most visible aspects of anti-gay and anti-lesbian discrimination. Lesbian and gay sex and other expressions of same-sex love are repressed in several ways.

The first is denial. While heterosexual love is all around us every day in films, books, on television, in advertising, on the streets, etc, visible expressions of same-sex love are rare. And if they are seen and recognized as such, those who witness them often react with hostility, outrage or even violence. The problem is in principle the same in all Member States – the visibility of lesbian and gay affection is seen as offensive. However, the actual situation can differ enormously from place to place. In the Southern Member States, where demonstrations of affection between men are generally more accepted than in the Northern states, the sight of two men holding hands would not cause any stir (unless it was clear that this was a sign of homosexual affection). In the Northern countries, however, such a scene would most likely be interpreted as homosexual – and offensive.

A second form of repression of the expression of same-sex love is the active prosecution of such expressions by state institutions. In several Member

---

14   In a survey of 416 young lesbians and gay men in London, 80 (19%) said they had attempted suicide because they were gay (Trenchard and Warren 1984). A US government Department of Health and Human Services report concluded that young lesbian and gay people are 'two to three times more likely to attempt suicide than other young people' and 'may comprise up to 30% of completed youth suicides annually' (Gibson, 1989). See also: Commissional Paper, US Department of Health and Human Services: *National Institute of Mental Health, Task Force on Youth Suicide* (National Conference on Prevention and Interventions in Youth Suicide, 11-13 June 1986, Oakland, California) and Khayatti, 1993.

States, various laws and regulations are used to criminalize such expressions, ranging from total bans on same-sex encounters to regulations forbidding kissing in public.[15] The police play a major role in the enforcement of these laws and regulations. Their enforcement depends largely on the amount of time and energy the police put into the pursuit of such 'crimes'.[16]

A third form of repression of the expression of same-sex love is anti-lesbian and anti-gay violence. This can range from verbal and physical abuse to robbery, assault, vandalism and even murder. This violence – where the aggressor believes that the sexuality (or perceived sexuality) of his victims justifies his violent behaviour – is a serious problem in all Member States.[17] A gay-basher in the Netherlands, arrested by the police for shoplifting, told police: 'I am not as bad as you think: I helped you with cleaning up gays'.[18] Gay-bashers feel themselves justified by society's anti-gay and anti-lesbian attitudes. With lesbian expressions of love, the sexual component of lesbian relationships is often ignored, but if it is recognized as such, it is often repressed with violence.[19] Men looking for contact with other men in public space ('cruising'), often face severe violence. Some police forces and gay and lesbian organizations monitoring violence against gay men in public places come up with hundreds of cases of violence (including police brutality)[20] against these men, knowing that even their numbers are probably only the tip of the iceberg.[21] Dutch and Spanish

15   Paragraph 2.6 of *Iceberg* 1991 gives examples of: women arrested for kissing each other, in Spain (*ILGA-bulletin*, 1987, No. 2, 22), Italy (*Sek*, November 1981, 20) and the United Kingdom (Crane 1982, 19); men arrested for kissing each other, in the United Kingdom (1 *Weekly Law Reports* 1986, 1017-1024; *Gay Times*, August 1986, 19) and Germany (*De Gay Krant*, 10 September 1988, 14); and men beaten up for kissing each other in public in the United Kingdom (*De Gay Krant*, November 1988, 10).

16   See paragraph II.A. of Chapter Three by Waaldijk for some law enforcement figures.

17   *Iceberg* 1991 contains numerous examples of anti-homosexual violence from most member states: assault (paragraph 11.1), murder (paragraph 11.3), robbery (paragraph 11.4), arson and bombing (paragraph 11.5). See also Van der Veen and Dercksen, 1990.

18   See Van der Veen, 1992.

19   A first inventory of the experiences of lesbians in the Netherlands showed that lesbians who show their affection in public are confronted with several forms of violence, such as sexual violence (motivated by the notion: 'if you have – forced – sexual intercourse with a man your 'wrong' feelings will disappear') and verbal and physical abuse (Van Oort, 1992).

20   Police raids on gay cruising areas are reported regularly. Paragraph 8.4 of *Iceberg* 1991 gives examples from Greece (*Sek*, August 1981, 15, October 1982, 20; *IGA-bulletin*, 1984, No. 1, 20; *Gai Pied Hebdo*, 1984, No. 146, 7) and France (*Sek*, December 1981, 13, March 1982, 10, September 1985, 9; *Gai Pied Hebdo*, 29 October 1983, 6, 1989, No. 368, 8-9).

21   Anti-gay violence is slowly becoming more visible through special projects in e.g. Germany, France, the Netherlands, Spain and the United Kingdom, whereas much has yet to be discovered on anti-lesbian violence. The aims of the projects are to uncover anti-gay and anti-lesbian violence, to encourage victims to report such crimes to the police, and to persuade the police to be more sympathetic towards lesbians and gay men. In the Netherlands, as a result of this kind of change in attitude, the police are now more able

research showed that 90% of this violence is not reported to the police or to lesbian and gay organizations, and found that more than half of the gay men interviewed had experienced anti-gay violence.[22] Dutch research showed that one in three lesbians has experienced anti-lesbian violence.[23] Lesbians and gay men are particularly reluctant to report violence inflicted on them in countries where there are laws criminalizing gay or lesbian behaviour.[24] This makes them an easy target. Young men even organize special gay-bashing groups and go to known cruising places to molest and rob these men. Many 'cruisers' are verbally and physically attacked or even murdered by them.[25]

In short: the idea that homosexuals are outlaws is an incentive for the victimisation of gay men. A gay man can more easily be blackmailed and he will be less willing to report violence against him, which makes gay-bashing more attractive. The criminalization of expressions of homosexual affection and sexuality also creates a low sense of self-esteem among lesbians and gay men and may easily lead to feelings of deprivation, isolation and severe depression.

The second form of repression (by the state) and the third form (violence) combine to reinforce each other. For example it is not known whether it is mainly fear of arrest and prosecution, or fear of social disapproval, hostility or violent attacks from onlookers which prevent most same-sex couples from holding hands or kissing in public. But what is clear is that fear of hostility from the general public plays a significant role in this self-censorship; and this means that those individuals who do choose to demonstrate openly their affection are all the more obvious – all the more likely to become targets for repression.

to control this kind of violence, and gay men are more willing to report crimes against them (see Van der Veen, 1984).

22 See Van der Veen, 1992, 23-26; and *Aspectos juridico-legales de la homosexualidad* (Barcelone 1992).
23 Van Oort, 1992.
24 In the Netherlands lesbians and gay men are more willing to report anti-homosexual experiences – knowing the police will help to protect them. In the United Kingdom the offenders are more likely to go to the police – knowing the police will help them to arrest the victims for indecent behaviour (see Van der Veen, 1992).
25 In some Member States some police forces (including at least 34 forces in the Netherlands, two in Germany, and one in the United Kingdom) have started to recognize the extent of the problem and have tried to develop strategies for the prevention of this large-scale violence. However, small scale studies in cities in the Netherlands and Spain have shown most violence is not reported (see note 21).

B. Partnership

The legal and social recognition of same-sex relationships ('partnerships') is currently the subject of much debate, both within and outside the lesbian and gay movement in many European countries.

Within the lesbian and gay communities it is still being debated whether the recognition of same-sex partnerships as equivalent to marriage is a legitimate goal for the movement.[26] Some lesbians and gay men see marriage as an institution which reinforces the unequal position of women and of homosexuals in this society; not an institution they would want to emulate. Some favour the individualization of rights, and would prefer to remove the special legal and social benefits from marriage. Others feel that such a social revolution is unlikely, and think it more important that lesbians and gay men are no longer excluded from the institution of marriage and the social and legal privileges it brings. Many prefer the term 'partnership' to 'marriage' and are not interested in religious recognition; but some, in particular those who are themselves religious may also see this as important.

There is an increasing variation in the lifestyles of EC citizens. Traditional marriage is becoming but one choice out of many; it is becoming more acceptable not to marry, to live alone, or to live with a partner outside marriage. Nevertheless, many lesbians and gay men are living in a traditional family i.e. married or living with their parents. The last two situations are probably less common in Southern Europe than in Northern European countries, where it is probably easier for lesbians and gay men to live with their partner.[27]

Social discrimination against same-sex couples affects the everyday life of many lesbians and gay men. They are excluded from social benefits that come with marriage, and they are often forced to keep quiet about their relationship. Lesbian and gay couples are excluded from marriage in all Member States and are therefore excluded from many of the legal rights that come with marriage. Apart from the legal benefits that flow from marriage, the enforced single status of lesbian and gay couples has many social consequences in areas such as access to housing, acceptance of the partner at work, and in the partner's family, and in other everyday situations.

---

26 See Waaldijk, 1992.
27 In a report from the Federal Department of Housing in Germany of 5 December 1989 it was estimated that 50% of lesbians and gay men have a steady relationship, and one third of these are living together. In the Netherlands, for 1989, the number of same-sex couples living together is estimated to be around 35,000. That is 8.5% of the total of households of non-married couples with or without children. Around 1 in every 10 couples living together (with or without children) is not married (see Vrooman, 1992, 1398 - 1399).

However, the acceptability of co-habitation differs largely from country to country and place to place.[28] In recent years there has been a slow shift towards acceptance of lesbian and gay relationships.[29] In many Member States, organizations such as employers, public transport operators, insurance companies, and pension funds have begun to accept same-sex relationships as equivalent to heterosexual relationships.[30] Also some religious denominations and some individual churches have started to accept same-sex couples in their ritual celebrations of relationships.[31]

C. Parents and Children

1. Lesbian and Gay Parents

Unexpected as it may seem, many European children are raised by one or two lesbian, gay or bisexual parents. The reason is that there are many forms of homosexual parenthood. We will mention the three major forms.

(a) One (or two) homosexual or bisexual parent(s) in a traditional marriage

This is probably the most common form. Some homosexual people who are married will hardly ever expose this aspect of their lives. Others will lead a partially homosexual lifestyle. Children from such marriages are raised by one (or two) homosexual parent(s).

---

28   Paragraphs 3.1 and 3.2 of *Iceberg* 1991 contain many examples of inequality between heterosexual and homosexual relationships
29   Opinion polls in the Netherlands have suggested that the percentage of the population approving of gay or lesbian couples living together has increased from 44% in 1980, to 55% in 1985 and 68% in 1991; those disapproving went down from 17% to 16% to 13% (*Sociaal en Cultureel Rapport* 1992, Rijswijk: Sociaal en Cultureel Planbureau, 1992, 462.)
30   Paragraphs 3.1 and 3.2 of *Iceberg* 1991 contain several examples of this increasing recognition: mostly in law, but also in some private pension schemes (United Kingdom, *Capital Gay*, 24 March 1989, 12; Netherlands: Martens and Van Straaten, 1992, 128); and by private companies offering rebates to 'families' (Denmark, *Pan*, 1981, No. 3, 3), etc.
31   Paragraph 3.4 of *Iceberg* 1991 contains examples from Belgium (*De Gay Krant*, 17 November 1990, 19); France (*Gai Pied Hebdo*, 1985, No. 157, 23 and 66); Germany (*Lambda Nachrichten*, 1986, No. 3, 29; *De Gay Krant*, September 1984, 7, August 1988, 14); and the United Kingdom (Lesbian Information Service, October 1987, 8). Some small Christian denominations (the Evangelische Kirche in the former GDR; the Remonstrantse Broederschap in the Netherlands; see Geurtsen, Hofmeijer and Zondervan 1991) and some non-religious denominations in the United Kingdom, Belgium and the Netherlands (humanist associations) officially recognize homosexual couples and pro-vide affirmation services.

*(b)   One parent living a homosexual lifestyle following divorce, and
     continuing to take part in raising the children of their marriage*

This is not uncommon. In some cases (usually where the mother is a lesbian) the children are raised within a lesbian or gay relationship; in other cases they only see their homosexual parent on visits. Due to common resistance to homosexual parenthood, the homosexual partner is sometimes less likely to get the custody of the children than the heterosexual partner.[32] This is particularly likely where the father comes out as gay.

*(c)   Homosexuals who decide to raise children within a same-sex
     relationship, or as a single person*

Although there are no Member States where lesbians and gay men have the same parental rights as heterosexuals,[33] this does not prevent many of them from choosing to bring up children. This is the third major form of homosexual parenthood.

In some cases a lesbian may decide to have a child on her own, or a lesbian couple will decide to have children and raise them within their relationship. They may become pregnant by self-insemination, if they can find a man willing to donate semen. The man may be a friend or a complete stranger, and may or may not play a role in raising the child, depending on the arrangement. For gay men such an arrangement may be their only chance of having children.

Alternatively, lesbians may use the services of clinics providing artificial insemination by donor (A.I.D.), although many clinics refuse to provide this service to lesbians or single women.[34]

Finally, in a few countries it is possible for lesbians and gay men to adopt or foster children although it is usually very difficult even where it is legally permitted. Sometimes lesbians and gay men are allowed to foster so-called 'hard-to-place' children i.e. older children or children with disabilities or AIDS whom no one else wants. The idea seems to be that it is better for the child to have any home, even an 'abnormal' one, than to remain in an institution.

---

32   See Chapter Three by Waaldijk for examples of divorce-cases where the homosexuality of one parent was taken into account in decisions relation to custody or visiting.

33   The non-biological parent in a same-sex couple is excluded from parental rights (including custody, inheritance, access). This can create great difficulties in cases where the biological parent for whatever reason can no longer take care of the children. In all Member States same-sex couples are excluded from joint adoption. Adoption by one individual is possible in many countries, but in practice lesbians and gay men are hardly ever accepted as adoptive parents.

34   See paragraph 4.3 of *Iceberg* 1991.

2. Controversial Parenthood

There is resistance to gay men or lesbians raising children in all Member States. Opponents feel that children will be set a bad example, and that the children are likely to turn out to be homosexual themselves. Children who are brought up within a same-sex relationship, it is argued, will miss the presence of the opposite sex as a point of reference. Their identity development might suffer as a result. These arguments are seldom applied to children who are raised by a single parent who is heterosexual.

There is no evidence to support such beliefs. But the existence of strong opposition to lesbians and gay men parenting makes it difficult to conduct research into the welfare of children raised within same-sex relationships – many lesbian and gay parents are understandably reluctant to get involved in studies where their ability to parent will be questioned just because of their sexuality. Exploratory research in the Netherlands into lesbian couples who chose to bring up children did show that the initial resistance of their peer-group disappeared after the child was born. The researchers found no signs of negative consequences for the children. The quality of the upbringing proved to be far more important than the gender or sexual orientation of the parents.[35] This was also the conclusion of British research comparing the psychological development of children of lesbian mothers with children of single heterosexual mothers.[36]

In some Member States (including the Netherlands, Denmark and the United Kingdom) organizations have been set up to help lesbian and gay parents in the above-mentioned situations. One can notice a slow shift towards acceptance of homosexual parenthood in most Member States. The discussion on the issue has moved into the public domain.

3. Lesbian and Gay Youth

One of the most serious problems for lesbians and gay men throughout the EC is that of the situation of lesbian and gay youth. The situation for adult lesbian and gay men is on the whole slowly improving. This cannot be said of the situation of young lesbians and gays.[37]

Why are young lesbians and gays so vulnerable? In puberty, when boys and girls are preoccupied with sexuality, young lesbians and gays need to go through a process of *coming out*.[38] In most cases this is a period of

---

35   Geerlings and Van der Meer, 1989.
36   See Golombok, Spencer and Rutter, 1983; Tasker and Golombok, 1991.
37   Research in the (comparatively tolerant) Netherlands has shown that the problems of young homosexuals have hardly changed over the last decade (Van der Veen and Dercksen, 1990, 140-141).
38   'Coming out' is the process of labeling the same-sex attraction that you are experiencing as homosexual, both for yourself and for others.

uncertainty and depression. Unlike young heterosexuals, young lesbians and gays lack positive role models. Like everybody, they are brought up with negative images of homosexuality. This means when they are coming out they especially need the support of those closest to them. However, family and friends are often more likely to reject them than support them. This, of course, makes their situation even more difficult and lonely.

The reaction of the parents is of great importance in this period. Unfortunately many of the family, friends in the neighbourhood, pupils and teachers at school do not support the young person in the process of coming out. Indeed, their relationship with these persons can be severely damaged. Many young people are verbally or physically attacked, thrown out of the house, or told that they are mistaken or just going through 'a phase'.[39] In countries with a higher age of consent for gay sex (the United Kingdom and Germany), and in Ireland, where all gay sex remains illegal, there is also the threat of criminal sanctions.[40] Even in more tolerant societies like the Netherlands and Denmark, many cases of negative reactions are still reported.[41] Little progress appears to have happened in this area.

In some countries the problems of lesbian and gay youth have been recognized and lesbian and gay youth organizations set up to help. The Council of Europe financially supports the International Gay and Lesbian Youth Organization, which organizes – among other things – annual gatherings for European lesbian and gay youth.

D. Employment

Lesbians and gay men face discrimination in employment in all the Member States. A few countries have laws against such discrimination, and these days few employers will explicitly exclude lesbians and gay men from their workforce. Nevertheless being lesbian or gay still lowers one's chance of getting a job, keeping a job and getting promotion. Many lesbians and gay men have fewer opportunities on the labour market simply because of their sexuality.[42]

The conditions at work are often hostile toward homosexuality.

---

39   Geerlof, 1992, found the following figures for different types of parental response to their child coming out to them: 26% experienced immediate acceptance, 34% acceptance after a while and 40% experienced permanent rejection.
40   The existence of such laws also tends to reinforce and justify negative social attitudes towards adolescent homosexuality.
41   For the Netherlands, see Geerlof and Tielman, 1986.
42   In a survey by the German magazine *Wiener* in 1989, 41% of gay men responding said their career had been negatively affected as a result of their sexuality (*De Gay Krant*, 26 August 1989, 13). 11% of gay men in Ireland responding to a survey by Gay Health Action in 1988 had been discriminated against in work because of their sexuality (see paragraph 5.1 of *Iceberg* 1991).

It is outside the limits of this chapter to differentiate between the different Member States and between types of employment.[43] There might be great differences between for example different sectors of industry and between civil servants and other employees.[44] Furthermore in some countries special regulations apply to people working in the armed forces, the Diplomatic Service, the judicial system or the church. Further research would be needed to establish in which sectors (and in which regions of the EC) anti-homosexual employment discrimination is most prevalent.

Research in the Netherlands[45] suggests that employment discrimination against lesbians and gay men is concentrated at four main levels:
(1) recruitment, promotion and dismissal;
(2) social conditions in the workplace;
(3) terms of employment;
(4) the availability of complaints procedures.

1. Recruitment, Promotion and Dismissal

Access to employment is difficult for minority groups – including lesbians and gay men, who may face discrimination at the stage of recruitment, or when applying for promotion, or may even face dismissal if it comes out that they are lesbian or gay.[46]

Such discrimination may be based on the belief of employers:
– that lesbian and gay employees will constitute a problem in the workplace, or
– that lesbians and gay men will not function properly because of their assumed unstable and multiple relationships, or

---

43   See chapter 5 of *Iceberg* 1991.
44   For discrimination against teachers, see paragraph II.E.2; for discrimination against health-workers, see paragraph II.F.2; and for discrimination against church-workers, see paragraph II.H.
45   Dercksen, 1992; Bonfrère, 1992; Van Odijk, 1988.
46   Paragraphs 5.1 and 5.4 of *Iceberg* 1991 give examples of *discriminatory recruitment* in the following sectors and countries: the Diplomatic Service in the United Kingdom (*The Guardian*, 19 January 1990); the merchant navy in Greece (*Gai Pied Hebdo*, 1984, No. 70, 113); the armed forces in the United Kingdom (Crane, 1982, 184), Germany (*Bundestag Drucksache* 11/7197, 14), Italy (*Unità*, 23 December 1987; *ILGA-bulletin* 1988/3) and Greece (*Gai Pied Hebdo*, 1983, No. 70, 13). Paragraphs 5.3 and 5.4 of *Iceberg* 1991 give examples of *discrimination in internal selection and promotion* in the following sectors and countries: banking in Italy (*Babilonia*, April 1986, No. 35, 6, April 1989, No. 66, 52-53); the civil service in the United Kingdom (*Gay Times*, October 1987; *The Guardian*, 19 January 1990); the armed forces in Germany (*Neue Juristische Wochenschrift*, 1991, Heft 17, 1127; *De Gay Krant*, 30 July 1988, 12). Paragraphs 5.2 and 5.4 of *Iceberg* 1991 give examples of *discriminatory dismissal* in the following sectors and countries: bar work in Spain (*Lambda*, April 1980, 2); youth work in the United Kingdom (Crane, 1982, 105-106); the armed forces in the United Kingdom (Crane, 1982, 184).

- that customers will stay away if they find out the company employs lesbians or gay men, or
- that lesbian and gay employees can be blackmailed easily and will thus be a security risk, or
- that lesbians and gay men have a problematic private life which will influence their productivity.

Employers will hardly ever explicitly fail to select, or dismiss, or fail to promote someone because of his or her sexual orientation. More often the reason given for not appointing, or not promoting, or for dismissing a lesbian or gay man will be, for example, that they would not or did not 'fit in with the team'.[47]

2. Social Conditions in the Workplace

Once employed, the social conditions of the organization in which a gay man or lesbian is employed will have a great influence on his or her well-being and productivity. Dutch research shows that a non-discriminatory and positive attitude of superiors, a relatively large number of women in the team or organization and a non-competitive but co-operative atmosphere have a positive influence.[48] The written and unwritten codes of behaviour are very important.[49] Not all lesbians and gay men are equally capable of adjusting to a hostile environment at work; accordingly their success in work varies. Different types of work, different sectors and different levels of education mean that different problems arise. There are reports of lesbians and gay men throughout the EC who get sick, resign or are dismissed as a consequence of the negative attitudes towards homosexuality which they encounter at work.[50] It is very difficult to make the discriminatory aspects visible.[51]

47 See the example from Denmark given in paragraph 5.2 of *Iceberg* 1991: a man had been dismissed, officially because there were difficulties in the co-operation between him and his colleagues, but it later transpired that the actual reason had been that his colleagues had complained about his being gay (*Pan*, 1980, No. 5/6, 26).
48 Van Odijk, 1988; Dercksen, 1992; Bonfrère, 1992.
49 In this context the importance of the explicit condemnation, in the EC Code of Practice on Protecting the Dignity of Women and Men at Work, of sexual harassment against lesbian and gay employees as 'unacceptable' should not be underestimated. See Chapter Seven by Byre and Chapter Fourteen by Betten.
50 Paragraph 5.3 of *Iceberg* 1991 gives an example from the United Kingdom of harass-ment of a lesbian woman at work, in which the woman in the end decides to leave her job (*Lesbian Information Service*, November 1987, 8, August/September 1989, 16).
51 Research in the Netherlands: Dercksen, 1992, Van Odijk, 1988, Bonfrère, 1992; in Ger-many: Lautmannn, 1977, and Zillich, 1988; in France: Cavailhes, Dutey et Bach-Ignasse, 1984.

3. Terms of Employment

Terms of employment often discriminate directly or indirectly against lesbian and gay employees. Most evidently this is the case in pension schemes and in regulations for leave from work (and for other 'spousal benefits') which make a distinction between married and unmarried employees.[52] In effect such terms and conditions of employment mean that many lesbians and gay men are paid less than their heterosexual colleagues for the same work.

4. The Availability of Complaints Procedures

If colleagues find out that an employee or manager is lesbian or gay, this may cause serious problems. The employee may be harassed to such a degree that dismissal or transfer to another department seems to be the only solution.

In all Member States there are very limited possibilities for lesbian and gay employees to get help in cases where their work is being complicated by discriminatory behaviour of colleagues or superiors or discriminatory regulations. Dutch research shows that company doctors, welfare workers and other company advisors are not able or willing to change discriminatory attitudes in the organization.[53]

Self-organization by lesbian and gay employees within labour unions and active anti-discriminatory company-policies may be a motor for change. In some Member States these types of actions are growing in number.[54]

E. Education

The social situation of homosexuality in the area of education can best be described in three paragraphs: one on the situation of pupils, one on that of teachers and one on educational material.

---

52   Paragraph 5.3 of *Iceberg* 1991 gives several examples of transport companies excluding same-sex partners from free travel arrangements for the 'family' of their employees in France (*Gai Pied Hebdo*, 1985, No. 191, 9-10), in Belgium (*De Gay Krant*, October 1988, 9) and in the United Kingdom (*Capital Gay*, 21 April 1989, 3).
53   Dercksen, 1992.
54   Paragraph 5.1 of *Iceberg* 1991 gives examples from Ireland (*Lesbian Information Service*, December 1987, 13, *Gay Times*, July 1988) and Italy (*Babilonia*, March 1986, 9).

1. Situation of Pupils

In the paragraph on lesbian and gay youth, we already mentioned the difficulties facing young lesbians and gays. These difficulties are not limited to the family situation. In school, too, lesbian and gay pupils face many problems, caused by the combination of a hostile or non-accepting school environment and the vulnerability of many homosexual pupils. There are some obvious cases of discrimination, where pupils are refused education because of their homosexuality, but in most cases discrimination is more covert, ranging from schools failing to tackle anti-gay or anti-lesbian bullying or violence, to lesbian and gay pupils badly underachieving, feeling isolation or being forced to be silent about their homosexuality.[55] Where they exist, lesbian and gay youth organizations play an important role in helping lesbian and gay youth at schools. But it is only a small minority of young lesbians and gays who can turn to such an organization.

2. Situation of Teachers

What is true concerning the situation on the labour market of lesbians and gay men in general, is also true of lesbian or gay teachers.[56] Many teachers have to pretend to be heterosexual, or be silent about their sexual orientation, to avoid the risk of dismissal or other problems at school. Pupils, their parents, colleagues or management often object to teachers being openly homosexual.[57] Some schools with negative views on homosexuality explicitly bar lesbians and gay men from teaching – for instance on the basis that such teachers would set a bad example or turn their pupils into homosexuals. For similar reasons, many educational institutions have special demands for teachers concerning their lifestyle, their convictions and beliefs. Gay teachers are also judged far more severely than their heterosexual colleagues and are more likely to be falsely accused of sexual harassment against pupils.[58]

Teachers can play an important role in showing and creating tolerance towards homosexuality by discussing it in a non-prejudiced way. Lesbian

---

55   In several Member States one can find schools, especially religious schools, where lesbian and gay pupils or students will be refused entry and where it is forbidden to speak positively about homosexuality. Paragraph 9.4 of *Iceberg* 1991 gives examples from the United Kingdom (*Gay Times*, April 1990, 7, August 1990, 5) and Italy (*De Gay Krant*, March 1984, 16; *Babilonia*, June 1986, 7).

56   See paragraph II.D.

57   Paragraphs 5.1 and 5.2 of *Iceberg* 1991 give examples of discriminatory non-recruitment and dismissal from: Denmark (*Pan*, 1983, No. 1, 4); the United Kingdom (Crane, 1982, 106-107; Colvin, 1989, 53); and Belgium (*ILGA-bulletin*, 1988, No. 4, 15-16). Research in the Netherlands (Tielman, Kersten and Van der Ploeg, 1990) showed that lesbian and gay teachers enjoy less freedom than their heterosexual colleagues.

58   Tielman, Kersten and Ploeg, 1990.

and gay teachers can also help lesbian and gay pupils come to terms with their sexuality, by showing them positive role models. The advantages of openly gay and lesbian teachers cannot be over-emphasized.

3. Educational Materials

Moves towards equality for lesbians and gay men are seriously obstructed by the lack of unbiased education materials. Very few schools offer their pupils reliable and unbiased information on homosexuality. Either homosexuality is not mentioned at all, or it is dealt with in a negative sense and presented as a problem. Only in a few educational programmes is information on homosexuality integrated into the programme. In British schools a special law forbids the 'promotion of homosexuality' in schools.[59] Although more educational materials on homosexuality are becoming available, it will still take some time to integrate the issue into every relevant programme, such as courses on sexuality, history, literature, social science, nature and biology, religion and ethics.[60]

Institutes of higher education, too, are confronted with a lack of material. Some universities and polytechnics have now started special programmes of teaching and research in the field of lesbian and gay studies.[61]

F. Health Care

1. Patients

As patients within the health-care system, lesbians and gay men are sometimes confronted with non-acceptance and negative attitudes and ideas. Health-care workers often look upon homosexuality as a psychiatric illness, despite the fact that in none of the European countries is homosexuality classified as an illness in the national registration.[62]

---

59   Section 28 of the Local Government Act 1988.
60   There are a growing number of organizations trying to change the situation. Some lesbian and gay organizations and educational institutions in e.g. Germany, the Netherlands and the United Kingdom, have developed special educational materials. Some lesbian and gay organizations offer special courses on homosexuality, where homosexuality is discussed with open lesbians and gay men. The EC Commission has given a grant to the Reading International Support Centre (in England) to produce an education pack under the title: *Human rights for all? A Global View of Lesbian and Gay Oppression and Liberation*, which appeared in 1992.
61   Universities in France, Germany, the Netherlands and the United Kingdom have set up or are creating lesbian and gay studies programmes. Under the EC ERASMUS programme, subsidies have been given for intensive summer courses in lesbian and gay studies with Belgian, Dutch, English, German and Italian Universities taking part.
62   See note 8 *supra*.

A minority of mental health-care workers try to convert homosexuals into heterosexuals. Such therapeutic treatments are usually unsuccessful and can cause major mental and physical problems for participants.[63] Although most therapists, however, do not try to 'cure', they are not always able to deal with homosexuality in a non-stigmatizing way, because of a lack of knowledge of lesbian and gay lifestyles and of specific psychological problems connected to the oppression faced by lesbians and gay men.[64]

Another problem is the non-acceptance of lesbian and gay relationships. Medical staff often refuse to inform same-sex partners or homosexual friends of a patient about his or her physical condition because they are not 'family'. Sometimes medical staff refuse visiting rights.

A third problem is the fear of AIDS. There are examples of refusal of treatment or of insurance to gay men as a perceived 'high risk group' for HIV infection. There are also examples of refusal of blood donations and examples of HIV tests being done without the patient's consent.[65]

In many countries lesbian and gay organizations are working on improving attitudes towards homosexuality within the health-care system by separate health-care programmes (counselling, AIDS self-help organizations, centres for sexually transmitted diseases, etc) for lesbians and gay men and by trying to influence health-care generally. Some of these organizations receive some state subsidies.

2. Workers

Negative attitudes towards homosexuality also influence the situation of lesbian and gay health-care workers. There are cases of discrimination in recruitment, bad treatment during work, health-care workers forced to keep quiet about their homosexuality, and dismissals. There have also been cases of patients objecting to being treated by lesbian and gay health-care workers. In some Member States lesbian and gay health care workers have created organizations to develop mutual support and to work towards changing the general attitude and behaviour towards homosexuality.

G. Housing and Recreation

In the areas of housing and recreation two mechanisms of social discrimination are prominent: one being the denial or refusal of access to goods and services, the other being anti-homosexual behaviour towards lesbian and gay users of housing and recreation services.

63   See Bayer, 1981.
64   See Schippers, 1989.
65   See Hendriks and Markestein, 1992, 197-203.

1. Housing

In the area of housing, there are two major problems. Firstly there is discrimination in access to housing and costs of housing. The second concerns hostility from neighbours once housing has been found.

Because many lesbians and gay men do not live in a traditional family structure, many of them fare badly in the housing market, depending on their social and financial situation and the place and country where they live. Especially in those areas where housing is scarce, landlords, real estate agents and other housing distributors often directly or indirectly advantage traditional families over others. Some housing authorities explicitly refuse to offer housing to lesbians and gay men.[66] In large urban environments anonymity may help to prevent such problems.

Attitudes of neighbours in a residential area can be a matter of concern. The non-acceptance of lesbians and gay men by some neighbours or sometimes the whole neighbourhood can cause several problems: lesbians and gay men are confronted with direct or indirect discrimination or even violent attacks by the neighbours.[67] These problems can be exacerbated by some housing-distributors, who tend to concentrate tenants fitting their traditional tenancy (married with children) into one area. Lesbian and gay men get housing in the so-called problem-areas, which, as examples have shown, can lead to extremely violent confrontations.

2. Recreation

Lesbians and gay men also face social discrimination in the area of recreation. Partly the same mechanisms that create discrimination at work or at home operate here.[68] What distinguishes recreation services from most other services is that the atmosphere created by the clients is part of the product. Recreational workers therefore selectively admit their clients. Homosexuals are often seen as a threat to the atmosphere.

66   In Germany the Green Party protested against the fact that public housing was in general only available for families and married couples. According to the Green Party, landlords from the private housing market make use of this situation to charge higher rents to lesbians and gay men (*Bundestag Drucksache* 11/1955, 7 March 1988, 4). Paragraph 6.2 of *Iceberg* 1991 also contains examples of housing discrimination from Belgium (*IGA-bulletin*, 1986, No. 2, 10) and the United Kingdom (Crane 1982, 140).
67   Dutch examples have been documented by CAdH.
68   See paragraphs 6.2 and 6.3 of *Iceberg* 1991 for examples of discrimination in sports centres, saunas, camping sites, hotels, restaurants, bars, etc.

H. Religion

Homosexuality has historically been condemned by most religious organizations. 'Sodomy', a word referring to several sinful non-procreational sexual acts including sexual acts between men, has been the subject of condemnation for centuries. People accused of sodomy were condemned or expelled from religious services and organizations. As explained in paragraph I.B.1 of this chapter, this condemnation still has strong effects on everyday discrimination within and outside the churches. However, now that the public attitude towards lesbians and gay men is changing, most religious organizations can no longer ignore the issue.[69] Lesbian and gay Christians have started to organize themselves. They are debating with various religious organizations. Although some smaller Christian organizations have responded very positively towards these efforts and are now changing their attitudes, most have kept their negative views. As a consequence of this development, we now see attitudes ranging from Christian churches that are supportive to lesbians and gay men (or that are even totally lesbian and gay), to very discriminatory denominations. The Roman Catholic hierarchy in particular remains very negative in its attitude towards homosexuality.[70]

Lesbians and gay men who seek recognition within the Christian churches are confronted with the following problems: lesbians and gay men are not accepted as or expelled as church members; priests refuse religious services to lesbians and gay men; homosexual clergy are not accepted or banned; church leaders display negative or hostile views on homosexuality.[71]

Unfortunately, little research is available on the current attitude within the Islamic, Hindu, Buddhist and Jewish communities in the EC. Although Islamic leaders often display very negative attitudes towards homosexuality, we do not know if this in practice also means that men and women are actually treated badly within the Islam communities in the EC.

---

69   Homosexuality has become a discussion issue in particular in some protestant churches in the Netherlands, Denmark, Germany and the United Kingdom.

70   See for example the Vatican document: *Some Considerations Concerning the Catholic Response to Legislative Proposals on the Non-discrimination of Homosexual Persons*, which was released on 25 June 1992 by the Office of the General Secretary of the Congregation for the Doctrine of the Faith (published in *L'Osservatore Romano*, 24 July 1992, and in the *National Catholic Reporter*, 31 July 1992).

71   Paragraphs 5.1., 5.2, 6.4, 8.1 and 10.2 of *Iceberg* 1991 contain several examples of discrimination by religious leaders, including the refusal to say a requiem mass for a murdered gay man (Italy, *De Gay Krant*, June 1986, 9), the refusal to let property to lesbian and gay organizations (France, *De Gay Krant*, May 1982; *Sek*, April 1982, 10), employment discrimination (Germany, *Leeuwarder Courant*, 7 December 1984; *Haagsche Courant*, 17 October 1989; France (*JCP*, 1991, 21724), and many verbal condemnations of homosexuality.

Most humanist organizations are more supportive of lesbians and gay men, and oppose anti-homosexual discrimination.

I. Association

Lesbian and gay men come together for a lot of reasons. They set up social, cultural and political organizations. They publish magazines. They organise parties, etc.

The diversity among lesbian and gay organizations is enormous. One can distinguish five major categories:
- campaigning organizations which aim to represent the interests of lesbians and gay men in society;
- organization which exist for a specific goal, such as publishing books, magazines or newspapers, organizing studies into homosexuality, counselling for lesbian and gay men, promotion of safe sex behaviour, lobbying;
- groups that organize specific categories of lesbian and/or gay men, such as groups for young people, for differently abled lesbians and gay men, for people from ethnic minorities, for lesbians and/or bisexual women only, for gay men who have AIDS or who are HIV-positive;
- lesbian and gay groups within larger organizations, such as political parties, trade unions, educational institutions, churches, the police, the armed forces;
- commercial enterprises, which aim at making profit by entertaining lesbians and/or gay men, such as bars, discos, hotels, bookshops, tour operators and travel agents, and businesses that serve as a forum for gay sexual pleasure (saunas etc).[72]

There are thousands of lesbian and/or gay (local, regional, national, international) organizations within the EC. In every Member State one or more lesbian and gay campaign is active. Almost all Member States have national lesbian and gay organizations.[73] These organizations may restrict themselves to simply creating a place for lesbians and gay men to socialize and be themselves, or they may extend to far-reaching political influence on society in general. Because of the invisibility of homosexuality, lesbian and gay organizations and meeting places are very important to isolated lesbians and gay men, providing both opportunities to meet others, and places where positive images of lesbian or gay lifestyles can be found.

In most Member States the importance of lesbian and gay organizations is recognized more and more; politicians and public authorities have recognized some organizations as representing the interests of lesbian and gay

---

72   This fifth category will not be discussed in the remainder of this paragraph.
73   Whether such national organizations are active in Portugal and Luxembourg, is unclear.

men. In Denmark and the Netherlands, national governments are developing their lesbian and gay policies in co-operation with these organizations; there and in Belgium some of these national organizations are subsidised on a regular basis. In these and in a few other countries several local and regional governments provide some support for lesbian and gay organizations. Recognition is also growing on an international level. In particular, the International Lesbian and Gay Association, active in all parts of the world, including the EC, has grown in influence, both amongst lesbians and gay men and with international institutions including the EC Commission, the European Parliament, the World Health Organization, Amnesty International, and the Department of Public Information of the United Nations.

Most lesbian and/or gay organizations have been and are confronted with negative attitudes and with actions motivated by anti-homosexual beliefs or feelings, for example:

- refusal of official recognition,
- refusal of funding or financial services,
- problems with renting or buying space to work in,
- violence against property (bombing, robbery, setting fire, anti-gay/-lesbian graffiti on their walls),
- violence against members by private persons, private organizations or by the police (raids),
- involuntarily closure.

There are examples of these types of problems from every member state.[74]

J. Information and Culture

Information is increasingly important in today's society. Information can be valuable and it can be dangerous. Information can be valuable in so far as it helps create a balanced idea about homosexuality and provides lesbians and gay men with positive images of lesbian and gay lifestyles. It is dangerous when it strengthens prejudices against homosexuality and legitimizes anti-homosexual discriminatory behaviour. This is still the situation in most Member States today. Analysis of media images of homosexuality has shown that it can contribute to a further stigmatization of homosexuality: homosexuality is most prominently presented in

[74] The London organization Pop Against Homophobia runs youth culture advertising campaigns worldwide. One of their aims is to introduce positive images of same-sex relationships into mainstream youth culture. The organization sells t-shirts, posters, badges, CDs, records etc. To go international the project needs financial facilities to accept international cheques and credit cards. In 1992 four banks refused to accept them after they had sent their catalogue. See paragraphs 8.1, 8.2 and 8.3 of *Iceberg* 1991 for many other examples of discrimination against lesbian and gay groups, bars, discos, etc.

combination with sensationalist news (perversion) and crime (blackmail, violence) or as a problem.[75] EC citizens who do not personally know lesbians and gay men, will tend to form an image of homosexuality based on these negative media images.

The situation varies from country to country. Research on the Dutch situation, for example, has shown that the general image in the press is positive, although many negative images persist.[76]

Information about homosexuality seems to be dominated by the fear of homosexuality – the irrational fear that positive or balanced information on homosexuality consciously or unconsciously persuades people to become homosexual.

Great cruelty has been perpetuated in the interest of the silencing of homosexuality. It took some twenty years for the German government to recognize that homosexuals were victims of the Nazi terror.[77] And only in the 1980s was the first commemoration plaque allowed for the homosexual victims of the concentration camps. In 1984, after countless refusals, the first plaque was placed in the former concentration camp of Mauthausen. The plaque in the shape of a pink triangle, the label the Nazis used for homosexuals, has the inscription: *Totgeschlagen, totgeschwiegen. Den homosexuellen Opfern des Nationalsozialismus.*[78]

Balanced information about homosexuality is not only important in making homosexuality visible and helping the general public to create their own image of homosexuality, but it also helps to inform lesbians and gay men about their situation and provides them with positive role models. Lesbian and gay media play an important role in this respect, but are frequently obstructed in their activities. Lesbian and gay newspapers, magazines, bookshops, and radio broadcasts have been confronted with censorship, seizures, etc. Censorship of homosexual publications, films and art is still an issue in several Member States. Thus, cultural expressions with a homosexual element and other means of positive information on homosexuality are still banned from everyday life in parts of the EC.[79]

75   Lautmann, 1977; Tielman, 1985.
76   Tielman, 1985 and Schedler *et al.*, 1989.
77   Only in 1987 did the German Parliament decide to make money available for *Wiedergutmachung* to be paid to 'forgotten' victims of the Nazi regime, including homosexuals (*De Gay Krant*, January 1988, 14).
78   'Beaten to death, silenced to death. To the homosexual victims of nazism.'
79   Chapter 9 of *Iceberg* 1991 includes several examples, including: the confiscation of foreign lesbian erotic videos in the United Kingdom (*Gay Times*, December 1990, 5); raids on lesbian and gay bookshops and seizure of some of their books and magazines in the United Kingdom (*Gay Times*, December 1984, 21, November 1990, 7; raid on a bookshop and seizure of almost the complete stock of gay books and magazines in Belgium (*Gai Pied Hebdo*, 1984, No. 146, 7, No. 147, 5); the confiscation of foreign gay magazines and books in Ireland (*Sek*, 1985/11, 7, 1986/8, 27); the ban in Ireland on the importing of a Danish book telling the story of a girl living with her father and his lover

Censorship reinforces the negative image of homosexuality as sick, despicable, dirty or sinful.

III. Conclusions

This chapter describes the social situation of lesbians and gay men and the attitude towards homosexuality within the Member States of the European Community, concentrating on social discrimination. After a description of the general causes, mechanisms and consequences of anti-gay and anti-lesbian discrimination, an overview is given of problems in ten major social areas. In this conclusion we will summarize our findings indicating some general trends, and conclude with some recommendations for policy and research.

A. Summary

The situation of the millions of EC citizens who are lesbian or gay is far from optimal. The lesbian and gay movement has been successful in combatting some discrimination, but anti-lesbian and anti-gay discrimination is still prominent in many areas. To varying degrees this discrimination is present in all Member States. Opinion polls from several countries, however, indicate slow shifts of public opinion towards acceptance of same-sex relationships, rejection of discrimination and tolerance of lesbian and gay lifestyles.

Social discrimination creates barriers to lesbians and gay men achieving social well-being and fully profiting from economic progress, and it limits their opportunities of participating in social life. Such discrimination finds its origin in a long history of condemnation of homosexuality – a history of negative views from religious, medical and legal sources. Many negative images of same-sex lifestyles persist in today's society, making homosexuality invisible, and stigmatizing and marginalizing lesbians and gay men.

(*Gay Times*, October 1990, 5); the threat of a prohibition on all publicity for a gay information magazine (*Gai Pied Hebdo*, 1987, No. 263, 6-18); the prosecution of the editors of a lesbian/gay magazine and of a lesbian/gay radio station, because of the content of personal adverts, in Belgium (*Gai Pied Hebdo*, 1989, No. 376, 2); the prosecution of the editors of gay magazines because of the content of these magazines in Greece (*IGA-bulletin*, 1984, No. 1, 3, 4 and 5); the cutting of kissing-scene from a gay radio-play in Germany (*De Gay Krant*, 25 February 1989, 17); the non-approval of gay films by board of censors in Italy (*Babilonia*, November 1983, 31) and in Greece (*Sek*, May 1980, 20); the scrapping of several gay and lesbian films from a film festival programme in Portugal (*Gai Pied Hebdo*, 1986, No. 249/250, 13; *De Gay Krant*, February 1987, 17).

Among the most visible results of these anti-gay and anti-lesbian sentiments are the denial and oppression of, and aggression against, expressions of same-sex love. Such expressions are effectively removed from everyday life by a process of denial or by active prosecution, and are silenced with anti-gay and anti-lesbian violence. Very many lesbians and gay men are, at least once in their lives confronted with anti-homosexual violence, ranging from verbal or physical abuse, blackmail, theft, robbery, battery, vandalizing, to murder.

Less visible, but equally powerful mechanisms of exclusion are denial, unequal opportunities and harassment in social areas such as education, health-care, housing, recreation and employment.

The employment situation for lesbians and gay men is bad, despite several anti-discriminatory measures. Lesbians and gay men face limitations in their access to employment, and once in work they may be confronted with the threat of non-promotion and dismissal, with being obliged to keep silent about their private life, with anti-gay and anti-lesbian sentiments and harassment in the workplace, and with discriminatory terms of employment. The seriousness of these problems differ from place to place and from sector to sector, but they do occur virtually everywhere.

Lesbian and gay couples often lack the social recognition that heterosexual couples take for granted. However the discussion on this form of discrimination has moved into the public domain, and one can see a slow shift towards acceptance. The same can be said for lesbian and gay parenthood. Many lesbian and gay parents, either living within a traditional marriage, or alone, or in a same-sex relationship, are beginning to demand their rights to have and bring up children. Resistance, based on irrational fears for the quality of the upbringing of children, limits the possibilities for homosexual parents.

The most urgent lesbian and gay problem throughout the EC is probably the situation of lesbian and gay youth. Lacking positive identification, facing rejection at home and at school, being vulnerable about their own feelings, their situation can be very insecure. The lack of balanced information on homosexuality and of positive images of lesbians and gay men (especially in the media and in educational materials), and in some countries the existence of laws which criminalize adolescent homosexuality, re-enforce anti-homosexual beliefs in society and thus may increase isolation of lesbian and gay youth.

Lesbian and gay organizations have been and will continue to be the best source of change towards improving the situation of lesbians and gay men in the EC. The efforts of these organizations have already improved the situation, but much remains to be done. On a European and international level, organizations of lesbians and gay men have come together in the International Lesbian and Gay Association.

In the EC as a whole, the major social problems for lesbians and gay men at this moment seem to be:
- a persistent lack of available, balanced and unbiased information on homosexuality and lesbian and gay lifestyles;
- the insecure situation of young lesbians and gays;
- the disadvantaged situation of lesbians and gay men in the workplace;
- a high level of anti-gay and anti-lesbian violence.

B. Recommendations

On the basis of this general overview of the social situation of lesbians and gay men within the Member States, the following recommendations for research, information and action seem appropriate.

Systematic and comparative research on the social situation of lesbians and gay men within the EC is a first step towards well-balanced anti-discriminatory policies. This calls for:
- a comparative study of the ideas about homosexuality that are held by the populations of the different regions of the EC, and of how these ideas do or do not form the basis of different forms of anti-homosexual discrimination;
- a study of how the well-being and productivity of lesbian and gay workers is affected by discriminatory attitudes and behaviour of their employers and their colleagues;
- a comparative study of the impact and effectiveness of programmes and strategies that have been applied to prevent anti-homosexual violence;
- a comparative study of the impact and effectiveness of different forms of lesbian and gay organizing on the social support for lesbians and gay men;
- a comparative study of the impact and effectiveness of programmes and strategies that have been applied to reduce the insecurity and isolation of young lesbians and gay men.

In the meantime the institutions and the Member States of the EC could take more direct measures to increase the visibility of homosexuality and to improve the social situation of lesbians and gay men. The national, regional and local governments and the various EC institutions could do this by:
- speaking out explicitly and publicly against the different forms of anti-homosexual discrimination;
- acting as a model employer, not only refraining from discriminating on the basis of sexual orientation (by recognizing, among other things, that

many of their employees have a partner of the same sex), but also taking positive steps to stop their employees from behaving in a discriminatory manner towards their lesbian and gay colleagues;

- supporting (financially and otherwise) the exchange of information on programmes and strategies that have been applied in different regions of the EC to prevent anti-homosexual violence, to reduce the insecurity and isolation of young lesbians and gays, or to counter other forms of homosexual discrimination.

Chapter Five
The Economic Situation in the Member States

by

RUSSELL CHILD*

*   Doctoral student, Management Centre, University of Bradford.

Table of Contents

I. The Economics of Homosexuality

A. Introduction

This chapter about the economic situation of lesbians and gay men in the EC is an exploration of what is different about homosexuals in an economic context. Such an approach to the situation of lesbians and gay men could be relevant to the EC, as it will provide a better understanding of the actual social position of lesbians and gay men in the Member States. It will also suggest steps the EC institutions could take to correct certain market distortions.

The economic situation of lesbians and gay men in the European Community is far from optimal and there are many possible ways in which the market could be distorted in an economic sense. These possible distortions form the basis of each section which follows.[1]

This chapter has been written by a gay man without a lesbian co-author and this inevitably has implications for the hypotheses that have been formulated. It is fair to assume that the position of lesbians will invariably be worse than that of gay men as lesbians are oppressed on the basis of their gender as well as their sexual orientation. Instead of prefacing each hypothesis with this statement the collective term of 'lesbians and gay men' has been used.

A word need also be said about the nature of what has been written. It will become increasingly apparent that it is discursive and questioning, rather than conclusive and answering, as I would obviously prefer. The main reason for this is the shortage of any previous research on this matter (which itself is a statement about the nature of economics as an academic discipline and about the status of lesbian and gay studies in the EC). In order therefore to write this chapter I have used data contained in the Iceberg-report,[2] some traditional economic theory, relevant statistics and literature and the expertise of others.

Compared to the previous two, this chapter will be even more exploratory, will contain less comparative material, and will focus not so much on examples of legal and social discrimination, but on the economic relevance of existing anti-homosexual discrimination and on the economic relevance of the lesbian and gay community.

---

1   The subjects to be dealt with (employment, income, migration, consumption, lesbian/gay businesses, lesbian/gay organizations, taxation, public expenditure) will, in some cases, follow the general lines of the previous two chapters, but certain issues are unique to the area of economics for reasons which will be explained in the relevant sections.

2   Waaldijk, draft-version 16 December 1991. References to this draft-report will be made via references to the previous two chapters.

B. The Nature of Economics

What follows is an attempt to assess what is different about homosexuals within an economic context and the effect of this upon the economy as a whole. Economic theory assumes that rational people make optimal decisions which lead to the highest possible welfare for society. In this context, optimal economic welfare could simply be defined as being the point where it would not be possible to produce more of at least one commodity without simultaneously producing less of another by merely re-allocating resources. This raises the question of whether or not the economy's resources are being fully utilised. If non-economic factors distort the decision-making process, then the welfare of society will be lower than it could or ought to be.

If distortion occurs then the performance of the market is said to be faulty. This does not mean that nothing good has happened, only that the best attainable outcome has not been achieved: welfare has not been maximised. In the case of 'the economics of homosexuality' the prime cause of such market failure is prejudice and discrimination. A possible role of the economist is to designate the costs and benefits of the distortions and of the corrective policies which are needed.

It could be argued that economics in the past has been 'blind' to gender, race and sexual orientation. Gradually feminists and anti-racists are forcing economics to take on the issues of gender and race.[3] Both have demonstrated convincingly that 'economics' (as a social process and as an academic analysis) can be used for those purposes outlined above with regard to the issue of sexual orientation.

C. Methodology

The methodological problems of data collection are horrendous if one wants to make quantitative statements about the economics of homosexuality. These problems relate to definition, identity/behaviour, sampling and the stigma on lesbian and gay research. They are not specific to *economic* research into homosexuality.

The main source of data is, of course, the lesbian and gay community itself, although this statement assumes that it is a homogenous unit which it quite plainly is not. Perhaps the first and most profound problem, in a methodological sense, is that of identity and definition.

To take just the 'gay community' as an identity: would this include the number of men who would define themselves as 'heterosexual' but have 'homosexual' experiences in public lavatories or gay saunas, for example, or would it only include those who lead wholly gay lifestyles in terms of

---

3   See, for example, Finer and Morgan, 1987, 376-392.

relationships, sexual experiences, political preferences and choice of friends? Homosexuality, then, as an identity appears to be a social construct which does not always correlate with the behaviour of individuals.

Assuming one solves this conflict between behaviour and identity in a way which is satisfactory, then there are a number of ways into the community for the collection of data – questionnaires, interviews, contacts with individuals, lesbian and gay organisations and magazines and through the 'snowball' sample thrown up by friendship groups. A further problem then arises of the sample. Can a hypothesis proven to be 'true' (or even 'false') in a study of a sample of lesbians and gay men then be said to be 'true' or 'false' for the lesbian and gay community as a whole? As most samples will invariably be self-selecting, then it most probably cannot.[4]

II. Five Fields of Economics

A. Employment and Income

1. The Economics of Employment

In dealing with these issues one is asking whether or not one is occupationally disadvantaged by being lesbian or gay. As a result of societal prejudice lesbians and gay men can experience anxiety, depression, worry and tension at work on account of their sexual orientation. In turn this can lead to lesbian and gay workers underperforming. Discrimination at work can be grouped into the following areas:
- recruitment, promotion and dismissal;
- terms of employment (pension schemes etc);
- social conditions at work (heterosexual harassment, anti-lesbian and anti-gay remarks, etc.).

All three categories of discrimination can result in a market distortion in so far as they may influence career choice, and someone who has their career-path blocked may end up less happy and therefore less productive than someone who continues to progress upwards in their chosen career. This could have a micro-economic impact in that lesbian and gay workers may

---

4   A purely random sample seems impossible: Could one choose 1000 names off an electoral register and send them a questionnaire designed to gain information about the economics of homosexuality? What if all 1,000 people claimed to be 'heterosexual'? What if there were lesbian and gay people in the 1,000 names but they were suspicious of a questionnaire which probed into a lifestyle which in some member states may be illegal? How do we know whether or not, quite simply, they will tell the truth? An alternative would be to distribute questionnaires among people in a lesbian/gay bar, or to use the 'snowball' method: starting perhaps with personal acquaintances and working outwards. Such sampling, though, would probably be self-selecting in terms of age, gender, class and region etc.

become less productive because they feel bad as a result of discrimination. Alternatively, the workforce may be less capable because good lesbian and gay candidates are excluded from it.

The type of discrimination in this context that can be most easily measured is *unequal pay*. Most pension schemes do not provide a pension for the surviving lesbian or gay partner of an employee, although the latter will have paid the same premiums. Together with the unavailability to the partners of lesbian and gay employees of other 'spousal benefits', this means that many homosexuals receive less pay than their heterosexual colleagues receive for the same work.

It would be useful to distinguish between economies in which virtually all employers discriminate to a similar degree and economies where only some employers discriminate significantly. The impact can be direct such as employers refusing to hire lesbian and gay workers, or indirect as potential employees avoid employment with employers who might discriminate. Such influences on career choice would have a negative impact on the quality of the workforce of the discriminating employers or sectors. It would thus also lead to an overall reduction of productivity.

In both type of economies, productivity will also be negatively influenced by other mechanisms than career-diversion:

- reduced well-being caused by discrimination, fear of discrimination or the threat of discrimination may lead to individual employees being less productive;
- exclusion from employment (non-hiring, non-promotion, dismissal, etc.) would lead to an under-representation of lesbian and gay workers.

Measuring the incidence of these types of behaviour in the economy as a whole could be problematic.

2. The Earnings Function

The traditional earnings function measures the productive capacity of a worker from formal schooling and training. It also includes additional factors to account for gender, experience, race and long-term illness.[5]

Empirical work could lead to an amended earnings function for lesbians and gay men with a lesbian/gay dummy which would be negatively impacted due to discrimination and positively due to a motivational factor.

---

5   The earnings function is an attempt to explain wage rates accounting for discrimination, stratification and imperfection in the labour market. It can be estimated as:
$$W = a + b\,EDC + c\,XP + d\,SQXP + e\,COL + f\,SIK + u$$
where W is the log hourly wage, a is a constant, EDC is schooling, XP is years of labour-market experience, SQXP is years of labour market experience squared, COL is a dummy for non-whites, SIK is a dummy for illness and u is a regression disturbance term. See Cameron, 1985, 36.

Classical theory assumes that the worker is paid according to the value of his or her marginal product which is the addition to the value of output brought about by that worker's employment. However, the presence of discrimination in the labour market in the form of refused employment or promotion or of dismissal from employment implies that the lesbian or gay worker is not working to her or his full potential and thus not receiving as high a wage as she or he might otherwise earn. Hence a distortion of the labour market which has a negative effect upon wage rates for lesbians and gay men.

Alternatively one could argue that because lesbians/gay men can hide their sexuality if they so desire then these points regarding discrimination become less relevant.[6] If this is the case then lesbian/gay workers are no worse off than their heterosexual counterparts and in the case of white gay men they may in fact be better off. A British survey found that the average white gay male was more likely to be in a professional job than his heterosexual counterpart.[7] This factor coupled with his lack of financial commitments in the form of a family would give the average white gay male considerable economic power. He would therefore have higher levels of personal disposable income available to him than his heterosexual counterpart and will have a higher propensity to consume.

So far, it is impossible to say whether the earnings function of white gay men is more positively or more negatively impacted. It is very unlikely that the earnings functions of lesbian women and of black gay men are more positively impacted. Whether certain categories of lesbians and gay men are over-represented among citizens living in poverty, is unknown.

3. Migration

Discrimination may cause people to emigrate to a more liberal region or jurisdiction. Many Irish gay men come to London and many English emigrate to Amsterdam. These people will take with them their economic power in terms of education, skills and experience. Of course, if the emigration is within the EC, then much of the loss is internalised and so, in aggregate terms, that overall cost is not so high but it leads to regions suffering extra brain-drain and to an irrational allocation of the EC workforce.

6   Although one could say that the very need to hide one's sexuality is in itself the result of discrimination and may lead to reduced well-being and productivity.
7   'The Homosexual Economy', in *The Economist*, 23 January 1982.

B. Consumption

1. Consumer Power

The use of the word 'power' in this context suggests that the lesbian/gay community is an economically active pressure group like trade unionists or French farmers. The lesbian/gay community can choose to operate in this way and occasionally tries to do so.[8]

The importance of lesbian and gay consumption is also illustrated by the emergence, in several member states, of a sizeable *pink economy* which continues to grow.[9] British research has suggested that white gay men are the single most affluent minority in the country.[10] This research found that the average white gay male earned more than his heterosexual counterpart and is more likely to be in professional employment. The gay man revealed in this survey therefore has considerable economic power. This affluence has a considerable allure for both gay owned and other businesses, the more so if it is the case that the typical white gay man has a stronger consumer interest in leisure and luxury facilities than his heterosexual counterpart.

The research also revealed that there was no comparable *pink economy* for lesbians, because most women do not have the spending power to generate and sustain one. Women generally earn less than men and also more often have responsibilities for children. Lesbians tend to have less economic power than heterosexual women since without dependence on men they do not benefit from male earning power. Unlike the specifically gay economy, the economic power of lesbians is found within the wider feminist economy. The feminist economy was found to have a different ethos to the pink economy with its motives being political rather than profit-making.

Even if some white gay men are indeed relatively wealthy (as was suggested by the research just mentioned), this does not necessarily mean that they are economically better off than their heterosexual counterparts, because some types of consumption are more expensive for consumers who are not part of a traditional heterosexual family unit. This is for example the case in sections of the housing market (see the following paragraph), and also in the market for pensions and other personal insurance cover, where most products are tailored towards the interests of traditional family units.[11] It should be noted that the same higher prices also apply for

8   For example the boycott of Marlboro cigarettes in the United States and several European countries by lesbians and gay men in protest at the activities of the US Senator Jesse Helms.
9   See paragraph II.C below.
10   See 'The Homosexual Economy', in *The Economist*, 23 January 1982 and 'Chasing the Pink Pound', in *The Guardian*, 14 May 1984.
11   See Chapter Three by Waaldijk and Chapter Four by Van der Veen & Dercksen for examples of marriage-related discrimination.

lesbians, for lesbian and gay adolescents, for black lesbians and gay men, and for people who for example have had their careers blocked after being open about their homosexuality.

2. Consumer Discrimination in Housing

The economics of housing includes the allocation of such facilities when in fact lesbians and gay men may be denied access to housing because of prejudice, fear of HIV-infection, etc. Where lesbian and gay couples are excluded by law or in practice from housing allocated by public authorities they will be driven into the private housing market. Where private landlords are aware of this they may put property rents up. This is, in itself, a distortion of the housing market.

Likewise the presence of lesbian or gay tenants can have a depressive effect on rents or house prices where their very presence is seen to be downvaluing adjacent accommodation. This is a further market distortion.

Each of these possibilities further diminishes the economic strength of lesbians and gay men in the housing market and may lead to higher rents being paid by lesbians and gay men.

3. Discrimination in Insurance

The insurance sector is traditionally quite conservative and likely to be more restrictive in the application of social attitudes then other sectors. This is particularly true in relation to the lesbian and gay communities. The perception of gay men in the context of HIV infection as a 'high risk' group has led to quite extensive discrimination in the provision of life insurance policies. Many who have ever tested for the presence of HIV antibodies may automatically be excluded from some life insurance policies. An assumption of a person's lifestyle (i.e. their perceived homosexuality) is used to discriminate economically against them. In many Member States life insurance policies may be required in order to be accepted for housing loans or mortgages. The discriminatory attitude affects the ability of homosexuals and gay men, in particular, from enjoying full economic freedom in the purchase of property.

C. Gay and Lesbian Businesses

If we assume that people derive utility from the proximity of other people of the same type then we can explain the desire for the collective consumption of lesbian or gay clubs, bars, restaurants etc. and also the importance of the provision of such services by lesbian or gay business.

Lesbian and gay business can be defined as businesses that cater for lesbians and/or gay men as consumers, and which are either owned by lesbians and/or gay men or which sell 'lesbian and/or gay products'. These businesses will have prime importance to local and national economies in terms of their likely success and their serving of the collective aspect of lesbian and gay consumption.[12]

Spatial issues are also of importance here. It is assumed that for lesbian and gay men it is often preferable to settle in large cities because anonymity permits lesbian and gay socialising more easily. As a result an urban lesbian and gay sub-culture has been shaped. For a sub-culture to thrive you need a certain number of people. There is a need to service this specific sub-culture in the form of clubs, bars, saunas, bookshops, cafes, etc. Hence the growth of large numbers of lesbian and gay businesses in key urban and holiday areas where this sub-culture will be especially large.[13] In these local economies it will be found that a large amount of money spent and goods and services provided (as a proportion of total expenditure and output) will come from the lesbian and gay community.[14]

Anti-homosexual legislation and acts of violence will have a negative impact on the success of these businesses. If this in practice means that a lesbian and gay club is liable to be raided by the police or a bookshop has literature seized by the authorities, then the utility derived from using these businesses will decline. So also will their profitability and their feasibility. Thus discrimination, also in the form of anti-lesbian and anti-gay violence (for example smashed windows, arson attacks on businesses), leads to distortion of the local economy as the businesses and the client base may decide to move somewhere else.

It would be less easy to conduct a police raid on a gay bookshop in San Francisco, because of the economic and political clout of the large gay community and gay business lobby in that city. Within the EC it may be possible for a lesbian and gay business lobby to become as economically significant. That could help the pink economy to co-exist with and enhance

---

12   See paragraph II.A.2 above. In Britain, the annual turnover of the lesbian and gay busi-
      ness community is estimated to be over £50 million [see *GLC handbook*, 1986]. It is
      estimated that of all 25,000 jobs in the Amsterdam tourist industry 3,000 are directly or
      indirectly resulting from gay/lesbian tourism (see the report *Album Amsterdam – Een kijk
      op je voorkeur in de stad van je voorkeur – Adviesnota voor de vestiging in Amsterdam
      van een internationaal expositie- en informatiecentrum,* presented to the City of Amster-
      dam in September 1992 by Stichting *Album Amsterdam,* 9.)
13   For instance in London, Manchester, Brighton, Paris, Berlin, Cologne, Gran Canaria,
      Ibiza, Barcelona, Antwerp, Amsterdam.
14   It is estimated that homosexual tourists account for at least 14% of all tourists visiting
      Amsterdam (see *Adviesnota Album Amsterdam supra* note 12).

mainstream enterprises and safeguard itself from attacks under obscenity legislation.[15]

D. Gay and Lesbian Organizations / Associations

Many lesbian and gay groups suffer intense funding problems and must raise funds from predominantly private sources. Public sector funding is minute in relation to public sector income from lesbians and gay men. One method used by groups to offset expenses is to apply for charitable status. In the UK, application for charitable status by lesbian and gay groups was generally refused until a test case by CHE (Campaign for Homosexual Equality) in 1984 was successful. This refusal to grant charitable status to UK groups certainly affected their ability to raise funds from corporate and charitable sources and thus effectively discriminated economically against the groups.

Additionally, many lesbian and gay groups find that suppliers (of services, such as legal or accounting or products, such as T-shirts or liquor) will refuse to advance credit facilities to them. Distrust of dealing with lesbians or gay men is frequently not overcome by that great social leveller – cash. A successful lesbian and gay organisation must have a much more solid credit record than the equivalent non-lesbian or non-gay organisation before being offered credit facilities such as overdrafts, credit card transactions or extended repayment terms.[16]

E. Public Finance

1. Taxation

If – by hiding their sexual orientation – lesbians and gay men take their 'normal' place in the economy, then there is nothing remarkable in their contribution to output, growth and tax revenues. However, if it is the case that the typical white gay male has a higher level of disposable income and higher levels of expenditure in the leisure and luxury areas of the economy than his heterosexual counterpart, then it is also the case that he will contribute more to tax revenues (like VAT). Likewise the burgeoning gay and lesbian business sector which services the needs of the lesbian and gay community has a significant and growing contribution to make to output, growth and tax revenues.

---

15 Organizations of gay (and lesbian) businesses exist in London (Gay Business Association), Paris (Syndicat National des Entrepreneurs Gai – SNEG) and Amsterdam (GALA – The Gay and Lesbian Association – Amsterdam).
16 Gay Business Association 1991/1992, London.

2. Expenditure on Discrimination and Anti-Discrimination

Gay men in some Member States are likely to find themselves prosecuted
for a wide range of offences that, in practice, have no heterosexual equivalent: such as cottaging and cruising, affection in public, and sex with
someone under the age limit for homosexual sex.

Gay men have been arrested as a result of the use of plain clothes *agents
provocateurs*, covert surveillance, spy-holes, mirrors, broom cupboards and
stake-outs lasting months. Not only does this represent an over-concentration of already scarce police resources on homosexual offences, but it is
also carried out along with court cases and imprisonment at considerable
public expense.[17]

Compared to that, the sums paid in subsidies to lesbian and gay organisations in some Member States are very small.[18]

III. Conclusions

A. Summary

Traditional *classical economic theory* has been blind to minorities such as
blacks, women, lesbians and gay men, assuming that the economic behaviour of these groups can be explained by existing theories. Only recently
have attempts been made to challenge this situation. Therefore any comments made in this chapter have been tentative and discursive rather than
assertive and conclusive.

---

17   Peter Tatchell has estimated the total cost of the prosecution of 3,900 men (and the im-
     prisonment of 200) for homosexual offences in England and Wales in 1989 at £13 mil-
     lion (see Tatchell, 1992, 88).
18   The national Danish organization for gays and lesbians, *LBL/F-48*, received 1.5 million
     Danish Crowns from the national government in 1988; each year they receive around
     80.000 Crowns from the national government for specific lesbian/gay purposes (plus
     around 7 million Crowns for their HIV and AIDS work), and some grants from local
     governments, for examples 200.000 Crowns from the city of Copenhagen in 1990 and
     1991 (data provided in a letter of 2 March 1992 from LBL/F-48 to Kees Waaldijk, Ice-
     berg-project).
     In subsidies to various Dutch lesbian and gay organizations the Dutch government has
     paid 2.5 million Guilders in 1989, 2.8 million in 1990, and 2.4 in 1991; the figure for
     1992 will be considerably less (data provided to parliament on 13 May 1992 by the co-
     ordinating minister for homosexual emancipation, in *Kamerstukken II*, 1991-92, 19504,
     No. 21, 12).
     However, in the UK the level of funding of lesbian and gay groups is minimal. No
     single group has received more than £10,000 since the GLC (Greater London Council)
     was abolished. Indeed Section 28 of the Local Government Bill makes it effectively
     illegal to fund lesbian and gay groups which may be seen to be 'promoting' lesbian and
     gay lifestyles. Since 1988 (when Section 28 became law) funding subsidies for lesbian
     and gay groups from public finance has been negligible.

Direct and indirect *employment* discrimination against lesbians and gay men occurs in all EC Member States with corresponding negative effects on incomes, economic power, productivity, etc., and resulting in market distortions such as career-diversion to other sectors and migration to other regions. It is possible that there are also some positive motivational factors.

Lesbian and gay *consumption* is of importance to the whole of the EC given the size of the 'pink economy' and the potential for a large impact on macro-economic factors, such as output, income and employment. There is some evidence that lesbians and gay men may have to pay higher prices for housing.

The lesbian/feminist as well as the gay *business sector* is already large in some Member States and has the potential to grow still further. It is currently hampered by legal oppression and illegal violence which deters many from entering it and encourages many to leave.

Lesbian and gay organiszations experience great difficulty in getting funding, charitable status and commercial credit.

The contribution to taxes from the lesbian and gay community in general, and from lesbian and gay businesses in particular, should not be underestimated. The use of *state resources* to police, prosecute and imprison members of the homosexual community represents an over-concentration of these financial and non-financial resources in this area of the law. Compared to this, all state subsidies designed to facilitate the emancipation of lesbians and gay men are minimal.

B. Recommendations

The first conclusion from this chapter could be that not only lesbians and gay men suffer the consequences of anti-homosexual discrimination, but that in an economic sense other sections of society (including the public purse) are also negatively affected by such discrimination. This could well be considered as an *extra* reason for both the Member States and the Institutions of the EC to combat the various forms of social and legal discrimination, and thus end the market distortions and irrational allocation of resources caused by it.

Due to the lack of previous research on the economics of homosexuality many of the hypotheses contained in this chapter could only be tentative, and certainly not quantified. The second conclusion of this chapter therefore is that further research and investigation is needed in areas such as the following:

- the inequality of pay resulting from the exclusion of same-sex partners and of other unmarried partners from many pension schemes and from other benefits for employees' partners;

- the extent of productivity losses caused by the fear or threat of discrimination against lesbian and gay workers;
- the extent of career-diversion due to anti-homosexual discrimination, and the productivity losses to those sectors from which lesbians and gay men are diverted;
- the extent of migration due to anti-homosexual discrimination, and the economic losses (in terms of skills, income, output, taxation, etc.) to those regions from where lesbians and gay men emigrate;
- the relative wealth or poverty of categories of lesbians and gay men (living alone or together with a partner) compared to their heterosexual counterparts;
- possible differences in the propensities to consume, invest and save between categories of lesbians and gay men and their heterosexual counterparts;
- price differences between goods and services (such as housing and insurance) for heterosexual couples (with or without children) and the same services for lesbian and gay couples (with or without children);
- the size of the lesbian and gay business sector and its contribution to output, income, growth and taxation in different regions of the EC;
- the impact of discriminatory violence, laws and practices on the feasibility and profitability of lesbian and gay businesses in different regions of the EC;
- the total cost to the Member States of the enforcement of anti-homosexual laws.

Chapter Six
The Treatment of Homosexuals under the European Convention on Human Rights

by

PIETER VAN DIJK *

*   Member of the Council of State of the Netherlands. Chairman of the Netherlands
Institute of Human Rights (SIM).

Table of Contents

I. Introduction

The right to self-determination of the individual is a basic human right. To quote from an opinion of Judge Martens, a member of the European Court of Human Rights:

> The principle which is basic in human rights and which underlies the various specific rights spelled out in the Convention [i.e. the European Convention on Human Rights] is respect for human dignity and human freedom. Human dignity and human freedom imply that a man should be free to shape himself and his fate in the way that he deems best fits his personality. [1]

The fact that this right to self-determination of the individual is not included in the human rights catalogues of the international and regional treaties dealing with human rights, does not mean that it is not internationally recognized. Like the right to self-determination of peoples, which is expressly mentioned in the two International Covenants on Human Rights of the United Nations,[2] the right to self-determination of the individual is a pre-condition for an effective and full enjoyment of other human rights, both civil and political, and economic, social and cultural rights.[3]

In this perspective it is significant that the right to self-determination of peoples is not listed among the human rights, but forms part of the introductory provisions concerning implementation and full realization of these rights. The right to self-determination of the individual might very well have also been mentioned in these introductory provisions. Anyhow, it is reasonable to assert that this right was assumed to exist by the drafters of the relevant treaties. Indeed, when discussing the inclusion of the right to self-determination of peoples, the Brazilian delegation argued that an express mention was not necessary since an implied recognition of that right could be assumed.[4] For political reasons it was nevertheless included and even given the utmost emphasis by making it the first provision of both Covenants.

The human-rights aspect of homosexuality in reality comes down to the issue of the recognition of the right to self-determination of homosexuals: the right to express and practice their sexual orientation and have homosexuality legally and socially recognized as a way of life of equal legitimacy and value as heterosexuality. A homosexual, too, has 'the right to establish and to develop relationships with other human beings, especially in the

---

1   Dissenting opinion in the *Cossey* case, Series A, No. 184, 24-25.
2   Article 1 of both the International Covenant on Civil and Political Rights and the International Covenant on Economic, Social and Cultural Rights.
3   See Cassese, 1981, 92-113 at 101-102.
4   Ibid. at 93.

emotional field, for the development and fulfillment of one's own personality.'[5]

Although, as said above, the pre-condition for the recognition of self-determination applies to all human rights, both civil and political, and economic, social and cultural rights, there are certain human rights and fundamental freedoms which have a specially strong link with the right to individual self-determination of homosexuals: the right to respect for one's private and family life, the prohibition of degrading treatment and the prohibition of discrimination as a separate right and in combination with other rights like the right to marry, freedom of expression and freedom of association. These rights and freedoms, therefore, also have a special relevance for the theme of this chapter. They have found recognition in the European Convention for the Protection of Human Rights and Fundamental Freedoms (ECHR) of the Council of Europe, *viz.* in Articles 8, 3 and 14 (in conjunction with Articles 10, 11 and 12) respectively.

Before these provisions of ECHR and their interpretation and application in relation to homosexuals in the case-law of the European Commission of Human Rights (the Commission) and the European Court of Human Rights (the Court) are discussed, some basic information about the ECHR will first be given here.

II. The European Convention on Human Rights

Individuals who are, or were at the decisive moment, under the jurisdiction of any of the States Parties to ECHR, have the right to file complaints against these States with the Commission in Strasbourg if they are of the opinion that any of their rights under ECHR has been violated by that particular State through its legislation, its administration or a decision of one of its courts. There are two main pre-conditions:

(1) the State against which the complaint (the official term used in the ECHR is petition) has been lodged, has declared that it recognizes the competence of the Commission to receive such complaints (Article 25); a condition which now has been fulfilled by all the 26 Contracting Parties;[6]

(2) before an individual complaint can be lodged, first any remedies which the legal system of the State concerned provides must have been

---

5   Quotation from a decision of the European Commission on Human Rights concerning heterosexuals, *Application 6959/75, Brüggeman and Scheuten v. Federal Republic of Germany*, Yearbook XIX (1976) 382 at 414.

6   See Van Dijk & Van Hoof, 1990, 37. For the other complaint procedure, that of inter-State complaints, see ibid., 33-36. Poland has indicated it will also grant recognition when they ratify the Convention.

exhausted in vain, unless the available remedy would cause an undue delay or would clearly not be effective.[7]

The right of complaint is open to any alleged victim of a violation of a Convention provision, irrespective of his or her nationality, provided that he or she was under the jurisdiction of that particular State at the relevant moment.

This procedure opens the possibility for those homosexuals, irrespective of their nationality and country of residence, who consider that they have been treated by the authorities[8] of any of the States Parties to ECHR – or feel threatened by the mere existence of its law and regulations[9] – in a way which violates one or more of the rights which they, as homosexuals, claim under the ECHR, to take their case to Strasbourg if they are of the opinion that the national courts have not given them full satisfaction. What does this mean in practice? Is it mainly a waste of energy, time and money – apart from an interesting experience and possibly a visit to the pleasant city of Strasbourg – or are there real prospects for an effective remedy under the ECHR? To answer this question, a survey of the most relevant Strasbourg case-law is given here.

III. The Right to Respect for Private and Family Life

Article 8 of ECHR lists under what may be called the right of privacy the right to respect for private life, family life, home and correspondence. The distinction between private life and family life appears to be of special significance for our subject.

A. Private Life

It is established case-law of both the Commission and the Court that the prohibition by law of homosexual acts in private between consenting individuals constitutes an interference with the exercise of the right to respect for private life as guaranteed in Article 8, paragraph 1 ECHR.[10] Although an interference can only be said to exist if there is a real risk of the legislation being applied, the mere fact that the implementation has not led to criminal convictions for a long time, does not of itself negate the possibility that it

---

7   Ibid., 81-98. For the other conditions of recevability of individual complainst, see ibid., 67-81 and 98-107.
8   Complaints can only be directed against States. Consequently, these complaints must relate to acts for which the State can be held responsible. See ibid., 76-78.
9   That this status of 'potential victim' is sufficient for admissibility of the application was recognized, *inter alia*, in the *Dudgeon* case, to be discussed later.
10   See, e.g., the judgment of the Court of 22 October 1981, *Dudgeon*, Series A, No. 45, 18.

has effects amounting to interference with private life, since a primary purpose of any such legislation is to prevent the conduct it proscribes, by persuasion or deterrence, while it also stigmatises the conduct as unlawful and undesirable.[11]

However, the second paragraph of Article 8 allows for such interferences by public authorities with the exercise of the right guaranteed in the first paragraph as are in accordance with the law and are necessary in a democratic society in the interests of national security, public safety or the economic well-being of the country, for the prevention of disorder or crime, for the protection of health or morals, or for the protection of the rights and freedoms of others.

In its *Dudgeon* judgment, which concerned the legislation forbidding sexual conduct between male homosexuals, the Court stated as follows with respect to these interferences:

> There can be no denial that some degree of regulation of homosexual conduct, as indeed of other forms of sexual conduct, by means of the criminal law can be justified as 'necessary in a democratic society'.[12]

This necessity of some degree of control, according to the Court, may even extend to consensual acts committed in private, notably – and there the Court quoted from a report referred to by the British Government, the 'Wolfenden Committee Report' –

> to provide sufficient safeguards against exploitation and corruption of others, particularly those who are especially vulnerable because they are young, weak in body or mind, inexperienced, or in a state of special physical, official or economic dependence.[13]

Furthermore, the Court referred to its statement in the *Handyside* judgment that

> by reason of their direct and continuous contact with the vital forces in their countries, State authorities are in principle in a better position than the international judge to give an opinion on the exact content of (the requirements of morals).[14]

---

11 Report of the Commission of 3 December 1991, *Modinos*, not yet published, para. 36.
12 Ibid., 20.
13 Ibid..
14 Judgment of 7 December 1976, *Handyside*, Series A, No. 24, 22.

However, the Court added here the very important observation that:

> not only the nature of the aim of the restriction but also the nature of the activities involved will affect the scope of the margin of appreciation. The present case concerns a most intimate aspect of private life.[15]

And another important observation made by the Court was the following one:

> As compared with the era when that legislation was enacted, there is now a better understanding, and in consequence an increased tolerance, of homosexual behaviour to the extent that in the great majority of the member States of the Council of Europe it is no longer considered to be necessary or appropriate to treat homosexual practices of the kind now in question as in themselves a matter to which the sanctions of the criminal law should be applied; the Court cannot overlook the marked changes which have occured in this regard in the domestic law of the member States.[16]

In its final conclusion the Court held only with respect to the penalisation of homosexual conduct between consenting male persons *over 21 years of age*, that this part of the law could not be deemed necessary in a democratic society for the protection of morals. Although the Court re-stated its view that it is for national authorities, in the first instance, to fix the age under which young people should be protected by criminal law, it considered that this issue did not arise here and therefore refused to comment on whether a prohibition on homosexual conduct *under the age* of 21 was justifiable.[17] The Court reaffirmed this position seven years later in the *Norris* case, which concerned Irish legislation penalising homosexual acts in private between consenting males. Here again the Court held that, also as regards Ireland, it could not be maintained that there was a pressing social need to make homosexual acts between consenting adults criminal offences, and that such justifications as there were for retaining the law in force unamended were outweighed by the detrimental effects which the very existence of the legislative provisions in question could have on the life of a person of homosexual orientation like the applicant.[18] The *Modinos* case, which concerns comparable legislation in Cyprus, has not yet been decided by the Court; the Commission, in its report, follows the judgments in the *Dudgeon* case and the *Norris* case.[19]

Although not everybody will be satisfied with the present case-law, in so far as the Court and the Commission restrict their condemnation to the penalisation of homosexual acts between persons of 21 years and older, it

15   *Supra* note 10, 21.
16   Ibid., 23-24.
17   Ibid., 24-25.
18   Judgment of 26 October 1988, *Norris*, Series A, No. 142, 21.
19   Report of 3 December 1991, not yet published.

is submitted that much has been gained. The Strasbourg organs have set clear limitations to the margin of appreciation to be left to the national legislature and other national authorities in interfering with the private sexual life of individuals, heterosexuals as well as homosexuals. Moreover, they have clearly indicated that the necessity of interferences in a democratic society has to be judged in the light of changed views and attitudes, in which respect the views and attitudes in the country concerned are not necessarily of decisive importance. By contrast with the decision in the *Handyside* case,[20] the protection of morals has been recognized as an autonomous concept to a certain extent.

This case-law is, however, only a first step in the direction of protecting homosexuals against discriminatory legislation and/or administrative practices. Further steps are required. In particular, the Strasbourg organs should scrutinize the legislation and practice of national authorities more thoroughly and not accept the justifications and aims advanced by them uncritically. This kind of a critical approach was, in my opinion, lacking on the part of the Commission in an unpublished decision on *Application 10389/83.*

The complaint concerned Section 1 of the Sexual Offences Act, as amended in 1967, prohibiting homosexual acts in private between consenting males of 21 years and older in England and Wales, when more than two persons take part or are present. The applicant had been arrested when organizing a gay party in his flat. His complaint about the arrest was not accepted by the Commission as the six months time-limit on bringing a complaint provided by Article 26 of ECHR had lapsed. He also complained, however, that the mere existence of the challenged legislation continuously and directly affected his private life. Although the United Kingdom government had stated before the Commission that the police had arrested the applicant because they reasonably suspected him of procuring homosexual acts, the Commission did not consider this kind of police action to be an interference with the applicant's private life. Its reasoning was the following:

> It is not [...] contended before the Commission that the applicant has, has had or wished to have homosexual relations with a male under 21 and that being so the legislation does not continuously and directly affect his private life. [...]
>
> The Commission recalls that the applicant has not alleged that he is disposed to the commission of homosexual acts when more than two persons take part or are present. Nor is there evidence that such acts took place in the applicant's home on 3 October 1982.
>
> The Commission therefore concludes that there is no indication that in the personal circumstances of the applicant the existence of the legislative provision making it an offence to commit a homosexual act when more than two persons

20   Judgment of 7 December 1976, *Handyside*, Series A, No. 24, 22.

take part or are present continuously and directly affects his private life and his home. Accordingly, the existence of this legislation does not constitute an interference with his right to respect for his private life or his home.[21]

What other indication of an interference in the applicant's private life and home than the police raid and the arrest on suspicion of having violated the provision concerned does the Commission need? It was precisely the actual practice – a practice which could lead to police action on the basis of an anonymous telephone caller and could result in arrest on the mere fact that the persons gathered together appeared to be gay – that should have led the Commission to the conclusion that the legislation concerned constituted a continuous threat of interference for any homosexual. The actual activities or inclinations of the person concerned seem totally irrelevant for the existence of an interference or threat of interference.

One cannot but conclude that the Commission evaded the real issues at stake and upheld legislation which amounted to a clear interference with any homosexual's private life without even examining the justification of this interference under the second paragraph of Article 8.

B. Private and Family Life; Non-Admission and Expulsion of Aliens

The ECHR does not contain a general right of admission into and residence in a contracting State for aliens,[22] nor does it contain a prohibition of expulsion of non-nationals except in the case of collective expulsion.[23] However, there are certain provisions in the ECHR which, on their own or in conjunction with one of the other provisions, imply elements which may be directly related to such a right. One of these provisions is Article 8, since it has been recognized in the Strasbourg case-law that non-admission or expulsion may constitute an interference with the exercise of the right to respect of family life of the person concerned.[24]

According to the Commission, however, a relationship between homosexuals does not qualify as family life in the sense of Article 8, paragraph 1. In a decision of 3 May 1983 the Commission stated:

Despite the modern evolution of attitudes towards homosexuality, the Commission finds that the applicants' relationship does not fall within the scope of the right to respect for family life ensured by Article 8.[25]

---

21   Application 10389/83, *X v. United Kingdom*, unpublished.
22   For nationals, Article 3, paragraph 2 of the Fourth Protocol provides that 'No one shall be deprived of the right to enter the territory of the State of which he is a national'.
23   Article 4 of the Fourth Protocol.
24   Judgment of 21 June 1988, *Berrehab*, Series A, No. 138, 14.
25   Application 9369/81, *X and Y v. United Kingdom*, (1983), DR 32, 220, at 221.

And even in a case where a lesbian couple had a baby, conceived through artificial insemination, the Commission denied the existence of a 'family' and thereby the protection of the immigration law concerned.[26]

This restrictive attitude towards the concept of 'family life' is difficult to understand in the light of the otherwise very extensive, autonomous interpretation of that concept in the Strasbourg case-law.[27] 'Family life' is not restricted to relationships between married couples and the children born out of a marriage, but is held also to cover relations between couples who are not married but have a common household,[28] between brothers and sisters and other relatives,[29] and between parents and their children born outside of marriage or after divorce.[30] Therefore, the argument that Article 8 aims at protecting the family in its traditional form – whatever that is – has no sound foundation in the case-law, and a homosexual relationship between two persons who actually live together would seem to fit very well into the broad, autonomous concept developed by Commission and Court. Even less convincing and satisfactory, in a decision of several years later, the Commission confined itself to repeating the above-quoted phrase without showing that it had investigated if and to what extent the 'modern evaluation of attitudes towards homosexuality' had in the meantime reached a point where it should take a different stand.[31] The approach by the Commission was the more disappointing as the Commission indicated that it did take into account the modern evaluation of attitudes towards heterosexuality by expressly stating that 'the relationship of heterosexual unmarried couples living together as husband and wife' could be assimilated to 'family'.[32] It is worth mentioning at this point that the Dutch Supreme Court, in a judgment of 19 October 1990, expressly rejected this narrow interpretation by the Commission of 'family life' in relation to homosexuals.[33]

Be this as it may, when a homosexual relationship is relied upon for requesting a residence permit, the private life of the persons concerned is at stake as was recognized by the Commission in the same decision on

---

26   Application 14753/89, *X and Y v. United Kingdom*, unpublished. For the same reason the Commission declared inadmissible the application by a lesbian couple and the son of one of them, who complained that their right to respect for their family life had been interfered with in that the first applicant could not be vested with the parental authority over the third applicant (the second applicant's son); *Application 15666/89, Kerkhoven, A.M. Hinke and S. Hinke v. the Netherlands,* not yet published.
27   See Van Dijk & Van Hoof, *supra* note 6, 378-386.
28   See, e.g., Applications 7289/75 and 7349/76, *X and Y v. Switzerland,* Yearbook XX (1977) 168 at 172.
29   Judgment of 13 June 1979, *Marckx*, Series A, No. 31, 21.
30   Ibid., 14.
31   Application 11716/85, *S v. United Kingdom*, (1986), DR 47, 274, at 277-278.
32   Ibid., 279.
33   NJ 1992 No. 129.

Application 9369/81,[34] and there is no reason why the private life of the two partners concerned would be entitled to less protection against interferences than a 'family life' relation. In fact the Commission indicated that it adopted 'the same factual approach'. This led the Commission nevertheless to the following astonishing observation:

> the applicants are professionally mobile: the first applicant did not hesitate in joining the second applicant in the United Kingdom although he had employment in his native country. The second applicant has travelled and worked in other parts of the world. The Commission finds that it has not been shown that the applicants could not live together elsewhere than the United Kingdom, or that the link with the United Kingdom is an essential element of the relationship.[35]

At first sight this reasoning seems to be in conformity with the traditional case-law concerning respect for family life under Article 8: non-admission or expulsion does not interfere with the right of respect for family life if the persons concerned may reasonably be expected to continue their relationship in the country of origin of the alien.[36] However, the Commission's decision does not contain any indication that it took into consideration the applicants' claim that they could not live in Malaysia because (1) the second applicant would not be given indefinite leave to remain there and would not find employment – as had become evident during an earlier stay there – and (2) they would be in constant fear of harassment and prosecution if it became known that they had a homosexual relationship, since even among consenting adults this constituted a criminal offence under Islamic-orientated Malaysian law.[37] It was precisely the homosexual factor that made the case a special one and this factor was neglected by the Commission. After all, the argument that the applicants could live together elsewhere could only reasonably refer to Malaysia since there was no reason why any other country would be any more appropriate as a country of residence than the United Kingdom, the national State of one of them.

The decision was repeated in a more recent case, where the country of origin of one of the applicants was not Malaysia but New Zealand. The request for indefinite leave to remain in the United Kingdom was based on the ground that the first applicant had been living there with the second applicant in a stable homosexual relationship. It was decided by the Home Secretary that the Immigration Rules made no provision for a person to remain in the United Kingdom on that basis. The second applicant stated that he would not be admitted to New Zealand to work, since enquiries had revealed that he would not be considered eligible for the 'occupational

---

34   *Supra* note 25.
35   Ibid..
36   See Van Dijk & Van Hoof, *supra* note 6, 386-389.
37   *Supra* note 25.

priority list'. The applicants claimed an unjustified interference with their private lives in requiring the first applicant to leave the country, since the law in the United Kingdom permitted homosexual acts in private between consenting adults and consequently no issue of public policy or morality arose justifying the interference.

The Commission's way of reasoning was quite simple:

(1) homosexual relationships do not fall within the ambit of family life but rather within the notion of private life;
(2) the inevitable disruption of a person's private life by refusing to allow him to remain in the country cannot, in principle, be regarded as an interference with the right to respect for private life, unless the person concerned can demonstrate that there are exceptional circumstances in his case justifying a departure from that principle;
(3) the absence in the law of the United Kingdom of settlement rights for non-nationals in respect of their stable, private relationships, other than family relationships, does not, of itself, disclose any appearance of a violation of Article 8; the applicants have not provided any substantiation of their claim that it would be impossible to live together in New Zealand or elsewhere.[38]

This reasoning raises the following questions:

(1) Why does a 'disruption' of private life constitute an 'interference' with respect for private life in 'exceptional circumstances' only?
(2) Why is the stable homosexual relationship that will be disrupted by the decision challenged not considered an 'exceptional circumstance'?
(3) What substantiation of their claim that they could not live together in New Zealand, other than the enquiries made should have been provided by the applicants? Why should New Zealand immigration law be any more flexible than the law in the United Kingdom with respect to homosexual relationships?
(4) How can the applicants provide any information about possibilities for them to live in any other country than New Zealand and the UK, the only two countries with which they have some special connection; and why should they?

All in all, the reasoning followed by the Commission seems not very convincing and gives the impression that, here too, the element of the homosexual relationship and the issue of the protection it deserves was in fact ignored.

---

38   Decision of 13 July 1987 on Application 12513/86, *X and Y v. United Kingdom*, unpublished.

IV. Prohibition of Discrimination

As is well known Article 14 does not contain an autonomous provision prohibiting discrimination. It only prohibits discrimination in relation to the enjoyment of the rights and freedoms set forth in the ECHR.[39] Although, at first sight, this would seem to have rather serious implications, that is not the case. First of all, Article 14 has been significantly 'emancipated' in the Strasbourg case-law in this respect. And secondly, in cases of discrimination against homosexuals it will almost always be possible to make a connection with any of the rights or freedoms laid down in ECHR, in particular the rights to respect for one's private life under Article 8. Moreover, for most Contracting Parties Article 26 of the International Covenant on Civil and Political Rights, which does contain a general prohibiton of unequal treatment, will serve as a supplementary rule as provided for in Article 60 of ECHR.

A. The 'Emancipation' of Article 14

Although Article 14 is not of an 'autonomous' but of an 'accessory' character, since it can be invoked only in connection with any of the rights or freedoms laid down in ECHR, the view has been developed in the Strasbourg case-law that for Article 14 to be applicable it is not necessary that one of these rights and freedoms has been violated on its own. It may be that

> a measure which in itself is in conformity with the requirements of the Article enshrining the right or freedom in question may however infringe this Article when read in conjunction with Article 14 for the reason that it is of a discriminatory nature.[40]

This development in the case-law makes Article 14 of special importance for our subject. Even if interferences by public authorities in the private sexual life of individuals could find their justification in any of the grounds listed in Article 8, paragraph 2, or for that matter in Article 9, paragraph 2 (freedom of thought), Article 10, paragraph 2 (freedom of expression), or Article 11, paragraph 2 (freedom of assembly and association), these Articles 8 to 11 may nevertheless be violated when read in conjunction with Article 14, should the interferences occur in a discriminatory way.

---

39   See Van Dijk & Van Hoof, *supra* note 6, 532-533.
40   Judgment of 23 July 1968, *Belgian Linguistic Cases*, Series A, No. 6, 33.

B. Equal Treatment of Homosexual Relationships in General; the 'Objective and Reasonable Justification' Test

The Court avoided pronouncing upon the issue of equal treatment of homosexual relationships under Article 14 in the *Dudgeon* case by holding that this aspect of the case amounted in effect to the complaint which the Court had already considered in relation to Article 8.[41] This approach, although understandable, is to be regretted in view of the importance of the issue involved. Moreover, the Commission, in its report in the same case, *had* pronounced itself on the issue and had done so in a way which, in my opinion, required modification by the Court.[42]

The Commission had referred to its established case-law that the criterion of social protection provided objective and reasonable justification for the restriction on male homosexual conduct, in so far as it related to acts involving persons under twenty-one years of age, and so to that extent the difference of treatment between male homosexuals and female homosexuals, and between homosexuals and heterosexuals was not discriminatory.[43] As to this criterion of social protection, in an earlier decision the Commission had referred to

> Studies [...] made on several occasions in the Federal Republic of Germany both on adult homosexual behaviour and on the effects on the personality of adolescents of homosexual relationships with adults. They have led to convincing conclusions as to the existence of a special social danger in the case of masculine homosexuality. This danger results from the fact that masculine homosexuals often constitute a distinct socio-cultural group with a clear tendency to proselytise adolescents and that the social isolation in which it involves the latter is particularly marked. The Commission therefore considers that the criterion of the need for social protection is, in the field in question, an objective criterion.[44]

Quod erat demonstrandum! Who is convinced? In my opinion, the reasoning indicates that the majority of the Commission could not sufficiently dissociate themselves from certain prejudices on the matter in society, which constitutes a weak foundation indeed for an objective and reasonable justification.

In a decision of almost two years later the Commission showed some recognition of the fact that opinions about the character and effects of homosexual acts may develop. With respect to the justification advanced by the government of the United Kingdom, which was based on opinions expressed in the above-mentioned 'Wolfenden Committee Report' of twenty

41   *Supra* note 10, 26.
42   Ibid., 26.
43   Report of 13 March 1980, *Dudgeon*, Series B, No. 40, 42.
44   Application 5935/72, *X v. Federal Republic of Germany*, Yearbook XIX (1976) 276 at 286-288.

years before, the Commission pointed out, as the central issue, whether these opinions remained valid 'for a moral and cultural climate which has evolved significantly since then'.[45] However, in its report in that same case, the Commission nevertheless relied to a large extent on the Wolfenden Committee Report. It added as its own view:

> that there is a realistic basis for the respondent Government's opinion that, given the controversial and sensitive nature of the question involved, young men in the eighteen to twenty-one age bracket who are involved in homosexual relationships would be subject to substantial social pressures which could be harmful to their psychological development.[46]

This led the Commission again to the conclusion that an objective and reasonable justification existed in the criterion of social protection for the unequal treatment of male homosexuals as compared to female homosexuals and to heterosexuals.[47] The Commission did not discuss at all the, in my opinion highly relevant, question whether social pressure was caused by the homosexual relationships themselves or by the biased attitude of society towards homosexuality.[48]

The same criticism applies in my opinion to the holding by the Commission in a 1983 decision that

> homosexual conduct by members of the armed forces may pose a particular risk to order within the forces which would not arise in civilian life

and that, therefore, it might

> properly be considered necessary in a democratic society 'for the prevention of disorder' to maintain stricter rules over homosexual conduct in the military sphere than would be justifiable in the civilian sphere.[49]

The Commission only referred to a statement by the Ministry of Defence but did not investigate itself, what exactly would cause this particular risk to order and why comparable risks would not be caused by heterosexual relationships within the forces or during military service. Since masculinity

---

45   Application 7215/75, *X v. United Kingdom*, (1978), DR 11, 36, at 44.
46   Report of 12 October 1978, (1980), DR 19, 66, at 78.
47   Ibid., 79. That position was reaffirmed several times: *Application 9721/82, Desmond v. United Kingdom*, unpublished; Application 17279/90, *Zukrigh v. Austria*, not yet published. In no decision was there any reference to the recommendation of the experts at the Council of Europe's Fifteenth Criminological Research Conference on 'Sexual Behaviour and Attitudes and their Implications for Criminal Law' (November 1982) that there was no scientific justification for difference in the age of consent.
48   The Commission upheld its opinion in a decision of 1 March 1982 on Application 9484/81, *X v. Belgium*, unpublished.
49   Application 9237/81, *B v. United Kingdom*, (1983), DR 34, 68, at 72.

prejudices still prevail in army circles the Commission should have found reasons for critically evaluating any views from those circles.

In a 1986 decision the Commission further specified its justification of differential treatment between on the one hand heterosexuals and female homosexuals and on the other hand male homosexuals. To that end, it quoted from a report of the British Criminal Law Revision Committee which stated that:

> homosexual relationships tended to arise later in life among women than among men; [...] there was no comparable group of 16 to 18 year old girls whose sexual orientation had not yet become fixed and who were consequently in need of protection by the criminal law; and [...] adolescent girls did not seem especially attractive to older women in search of a partner of the same sex, there being greater emphasis in male homosexual culture on this age group.[50]

On the basis of this report the Commission, 'while recognising the changing and developing views on the issue of the age of consent for male homosexuals', was of the opinion that the difference in treatment satisfied the test of proportionality.[51] The question whether the differential treatment between heterosexuals and homosexuals could be justified by the – most unlikely – fact that adolescent girls are also not especially attractive to older men, was not answered by the Commission. In my opinion, the kind of reasoning followed by the Commission is not very satisfactory, to say the least; it leaves the impression that the conclusion reached determines the arguments used, rather than the other way around. National reports drafted in the country against which the complaint has been lodged, would seem to be not the most convincing basis for an international assessment. In this context it is quite remarkable and would seem to be relevant for the Strasbourg organs that both the Parliamentary Assembly of the Council of Europe and the European Parliament have urged the Member States to apply to homosexuals the same age of consent as for heterosexual acts.[52] This appeal 'has not fallen on deaf ears', as Laurence Helfer puts it in a comprehensive study on the homosexual age of consent issue, in which he indicates that recent modifications in the relevant laws of most Member States of the Council of Europe have led to a result in relation to which the Strasbourg case-law lags behind.[53]

---

50   Application 10389/83, *X v. United Kingdom*, unpublished.
51   Ibid.
52   Parliamentary Assembly, Thirty-third Ordinary Session, Recommendation 924 (1981) of 1 October 1981 and Resolution 756 (1981) of 1 October 1981; European Parliament, 1984-85 Debates (Doc. Nos. 1-311, 12), Resolution of 13 March 1984. OJ 1984 C 104/46-48.
53   Helfer, 1990, 1044-1100, especially 1086-1092.

C. Equal Treatment of Homosexuals under Immigration Regulations

In a number of immigration cases the issue of discrimination also arose, since in most immigration regulations there are special provisions for 'family reunification' that are not applied to homosexual relations. In the case of *X and Y v. United Kingdom*,[54] referred-to above, the Commission rejected the allegation of discrimination in violation of Article 14 in the following words:

> even if the separation of the applicants, as a possible consequence of the deportation proceedings, is alleged to be discriminatory, the question arises: compared with whom have the applicants suffered discrimination?
> (...) it is necessary to compare like with like. The Commission has above rejected the contention that the applicants' relationship constitutes family life within the meaning of Article 8, thus no comparison can be made with the differential treatment afforded to relationships classed as family life by United Kingdom immigration legislation and practice. In the realm of private life, the applicants have not submitted any evidence of discrimination on grounds of sex, the only comparable group being that of lesbians, but a stable lesbian couple would, in principle, have been treated in the same way as the applicants.[55]

With all due respect, here the Commission's reasoning leads *ad absurdum*. Leaving apart the argument for the moment that, as was explained above, the non-recognition of a stable homosexual relationship as 'family life' in the sense of Article 8 is too restrictive an interpretation of that provision; since the only ground for the differential treatment is the homosexual character of the relationship, the Commission cannot confine itself to the argument that the cases are not equal, but should have investigated if there is an objective and reasonable ground for treating heterosexual and homosexual couples differently.

In two more recent decisions the Commission followed a more correct line of reasoning in this respect. It started from the recognition that there was differential treatment and investigated whether there was an objective and reasonable justification:

> The Commission finds that the aim of the legislation in question was to protect the family, a goal similar to the protection of the right to respect for family life guaranteed by Article 8 of ECHR. The aim itself is clearly legitimate. The question remains, however, whether it was justified to protect families but not to give similar protection to other stable relationships. The Commission considers that the family (to which the relationship of heterosexual unmarried couples living together as husband and wife can be assimilated) merits special protection in society and it sees no reason why a High Contracting Party should not afford particular assistance to families. The Commission therefore accepts that the difference in treatment between the applicant and somebody in the same position

---

54   Application 9369/81, *supra* note 25.
55   See *supra* note 25; the relevant part of the decision has not been published.

whose partner had been of the opposite sex can be objectively and reasonably justified.[56]

The validity of the above reasoning depends, of course, completely on the correctness, or at least acceptability, of the Commission's assumption that the 'family' which 'merits special protection' does include heterosexual unmarried couples but not homosexual couples. As has been set out above, this view adopted by the Commission is not self-evident and does not ensue compellingly from the autonomous and broad concept of 'family life' developed in the Strasbourg case-law.

D. Equal Treatment of Homosexuals and the Right to Marry

In the *Rees* case the Court delivered its unanimous opinion that:

> the right to marry guaranteed by Article 12 refers to the traditional marriage between persons of opposite biological sex. This appears also from the wording of the Article which makes it clear that Article 12 is mainly concerned to protect marriage as the basis of the family.[57]

With due respect I submit that the above position amounts to an *a priori* reasoning. The fact that the ECHR guarantees the right to marry and the right to found a family in one and the same provision does not necessarily carry with it the implication that the former is connected with the latter. If, as the Court's case-law indicates, the concept of family is not necessarily linked with that of marriage,[58] why should the opposite be the case? Article 11 of the ECHR also includes two rights: the freedom of assembly and the freedom of association; that does not mean that assemblies by groups of people who do not form an association are not protected. As it was put later on by Judge Martens in his dissenting opinion in the *Cossey* case:

> it cannot be assumed that the stated purpose of the right to marry (to protect marriage as the basis of the family) can serve as a basis for its delimitation: under Article 12 it would certainly not be permissible for a member State to provide that only those who can prove their ability to procreate are allowed to marry.[59]

But even if a link between the right to marry and the right to found a family was intended by the drafters of Article 12, that would not imply that the right to marry 'refers to the traditional marriage' since the character and scope of that right would then be affected by the dynamic interpretation of 'family'.

---

56   Application 11716/85, *S v. United Kingdom*, (1986), DR 47, 274, at 279.
57   Judgment of 17 October 1986, *Rees*, Series A, No. 106, 19.
58   Judgment of 13 June 1979, *Marckx*, Series A, No. 31, 14.
59   Series A, No. 184, 32.

The Court repeated its position in the *Cossey* case, again concerning an application by a transsexual. The Court held that the developments which had occurred in the contracting States could not be said to evidence any general abandonment of the traditional concept of marriage.[60] It is submitted that by requiring such evidence of a general abadonment the Court sets a limitation to its powers to adopt a dynamic approach in its case-law which it has clearly transgressed in many other cases. After all, in the *Dudgeon* case and the *Norris* case there was also no general abandonment of the penalisation of homosexual acts between adults. Application of the 'European consensus inquiry'[61] in its extreme would exclude the possibility of finding any national legislation in violation of the ECHR. As Judge Martens puts it in his dissenting opinion:

> In such cases [concerning family law and sexuality] the Court's policy seems to be to adapt its interpretation to the relevant societal changes only if almost all member States have adopted the new ideas. In my opinion this caution is in principle not consistent with the Court's mission to protect the individual against the collectivity and to do so by elaborating common standards [...]. Caution is indeed called for, but in another direction: if a collectivity oppresses an individual because it does not want to recognize societal changes, the Court should take care not to yield too readily to arguments based on a country's cultural and historical particularities.[62]

While Judge Martens' observations concern transsexuals, they may also become relevant for homosexuals now that there is a growing movement in Member States of the Council of Europe towards making some form of legal recognition and registration of homosexual relationships possible, precisely in order to remove the legal (and psychological) disadvantages which non-recognition implies.

E. Non-Discrimination as an Element of the 'Proportionality' Test

Finally, a decision of the Commission should be mentioned in a case in which Article 14 was not raised but the issue of discrimination, in my opinion, should nevertheless have played some role. The case concerned a female teacher who was fired after she had described, in a tv programme, the negative repercussions which her being a homosexual had had on her professional career. She claimed violation of Article 10 of ECHR. The

---

60   Judgment of 27 September 1990, *Cossey*, Series A, No. 184, 18.
61   This term is borrowed from Helfer, *supra* note 53, 1056-1057.
62   Series A, No. 184, 37. In its judgment of 25 March 1992, *B. v. France*, Series A, No. 232-C, the Court reached the conclusion that Article 8 of the Convention had been violated by the refusal of the French *procureur de la République* to have the reference to sex of a transsexual changed in the civil status register of her place of birth. However, in

Commission reached the conclusion that the restrictions imposed upon her freedom of expression were justified in view of the special responsibilities which her profession imposed upon her and for the protection of the reputation of the institution where she exercised that profession and of the persons whom she had mentioned in the programme. In the Commission's opinion the principle of proportionality had been respected in this case.[63]

Although the Commission made the observation that no sanction was imposed upon the applicant for reason of her homosexuality, in my opinion the Commission should have investigated, when assessing the proportionality of the measure of dismissal, whether and to what extent homosexuality had played a role in the decision of the authorities to fire her. After all, even if Article 14 is not relied upon and therefore does not require separate discussion, non-discrimination is an inherent element of proportionality.

V. Prohibition of Inhuman or Degrading Treatment or Punishment

In cases where it is not possible to make a link between Article 14 and one of the other rights and freedoms laid down in ECHR, discrimination on the basis of homosexuality may still raise an issue under the ECHR, *viz.* under Article 3: prohibition of torture or inhuman or degrading treatment or punishment.

A. Racial Discrimination as a Form of Degrading Treatment

So far the link between discrimination and degrading treatment has been made in the Strasbourg case-law only with respect to discrimination based on race. However, there would seem to be no reason why the underlying arguments do not apply equally to discrimination on the basis of homosexuality. In a decision of 1970 the Commission held as follows:

> Whereas, however, the Commission is of the opinion that, quite apart from any consideration of Article 14, discrimination based on race could, in certain circumstances, of itself amount to degrading treatment within the meaning of Article 3 of ECHR; whereas the Commission considers that it is generally recognized that a special importance should be attached to discrimination based on race, and that publicly to single out a group of persons for differential treatment on the basis of race might, in certain circumstances, constitute a special form of affront to human dignity; whereas, therefore, differential

that case the complaint based on Article 12 of the Convention had been rejected by the Commission on the ground of failure to exhaust domestic remedies.
63   Decision of 3 May 1988 on Application 11389/85, *X v. Belgium*, unpublished.

treatment of a group of persons on the basis of race might be capable of constituting degrading treatment in circumstances where differential treatment on some other ground, such as language, would raise no such question.[64]

It is self-evident that discrimination is not equally degrading in all cases. This depends largely on the ground of differentiation, the purpose aimed at and the effects of the differential treatment for the person concerned. Nevertheless it is far from self-evident that discrimination on the basis of race should take an exclusive position in this respect. Discrimination on the basis of homosexuality, without there being any objective and reasonable ground for it, in my opinion may be equally degrading for the person concerned, depending on the kind and measure of the discrimination involved.

B. Discrimination on the Basis of Homosexuality as a Form of Degrading Treatment

For breaking down the exclusivity of racial discrimination a parallel may be drawn to the Commission's case-law concerning transsexuals. In its report in the *Van Oosterwijck* case the Commission indicated that the refusal by the authorities to enter the change of sex of the applicant into the registers, which made it impossible for her to get married, could raise an issue under Article 3. However, the Commission did not reach a decision on the issue, because it already found a violation of Articles 8 and 12 of ECHR.[65] This raises the possibility that if, for instance, homosexuals complain about discrimination, because their relationships are not treated the same way as marriages and relationships of heterosexuals other than marriages, and if the present case-law is upheld that their relationships are not covered by the right to respect for family life under Article 8 nor by the right to marry and found a family under Article 12, their complaint may also be examined under Article 3.[66]

---

64 *East African Asians v. United Kingdom*, Yearbook XIII (1970) 928 at 994.
65 Report of 1 March 1979, *Van Oosterwijck*, Series B, No. 36, 28-29. The Court did not decide the merits of the case at all, because it held that the local remedies had not been exhausted.
66 See the Resolution of the European Parliament on discrimination against transsexuals; Council of Europe, *Human Rights; Information Sheet No. 25*, Strasbourg 1990, 143-145. There the European Parliament, regretting that transsexuals everywhere are still discriminated against [...]; Calls on the Council of Europe to enact a convention for the protection of transsexuals; [...] Calls on the Council and the Member States, when harmonizing the right of asylum, to recognize persecution on the grounds of transsexuality as grounds for asylum'.

C. State Responsibility for Inhuman and Degrading Treatment in Other Countries

Although the above-quoted statement of the Commission on racial discrimination as a form of degrading treatment is phrased in a general way, the Strasbourg case-law has examined discrimination under Article 3 almost exclusively in cases of non-admittance to or expulsion from a country.[67]

It is important to note that in those cases it is not always the situation in the respondent State that is at issue; the case may also concern the treatment which the applicant has to fear in the country to which he or she is (threatened to be) expelled or will have to return after refusal of entry. In the latter cases the State which decides to expel or which refuses entry is held responsible for the resulting inhuman or degrading treatment in that other country. As the Court stated it in the *Cruz Varas* case:

> In its *Soering* judgment of 7 July 1989 the Court held that the decision by a Contracting State to extradite a fugitive may give rise to an issue under Article 3, and hence engage the responsibility of that State under ECHR, where substantial grounds have been shown for believing that the person concerned, if extradited, faces a real risk of being subjected to torture or to inhuman or degrading treatment or punishment in the requesting country.[68]

Although the establishment of such responsibility involves an assessment of conditions in the requesting country against the standards of Article 3, there is no question of adjudicating on or establishing the responsibility of the receiving country, whether under general international law, under the ECHR or otherwise. In so far as any liability under the ECHR is or may be incurred, it is liability incurred by the extraditing Contracting State by reason of its having taken action which has as a direct consequence the exposure of an individual to proscribed ill-treatment.[69]

Although the present case concerns expulsion as opposed to a decision to extradite, the Court considers that the above principle also applies to expulsion decisions and *a fortiori* to cases of actual expulsion.[70]

This interpretation of the scope of responsibility under Article 3 raises the possibility that a contracting State violates Article 3, if it decides to expel an alien to a country where he or she faces degrading treatment on the basis of homosexuality.[71] In this context it is also important to note that, while under the ECHR claims can only relate to acts of omissions by

---

67   See Van Dijk & Van Hoof, *supra* note 6, 240.
68   Series A, No. 161, 35, para. 91.
69   Ibid., 36, para. 91.
70   Judgment of 20 March 1991, *Cruz Varas e.a.*, Series A, No. 201, paras. 69-70.
71   Discrimination on the basis of homosexuality may amount to 'persecution' of persons belonging to a 'social group' in the sense of Article 1(A) of the Refugee Convention. See, e.g., Netherlands Council of State, decision of 13 August 1981, RV 1981, No. 5.

persons and bodies for whom the State can be held responsible,[72] in cases of expulsion or refusal of entry the State is responsible for the resulting degrading treatment in another country irrespective of whether that treatment is to be expected from the authorities or from private persons.[73]

VI. Some Concluding Observations

After this short exposé I return to the question raised in the introduction: are there real prospects for an effective remedy under ECHR?

In my opinion the European Convention has great potential in offering national and international remedies against interferences with the public and private life of homosexuals and against discrimination of homosexuals:

(1) it has been recognized that private sexual life is covered by the right to respect for private life in Article 8, and it is not unlikely that the Court will decline to follow the Commission in its opinion that homosexual relationships are not also covered by the right to respect for family life;

(2) the prohibition of discrimination under Article 14 has been given a rather autonomous character and, moreover, the opening has been made in principle that discrimination may take the form of degrading treatment in the sense of Article 3.

Since the Strasbourg case-law shows that it is in principle recognized by the Commission and the Court that Article 14 of the ECHR prohibits discrimination on the basis of sexual orientation – otherwise an investigation of the justification of such discrimination would have been unnecessary – there seems to be no need for a separate protocol to the ECHR for that purpose, as has been proposed.[74] Such a step might well turn out to be counterproductive. It would take a long time for such a protocol to enter into force, while certain States most probably would never ratify it. In the meantime, the drafting and adoption of a separate protocol for this category would provide ground for the argument that Article 14 does not after all cover unequal treatment between heterosexuals and homosexuals.

Of course, Article 14 is not a fully autonomous anti-discrimination provision, connected as it is to the rights and freedoms of the ECHR. Consequently, it cannot serve to challenge discrimination against homosexuals in such fields as employment in the private sector, housing, health care etc.,

---

72   See Van Dijk & Van Hoof, *supra* note 6, 76-78.
73   Application 10040/82, *X v. Federal Republic of Germany*, not published: 'it is not necessary for the application of Article 3 that the danger emanates from the Government of the State which requires extradition'.
74   See Ashman, 1990. See also European Parliament, Resolution of 11 June 1986 on violence against women, paragraph 12; Doc. A2-44/86, OJ 1986 C 176/75.

unless the discrimination concerned takes such serious forms that it amounts to an inhuman or degrading treatment in the sense of Article 3. However, that fact presents a problem of a more general character and should not be solved by a separate protocol concerning homosexuals, but either by amending Article 14 into a general and independent provision concerning equal treatment, similar to Article 26 of the International Covenant on Civil and Political Rights[75] or by including some of the most relevant economic, social and cultural rights into the ECHR. Any proposal to remedy the situation especially for homosexuals might very well raise unwelcome opposition at both governmental and non-governmental level.[76]

In the same way, the inclusion of special rights and freedoms concerning homosexuals might provide a basis for the *a contrario* argument that the general rights and freedoms embodied in the ECHR do not apply, or not in all respects, to homosexuals. This could be avoided only, it would seem, by drafting a separate convention. That solution, which has been opted for within the United Nations framework, for instance with respect to racial discrimination and discrimination against women, and with respect to children as a separate category, would certainly not lead to any constructive results for homosexuals for a long time, if ever.

The ECHR as it stands, if treated as a 'living instrument'[77] and interpreted in a dynamic way in view of developments which take place in society, provides an adequate basis for the protection of the rights of homosexuals. What is missing at the moment is this dynamic attitude on the part of the Court, and even more so on the part of the Commission, in matters relating to homosexuality.

The main issue at the moment is how broad a margin of discretion the Strasbourg organs, in the application of Article 8, and of Article 14 in connection with other articles like Articles 9 to 12, are prepared to leave to the national authorities and how far they wish to go in making an independent and detailed investigation of the necessity and proportionality of the interferences, and of the objectivity and reasonableness of the justification

75 That provision has been interpreted as not only relating to civil and political rights; Human Rights Committee, 9 April 1987, *Broeks v. Netherlands,* CCPR/C/29/D/172/ 1984. It should be noted that the general scope of Article 26 applies to those Contracting States which are also parties to the Covenant; see Article 60 ECHR.

76 In this respect it is interesting to note in relation to transsexuals that the Parliamentary Assembly, although in its Recommendation 1117 (1989) on the condition of transsexuals it refers to a resolution of the European Parliament calling on the Council of Europe to enact a convention for the protection of transsexuals, limits itself to recommending 'that the Committee of Ministers draw up a recommendation inviting member states to introduce legislation whereby, in the case of irreversible transsexualism [...] all discrimination in the enjoyment of fundamental rights and freedoms is prohibited in accordance with Article 14 of the European Convention on Human Rights'.

77 See the example given by the Court in its judgment of 25 April 1978, *Tyrer,* Series A, No. 26, 16.

advanced for unequal treatment. In relation to Article 3, the main issue is whether a sufficiently broad scope will be given to the concept of inhuman and degrading treatment to cover discrimination on the basis of homosexuality.

These issues can only be put to a further test, and the Strasbourg case-law can only develop, if new, well-founded and well-prepared cases are brought to Strasbourg. Such test-cases are needed all the more as the Court is not much inclined to give abstract definitions and include *obiter dicta* in its judgments. This makes the case-law a rather slow instrument of law creation. But an instrument it is, and for the moment the most efficient and effective one within the Council of Europe. The Parliamentary Assembly, which has dealt with the rights of homosexuals in the past,[78] has recommendatory powers only. For the implementation of its recommendations the Parliamentary Assembly – and the same holds true for the Committee of Ministers – depends on the legislatures of the contracting States and, within a certain scope, on the Court and the Commission.

The fear that new decisions by the Commission or the Court may block developments and may constitute an excuse for national courts to take a rather restrictive approach, is not unjustified. However, the present Strasbourg case-law – especially that of the Court – in my opinion offers sufficiently promising perspectives, at least as compared to the case-law in some of the contracting States, to make it worth the risk. Therefore, my conclusion is that strong test-cases should be prepared and individual applicants should be supported by collective interest groups. It may be true that, at the present moment, one can still not be very optimistic about the prospects of prompt and appropriate remedies for the person in question; it is nevertheless worthwhile, and for the emancipation of homosexuals even necessary, that complaints are lodged in Strasbourg to elicit a case-law which is more favorable to the recognition of the rights of homosexuals and which may have a positive impact on the law and practice in the Member States of the Council of Europe.

The ECHR may also be 'mobilized' before national courts. This holds good in particular for those contracting States where the ECHR has internal effect. However, in 'dualist' States the ECHR may also have a certain legal effect as an important frame of reference for the interpretation of domestic law. The national courts are bound by the interpretation given by the Court, as the Court's case-law constitutes an integral part of the ECHR and shares its binding force. They may, however, take a more liberal approach, if they can base themselves on provisons of domestic law or of other treaties

---

78 See Recommendation 924 (1981) and Resolution 756 (1981) on discrimination against homosexuals, based on the Voogd Report, and adopted on 1 October 1981, *supra* note 52.

(Article 60 of the ECHR). Moreover, in my opinion, the national courts are bound by a restrictive interpretation by the Court only if the case-law concerned is unambiguous and well developed in that respect. After all, the Court itself is prepared to revise its own interpretations, taking into account, *inter alia,* developments in the national case-law of the contracting States. Therefore, by adopting an approach that is not expressly and unambiguously rejected by the Court, the national courts can make their contribution to a dynamic interpretation of the ECHR.

Chapter Seven
Equality and Non-Discrimination

by

ANGELA BYRE[*]

*   Research Fellow, London Policy Institute.

Table of Contents

I. Acquired Rights

A. Basic Treaty Provisions

European Community legislation and action programmes in the field of discrimination and equal treatment have been wide-ranging and detailed in content and much developed over the last decade and a half. Aside from provisions specifically relating to nationality and free movement principles, however, Community initiatives in the discrimination field have concentrated on one major type of discrimination – namely discrimination on grounds of sex.

The primary legal provisions here are to be found in the EEC Treaty, *Article 119* of which requires Member States of the Community to 'ensure and maintain the application of the principle that men and women should receive equal pay for equal work'. The European Court of Justice confirmed the social as well as the economic objectives of Article 119 in an early case referred from Belgium for a preliminary ruling *(Defrenne II)*.[1] The Court declared that

> this provision forms part of the social objectives of the Community, which is not merely an economic union, but is at the same time intended, by common action, to ensure social progress and seek the constant improvement of the living and working conditions of their peoples, as is emphasized by the Preamble to the Treaty.

The Court subsequently emphasized not only the 'social progress' aspect of the Article 119 equality provisions, but also their 'fundamental' nature. In the third *Defrenne* judgment,[2] the Court stated that:

> respect for fundamental personal human rights is one of the general principles of Community law... There can be no doubt that the elimination of discrimination based on sex forms part of those fundamental rights.

This recognition of the fundamental and progressive nature of the basic equality provisions in the EEC Treaty underlies the way in which the European Court has interpreted and developed the equality principles of the Treaty and its follow-up Directives.

---

1   Case 43/75, *Defrenne v. Sabena II* [1976] ECR 455.
2   Case 149/77, *Defrenne v. Sabena III* [1978] ECR 1365.

B. Development of the Equal Treatment Principle

During the period from 1975 to 1986, as the social side of EC policies began to be developed, the Article 119 Treaty provisions were built upon and added to in a series of binding Council Directives on specific aspects of sex equality. Five Directives were adopted: the first amplifying the Treaty provisions on equal pay (most notably by introducing the concept of equal pay for work of equal value); and subsequent Directives applying the principle of equal treatment for men and women and prohibiting discrimination on grounds of sex in employment and working conditions, statutory social security schemes, occupational social security, and the self-employment field.[3]

Of the existing corpus of Community legislation, the provisions in the *1976 Equal Treatment Directive*[4] are those of most potential relevance to lesbians and gay men and the problems they are likely to encounter in a work environment – such as difficulties in securing work or promotion, harassment at the workplace, and unfair dismissal. The Directive was adopted to implement 'the principle of equal treatment for men and women as regards access to employment, vocational training and promotion and working conditions'. The Directive's scope is intended to cover all stages of employment – from recruitment, through the working conditions applied while in employment, to dismissal and termination of employment. The principle of equal treatment in the Directive is defined as meaning that 'there shall be no discrimination whatsoever on grounds of sex either directly or indirectly by reference in particular to marital or family status' (Article 2). The Directive does not itself lay down particular sanctions or provide a wronged individual with specific compensation or forms of redress. However, the ECJ has ruled that where an EC Member State's implementing legislation provides for compensation in cases of proven sex discrimination, such compensation must be 'adequate' in relation to the damage sustained and amount to more than purely nominal compensation in order to be effective and have a deterrent effect.[5]

The ECJ has given a number of important rulings, mostly in response to requests for preliminary rulings on issues of interpretation of the Community provisions from national courts under Article 177 of the EEC Treaty. For example, the concept of indirect discrimination – not defined in the Directive itself but a potentially important means of challenging employment structures and practices which perpetuate discrimination – has been clarified by the Court. In the *Bilka* judgment,[6] the Court held that a practice which

3   These Directives are, respectively, Nos. 75/117, 76/207, 79/7, 86/378 and 86/613.
4   Directive 76/207/EEC of 9 February 1976, OJ L 39 of 14 February 1976.
5   Case 14/83, *von Colson and Kamann v. Land Nordrhein-Westfalen* [1984] ECR 1891.
6   Case 170/84, *Bilka Kaufhaus v. Weber* [1986] ECR 1607.

excluded part-time workers and in practice affected a far greater proportion of women than men, would be unlawful indirect discrimination unless the employer could provide objective justification for the practice unrelated to any discrimination on grounds of sex. In order to justify such a practice along these lines, it would be necessary to show that the means chosen for achieving the employer's objective corresponded to a real need on the part of the undertaking, were appropriate to achieving the objective and were necessary to that end. The Court thus laid down the ground-rules for applying the indirect discrimination concept, and placed the onus on employers to explain their policies on an objective basis.[7] In another important judgment (the *Dekker* case 177/88),[8] the ECJ ruled that the refusal to hire a woman on the grounds of her pregnancy was contrary to the equal treatment/non-discrimination principles of the 1976 Directive, even though the Directive does not specifically refer to pregnancy discrimination.

These and many other European Court rulings show that the principles of the EEC Treaty and of the specific equality Directives, and their potential scope, are gradually being developed and elaborated on – a process that is likely to continue in the future, with many issues still to be tested and explored. The 1976 Directive and the Court rulings on it have not, to date, specifically referred to the treatment of lesbians and gay men or to possible discrimination on grounds of sexual orientation. However, it is arguable that the basic equal treatment principle and the prohibition of discrimination on grounds of direct or indirect sex discrimination could be invoked in respect of unfair treatment of men and women at work linked to their sexual orientation (see further in section II below). The scope of the non-discrimination principle has yet to be tested in this area. If the principle can be interpreted broadly so as to cover discrimination on these grounds, the aspects of employment to which the 1976 Directive's principles may be applied would appear to include the main problem areas for lesbians and gay men in the work field – namely, refusal to hire, unfair dismissal, and discriminatory treatment in relation to working conditions including forms of harassment.[9]

C. Non-Legislative Provisions

Aside from what may be termed the 'hard' law of Community equality Directives – which represent binding legal provisions and some elements of which, if sufficiently precise and unconditional, may be directly relied on

---

7   See also Case 109/88, *Danfoss* [1989] ECR 3199.
8   Case 177/88, *Dekker v. VJV – Centrum plus* [1990] ECR 3941.
9   See Chapters Three, Four and Fourteen by Betten for detailed examples of such workplace discrimination.

by individuals in their national courts – the EC bodies have initiated other non-binding, non-legislative measures to promote non-discrimination and equality in all aspects of employment and working life. A 16-point Action Programme on the promotion of equal opportunities for women was approved by the EC's Council of Ministers for the period 1982-85; subsequent approval was given for a Medium-Term Programme for the period 1986-90 following up the earlier strategy; and a Third Action Programme has recently been approved to pursue the Community's strategic objectives in the equality field for the period 1991-95. The Programmes cover a wide range of actions at both national and Community levels aimed at furthering equality goals. While many of the actions called for in these Programmes do not have any legal force in themselves, they may stimulate legal changes in the future.

The *Third Action Programme*[10] follows up commitments in the Community's 1989 Charter of the Fundamental Social Rights of Workers[11] – itself a statement of intent rather than a measure with any legal force – to an intensification of action aimed at promoting equality of opportunity as the EC moves towards completion of its barrier-free Single Market. The Third Action Programme has three main objectives, namely: further implementation and development of the law; the integration of women into the labour market; and improving the status of women. On the legislative front, there are plans to increase awareness and understanding of existing legal rights and obligations, and to extend and strengthen the body of Community equality law (by pursuing proposals for Directives on the burden of proof, parental leave and further social security measures). There are no plans, however, to make specific additions or improvements to the 1976 Equal Treatment Directive or to bring forward new measures to tackle the issue of appropriate sanctions and forms of redress in cases of proven discrimination contrary to the Directive. One issue which is addressed in the non-legislative sections of the Third Action Programme is that of sexual harassment. Among measures 'to improve the working conditions and the reconciliation between work and family responsibilities for men and women' is provision for the European Commission to draw up 'a code of good conduct on the protection of the dignity of women and men at work'.

The new sexual harassment *Code of Practice,*[12] which was adopted in November 1991 along with a European Commission Recommendation

10 Third Action Programme on Equal Opportunities for Women and Men: COM (90) 449 final, 6 November 1990.
11 Community Charter of the Fundamental Social Rights of Workers: COM (89) 568 final, November 1989.
12 The final text of the 'Commission Recommendation of 27 November 1991 on the protection of the dignity of women and men at work', which includes 'A Code of Practice on Measures to Combat Sexual Harassment', was published twice: OJ 1992 C 27/04 and OJ 1992 L 49. The Recommendation is based on a Council Resolution of

advocating supportive action by EC Member States in this area, has no legal force of its own. The Code aims to give 'practical guidance' to employers, trade unions and employees on 'the protection of the dignity of women and men at work'. It seeks to 'ensure that sexual harassment does not occur and, if it does occur, to ensure that adequate procedures are readily available to deal with the problem and prevent its recurrence'. The Code draws on best practice and experience in the Member States, and represents a deliberate choice by the Community bodies to go for voluntary action backed by EC-level guidance rather than a formal regulatory approach to issues generally regarded as sensitive and covered to some extent by existing equal treatment legislation. The Code defines sexual harassment as 'unwanted conduct of a sexual nature, or other conduct based on sex affecting the dignity of women and men at work. This can include unwelcome physical, verbal or non-verbal conduct.' Sexual harassment is regarded as a form of sex discrimination' because the gender of the recipient is the determining factor in who is harassed'.

The Code was not initially concerned with the problems experienced by lesbians and gay men at the workplace, and early drafts of the Code made no specific reference to them. However, the final version of the Code rectifies this omission. It notes that 'some specific groups are particularly vulnerable to sexual harassment', and that research indicates that lesbians and gay men are among the groups especially at risk of such harassment. The Code adds: 'It is undeniable that harassment on grounds of sexual orientation undermines the dignity at work of those affected and it is impossible to regard such harassment as appropriate workplace behaviour'.

II. Extensions

In considering the question of how existing Community equality/non-discrimination provisions could be extended or developed to secure adequate protection for lesbians and gay men at work, it is also relevant to consider what is likely to be most practicable as well as desirable in terms of achieving this objective. To date, the Community has adopted basic sex equality legislation (on equal pay, and equal treatment in employment and in the social security field), but has largely left development of these basic laws to implementing national legislation and the interpretation of the courts, especially the European Court of Justice. Attempts to introduce EC-level measures to extend or amplify the existing Directives, as most notably in the case of proposals regarding the burden of proof which should apply

29 May 1990 (OJ 1990 C 157/02), and has been endorsed by a Council Declaration of 19 December 1991 (OJ 1992 C 27/01).

in equal treatment cases, have not succeeded in getting the necessary degree of political support and being adopted. Moreover, where issues are regarded as particularly sensitive in nature, as in the case of sexual harassment, the Community bodies have sought to highlight the issues in a non-regulatory way through guidance and codes of practice rather than through extended or new legislation. The following approach is therefore suggested as the most appropriate in terms of securing specific Community rights for lesbians and gay men in the employment field.

Test Cases. First, the existing provisions of the 1976 Equal Treatment Directive should be tested to establish whether the principle of non-discrimination 'on grounds of sex' can be interpreted in a sufficiently broad way to encompass discrimination on grounds of sexual orientation. A number of different issues could be tested. For example, at the access to employment stage, a *refusal to hire* involving anti-homosexual discrimination based on gender role expectations and stereotyping could be challenged as a form of direct discrimination contrary to the Directive. It could be argued that a refusal to hire say, gay men, constituted such discrimination since general gender-based assumptions that homosexual men would be unreliable workers, etc, took no account of an individual's suitability for a particular job and would not be applied to female applicants.

Similarly, *harassment* of lesbians or gay men in the course of their employment (including verbal abuse) could be challenged as a form of direct discrimination contrary to the 1976 Directive. The fact that the European Commission's 1991 Recommendation and accompanying Code of Practice on sexual harassment acknowledge that: 'conduct of a sexual nature or other conduct based on sex affecting the dignity of women and men at work may be contrary to the (legal) principle of equal treatment', and specifically include the harassment of lesbians and gay men within the scope of sexual harassment, should provide useful back-up for such a challenge. Moreover, the European Court's *Grimaldi* judgment has confirmed the persuasive authority of such non-binding provisions.[13] The fact that the Directive itself does not specifically refer to discrimination on grounds of sexual orientation should not be fatal to such a challenge, since pregnancy discrimination is similarly not mentioned in the Directive but has been held to be capable of constituting discrimination covered by the Equal Treatment Directive.[14]

Other issues which could be the subject of test cases would include *dismissal discrimination* on grounds of sexual orientation (where similar direct

13   Case C-322/88, *Grimaldi v. Fonds des maladies professionelles* [1989] ECR 4407. In the *Grimaldi* case, the European Court held that national courts are bound to take Community Recommendations into consideration in order to decide disputes submitted to them, in particular 'where they are capable of casting light on the interpretation of other provisions of national or Community law.'

14   See *Dekker, supra* note 8.

discrimination arguments could be advanced to those used for gender-based assumptions at the hiring stage); and discrimination based on *marital status* – as, for example, where employment benefits such as travel concessions or certain pension benefits are made available to employees and their spouses but denied to the partners of employees in same sex couples who cannot get married. The 1976 Equal Treatment Directive outlaws discrimination on grounds of sex 'by reference in particular to *marital* or family status' (my emphasis).

Test cases on these and other problem areas should be referred from national courts to the European Court of Justice for preliminary interpretative rulings, under the established Article 177 EEC Treaty procedures. If the Court affirms that the 1976 Directive's provisions are to be broadly interpreted to cover sexual orientation, the European Commission could then draw up a guidance note or memorandum to ensure general awareness of the implications of the Court's rulings.

Practical guidance. In parallel to the test case approach outlined above, active use should be made of the European Commission's new sexual harassment Code which now includes the harassment of lesbians and gay men within its scope. The Code aims to encourage the development and implementation of policies and practices 'which establish working environments free of sexual harassment and in which women and men respect one another's human integrity'. The practical guidance given in the Code to employers, trade unions and employees should be widely disseminated and the guidance could be elaborated on – perhaps by supplementary EC-level guidance from the European Commission – to show specifically how the workplace problems faced by lesbians and gay men should be tackled.

Legislative amendments. If the European Court's rulings in the Equal Treatment Directive test cases are negative and indicate that the Directive cannot, in its present form, be interpreted as applying to discrimination on grounds of sexual orientation, consideration should be given to formulating proposals for amendments to the Directive to secure such application. At the same time, consideration could be given to making the application of the Directive to harassment at the workplace, including harassment on grounds of sexual orientation, more explicit by appropriate amendments to the basic Directive.

This step-by-step approach to securing rights for lesbians and gay men in the employment field takes account of the existing legal framework on equality in the Community, and seeks to build on its foundations rather than constructing an entirely new base for these rights. The emphasis has been deliberately on legal provisions, backed by voluntary initiatives where appropriate, as this would appear to offer the best possibility of securing adequate and standard protection for the individuals concerned.

III. Additions

In the past, it has proved difficult to get the necessary unanimity required in the EC's Council of Ministers for many social legislation proposals, including equality proposals. Prior to the December 1991 *Inter-Governmental Conferences* on EC Treaty reforms, health and safety measures and those directly linked to the completion of the Community's Single Market were the only ones to which majority voting could apply in the social field. The agreements reached at the December 1991 meetings in Maastricht, if ultimately ratified by all the EC member states, will, to a limited extent, open up the majority voting possibilities. While work on the Community's 1989 Charter of the Fundamental Social Rights of Workers, and its Action Programme, is likely to continue on the basis of trying to get full agreement by all 12 EC Member States, a *special Agreement* signed at Maastricht by all Member States except the United Kingdom will, if Danish ratification difficulties are resolved and the Maastricht agreements are fully ratified, enable those Member States to proceed with certain new proposals to implement the Social Charter objectives on a qualified majority voting basis.

Among the issues which the special Agreement allows the 11 signatory Member States to proceed with on a *qualified majority voting* basis are issues concerning 'equality between men and women with regard to labour market opportunities and treatment at work'. These new majority voting opportunities could enable equal treatment amending legislation along the lines indicated above to be adopted more easily. New issues could also be addressed – such as the issue of appropriate sanctions and forms of redress across the Community for individuals having suffered unlawful discrimination. However, any such new legislative proposals which might ultimately be approved by majority voting among the 11 Member State signatories to the Agreement, would not affect the rights of workers in the United Kingdom (the non-signatory Member State, not agreeing to be covered by the Protocol). This would mean that a *two-tier situation* would be created, with differing equality rights and obligations in the UK and elsewhere in the European Community. It would seem desirable, therefore, to proceed with the strategy (outlined in section II above) of clarifying and elaborating on the existing EC equality legislation which applies to *all* EC Member States, rather than seeking to open up a two-tier approach in the short term. If and when the EC Treaty reforms and the special Agreement are ultimately ratified and take effect, the situation could be *reviewed* to see how effectively the rights of lesbians and gay men in the employment field throughout the European Community were being served by the existing EC-wide measures. If problems still remained, efforts should be made to secure the agreement of all EC Member States for new legislative and non-legislative action. Only if such agreement proved impossible should consideration be given to utilising the new Agreement procedures and embarking on a two-tier approach (which, in the author's opinion, would be undesirable and very much a last option).

Chapter Eight

Subsidiarity: an Aspect of European Community Law and its Relevance to Lesbians and Gay Men

by

FRANCIS SNYDER *

with the collaboration of HAN SOMSEN and HENRIK DUEDAHL HOYER

* Professor, University College, London; European University Institute, Florence.

Table of Contents

I. Introduction

Chapters Eight, Nine and Ten are concerned with two aspects of European Community (EC) law which, so far at least, have remained relatively unexplored with regard to the needs of lesbians and gay men. The first is the principle of subsidiarity. The second, stemming from the role of the EC as employer, is the Staff Regulations.

At first glance these two aspects of EC law may appear to be unrelated. It may be suggested, however, that, from the standpoint of legal doctrine or legal technique, they share at least one important feature. Each represents a kind of organizing device, which, alone or in conjunction with other elements of EC law, establishes a general normative framework. In turn, this normative framework, whether extremely broad or narrowly defined, governs, at least in principle, a particular area of behaviour.

The principle of subsidiarity is procedural, general, and overarching; the Staff Regulations, giving rise to substantive rights, are specific and detailed. But each helps to establish – or forms in itself – a particular normative framework. Subsidiarity is a basic constitutional principle, which together with other concepts and principles defines the EC legal order.[1] The Staff Regulations, as periodically amended, comprise a veritable employment code for EC officials and other EC servants; their application is limited to this group of people.

Viewed as legal norms and techniques, therefore, the topics discussed in these chapters differ substantially from the typical categories of EC economic and social law, such as the law concerning the free movement of workers, or even the principle of non-discrimination, which potentially confer directly enforceable rights upon all citizens (including lesbians and gay men) of the EC Member States.

II. Subsidiarity

A. Background and Definitions

The potential relevance of the principle of subsidiarity to the concerns of lesbians and gay men may be summarized, perhaps, in two questions. Does the EC have the legal competence (or power) to further the needs of lesbians and gay men? If so, to what extent? This way of considering the matter may however be misleading. Strictly speaking, the principle of subsidiarity

---

1 On the EC legal order: Weiler, 'The Transformation of Europe', 1 *Yale Law Journal* (1992) 1; Snyder, 'The Effectiveness of European Community Law: Institutions, Processes, Tools and Techniques', 56 *Modern Law Review* (1993) 19.

is concerned, not with the EC's legal competence, but rather with the delineation of the roles of the EC and the twelve EC Member States. In other words, instead of helping us to determine whether the EC has legal competence to deal with the concerns of lesbians and gay men, it presumes that the EC has legal competence and is concerned only with the exercise of this power. For present purposes, however, it is nonetheless useful to consider both the issue of EC competence and the issue of the exercise of this competence, since this will illuminate more clearly the role of the principle of subsidiarity in the EC constitutional order.

To the extent that the principle of subsidiarity concerns the allocation of decision-making power between the EC and the Member States, it may be argued that, in practice, subsidiarity has always been part of the EC constitutional order. Nevertheless, recent years have witnessed an increasing emphasis on subsidiarity, not only in practice but also as a fundamental principle of EC constitutional law.

The principle of subsidiarity was expressly formulated by the Single European Act. The Single European Act was agreed in 1986 and came into force on 1 July 1987. Article 25 Single European Act amended the EEC Treaty (Treaty of Rome) by inserting, *inter alia*, a new Article 130r EEC regarding environmental policy. Article 130r(4) provides that

> The Community shall take action relating to the environment to the extent to which the objectives ... can be attained better at Community level than at the level of the individual Member States...

More recently, as a result of the Inter-Governmental Conference on Political and Monetary Union held in Maastricht in December 1991, subsidiarity now features among the general principles of EC constitutional law. Article B of the new Common Provisions of the Maastricht Treaty on European Union provides, *inter alia*, that

> The objectives of the Union shall be achieved as provided in this Treaty and in accordance with the conditions and the timetable set out therein while respecting the principle of subsidiarity as defined in Article 3b of the Treaty establishing the European Community.

This Article 3b (inserted by Article G of the Maastricht Treaty) is among those setting out the principles of the EC. Hence the potential application of the principle of subsidiarity is no longer limited to the domain of environmental policy.

According to Article 3b, subsidiarity means that

> the Community shall take action ... only if, and in so far as the objectives of the proposed action cannot be sufficiently achieved by the Member States and can

therefore, by reason of the scale or effects of the proposed action, be better achieved by the Community.

Article 3b also provides that

Any action by the Community shall not go beyond what is necessary to achieve the objectives of this Treaty.

This provision expresses the principle of proportionality. It is directly relevant to subsidiarity. Even when the Community does act, the principle of proportionality as currently understood, requires that this action take the form of the least restrictive alternative. Hence, if possible, a directive should be used instead of a regulation. Similarly, a measure which is not legally binding should be preferred to a legally binding measure, if the two are equally effective in achieving a given objective.

It is not surprising, therefore, that subsidiarity has come to be regarded as the principle *par excellence* which may aid the delimitation of the respective competences of the Community and the Member States. Hence, it would seem logical to consider the possibility of EC action regarding lesbians and gay men from the standpoint of the principle of subsidiarity.

A widespread consensus exists as to the desirability of the principle of subsidiarity in the EC legal order. This does not necessarily imply, however, that the term posesses a single agreed meaning. In fact, the converse is true. Rather like the emperor's new clothes, the fact that the term lacks any clear meaning is among its most important qualities. In the past an amorphous concept as 'political union' served to build a consensus as to the desirability of a change in direction for the EC; subsidiarity may now perform a similar function.

It is therefore not as strange as it may seem to consider and perhaps to question the practical significance of this principle. To what extent is it useful in determining the equilibrium between the exercise of powers by the EC, on the one hand, and by the Member States, on the other hand? The current discussions regarding subsidiarity remain relatively unfocussed. In this context, an enquiry as to the practical significance of the principle of subsidiarity is essential in order to ascertain its relevance, if any, to the interests of lesbians and gay men.

B. The Question of the EC's Legal Competence

A logical starting point for the purpose of delimiting the legal competence of the EC, and thus of demarcating the EC's powers from those of the Member States, is *Article 4* EEC. It is placed in Part One of the EC Treaty entitled 'Principles'. Article 4, first paragraph, provides:

The tasks entrusted to the Community shall be carried out by the following institutions:
- an Assembly
- a Council
- a Commission
- a Court of Justice
Each institution shall act within the limits of the powers conferred upon it by this
Treaty.

This part of Article 4 EEC remains largely unchanged by the Treaty on
European Union (Maastricht Treaty).

However, after the entry into force of the Maastricht Treaty, Article 4
EEC will be supplemented by various provisions. Article E in the new
Common Provisions of the Maastricht Treaty provides, *inter alia*, that

The European Parliament, the Council, the Commission and the Court of Justice
shall exercise their powers under the conditions and for the purposes provided
for, on the one hand, by the provisions of the Treaties establishing the European
Communities, the subsequent Treaties and Acts modifying and supplementing
them and, on the other hand, by the other provisions of this Treaty.

Article 3b states, with regard to the EC's legal competence, that

The Community shall act within the limits of the powers conferred upon it by
this Treaty and of the objectives assigned to it therein... Any action by the
Community shall not go beyond what is necessary to achieve the objectives of
this Treaty.

It may be suggested that, for present purposes, these new provisions do not
change fundamentally the basic principle set out in Article 4 EEC. This Article is regarded by many as a manifestation of the so-called principle of attributed powers (*principe d'attribution des compétences*). As commonly understood, it means that the limits of the EC's competences are conditioned
by the objectives and powers laid down in the Treaty. In fact, this principle
has two aspects. The first concerns the delimitation of the respective powers
of the EC and of the Member States. The second concerns the respective
powers of the different EC institutions; though this question of the so-called
'institutional balance' among EC institutions differs fundamentally from
the first question in some respects, the two are of course closely related.

Phrased negatively, the principle of attributed powers means that the EC
has no powers other than those laid down in the Treaty. The rule that legal
competence resides with the Member States unless the Treaty (or provisions
derived from the Treaty) provide otherwise is not unlike the rule found in
Article 30 of the German Basic Law and the Tenth Amendment to the
United States Constitution.[2]

---

2   Article 30 of the Federal German Grundgesetz reads:

Further support for the rule that the EC generally does not possess powers other than those expressly provided in the Treaty is also often derived from the fact that the Treaty requires that EC legislation state its legal basis, that is, it must be expressly based on one or more Articles of the Treaty.[3] It is noteworthy that the notion of subsidiarity as embodied in Article 3b inserted by the Maastricht Treaty on European Union similarly maintains the dichotomy of the objectives pursued by the Treaty and the powers at the disposal of the institutions to carry out those objectives.

The European Court of Justice (ECJ) has ruled that the EC possesses certain implied powers, which should not be confused with those laid down in Article 235 (to which we will turn later).[4] This jurisprudence qualifies the principle of (expressly) attributed powers. In addition, the general theory that the EC possesses only those powers specifically granted to it by the Treaty has been substantially eroded, in practice, and sometimes virtually abandoned, in the past decade or so. Nevertheless, the principle may still provide a useful starting point in our discussion of EC competence to further the interests of lesbians and gay men.

In seeking to establish whether the EC has the legal competence to protect the interests of its lesbian and gay citizens, it is therefore necessary to ascertain, first, whether this concern forms part of the objectives of the Community and, second, if it does, what powers are placed at the disposal of the EC institutions to carry out this task. Only once this fundamental question has been addressed is it necessary to turn to the problem of which level of government in the EC system should exercise power, the EC or the Member States. In other words, the principle of subsidiarity as a possible aid in establishing which authority should exercise power will only arise insofar as the EC's competence is not exclusive, that is, in those spheres where the Member States may have already lost all their powers.[5] The principle of subsidiarity can only play a role in those fields where the EC and the Member States enjoy concurrent competence.

> The exercise of governmental powers and the discharge of governmental functions shall be incumbent on the Lander in so far as this Basic Law does not otherwise prescribe or permit.
>
> The Tenth Amendment formulated the same principle thus:
>
> > The powers not delegated to the United States by the Constitution or prohibited by it to the States, are reserved to the States respectively or the People.

3   Article 190 EEC.
4   The Court first accepted the Community's implied powers in Case 8/55, *Fédération Charbonnière de Belgique v. High Authority* [1956] ECR 245 and later more extensively in Case 41/69, *ACF Chemiefarma NV v. Commission* [1970] ECR 661 and Case 281, 283-285, 287/85, *Germany, France, the Netherlands, Denmark and the United Kingdom v. Commission (Re Migration Policy)* [1987] ECR. The doctrine is most pronounced in the field of the Community's external powers: see Case 22/70, *Commission v. Council* [1971] ECR 263; Joined Cases 3, 4, 6/76, *Kramer et al.* [1976] ECR 1279; and Opinion 1/76 on *The Laying-up Fund for Inland Waterway Vessels* [1977] ECR 741.
5   Cf. Article 3b of the Treaty on European Union, *supra* note 2.

C. The Objectives of the EC

1. The Preamble

For the answer to the first limb of our question, that of the extent to which the Community's objectives encompass the protection of interests of lesbians and gay men, it seems proper to devote special attention to the Preamble to the Treaty of Rome and the principles listed in Part One. It is here that the EC's objectives are expressed most clearly.

The Preamble has been of great assistance to the ECJ in interpreting the Treaty, and its legal significance should therefore not be under-estimated. Its main value perhaps has been to emphasize the dynamic character of the EC, which in turn has helped to justify a dynamic, extensive interpretation of EC competence.[6] In the Preamble the Member States confirm as 'the essential' objective of the Treaty of Rome 'the constant improvement of the living and working conditions of their peoples'. Such a recital – which by itself lacks any operative effect – may in conjunction with other provisions of EC law become a vehicle for action which may eventually even develop into a fully fledged EC policy.

A good example of how, aided by the Preamble and the provisions in Part One, a certain area of policy may, despite the absence of firm commitments in the Treaty, come to be embraced by the EC is provided by environmental policy. Although until 1986 the Treaty did not contain any reference to the natural environment, by that time about 100 Directives had been unanimously adopted, covering a wide spectrum of environmental problems. Scholars have always stressed that the Preamble, in conjunction with Article 2 EEC, provide a basis for EC action in this field. This line of reasoning was eventually accepted by the Community's institutions, including the ECJ.

With the adoption of the Maastricht Treaty on European Union the EC's prime objective no longer consists solely – nor even primarily – of the establishment of an internal market. This shift becomes clear especially in the common provisions to the new Treaty. Although this is not the place to examine the legal significance of these common provisions, the precise language in which they are phrased would seem to suggest that their legal importance is more prominent than the vaguer provisions of the Preamble to present Treaty.

---

6   Cf. Case 26/62, *Van Gend & Loos v. Nederlandse Administratie der Belastingen* [1963] ECR 1, where the Court explained:

> To ascertain whether the provisions of an international treaty extend so far in their effects it is necessary to consider the spirit, the general scheme and the wording of those provisions.

Note that the Court reversed the order as laid down in Article 31 of the 1969 Vienna Convention on the Law of Treaties.

The task of the Community is, in the words of Article A, '... to organize, in a manner demonstrating consistency and solidarity, relations between the Member States and between their peoples.'

The objectives listed in Article B include, *inter alia*, 'to strengthen the protection of the rights and interests of the nationals of its Member States through the introduction of a citizenship of the Union.' Furthermore, Article F provides that the Union

> shall respect fundamental rights, as guaranteed by the European Convention for the Protection of Human Rights and Fundamental Freedoms signed in Rome on 4 November 1950 and as they result from the constitutional traditions common to the Member States, as general principles of Community Law.

The fact that such fundamental rights form part of the EC legal order has long been accepted by the ECJ,[7] but the explicit reference to these rights will undoubtedly reinforce their position in the context of EC law-making. It may be suggested that the right as guaranteed in Article 8 of the Convention for the Protection of Human Rights and Fundamental Freedoms to a private and a family life may be of special importance in the present context.[8]

In brief, from the Treaty's Preamble and most notably from the common provisions in the Treaty on European Union, it appears that the EC Treaty aims to protect and strengthen the rights of its citizens. That this includes the rights of lesbians and gay men follows, *inter alia*, from the pledge that the Union's objectives shall be implemented 'in a manner demonstrating consistency and solidarity' as well as from references to fundamental rights.

As has already been indicated above, however, the Preamble by itself cannot give rise to EC competence. To argue convincingly that the EC is competent to take specific action to protect the rights and meet the needs of lesbians and gay men, it is necessary to point to specific empowering provisions in the Treaty. It is no doubt for this reason that the Commission in its action programme for a Community Social Charter stressed the

---

7   See in particular Case 11/70, *Internationale Handelsgesellschaft* [1970] ECR 1125; Case 4/73, *Nold v. Commission,* ECR 491; Case 44/79, *Liselotte Hauer v. Land Rheinland-Pfalz* [1979] ECR 3727; Joined Cases 60 and 61/84, *Cinéthèque and others* [1985] ECR 2605; Case C-260/89, *Elliniki,* judgment of 18.6.1991 (not yet reported); Case C-159/90, *Society for the Protection of Unborn Children Ireland (SPUC) v. Grogan* [1991] 3 CMLR 849.

8   Article 8 provides:
     (1) Everyone has the right to respect for his private and family life, his home and correspondence.
     (2) There shall be no interference by a public authority with the exercise of this right except such as is in accordance with the law and is necessary in a democratic society in the interests of national security, public safety or the economic well-being of the country, for the prevention of disorder or crime, for the protection of health or morals, or the protection of the rights and freedoms of others.

economic importance of the integration of the disabled, thus attempting to bring a policy for the disabled squarely within the ambit of the Treaty.

2. Principles

The principles of the EEC are stated in Part One of the Treaty of Rome. For our purposes the most important provisions are Articles 2 and 3. It is important to read these two Articles together. Article 2 states the objectives of the EEC and means by which they are to be achieved. Article 3 states various activities which are to be undertaken in order to achieve these objectives. Article 2 provides that the task of the Community is

> to promote throughout the Community a harmonious development of economic activities, a continuous and balanced expansion, an increase in stability, an accelerated raising of the standard of living and closer relations between the States belonging to it.

It should be noted however that the list of objectives in Article 2 is not exhaustive. For example, the Community's environmental objectives are found not in Article 2 but in Article 130r EEC.[9]

The same Article 2 makes clear that the Community's objectives are to be achieved 'by establishing a common market and progressively approximating the economic policies of the Member States'. Whereas 'an accelerated raising of the standard of living' concerns homosexuals as much as others and may legitimize Community measures especially aimed at lesbians and gay men, the primarily economic instruments advanced to achieve this goal at the same time would seem to restrict the possible scope for such action. Article 3 enumerates these instruments in more detail.[10]

---

9   Other examples are Articles 29, 39, 104, 110, 117, 123.
10   Article 3 provides:
      For the purposes set out in Art. 2, the activities of the Community shall include, as provided in this Treaty and in accordance with the timetable set out therein:
      (a) the elimination, as between Member States, of customs duties and of other measures having equivalent effect;
      (b) the establishment of a common customs tariff and of a common commercial policy towards third countries;
      (c) the abolition, as between Member States, of obstacles to freedom of movement of persons, services and capital;
      (d) the adoption of a common policy in the sphere of agriculture;
      (e) the adoption of a common policy in the sphere of transport;
      (f) the institution of a system ensuring that competition in the common market is not distorted;
      (g) the application of procedures by which the economic policies of Member States can be coordinated and disequilibria in their balances of payments remedied;
      (h) the approximation of the laws of Member States to the extent required for the proper functioning of the common market;
      (i) the creation of a European Social Fund in order to improve employment opportunities for workers and to contribute to the raising of their standard of living;

Only a few of these would appear *prima facie* to be of direct importance to homosexuals.[11]

As a result of the Maastricht Treaty, the amended Articles 2 and 3 are much wider in their scope and the 'economic' emphasis of the instruments provided for the attainment of the Community's objectives has been further diluted. Thus, according to the new Article 2 the Community shall have as its task

> ... to promote throughout the Community a harmonious and balanced develop-
> ment of economic activities, sustainable and non-inflationary growth respecting
> the environment, a high degree of convergence of economic performance, a high
> level of employment and of social protection, the raising of the standard of living
> and the quality of life, and economic and social cohesion and solidarity among
> Member States.

This, in turn, is to be achieved by 'establishing a common market and an economic and monetary union and by implementing the common policies or activities referred to in Articles 3 and 3a'.[12] As already mentioned, these policies are to be implemented in accordance with the principle of subsidiarity. Though not exclusive, Article 3 as formulated in the Treaty on European Union may justifiably be viewed as the most recent expression of what are regarded the 'tasks entrusted to the Community'. The principles of the EC also include the duty of Community loyalty. It is stated in Article 5 EEC. This Article provides that

> Member States shall take all appropriate measures, whether general or particular,
> to ensure fulfilment of the obligations arising out of this Treaty or resulting from
> action taken by the Community. They shall facilitate the achievement of the

(j)   the establishment of a European Investment Bank to facilitate the economic expan -
      sion of the Community by opening fresh resources;
(k)   the association of the overseas countries and territories in order to increase trade and
      promote jointly economic and social development.

11   This is to be distinguished from those measures which affect all Community citizens
      equally, which are dealt with in other chapters.
12   Compared to the present Article 3, the most important innovation brought about after
      the entry into force of the Treaty on Political Union will be the inclusion of the follow-
      ing activities:
      –   measures concerning the entry and movement of persons in the internal market as
          provided for in Article 100c;
      –   the strengthening of economic and social cohesion;
      –   a policy in the sphere of the environment;
      –   the strengthening of the competitiveness of Community industry;
      –   the promotion of research and technological development;
      –   encouragement for the establishment and development of trans-European networks;
      –   a contribution to education and training of quality and to the flowering of the cul -
          tures of the Member States;
      –   a policy in the sphere of development cooperation;
      –   a contribution to the strengthening of consumer protection;
      –   measures in the spheres of energy, civil protection and tourism.

Community's tasks. They shall abstain from any measure which could jeopardize the attainment of the objectives of this Treaty.

As interpreted and applied by the ECJ, this Article is one of the central principles of the EC's constitutional order, constraining the Member States in the fulfilment of their Treaty obligations.[13] Consequently, even if action regarding lesbians and gay men were taken at the national level, the Member States would be bound by Article 5 in so far as such action derived from or related to obligations arising out of the Treaty or resulted from action taken by the Community.

The only provision in Part One which has operative legal effects is Article 7, which prohibits any discrimination on grounds of nationality. Although the scope of this provision may at first sight seem too narrow to be of any real significance for homosexuals, the provision has already been invoked once in circumstances that are of direct importance in this context. In a case which involved the application for a residence permit by the unmarried companion of an English worker in the Netherlands, the European Court was asked to pronounce on the interpretation of the term 'spouse' in Article 10(1)(a) of Regulation 1612/68, which enumerates the categories of persons which have the right to install themselves with a worker who is a national of one Member State and who is employed in the territory of another Member State.[14] Although the Court decided that the term 'spouse' only refers to a marital relationship, it ruled that where Member States grant residence permits to foreign cohabitants of their nationals (which the Court construed as a 'social advantage' within the meaning of Article 7(2) of Regulation 1612/68), Article 7 EEC extends this right to cohabitants of nationals of other Member States.[15] Consequently, the prohibition of discrimination on the grounds of nationality of Article 7 EEC may extend certain rights enjoyed by lesbians and gay men in one Member State to lesbians and gay men of other nationalities within that Member State.

In addition, it may be argued that a more general principle of non-discrimination forms part of the 'constitution' of the Community.[16]

After this review of some general principles, the remainder of this Chapter will be organized as follows. First, those activities enumerated in (the amended) Article 3 which are of *prima facie* importance to lesbians and gay men will be considered, together with the specific and general powers provided in the Treaty to implement these tasks. This review will then be

---

13   For further discussion of this Article and some of its implications, see Temple Lang, 'Community Constitutional Law: Article 5 EEC Treaty,' 27 *CML Rev.* (1990) 645.
14   Case 59/85, *Netherlands v. Ann Florence Reed* [1986] ECR 1283.
15   Article 7(2) of Regulation 1612/68 provides that in the host state a worker who is a national of another Member State must enjoy the same social and tax advantages as national workers.
16   See Chapter Seven by Angela Byre.

followed by a discussion of the principle of subsidiarity. The main aim of this Chapter is to reach conclusions concerning the expected impact with regard to EC policies concerning lesbians and gay men of the inclusion in the Treaty of the principle of subsidiarity.

D. EC Competence and the Interests of Lesbians and Gay Men

Of the activities listed in Article 3, the most relevant for lesbians and gay men is probably the abolition of obstacles to the freedom of movement of persons. The right to move freely within the Community so as to seek employment,[17] or to accept offers of employment actually made, as secured in Article 48, undoubtedly is intended to apply equally to lesbians and gay men as well as to all other workers. In practice, however, lesbians and gay men encounter a number of real and potential obstacles to the exercise of their rights. As is explained in other chapters,[18] these obstacles may result from, *inter alia*, restrictive interpretations of the secondary legislation conferring rights upon the gay workers's 'family',[19] as well as from the margin of discretion left to the national authorities under Article 48(3) to restrict the free movement of workers on the grounds of public policy, public security or public health.[20] There can be little doubt that, as these obstacles hamper the establishment of the internal market (Article 100a and 8a) or the establishment or functioning of the common market (Article 100), the Community has the power and arguably even the duty to propose harmonizing legislation, in accordance with Article 3(h), aimed at removing these obstacles.[21]

---

17   That Article 48(3)(b) also encompasses the right to look for employment was accepted by the Court in Case 48/75, *Procureur du Roi v. Royer* [1976] ECR 497. See more recently, Case C-292/89, *Antonissen* [1991] ECR I-745.

18   See Chapter Twelve by d'Oliveira and Chapter Fourteen by Betten.

19   In particular, in *Reed*, the ECJ limited the term 'spouse' in Article 10(1)(a) of Regulation 1612/68 to a marital relationship only. But see also Chapter Fifteen by Emmert.

20   Cf. Directive 64/221 on the *Co-Ordination of Special Measures Concerning the Movement and Residence of Foreign Nationals which are Justified on Grounds of Public Policy, Public Security or Public Health*. It should be noted, however, that this margin of discretion has been curtailed by the ECJ to an extent that it would seem very doubtful whether there remains any scope for the refusal of a residence permit or its renewal or expulsion from the territory of a worker on the sole ground of his or her sexual orientation. See especially Case 36/75, *Rutili v. French Minister of the Interior* [1975] ECR 1219 and Case 30/77, *R. v. Bouchereau* [1977] ECR 1999, after which restrictions cannot be imposed unless his or her presence or conduct constitutes a 'genuine and sufficiently serious threat to public policy' and the grounds invoked must affect 'one of the fundamental interests of society'. Any restrictions here are likely to be based on a criminal conviction for homosexual activity or HIV status.

21   An example may be provided by Member States' uncoordinated policies aimed at restricting the spread of HIV infection and AIDS which could seriously undermine the free movement of gay workers. It may be argued that the Commission should propose a

The Treaty provisions regarding the freedom of establishment and the freedom to provide services have, generally speaking, been interpreted in a manner analogous to those concerning the free movement of workers. Consequently, the same conclusion in respect of the Community's powers to ensure that lesbians and gay men benefit as well as others from these rights should apply.

The European Social Fund, referred to in Article 3(i), is aimed at improving employment opportunities for workers and to contributing to the raising of their standard of living. It could be made to be of special importance for lesbians and gay men, though at present there are no practical examples of such initiatives. Such an initiative, however, might include a project involving vocational training courses to improve employment opportunities for lesbians and gay men or innovatory projects adopted by the Council.

It is difficult to predict how the EC's 1989 Charter of Basic Social Rights for Workers is to be implemented.[22] However, it offers at least the potential opportunity to devote special attention to the needs of lesbians and gay men in the EC. This seems clear from the following recital:

> Whereas, in order to ensure equal treatment, it is important to combat *every form of discrimination*, including discrimination on grounds of sex, colour, race, opinions and beliefs, and whereas, in a spirit of solidarity, it is important to combat social exclusion.[23]

The Social Charter is a 'soft law' declaration and not a legally binding instrument.[24] This is not to say, however, that it produces no legal effects. Indeed 'soft law' now plays a significant role in the Community system. The Commission has increasingly used 'soft law' in areas where the boundaries of EC competence are not entirely clear, and the distinction between 'soft law' and 'hard law' remain to some extent to be defined.[25] In addition, the European Court of Justice has recognized that recommendations, though lacking legal force under Article 189 EEC, can produce legal effects. More specifically, national courts are bound to take EC recommendations into consideration in order to decide disputes submitted to them, particularly where the recommendations cast light on the interpretation of national measures adopted in order to implement them or where the recommendations are designed to supplement binding Community provisions.[26]

---

harmonizing directive so as to ensure that the free movement of gay workers is safeguarded.

22   See Chapter Seven by Angela Byre. See generally Bercusson, 1990; Hepple, 1990.
23   Community Charter of the Fundamental Social Rights of Workers, Luxembourg, Office for Offical Publications of the European Communities, 1990 at 10 (emphasis added).
24   See Hepple, 1990, 643-654 at 644.
25   See Snyder, *supra* note 1.
26   Case C-322/88, *Grimaldi v. Fonds des Maladies Professionelles* [1989] ECR 4407.

It is also important to note that the Commission considered that the implementation of the Charter did not entail an extension of the Community's powers as defined in the Treaties. This would seem to imply that the Charter, adopted by 11 of the Heads of State or Government of the Member States of the European Community, contains objectives which fall within the ambit of Article 235 in particular, to which we will return briefly below.

Another important area of EC law concerns the free movement of goods, in particular the elimination of customs duties, quantitative restrictions and equivalent measures. It is not possible here to consider this area in detail,[27] but it is worth mentioning that questions may arise as to the extent to which Member States remain free to prohibit products specifically aimed at the lesbian and gay market. Under Article 36 EEC, Member States are entitled to restrict imports if such restrictions can be justified, *inter alia*, on grounds of public morality, public policy or public security'.[28] Any restrictions may not however constitute a means of arbitrary discrimination or a disguised restriction on trade between Member States. In principle, it is for each Member State to determine in accordance with its own scale of values and in the form selected by it, the requirements of public morality in its territory.[29] However, a Member State may not rely on grounds of public morality within the meaning of Article 36 EEC in order to prohibit the importation of certain goods on the ground that they are indecent or obscene when its legislation contains no prohibition on the manufacture and marketing of the same goods on its territory.[30] As with the public policy provisos in Articles 48(3) and 56(1), although the scope of Article 36 has been restricted significantly by the ECJ, frequent reliance on the provision in order to restrict importation of literature may ultimately justify recourse to Article 100a or Article 100.

Any credible policy to establish equal treatment between lesbians and gay men and other European citizens should include education, especially of young people. It is therefore important to note that the amended Article 3 refers to education. However, education is a field in which the competence of the EC has traditionally been questioned.[31] Only in the sphere of incentive measures, especially those which promote movement of students and

27 See Chapter Thirteen by De Witte.
28 Article 36 provides:
    The provisions of Articles 30 to 34 shall not preclude prohibitions or restrictions on imports, exports or goods in transit justified on grounds of public morality, public policy or public security; the protection of health and life of humans, animals or plants; the protection of national treasures possessing artistic, historic or archeological value; or the protecion of industrial and commercial property. Such prohibitions or restrictions shall not, however, constitute a means of arbitrary discrimination or a disguised restriction on trade between Member States.
29 Case 34/79, *Henn & Darby* [1979] ECR 3795.
30 Case 121/85, *Conegate Limited v. HM Customs and Excise* [1986] ECR 1007.
31 See generally De Witte (ed.), 1989; Lonbay, 1989.

teachers, has the Community been able to make inroads. This trend has been codified in the new Treaty.[32] The objectives of EC action to be undertaken are all restricted to exchange of people, ideas and experience and/or the development of a European dimension in education. Any harmonization of laws is specifically excluded.[33] Hence it would appear that – regardless of what Article 3b may entail – a Community education policy aimed at, for example, removing prejudices against lesbians and gay men would find some difficulty in being based on these provisions.

From this brief examination of Community competence to pursue the interests of lesbians and gay men, it might therefore appear that, despite recent amendments, the objective of 'an accelerated raising of the standard of living' leaves little more room for specific EC action than do the instruments previously provided to implement this objective.

However, to the extent that the specific concerns of lesbians and gay men fall within the EC, the mere fact that Article 3 does not refer to all the activities which are necessary for the implementation of these objectives is not in itself a bar to EC action. In such instances the EC has made use of Article 235 EEC, the EEC Treaty's residual powers clause. This Article provides that, if action by the Community should prove necessary to attain, in the course of the operation of the common market, one of the objectives of the Community, and the Treaty has failed to provide the necesssary powers, the Council, acting unanimously on a proposal from the Commission and after consulting the European Parliament, may take the appropriate measures.

Extensive use has been made of this provision, notably in the field of the Community's environmental policy.[34]

An example of how an EC policy aimed at a 'minority' may be legitimized in this way despite the apparent lack of EC competence in that field may be found in the Commission's (relatively unsuccessful) attempts to establish a Community for the disabled. Thus, in its proposals for Decisions concerning vocational training and economic and social integration of people with disabilities, the Commission submitted:

---

[32]   According to the Treaty on European Union Article 126(1) will provide that:
       The Community shall contribute to the development of quality education by en -
       couraging cooperation between Member States and, if necessary, by supporting and
       supplementing their action, while fully respecting the responsibility of the Member
       States for the content of teaching and the organization of education systems and
       their cultural and linguistic diversity.
[33]   Cf. the new Article 126(4)
[34]   See Schwarze, 1978, 614-628.

... disabled people have the same right as all other workers to equal opportunity in training and employment, and ... special measures are needed at Community and national levels if these are to be achieved.[35]

More recently, in its action programme relating to the implementation of the Community Charter of Basic Social Rights for Workers, the Commission has sought a direct link with the more traditional objectives of the Treaty:

> The social and economic integration of disabled people is an important element of the social dimension of the single market to be completed by 1992. It is not only a question of social justice. It is also an *economic* issue in so far as their occupational integration in a regular working environment may often represent an asset for the Community.[36]

The same reasoning, it would appear, could apply to specific policies concerning lesbians and gay men. The statement in the Preamble that the Community is constantly to improve its peoples' working and living conditions could work as a reminder to this effect.

However, an extensive use of Article 235 EEC is unlikely, at least in the short term. This is because of the emerging consensus concerning the desirability of subsidiarity, one function of which is to serve as a safeguard against the further expansion of EC powers and their exercise. It is questionable whether Article 235 will be afforded the same important role as in the past. Recently, it has even been suggested that the provision should be deleted from the Treaty as it no longer accords with current thinking as regards the extent of Community competence.[37]

Another, perhaps more useful precedent for Community action on lesbian and gay issues may be found in the Council Resolution of 29 May 1990 on the Fight Against Racism and Xenophobia.[38] This Resolution refers to the Treaties as a whole, rather than a specific article, as its legal base. Its Preamble emphasizes the importance of the protection of fundamental human rights. It also states that it 'behoves the institutions of the Community and the competent authorities of the Member States, each in keeping with its powers, to take the necessary measures to implement this resolution.[39] The text of the Resolution refers to several relevant legal instruments and states numerous principles, objectives and methods, as well as inviting the Member States to take specific action. This form of

---

35   COM (87) 544 final, 10 November 1987, 5.
36   COM (89) 568 final, 19 November 1989 (emphasis added).
37   Wilke and Wallace, 1990.
38   Resolution of the Council and the Representatives of the Governments of the Member States, meeting within the Council, on 29 May 1990, on the Fight Against Racism and Xenophobia, OJ 1990 C 157/1, 27 June 1990 .
39   Ibid., Preamble, 9th recital.

Community 'soft law', recognizing the respective roles of the EC and the Member States, may provide a most useful model for EC and national action regarding lesbian and gay rights.

E. The Impact of Subsidiarity on the Exercise of EC Powers

1. The Wording of the Maastricht Treaty

Subsidiarity is a principle of choice as to the allocation of the exercise of decision-making power. In order to understand when the principle of subsidiarity applies, it is helpful to begin with the wording of the Maastricht Treaty. According to Article 3b inserted by the Maastricht Treaty, subsidiarity comes into play when two conditions are fulfilled: first, the EC and the Member States have concurrent competence; and, second, the objectives of the proposed action can be sufficiently achieved by the Member States, bearing in mind in particular the scale and effects of the proposed action. As this interpretation is based on reading the words negatively, it may be helpful to follow the Treaty words exactly, in other words, first to identify the domain in which the principle of subsidiarity does *not* apply.

The principle of subsidiarity does not apply in two instances: (i) it does not apply if the EC alone has legal competence; so there is no room for Member State action; (ii) it does not apply if the Member States alone have legal competence. Such an interpretation does not follow from a strict interpretation of the precise words of Article 3b, but commonsense and legal logic would both seem to indicate that in the latter case there is no room for EC action.

The principle of subsidiarity only applies when the EC and the Member States both are legally competent to act, in other words in those domains in which the EC and the Member States have concurrent powers. Here the EC shall act 'only if and insofar as the objectives of the proposed action cannot be sufficiently achieved by the Member States and can therefore, by reason of the scale or effects of the proposed action, be better achieved by the Community' (Article 3b). In all other instances the principle of subsidiarity applies: that is, the action is to be taken not by the EC but instead by the Member States.

The wording of the principle of subsidiarity in Article 3b of the Maastricht Treaty thus reverses what has often seemed in the past to be the presumption as to the appropriate level for legal action. It gives weight to the argument that EC intervention may now be viewed as *a priori* undesirable. This reversal of the presumption constitutes a striking departure from the final Dutch draft of the provision. The latter provided:

The Community shall take action, in accordance with the principle of subsidiarity, only if, and insofar as, these objectives can be better achieved by the Community than by the Member States acting separately, by reason of the scale or effects of the proposed action.

The negative form adopted at Maastricht would seem to leave very little room left for the application of the principle in its 'positive' sense, as advanced recently by Ranjault.[40]

2. Ambiguity and Interpretation

The principle (or concept) of subsidiarity in the Maastricht Treaty, as already noted, does not yet have any precise, universally accepted meaning. It has been suggested that the ambiguity of the principle has been one of its most valuable features. It has facilitated the building of a consensus on the general direction of the EC in the decades to come.

The idea that uncertainty as to the meaning or implications of certain fundamental principles or concepts in a legal and political order may actually facilitate efforts to reach agreement on substantive provisions is widely accepted among political scientists. For example, Brennan and Buchanan observe that

to the extent that a person faced with constitutional choice remains uncertain as to what his [or her] position will be under seperate choice options, he [or she] will tend to agree on arrangements that might be called 'fair' in the sense that patterns of outcomes generated under such arrangements will be broadly acceptable, regardless of where the participant might be located in such outcomes'[41]

Similarly, this 'veil of uncertainty' has been advanced as an important factor in explaining the formation of international regimes, or loose regulatory schemes, concerning the environment.[42]

For the same reason, the inclusion of the principle of subsidiarity has eventually enabled the adoption of the Treaty on European Union. Viewed from this perspective, it can be argued that the principle already has served its purpose.

However, with the elevation of subsidiarity as a principle justiciable by the ECJ under Article 173, the ambiguity of the concept is no longer

40   Cf. Ranjault, 1992, 49 arguing:
         ... subsidiarity refers not only to the idea of intervention 'at second hand', i.e. action to supplement (and arisising from) incapacities and failings by the lower group, and only in proportion to such incapacities and failings – but also to the idea of necessary support or protection, which means supplementary action as soon as the need for it makes itself felt, and in particular as soon as human dignity is deemed to be insufficiently secure.
41   Brennan and Buchanan, 29-30.
42   Young, 1989, Vol. 43, No. 3.

necessarily a virtue. Rather, as the legality of future Community legislation may be judged by the Court with Article 3b as a yardstick, the question as to the precise application of subsidiarity to individual cases can no longer be ignored. In these circumstances, the adequacy of the principle has been the subject of numerous views. It is useful briefly to contrast two positions.

On the one hand, well aware of the fact that the devil is usually to be found in the detail, many have been sceptical, if not cynical, as to appropriateness of the principle. Thus, the United Kingdom House of Lords Select Committee on the European Communities remarked:

> The Committee do not believe that subsidiarity can be used as a precise measure against which to judge legislation. The test of subsidiarity can never be wholly objective or consistent over time – different people regard collective action as more effective than individual action in different circumstances. Properly used, subsidiarity should determine not whether Community legislation is necessary or appropriate at all, but also the extent to which it should regulate or harmonize national divergencies, and how it should be enforced. But to leave legislation open to annulment or revision by the European Court on such subjective grounds, would lead to immense confusion and uncertainty in Community law.[43]

Numerous well respected scholars have voiced similar concern about the legal problems surrounding the application of the principle of subsidiarity.[44]

On the other hand, despite these warnings, subsidiarity has now been formulated in legally binding terms. Consequently, an attempt must be undertaken to examine the possible implications of the principle for the exercise of the Community powers to take action in the sphere of lesbian and gay concerns. From this standpoint, the principle of subsidiarity resembles many fundamental principles of constitutional law. The generality, vagueness or ambiguity of such principles rarely, if ever, prevent the judiciary or the administration from defining (or attempting to define) and applying them in individual instances. Indeed, the ambiguity of the principle may be an advantage in making it possible to legitimate different policies, to

---

43   30 October 1990, HMSO HL paper 88, 1.
44   See Heintzen, 'Subsidiaritätsprinzip und Europäische Gemeinschaft', 7 *Juristen Zeitung* Vol. 46 (1991) 318:

> Es kann angesichts dessen nicht ausgeschlossen werden, daß die Verankerung des Subsidiaritätsprinzips in den EG-Vertragen möglicherweise das Gegenteil dessen bewirkt, was man damit eigentlich bezweckt, daß sie nämlich weiteren Kompetenz-verlagerungen auf die Gemeinschaft Vorschub leistet mit dem Argument, die Gemeinschaft könne eine bestimmte Aufgabe wirkungsvoller erfüllen als die Mitglied-staaten je für sich'. [In the light of this, one cannot exclude the possibility that the incorporation of the subsidiarity principle into the EC Treaty will have the opposite effect from that intended; namely, it runs against the argument that the further shift in competence to the Community makes the Community more capable of perform-ing a specific task than are the Member States themselves at present.]

facilitate shifts in policy, and to enable the political, legal and social order in question to change and develop.

Currently, however, it is neither realistic nor feasible to attempt to apply – at least in the abstract – the principle of subsidiarity to the specific areas of EC competence set out above. Given the imprecise formulation of the principle, it must be agreed with Wallace and Wilke that:

> The Court can enunciate principles and settle individual cases. It cannot prevent differences of political interpretation and it must (if the rule of law is to be respected) move with the grain of changing economic and social realities. So no treaty text could define once and for all the boundaries between EC powers, member states' powers and concurrent powers. These issues depend at the end of the day on political judgment and political negotiation.[45]

This does not of course mean that the principle of subsidiarity would not apply in specific instances in the future. For example, it has been proposed that the Commission, the Council and the European Parliament adopt an Inter-Institutional Agreement setting out their definition of subsidiarity and its implications for EC action. Such an Agreement would be legally binding on the institutions but would probably not be legally enforceable by individuals. Once it is established that the EC and the Member States have concurrent competence to act with regard to a specific matter, it is not predetermined which level of government would in fact exercise its powers. As a preliminary guideline, however, it is useful to examine briefly the history of the concept of subsidiarity and several analogues in current EC law which are intended to serve similar purposes.

3. History and Current EC Law as Guidelines

A general idea of the impact of the principle of subsidiarity may be gained by a brief enquiry into the historical and legal precedents of the principle. Academic writings on the subject of subsidiarity usually credit Pope Pius XI with the first use of the notion. In his Encyclical Letter *Quadragesimo Anno* (1931) it was argued:

> It is an injustice, a grave evil and a disturbance of right order for a larger and higher society to arrogate to itself functions which can be performed efficiently by smaller and lower societies. This is a fundamental principle of social philosophy, unshaken and unchangeable.[46]

45   Wilke and Wallace, *supra* note 37, at 10.
46   Pius XI, 1931.

However, early 19th century manifestations of the principle have been found[47] and more generally, the underlying ideas may be said to be reflected in Thomastic philosophy.

Even though the origins of the principle of subsidiarity can thus be traced back to a variety of socio-political currents and philosophies, the sudden prominence of 'subsidiarity' in the European debate stems primarily from one concern: that of the unfettered expansion of the EC's exercise of its legal competence (especially based on Article 235), frequently at the expense of national, regional or local power. Or, in the words of Commissioner Millan, subsidiarity refers 'to the need to ensure that political decisions are not taken at any higher level than they need to be.'[48] Related to this prime concern are the fears that, first, the increasing exercise by the EC of its legally attributed powers will in fact lead to the expansion of the EC's legal competence; and, second, the expansion of EC involvement will necessarily result in increased uniformity, leaving no room for regional or national diversity.

It is not surprising that the most ardent support for the inclusion of subsidiarity amongst the EC's principles comes from the German *Länder*, which have long voiced complaints about an EC encroaching upon areas constitutionally reserved to them.[49] Indeed, a meeting convened by the *Länder* in Bonn in 1988 at which subsidiarity featured high on the agenda and which – significantly – was attended by the President of the Commission, Jacques Delors, is generally regarded as a turning point in the Commission's attitude towards the concept.

It would however be misconceived to consider that subsidiarity is the first or only EC response to these concerns. The need to allow for regional and national diversity, for example, has been safeguarded by numerous provisions, especially those introduced by the Single European Act, such as Articles 8c, 100a(4), 118(3) and 130t. Even before the Single European Act, the ECJ elaborated the principles of 'mutual recognition' and the so-called 'mandatory requirements', as legal devices designed to facilitate economic integration while simultaneously enabling Member States to maintain their own national measures within certain limits. The jurisprudence of the ECJ also offers other significant examples of such realism. As has been seen, in the *Reed* case the Court based its view that the term 'spouse' refers exlusively to marital relationships on differing national traditions.

---

47   Hofmeister, 1982.
48   Millan, Speech at Paisley College, 20 April 1990 as quoted from Spicker, *infra* note 51, at 3.
49   Classical examples are the broadcasting directive and various Community programmes in the field of education and training. For the German view on subsidiarity see for example Schelter, 1991, 138-140.

In any event, the underlying concerns which led eventually to the inclusion of the principle of subsidiarity in the Treaty are an important factor in the interpretation of the principle. There can be little doubt that the principle of subsidiarity is intended to minimize EC intervention unless no effective alternatives, within the scope of the Treaty language, are available. This is an important observation as definitions of subsidiarity based on a concept of 'effectiveness' (along the lines of the present Article 130r(4)) may actually stimulate the centralization of competence.[50]

Due to its roots in social and moral theory, the concept (now principle) of subsidiarity has proved a much more pursuasive argument against the expansion of EC competence or the exercise of EC powers than has the notion of 'sovereignty'.[51] Spicker correctly points out that the kind of measures which the Commission has proposed succesfully in the past with the prime objective of establishing a precedent for future action in a new policy field are likely to be the first victims of the principle of subsidiarity.[52] It may therefore be suggested that the incorporation of the principle of subsidiarity, as defined in the Maastricht Treaty, into EC constitutional law may be expected to hamper considerably any prospects for the incremental development of a general EC 'policy' aimed specifically at lesbians and gay men. The specific implications of this suggestion are elaborated somewhat more in the Conclusion (Chapter Ten). The extent to which the principle of subsidiarity may permit national authorities not to act at all, however, remains unclear. Nonetheless it may be suggested that a refusal by Member States to act in an area of concurrent competence would be tantamount to a demonstration that the objectives could not be sufficiently

50   For example Heintzen, *supra* note 44, at 320:
      Allgemeine Subsidiaritätsklauseln sind juristisch von zweifelhaftem Wert. Das Sub-
      sidiaritätsprinzip ist auf die Umsetzung in einer präzise ausformulierten justiziablen,
      nach Organisationseinheiten, Staatsfunktionen und Sachmaterien differenzierenden
      Kompetenzordnung angewiesen. Es bezeichnet ein Problem, enthält aber nicht die
      Lösung (...)
      [The legal value of general subsidiarity clauses is dubious. The principle of sub-
      sidiarity aims at a change in a precisely defined, justiciable and differentiated divi-
      sion of competence. Yet it reveals a problem without giving any answers...] Simi-
      larly, Geelhoed; Mackenzie-Stuart, 1991. See also the extremely extensive interpre-
      tation of what can be 'better' attained by the Community by Kramer, 'The Single
      European Act and Environmental Protection: Reflections on Several New Provisions
      in Community Law', *CML Rev.* Vol. 24 (1987) 665.
51   Cf. Spicker, 1 *Journal of European Social Policy*, Vol. 1 (1991) 10 remarking:
      But the idea of sovereignty is a blunt instrument, and those who wish to maintain
      their power and authority by opposing the extention of bus passes can be made to
      feel foolish in referring to it. (...) By contrast with sovereignty, the idea of
      'subsidiarity' is rooted in a rich, complex body of social theory with a strong moral
      foundation.
52   Spicker, ibid., at 10, using bus passes for the elderly and measures relating to cigarette
      packets as examples were the Commission attempts to incrementally establish a
      foothold in a certain policy field.

achieved by the Member States. If the action met the tests of scale or effects in the terms of Article 3b, it could also be suggested that the Community would be entitled to act in order to fulfil Community objectives. In this event, the Community action might involve recourse to the traditional means of EC actions, such as seeking to harmonize national legislation. Even in such case, however, the form of Community action will have to meet the test of proportionality expressed in the last sentence of Article 3b, that is, that it should be the least restrictive alternative means which is effective to achieve the objective in view.

Chapter Nine
The Community as Employer
Staff Regulations: an Aspect of European
Community Law and its Relevance to Lesbians
and Gay Men

by

FRANCIS SNYDER
with the collaboration of HAN SOMSEN and HENRIK DUEDAHL HOYER

Table of Contents

I. Introduction

This Chapter is concerned with the EC as an employer. It considers the EC's Staff Regulations, the formal name of which is the *Staff Regulations of Officials and the Conditions of Employment of Other Servants of the European Communities*. They are the rules determining the mutual rights and obligations of staff in the EC institutions. The Staff Regulations are composed of a series of Council regulations; the later ones are essentially modifications and amendments to the original.[1]

The Staff Regulations are extremely complex, and space limitations make it impossible to attempt a comprehensive survey of the subject. The purpose of this Part is rather to illustrate, by way of example, some of the ways in which the role of the EC as employer may affect the specific interests of lesbians and gay men. The following discussion is not concerned, except in passing, with the effects on lesbians and gay men of the basic EC principles concerning the free movement of workers; these principles are dealt with in other chapters.

II. Coverage

The Staff Regulations apply mainly to officials of the EC institutions. But the term 'official' is neither clear nor comprehensive. Similarly, the term 'institution of the European Communities' is also ambiguous.

The question as to who is an official of the EC is dealt with in Article 1 of the Staff Regulations. This Article was interpreted in *Vittorio Salerno and others v. Commission and Council.*[2] There the ECJ[3] said:

> With regard more particularly to the applicant's argument that they have been officials or servants of the Commission since they were engaged by the EAC (European Association for Cooperation), it must be pointed out that the first paragraph of Article 1 of the Staff Regulations of the Officials of the European Communities, provides that 'Official of the Communities' means any person, who has been appointed, as provided for in the Staff Regulations, to an

---

1   The first basic Staff Regulation was applicable from 5 March 1968, as laid down by Articles 2 and 3 of Council Regulation (EEC, EURATOM, ECSC) No. 259/68 of 29 February 1968 (OJ 1968 L 56): Council Regulation (EEC, Euratom, ECSC) 259/68 laying down the staff regulations of the Officials and the conditions of Employment of Other Servants of the European Communities and instituting special measures temporarily applicable to officials of the Commission (Staff Regulations Officials), OJ 1968 L 56/1. Since then it has been modified and amended on numerous occasions.
2   Joined Cases 87 and 130/77 and 22/83 and 9 and 10/84 [1985] ECR 2523.
3   The Court of First Instance now has jurisdiction with regard to disputes arising under the Staff Regulations. See Council Decision 88/591, OJ 1989 C 215/1.

established post on the staff of one of the Institutions of the Communities by an instrument issued by the appointing authority of that institution.

This case confirmed the distinction drawn by the Staff Regulations between the two basic groupings of EC employees, Officials and Other Servants. In order to involve an official, the employment relation must be established by means of an administrative act as described above. In contrast, the other servants of the European Communities are engaged by contract. The great majority of staff on the operating budget are permanent officials, although the budget also includes temporary posts.[4]

The group of persons who are covered by the Staff Regulations is in fact even more more extensive. Not everyone employed by the EC is taken on as an official. The rules governing temporary staff, auxiliary staff, special advisers and local staff[5] are not identical. In addition, for example, when people are married,[6] their spouses and children may be concerned, as may any person for whom the official has a legal responsibility to maintain and whose maintenance involves heavy expenditure may, exceptionally, be covered.[7] The question as to whether such rules referring to spouses apply to lesbian and gay partnerships has not, so far as is known, been answered. Moreover, special rules govern staff employed by the Commission outside the EC, eg. Washington, Tokyo. Furthermore, a person trying to become an official, by applying for a competition, is covered to the extent that, if dissatisfied, he or she may submit a claim.[8] Finally, the Staff Regulations also contain a pension scheme,[9] so pensioners are also covered. In fact, the Staff Regulations are so extensive that it extends beyond the officials lifetime by offering pensions to the officials widow(er)s[10] and orphans.[11] Again, the extent to which they apply to the partnerships of lesbians or gay men does not seem to be clear.

It is also necessary to refer briefly to the institutions covered by the Staff Regulations. The contemporary EC is the result of a merger of the institutions of the original three Communities: the European Coal and Steel Community,[12] the European Economic Community and the European

---

4   Hay, 1989, 35.
5   Section two of the Staff Regulations sets out the 'Conditions of employment of other servants of the European Communities'.
6   An example involving this term is discussed below.
7   Article 72 of the Staff Regulations Officials.
8   Case 52/85, [1986] 1555.
9   Article 77-84 and Annex VIII in the Staff Regulations Officials together with Article 33 paragraph 4 and Article 39 paragraph 2 of the 'Conditions of employment of other servants of the European Communities.
10   Article 79-79a in the Staff Regulation Officials and Article 36 in 'Condition of employment of other servants'.
11   Article 80 of the Staff Regulation Officials and Article 37 in the 'Conditions of Employment of other servants of the European Communities'.
12   The ECSC Treaty was signed on 18 April 1951 and entered into force on 25 July 1952.

Atomic Energy Community.[13] The Communities remain legally distinct, each being based on a separate treaty, but they share the same institutions, the officials and other servants of which are covered by the same Staff Regulations.

Currently there are six major EC institutions: the Commission, the Council of Ministers, the European Parliament, the Court of Justice (ECJ and Court of First Instance), the Court of Auditors and the Economic and Social Committee. For the present purposes, it is assumed that the general remarks in this Part will also apply, *mutatis mutandis*, to any new institutions which may result from the Maastricht Treaty.

According to Article 1 of the Staff Regulations, the Staff Regulations shall apply to the Institutions of the European Communities (the European Parliament, the Council, the Commission and the ECJ.) Article 1, paragraph 2, states that: 'Save as otherwise provided, the Economic and Social Committee and the Court of Auditors shall, for the purpose of these Staff Regulations, be treated as Institutions of the European Communities'. It should be noted that there have been several cases[14] in which it was argued that the Staff Regulations did not extend to the Economic and Social Committee or to the Court of Auditors. In all the cases the applicants' submissions were held to be unfounded. The Staff Regulations also concern the European Investment Bank.

III. Outline of Contents

The Staff Regulations have four main sections:

I – Staff regulations of the officials of the European Communities;
II – Conditions of employment of other servants of the European Communities;
III – other regulations of the Council/ of the Councils applicable to the officials and other servants of the European Communities; and
IV – Rules drawn up by agreement between the Institutions of the European Communities and applicable to officials and other servants of the European Communities.

The Staff Regulations are divided into distinct subject areas. For example, the Staff Regulations for officials start with some general provisions[15] which lay down basic notions, rules and principles. They define the status of an official,[16] the authority in the institution which takes decisions

---

13 Both the EEC and the EAEC Treaty was signed in Rome on 25 March 1957 and entered into force on 1 January 1958.
14 Under Article 1(2), Staff Regulations Officials.
15 Article 1-10a, Staff Regulations Officials.
16 Article 5, Staff Regulations Officials.

affecting the official, how a vacancy must be published before it is filled,[17] and the placing of an official in a grid of categories and grades on which his/her pay is ultimately based. One the most important provisions[18] mentions the principle of equality, to which recruitment is stated to be subject.

It should be noted that the principle of equality is not stated in the same terms or so directly with regard to the terms and conditions of employment as it is with regard to recruitment. No specific provisions appear to concern training. With regard to promotion, Article 43 provides that the ability, efficiency and conduct in the service of each official, with the exception of Grades A1 and A2, shall be the subject of a periodic report at least once every two years. The report must be communicated to the official, who is entitled to make any comments which he or she deems relevant. Advancement from one step to another within a grade is automatic every two years. (Article 44). According to Article 45, promotion is by decision of the appointing authority. With regard to dismissal the grounds for termination of employment are resignation, compulsory resignation, retirement in the interests of the service, dismissal for incompetence, removal from post, retirement, or death (Article 47). An official may be required to resign only *inter alia* (a) where he or she ceases to fulfil specified conditions, including producing the appropriate character reference as to his or her suitability for the performance of his or her duties (Article 49(8), 1st paragraph; Article 28(c)); or (b) where the spouse of an official is in gainful employment, the official's appointing authority considers that the nature of the employment is incompatible with that of the official, and the official is unable to give an undertaking that it will cease within a specified period (Article 49, 2nd para; Article 13). Reasoned decisions requiring officials to resign must be taken by the appointing authority after consulting the Joint Committee and hearing the official concerned (Article 49, 2nd paragraph). Article 50 provides that an official in Grades A1 or A2 may be retired in the interests of the service; no details are specified for this ground. It should also be noted that the Staff Regulations provide for the setting up, within each institution, of a Staff Committee, Joint Committees, Disciplinary Boards and a Reports Committee, which are intended, respectively, to represent the interests of the staff, be consulted on specified occasions, to be consulted in disciplinary proceedings and to provide opinions. Elaborate procedures are established for dealing with requests and complaints.

---

17   Article 4, Staff Regulations Officials. On the other hand there is no requirement to advertise vacant posts which are temporary. These posts often go to people who have good connections to the European Communities or to people who are located close to the Institutions of the European Communities and who therefore are not necessarily the best qualified candidates.

18   Article 7 together with Article 27. Article 27(2) says: 'Officials shall be selected without reference to race, creed or sex'.

A further section is entitled 'rights and obligations'.[19] The Staff Regulations lay down that an official must do his or her job properly, be discreet and be independent of outside influence or authorities. The official can also ask the institution to come to his or her assistance in specified instances. The Staff Regulations then deal with 'careers'[20] recruitment,[21] administrative status,[22] promotion[23] and termination of service.[24] One of the fundamental rules mentioned under administrative status is that the official may find himself or herself in one of five so-called positions, including activity (the most common), secondment and leave on personal grounds.

Title IV is concerned with working conditions (hours of work, leave and holidays);[25] examples of these provisions are given below. The final sections of the Staff Regulations deal with pay and social security benefits when the official is ill or has an accident, as well as the reimbursement of expenses arising on taking up appointment.[26] There are sections on pensions,[27] discipline[28] and complaints.[29]

These last provisions enable a person to request a decision by the administration (requests procedure) or to contest a decision already taken (complaints procedure). If all else fails, the official can go to the Court of First Instance by using Articles 90 and 91 of the Staff Regulations. The Court also has the task of resolving disputes between institutions of the EC and their employees. Article 179 EEC lays down that the Court of Justice has jurisdiction in any dispute between the Community and its servants within the limits and under the conditions laid down in the Staff Regulations or the conditions of employment. Appeals based on Article 179 of the EEC Treaty are subject to the time limits laid down in Articles 90 and 91 of the Staff Regulations.[30] It should be pointed out that Article 90 (2) of the Staff Regulations, in conjunction with Article 91, makes the admissibility of proceedings under Article 179 EEC subject to the condition that the contested measure should have adversely affected the applicant and that only those measures which are capable of directly affecting a specific legal situation may be regarded as adversely affecting the person concerned.[31]

---

19   Staff Regulations Officials, Articles 11-26.
20   Staff Regulations Officials, Articles 27-54.
21   Staff Regulations Officials, Articles 27-34.
22   Staff Regulations Officials, Articles 35-42.
23   Staff Regulations Officials, Articles 43-46.
24   Staff Regulations Officials, Articles 47-54.
25   Staff Regulations Officials, Articles 55-61.
26   Staff Regulations Officials, Articles 63-85a.
27   Staff Regulations Officials, Articles 77-84.
28   Staff Regulations Officials, Articles 86-89.
29   Staff Regulations Officials, Articles 90-91.
30   Case 257/85, *Dufay v. Parliament* [1987] ECR 1561, at. 21.
31   Joined Cases 269 and 292/84, *Fabro v. Commission* [1985] ECR 2983, at 9.

For officials who occupy posts in the field of nuclear science calling for scientific or technical qualifications, there is a special Title VIII – special provisions applicable to officials in the scientific or technical services of the communities.[32]

Finally, the Staff Regulations lay down a procedure for the adoption of inter-institutional subordinate rules, although the institution may also adopt its own subordinate rules to give effect to the Staff Regulations.[33]

IV. EC Staff, Recruitment and Career Structure

The staff of the EC are drawn from all twelve Member States. As of the 1989 Budget, the EC employed 23,432 staff. This total was divided by institutions as follows:

Commission: 16,309; Council: 2,165; European Parliament: 3,405; Court of Justice: 682; Court of Auditors: 377; and Economic and Social Committee: 494.

Each institution can hire staff independently, though sometimes other institutions share recruitment procedures with the Commission. Most recruitment[34] to the institutions is by open competitions held in all twelve Member States. Notices of competitions are published in the Official Journal of the European Communities and competitions are usually advertised in the main daily papers in the Member States. The competitions are held in all of the nine Community languages, based exclusively on qualitative criteria. The rules require that recruitment is to be conducted in as objective a manner as possible. No discrimination is allowed on the basis of race, creed or sex.[35] It should be clear that this provision should also prohibit discrimination on the ground that the applicant is a lesbian or a gay man, but there is no express legal provision to this effect, nor do there appear to be any judicial decisions which expressly consider the issue.

The recruitment procedure is normally in three stages. The first stage consists of multiple-choice eliminatory tests. These cover reasoning power; knowledge of the field covered by the competition and of current, particularly Community affairs; and knowledge of a second language. The second stage is a test of analytical and drafting ability. If a candidate is successful in both these written stages, the third stage is an oral test and, where

32 Staff Regulations Officials, Articles 92-101.
33 Staff Regulations Officials, Articles 102-110.
34 Staff Regulations Officials, Articles 27-34 concern recruitment and Annex III concerns competitions.
35 Staff Regulations Officials, Article 27. This may apply by analogy to the conditions of employment of other servants of the European Community, although not expressly mentioned there.

appropriate, a practical test (e.g., for secretarial posts). Like the written tests, the oral test is carried out in the candidate's native language, but the Selection Board may also check on his or her ability to speak a second language.

After passing these three stages, the successful candidates are placed on a reserve list. Listing does not guarantee the offer of a post. This will depend on the specific professional requirements of the various services and on the candidate's individual qualifications.

In principle, there are no national quotas,[36] but nationality may be decisive provided that it is first established by comparative examination that the qualification of candidates are clearly the same.[37] In practice there is a broad geographical and national[38] balance;[39] Nationality can be decisive when it is necessary to maintain or reestablish a geographical balance.[40] Judicial review of such matters is limited to ensuring that the exercise of discretion was within reasonable limits and not manifestly incorrect, but nationality is secondary, and only where merits and qualifications are equal may it be taken into account as one factor.[41] Generally, up to 60% of successful candidates will be offered posts before the expiry of the list, which normally has an overall validity of two to three years. Once taken on, an official is usually covered by the Staff Regulations.[42]

EC staff have a common career structure. It comprises four categories of staff corresponding to the minimum educational qualifications required[43] for entry to each: D category – primary certificate; C category – secondary educational qualifications; B category – university entrance level qualifications; and A and LA category – university degree.

Category A has mainly administrative functions. Category B is the executive grade. Category C is mainly the secretarial and clerical grade, and category D carries out service and manual functions. There is also an LA category for interpreters and translators. Each category is divided into grades, corresponding to different levels of responsibility. Category A has 8 grades, L/A has 6 grades, B and C each have 5 grades, D has 4 grades.

---

36   Staff Regulations, Article 7 says: 'that the appointing authority shall, acting solely in the interest of the service and without regard to nationality, assign each official by appointment...', and Article 27 says: 'no posts shall be reserved for nationals of any specific Member State'.
37   Case 85/82, *Schloh v. Council* [1983] ECR 2105.
38   Article 27(1) in the Staff Regulations Officials says: 'Recruitment shall be directed to securing for the institution the services of officials of the highest standard of ability, efficiency and integrity, recruited on the broadest possible geographical basis from among nationals of Member States of the Communities'.
39   Hay, 1989, 59.
40   Case 15/63, *Lassalle v. EP* [1964] ECR 31
41   Case 282/81, *Ragusa v. Commission* [1983] ECR 1245.
42   Staff Regulations Officials, Article 1.
43   Staff Regulations Officials, Article 5.

Each grade has two steps or grades.[44] In turn, each grade is divided into a limited number of salary steps over which advancement takes place every two years. Officials may be promoted from one grade to the next, after a minimum period in each grade. By internal competitions officials can move to a higher category.

The organizationnal hierarchy may be illustrated by the example of the EC Commission. The basic management structure is that a department inside a Directorate General is headed by an A3, A4 or sometimes even A5, official. Staff are grouped into these departments, in accordance with their different tasks and responsibilities. The head of unit will usually be under the authority of a director (A2), who in turn will normally report to a director-general (A1) who represents the highest level that an official may reach in each institution.

Pay scales[45] for Community servants are decided by the Member States meeting in the Council of Ministers in September every year.[46] The level is adjusted in accordance with movements in the levels of pay of national public servants. Pay is subject to tax (with a maximum rate of 45%), of which the proceeds are paid directly into the Community budget. Any other income a Community official may have is subject to national taxation in the country from which he or she was recruited. There was however an additional 'crisis levy' (an additional temporary tax, introduced in July 1981,[47] to contribute towards the costs of the economic crisis) which was deducted from salaries at a variable level that for most senior staff was 7.62%.[48]

V. Working Conditions and Related Matters

The Staff Regulations provide in detail for working conditions and related matters for officials and other servants, for example, hours of work, leave and public holidays. They also provide for emoluments and social security benefits, including remuneration and expenses, social security benefits, pensions and other matters. Detailed provisions governing these topics are set forth in annexes. For example, Annex VII covers remuneration and reimbursement of expenses, including such pre-requisites as installation allowance, removal allowance and others.

---

44   Staff Regulations Officials, Article 5.
45   Staff Regulations Officials, Articles 62-70a. Conditions of employment of other servants, Articles 19-27 (Temporary staff), Articles 61-69 (Auxiliary staff), Article 79 (Local staff), Article 82 (Special advisers).
46   Staff Regulations Officials, Article 65. Conditions of employment of other servants, Article 20 (Temporary staff), Article 64 (Auxiliary staff).
47   Initially only for a ten year period.
48   Hay, 1989.

In view of the complexity of the Staff Regulations, two examples will suffice to illustrate matters specifically affecting lesbians and gay men. Provided that certain conditions are satisfied, an official is entitled to family allowances. Such allowances include, *inter alia*, a household allowance (see Article 67(1)(a)). The amount and the conditions for receipt of the household allowance are provided in Annex VI, Article 1. This section provides that the household allowance shall be granted to (a) a married official; (b) an official who is widowed, divorced, legally separated or unmarried and has one or more dependent children; or (c) by special reasoned decision of the appointing authority based on supporting documents, an official who, while not fulfilling the conditions laid down in (a) and (b), nevertheless actually assumes family responsibilities. These conditions do not expressly include or exclude a household composed of lesbians or gay men; they would be included under (c). It should be noted however that this would require a special procedure, which differs and would appear to be more onerous than that applicable to the first two categories.

A second example asks whether a lesbian or gay male partner would be included within the term 'spouse' or any similar term. The Staff Regulations often define access to emoluments and other benefits in such terms. In Denmark two persons of the same sex may have their partnership registered.[49] The relevant Danish legislation raises several difficult issues. According to Section 2 Subsection (ii), 'A partnership can only be registered if both or one of the partners is domiciled in Denmark and has Danish Citizenship'. The requirement of Danish citizenship is likely to be found incompatible with EC law, in particular Article 7 EEC.

More problematic, however, and directly relevant to the concerns of this chapter, is the potential effect of the Danish legislation within the context of the Staff Regulations. The legal effect of a registration is set out in Sections 3 and 4. Section 3 states that

> With the exceptions mentioned in section 4, the registration of a partnership shall have the same legal effect as marriage...

One of the exemption clauses states that: 'Provisions in international treaties shall not be applicable to registered partnerships without the assent of the other contracting parties'. Consider the hypothetical example of an EC official, legally registered in Denmark with a person of the same sex, who claims that he or she is entitled to the same treatment under the Staff Regulations as a married official in a heterosexual partnership. Would the provision in Danish legislation to the effect that the partnership is to have the same legal effect as marriage be conclusive, or accepted, for the purpose

---

49   A law to provide for Registered Partnership was adopted by the Folketing (Danish Parliament) on 26 May 1989 and came into force on 1 October 1989.

of the Staff Regulations? What of the exemption clause, in respect of provisions in international treaties? Should the Staff Regulations be considered as a 'provision in an international treaty'? These questions illustrate some of the difficulties potentially faced by lesbians and gay men with regard to the Staff Regulations.[50]

---

50   It should be noted that the ECJ's definitions of 'spouse' have so far been reached within the context of the Treaty provisions on the free movement of workers. It is likely that such definitions would also be applied for the purposes of the Staff Regulations. However, the differences in the two contexts might mean that the use of the Staff Regulations of definitions of 'spouse' given for the purpose of the free movement of workers may be inappropriate. As is well-known, the ECJ often gives special emphasis to differences in context in interpreting identical words in two legal instruments, leading to the conclusion that each context requires its specific definition.

Chapter Ten
Conclusions of Chapters 8 and 9

by

FRANCIS SNYDER
with the collaboration of HAN SOMSEN and HENRIK DUEDAHL HOYER

Chapters Eight and Nine have aimed to provide an overview of two aspects of EC law in so far as they affect lesbians and gay men. The principle of subsidiarity now forms an essential part of the EC constitutional order. The Staff Regulations, though based on the Treaty, constitute a special code of employment for EC officials and other servants. Each of these legal instruments or concepts may affect lesbians and gay men. Although the impact in each case is not at all certain, it is likely to raise very complex legal issues. In most instances there is very little by way of precedent or guideline to help one find one's way, especially since the principle of subsidiarity in its present form is novel in EC law and since the Staff Regulations are relatively unknown except to a handful of specialists. It may be useful nevertheless to try to draw some brief conclusions.

With regard to the principle of subsidiarity, it is important to state that it follows from the EC's objectives, especially after ratification of the Maastricht Treaty, that the EC's aims encompass the protection of the interests of its lesbian and gay citizens. There can be no doubt that the realization of this objective may require the adoption of measures at EC level.

If we examine the powers in the Treaty to attain this objective, we can distinguish two groups of competence. The first group includes those powers which derive primarily from the objective of eliminating obstacles that directly affect the establishment or functioning of the internal market. These powers are found especially in Articles 100 and 100a. The other group comprises a residual category empowering the EC to take more comprehensive action on behalf of lesbians and gay men, based on Article 235 of the Treaty. The implementation of the objectives of the Social Charter, for example, may require recourse to this provision.

The impact of the principle of subsidiarity on the actual exercise of these powers would seem to differ as between these two categories.

The first group of measures, aimed primarily at removing obstacles to the establishment or functioning of the internal market created by discrimination against lesbians and gay men, should survive the test of subsidiarity laid down in Article 3b. That is, the EC may exercise its powers in these matters without any serious effects resulting from the principle of subsidiarity. These obstacles, by their very nature, cannot be removed by the Member States individually, and therefore 'by reason of the scale or effects' they should be dealt with at EC level.

The impact of the test of subsidiarity would be much more profound were the EC to propose, for example, a programme aimed at the social integration of lesbians and gay men in the EC. Such a programme would by no means be inconsistent with the EC's wider objectives. Perhaps the most obvious way of pursuing such a programme would be by means of the EC's powers in the field of education. However, as has been seen, it is open to serious question as whether these powers extend to the measures necessary to effect a programme of this kind. The application of the principle of subsidiarity may mean that such measures, if taken at all, would be taken by Member States.

Other comprehensive initiatives intended to further the interests of lesbians and gay men would necessarily be based on Article 235 EEC. Although the inclusion of Article 3b does not in itself rule out future recourse to Article 235, reliance on this provision so as to supplement action that can be justified under Article 100a will become exceptional. It should be pointed out that, as Article 235 requires unanimous approval of the Council, the argument of subsidiarity will be very effective even if employed by just one Member State.[1]

In addition, as previously noted, the likelihood of the Commission successfully establishing a comprehensive policy for lesbians and gay men within the EC by way of its tested 'step-by step' strategy has also been seriously undermined by the principle of subsidiarity. Previous attempts by Member States to prevent the Commission from exercising certain powers by relying on the notion of sovereignty often missed their target. However, it will be exactly these incremental and apparently insignificant proposals that might not stand up to the test of subsidiarity.

In the final analysis, however, the application of the principle of subsidiarity to individual policy areas is governed by policy and not by law. The fact that at present very few of the Member States (notably the Netherlands and Denmark) have deemed it necessary to pursue what may be termed a comprehensive policy for lesbians and gay men[2] makes it extremely unlikely that such a policy will be initiated at EC level within the foreseeable future. The force of this conclusion is likely to be strengthened, rather than diminished, by the political nature of the principle of subsidiarity.

With regard to the Staff Regulations, it is clear that the role of the EC as employer has a direct impact on its lesbian and gay officials and other servants. The legal means for dealing with this impact lie, first, in the Staff

---

1   For the impact of the inclusion of the notion of subsidiarity in the text of the Social Charter, see Spicker, 1991, 11 arguing:

> Subsidiarity has then, a major effect in limiting the scope for a European social policy, as it must limit the actions of any supranational body. The effect of accepting it could be to take issues like the provision of health care [...], personal social services, education and housing, largely outside the possible remit of the European Community. The potential for the Social Charter was enormously limited by the development of support for the concept.

2   These two groups have been treated together throughout this paper because of the initial definition of the mandate and terms of this report. This should not be taken to imply any conclusion that these groups necessarily have always the same aims or interests, even though certain aims or interests, such as freedom from discrimination, may be widely shared.

Regulations themselves and, second, in the fundamental principles of EC law concerning non-discrmination, human rights and the free movement of persons. The Staff Regulations contain numerous terms which define access to benefits, monetary and other, in terms which do not usually seem to apply easily to lesbians or gay men, especially in partnerships.

It is notoriously difficult to revise the Staff Regulations. Consequently it may be suggested that informal procedures, administrative rules and other means less formal than an EC regulation (such as the Staff Regulations) may be the most appropriate means of improving the position of lesbians and gay men covered by the Staff Regulations.

In addition, the Staff Regulations give legal rights to enable grievance resolution mechanisms to operate at two successive levels.

On the one hand, institutional mechanisms exist within the institutions designed to settle conflicts between the official and the EC. These mechanisms include, first, the procedures set out in Article 90(1) of the Staff Regulations concerning questions about them submitted by the staff. Second, they include the procedures set out in Article 90(2) of the Staff Regulations for dealing with complaints made by officials.

On the other hand, an official can seek judicial review by the Court of First Instance in Luxemburg. The official is required to respect the time limits laid down in the Staff Regulations. The official has three months to react after receiving the decision; the institution has four months to reply once it has received a complaint; and the official then has three months within which to make an appeal to the Court of First Instance.

Here, also, it is important to appreciate the limits of law and the importance of the social, political and economic context in which EC law operates in practice. This chapter has been concerned primarily with legal doctrine, but the context in which this doctrine is deployed by individuals, groups and institutions has not been very far in the background. In order to arrive at an accurate assessment of the role of EC law with regard to the rights of lesbians and gay men, however, it is essential to go further. The law has a role to play, especially in the emerging constitutional order of the EC in the post-Maastricht era, but this role is conditioned, circumscribed and shaped by contemporary European society.

Chapter Eleven
European Citizenship and the Rights of Lesbians and Gay Men

by

ANTONIO TANCA[*]

[*]   University of Florence.

Table of Contents

I. Introduction

This chapter concerns a fascinating – but difficult – topic: the relevance and role of the rights of lesbians and gay men in the context of European citizenship. It is fascinating because European citizenship is at the core of the process of European unification. The establishment of a truly European citizenship will presumably mark the passage from a mere international organization (no matter how tightly-knitted) to a federal State. It is difficult because this concept is at the moment little more than an empty box. Thus, talking about gay and lesbian rights with reference to it is, to paraphrase a famous poem by Pablo Neruda, like entering a transparent house through its walls, and hanging up pictures in the air.

The concept of European citizenship developed gradually. I shall first of all report about the debate taking place in the last few months in preparation for the inter-governmental conference on Political Union. Then I shall discuss the outcome of this debate in the drafting in the Maastricht treaty which contains, in Part II, a group of articles concerning the citizenship of the Union.[1]

After a general assessment of the scope and practical implications of these articles, I will then concentrate on the subjects which are more relevant to lesbians and gay men. I shall also briefly discuss other problems connected with the problem of citizenship, which seem especially important with reference to lesbian and gay rights.

II. European Citizenship

European citizenship is, as such, a notion which is yet to be precisely defined in legal terms. Under Community law a certain number of rights and duties, normally attributable to citizens of Member States, may be grouped in such a way as to constitute, in rough terms, a rudimentary form of European citizenship (a system of rights and duties of individuals under Community law). The two main pillars of this system are the free movement of workers on the one hand, and the protection of fundamental rights on the other.

---

1   The Articles in question, to be inserted in the EEC Treaty, are 8 to 8e. Article 8 states
     the following:
         1. Citizenship of the Union is hereby established.
         Every person holding the nationality of a Member State shall be a citizen of the
         Union.
         2. Citizens of the Union shall enjoy the rights conferred by this treaty and shall be
         subject to the duties imposed thereby.

Technically speaking, nevertheless, this is not yet citizenship. In fact, citizenship presupposes an individual's direct allegiance to her or his national State. Under the system mentioned above, the national State still acts as a necessary intermediate element between the individual and the Community: most of the rights in question existing under Community law, especially those inherent in the qualification of 'worker', may only be enjoyed by the citizens of Member States.

These two subjects, as well as the subject of family ties and equal treatment, are dealt with in other chapters of this report. So whereas many relevant issues concerning gays and lesbians will be dealt with by other more specific chapters (as far as the lex lata is concerned), the present chapter will not contain much reference to the *lex lata*.[2] The concept of European citizenship, as it is envisaged here, goes beyond the two dimensions already mentioned (freedom of movement for workers and fundamental rights). It began to take shape starting from several proposals put forward by the Spanish government and by various European institutions in preparation for the Intergovernmental Conference on Political Union. The 'common core' of these proposals has some implications for lesbian and gay rights: some of them may autonomously be defined *vis-à-vis* the rights already granted within existing Community law. It will be interesting to find out whether the introduction of European citizenship might actually add up to the rights already acquired or solve some of the problems left open by the existing legislation.

III. European Citizenship: the Debate Leading to Maastricht

The concept of European citizenship has made its 'official' appearance in a legal text in the Agreement on European Union, signed in Maastricht on 7 February 1992.[3] In the debate preceding it and in its preparatory documents it was seen as a necessary element in the building of Europe as a political union, something which could also psychologically mark – for the citizens of Member States – the feeling of belonging to the same political entity. The basic idea was that its practical operation would necessarily bring about an enlargement of the present Community competence as well as the

---

2   It is not possible at the moment (December 1992), to predict whether or not the Maastricht Treaty will in the end be ratified by all Member States. Hence, the norms included in it, concerning the citizenship of the Union, are not, as yet, *lex lata*. For the sake of argument, however, I will consider some of the relevant rights as acquired for our purposes, in the hope that the treaty will eventually come into force.

3   For the text in full see *supra*, note 1.

attribution to European citizens of additional rights beyond those already granted by the EC treaties. We shall see to what extent that proved true.

In the conclusions published by the Italian presidency of the Council of Ministers, it was stated that *'le Conseil est heureux de prendre note du con- sensus auquel sont parvenus les Etats membres en vue d'examiner le concept de citoyenneté européenne'*.[4] The first impulse in this sense had however come from the Spanish Government, which had made the first attempt to give specific content to this concept by drafting a concrete proposal. Accord- ing to this proposal, European citizenship is the personal status of citizens of Member States who, by the very fact of being part of the Community, acquire rights and duties which are part ('peculiar') of the Community framework.[5] The process of political unification being a dynamic one, Eu- ropean citizenship must necessarily entail a certain number of political, so- cial and economic rights limited in scope, which may, however, subse- quently be broadened in their scope as well as in their number.[6]

The idea of European citizenship was then officially endorsed by some Community institutions. In fact, it was already mentioned in a European Parliament Resolution containing a 'Declaration on Fundamental Rights and Freedoms', as well as in the Resolution of 12 December 1990 on 'The Constitutional Basis of European Union'.[7] The European Council of Rome (14-15 December 1990) noted with satisfaction that Member States had agreed to examine the notion of European citizenship.[8] Already in October

4   'The Council is pleased to take note of the consensus which the Member States have
     reached with a view to examine the concept of European citizenship'. Quoted by Solbes
     Mira, 1991, 168.
5   Ibid., 169. See also Diez-Hochleitner, 'Conferencia intergubernamental sobre la union
     politica: propuesta sobre ciudadania europea', 43 *Revista Espanola de Derecho Interna-
     cional* (1991) 262, which includes the complete text of the Spanish proposal on Euro-
     pean citizenship.
6   See, Solbes Mira, 1991, 269.
7   'E. considering that a European citizenship can exist only if every citizen enjoys the
     same protection of his/her rights and freedoms within the scope of application of Com-
     munity law,' (trans. from Italian mine), *Declaration on Fundamental Rights and Free-
     doms*, EP Doc. A 2-3/89, OJ 1989 C 120/51, 16.5.89. The EP Resolution on the
     'Constitutional Basis of European Union' is reproduced in 12 *HRLJ*, 54. Points 20 and
     21 concern citizenship. Point 20 reads as follows:
        The citizens of the Member States shall be citizens of the Union; no discrimination
        between citizens, particularly on grounds of nationality, shall be permitted. The cit-
        izens of the Union shall enjoy full freedom of movement within its confines; they
        shall be free, subject to the law of the Union and, when applicable, those of the
        Member States, to engage in whatever political economic, social, artistic or reli-
        gious activities they wish; foreigners legally registered as residents may, subject to
        conditions established by the laws, enjoy comparable rights; [...].
8   European Citizenship was the object of a special section of the Final Act. This section
     reads as follows:
        3. Citoyenneté européenne
        Le Conseil européen note avec satisfaction que les Etats membres sont d'accord
        pour que la notion de citoyenneté européenne soit examinée.

1990 the Commission had officially endorsed the Spanish proposal and had put forward a proposal in twelve articles defining the concrete content of the concept.[9] In June 1991 the Luxembourg presidency also put forward its own proposal, which coincided in part with that of the Commission, but was more limited in scope.[10]

The concrete content of the two proposals (for the parts which coincided) was as follows:

– European citizens are the citizens of Member States.
– They have the right to freely circulate and sojourn throughout the territory of the Community (a right which is unconditional, which is to say not linked to the fact of performing an economic activity).
– They have the right to vote and to run as candidates (in local elections, as well as in the elections for the European Parliament) in the place where they reside.
– Protection may be granted to European citizens by Community organs or by diplomatic and consular authorities of other Member States when they are on the territory of third States.
– They have a right of petition (for the concrete protection of the rights arising from their citizenship) to a special mediator ('ombudsman') or to the European Parliament (Luxembourg Proposal).

This is, so to speak, the kernel of European citizenship. The Commission proposal, however, went farther, insofar as it included other social and cultural rights, as well as an explicit statement of the principle of non-discrimination on nationality grounds (valid also against third parties, which is to say, prohibiting discrimination even by private persons on nationality grounds). A certain dissatisfaction with the proposal of the presidency of the Conference on Political Union was voiced by the European Parliament

---

Il invite la Conférence à examiner dans quelle mesure les droit ci-après pourraient être consacrés dans le traité en manière à concrétiser cette notion:
– droits civiques: participation aux élections du Parlement européen dans le pays de résidence; participations eventuelle aux élections municipales;
– droits sociaux et économiques: libre circulation et droit de séjour indépendamment du fait que l'on exerce ou non une activité économique, égalité des chances et de traitement pour tous les citoyens de la Communauté;
– protection commune des citoyens de la Communauté hors des frontières de celle-ci.
Il faudrait envisager la possibilité d'instituer un mécanisme pour la défense des droits des citoyens en ce qui concerne les questions communautaires ('ombudsman'). Lors de la mise en œuvre de chacune de ces dispositions, une attention appropriée devrait être accordée aux problèmes particuliers que connaissent certains Etats membres.

9   See text sent by the Commission to the Secretary-General of the European Parliament (25.2.91) containing the 'Working document' on European Citizenship (unpublished).
10   See 'Projet de Traité sur l'Union, document de référence de la Présidence luxembourgeoise', 18.6.1991, Conf-UP-UEM 2008/91.

which, on 14 June 1991, adopted a Resolution on the Citizenship of the Union, where the scope of the concept was much broadened.[11]

In all proposals European citizenship is deemed in any case to be complementary to national citizenships. In Gonzalez words, a concept which should *'prendre corps progressivement sans entamer en rien la citoyenneté nationale dont elle serait un complément et non un substitut'*, with a view to developing *'le sentiment d'appartenance à la construction européenne'*.[12]

IV. Two Visions of European Citizenship: Minimalist and Maximalist

Before looking at the actual outcome of this debate and its possible impact on the rights of lesbians and gay men, it is interesting to look at the possible implications of both conceptions: from the first, which I will call 'minimalist' and which resulted from the documents of the Presidency, to the 'maximalist' one, contained in the European Parliament's resolution. The 'working document' of the Commission can be situated somewhere in the middle. In fact, as the Maastricht treaty is not in force yet, whatever comment or observation one may make necessarily concerns the *lex ferenda*.

The draft resolution of the European Parliament certainly envisaged a much wider vision of European citizenship.[13] It could therefore be taken as an example of the maximalist concept. In the Resolution, great stress was put on the fact that European citizenship must be *defined in autonomous terms*. This seemed to imply that although European citizenship complements that of the Member States it must have an autonomous basis, and not necessarily be defined by reference to the citizenship of Member States. Accordingly, the Resolution hinted that in the mode of acquisition, the Union might establish certain criteria, which could possibly super-impose themselves upon those of Member States.[14] It also explicitly advocated

---

11 See EP Res. A 3-139/91, (PE 152.805) 14.6.1991, and *'Relazione interlocutoria della commissione per gli affari istituzionali sulla cittadinanza dell'Unione'* (or. It.) (PE 150.034), 23.5.1991.

12 'take shape progressively without in any way encroaching on national citizenship to which it would be complementary and not a substitute ... this feeling of belonging to the European construction.' Quoted in the 'Note Explicative' to the proposal of the Commission.

13 I am referring to the draft resolution on the Citizenship of the Union, issued by the Committee for Institutional Affairs, 5.9.1991, Doc. PE 153.099.

14 In the proposal of the Presidency, and in that of the Commission the identification between citizenship of the Union and of the individual member State is total. Article X 1.1 of the Working document of the Commission states: 'Est citoyen de l'Union toute personne ayant la nationalité d'un Etat membre'. And it adds in a footnote: 'Prévoir une déclaration de chaque Etat membre définissant la notion de nationalité', COM Doc., *supra* note 9.

common rules concerning the status of citizens of third States.[15]

The European Parliament draft also set out the right for every European citizen to have a *direct influence* in the formation of the rules affecting him/her. This necessarily implied greater powers for the European Parliament in the legislative process of the future Union.[16] The right to participate in the electoral process was formulated in broader terms, insofar as it entailed an explicit right of association for political purposes and participation in political parties. Moreover, the general freedom of movement and establishment was associated with a prohibition of discrimination *on any grounds* (and not only on nationality grounds).[17] Finally, the European Parliament resolution explictly mentioned the necessity of including in the future treaty a list of fundamental rights appertaining to every European citizen.[18]

V. European Citizenship in the Maastricht Treaty on European Union

It is probably no surprise that, considering the difficulties that Member States have encountered in agreeing on a common text, it was the 'minimalist' concept which prevailed in the Treaty on European Union. As said above, citizenship, and the criteria for its attribution, are among the most basic prerogatives of sovereign States. In a text which in certain aspects represents a compromise between two different concepts of the future Europe (a federal Europe as opposed to a Union of Sovereign States), a 'hard' notion of European citizenship, giving to European institutions the right to establish common criteria for the attribution of citizenship, or at least the power to limit, on the basis of European criteria, the corresponding

---

15   See article 3(b) of the Draft proposal. In fact article 3(a) of the proposal reads: 'Il Con-siglio fissa, all'unanimità, su proposta della Commissione e previo parere conforme del Parlamento Europeo, la nozione di persone residenti nell'Unione'. ['The Council shall, acting unanimously on a proposal from the Commission and in accordance with an opinion from the European Parliament, establish the notion of persons residing in the Union.'] This provision could bear some relevance with reference to the problem of ad-mission of third State citizens (particularly refugees) to the territory of the Union.
16   Such a provision was absent from the Commission's proposal.
17   Here, too, there is a discrepancy with the Commission's proposal, which limited the non-discrimination principle to nationality grounds.
18   The Commission's proposal, on the other hand, contained a reference to the European Convention of Human Rights. Article X_2 stated: '*Tout citoyen de l'Union peut se pré-valoir des droit garantis par la Convention européenne de sauvegarde des droits de l'homme et des libertés fondamentales, que l'Union fait sienne*'. Moreover, it contained two additional articles concerning respectively the right of every citizen '*de participer à l'expression de sa culture*', and the duty to respect the expression of that of others, as well as '*le droit à un environnement sain et le devoir de contribuer à sa protection*' (articles X_6 and X_7).

right of Member States, would have been unacceptable at least to some of the States (or perhaps to all of them at the present stage).

European citizens are therefore only the people whom Member States consider their nationals. The power to decide who is a citizen and who is not fully remains with Member States. Hence, European citizenship as such, technically speaking, does not exist. It does not exist even as a complementary citizenship to that of Member States for the reasons stated above.[19] This means that the loss, by a European citizen, of the citizenship of a Member State (occurring on the basis of that State's legislation) automatically entails the loss of European citizenship.[20] Whether or not the citizenship of the Union is in fact citizenship in the traditional sense of the word, the rights contained in the Maastricht Treaty under the heading 'citizenship of the Union' do have a certain degree of importance for lesbians and gay men. They are certainly worth a closer look.

Article 8(1) establishes the citizenship of the Union and attributes this citizenship to every person holding the nationality of a Member State.[21] From the wording of this Article (and especially of its second paragraph) it is clear that the concept of citizenship of the Union only encompasses a limited number of rights and duties, explicitly listed in the treaty, which are reserved for the nationals of Member States. In their nature, these rights do not differ from those arising under the EC Treaty or any other treaty conferring rights on individuals.

The most important of these rights is set out in Article 8a, which establishes the right for every citizen to move and reside freely within the territory of the Member States, subject to the limitations laid down by the Treaty and by the measures adopted to implement it.[22] This is a right of remarkable importance. It marks a step ahead of the traditional EC law concept of free movement of persons which, given the 'economic' character of the Community, was limited to workers. The right of an EC citizen to establish him/herself elsewhere in the Community was, and still is, limited by the necessity of looking for a job, being enrolled in a school, or

19   I am referring to possible European criteria for the attribution of citizenship which might supplant (or act as limits to) the national ones.

20   One might still wonder, however, whether the Court of Justice would not, in some cases, have a say in the matter in those cases where, for example, the loss of citizenship might entail the violation of certain basic principles of EC law, such as non-discrimination. The question cannot however be dealt with here.

21   For the text of Article 8, see *supra* note 1.

22   Article 8a:
         1. Every citizen of the Union shall have the right to move and reside freely within the territory of the Member States, subject to the limitations and conditions laid down in this Treaty and by the measures adopted to give it effect.
         2. The Council may adopt provisions with a view to facilitating the exercise of the rights referred to in paragraph 1; save as otherwise provided in this Treaty, the

beginning an economic activity. Thus this new right gives a practical meaning to the concept of European citizenship.[23] A European person will have an increased feeling of belonging to an entity called Europe by feeling free to go and stay wherever he/she likes on European territory.

The other 'pillars' of European citizenship may be found in the following articles. Article 8b establishes the right to vote and stand as a candidate in local and European elections for every European citizen residing in a country other than her or his own.[24] Article 8c provides for the so-called right of protection of European citizens in third countries by the diplomatic or consular authorities of States other than the State of which that person is a national.[25] Article 8d confers on every European citizen a right of petition to the European Parliament as well as the right to address complaints to a special Ombudsman.[26] Article 8e, finally, does not contain any other substantive right, but specifically provides for the possibility of adding new rights to this section or strenghtening the existing ones without amending the Treaty.[27]

Council shall act unanimously on a proposal from the Commission and after obtaining the assent of the European Parliament.

23   See *infra*, next paragraph.

24   These rights, contained respectively in the first and second paragraphs of article 8b are also subject to conditions on their implementation. Article 8b:

1. Every citizen of the Union residing in a Member State of which he is not a na-tional shall have the right to vote and to stand as a candidate at municipal elec-tions in the Member State in which he resides, under the same conditions as na-tionals of that State. This right shall be exercised subject to detailed arrangements to be adopted before 31 December 1994 by the Council, acting unanimously on a proposal from the Commission and after consulting the European Parliament; these arrangements may provide for derogations where warranted by problems specific to a Member State.

2. Without prejudice to Article 138(3) and to the provisions adopted for its imple-mentation, every citizens of the Union residing in a Member State of which he is not a national shall have the right to vote and to stand as a candidate in elections to the European Parliament in the Member State in which he resides, under the same conditions as nationals of that State. This right shall be exercised subject to detailed arrangements to be adopted before 31 December 1993 by the Council, act-ing unanimously on a proposal from the Commission and after consulting the Eu-ropean Parliament; these arrangements may provide for derogations where war-ranted by problems specific to a Member State.

25   Article 8c:

Every citizen of the Union shall, in the territory of a third country in which the Member State of which he is a national is not represented, be entitled to protection by the diplomatic or consular authorities of every Member State, on the same condi-tions as the nationals of that State. Before 31 December 1993, Member States shall establish the necessary rules among themselves and start the international negotia-tions required to secure this protection.

26   Article 8d:

Every citizen of the Union shall have the right to petition the European Parliament in accordance with Article 138d.

Every citizen of the Union may apply to the Ombudsman established in accordance with Article 138e.

27   Article 8e:

VI. Lesbian and Gay Rights and European Citizenship

Now that a relatively clear picture has been drawn concerning the substantive rights making up European citizenship, it is also possible to discuss their implications upon lesbian and gay rights. This survey will not be limited to the *lex lata* because, provided the Maastricht Treaty comes into force, it will be possible, thanks to Article 8e, to enlarge and deepen the rights which together make up this rudimentary concept.

A. Acquisition of Citizenship

The first observation which must be made concerns European citizens. As already stated above, the Articles included in the Maastricht Treaty do not establish common criteria for the attribution of citizenship. A reference to the necessity of reaching an agreement on such criteria was contained only in the proposal by the European Parliament.[28] According to the working document of the Commission, on the other hand, States were only required to list the criteria they adopted for the granting of citizenship. No mention was made of any limitation on such right, nor of any superimposition of European criteria upon national ones.[29] This is in fact an area where States are most reluctant to surrender portions of their sovereignty to a supranational body. It is therefore not surprising that no significant progress was made.[30] The choice – perhaps inevitable – not to establish any common

---

The Commission shall report to the European Parliament, to the Council and to the Economic and Social Committee before 31 December 1993 and then every three years on the application of the provisions of this Part. This report shall take into account the development of the Union.
On this basis, and without prejudice to the other provisions of this Treaty, the Council, acting unanimously on a proposal from the Commission and after consulting the European Parliament, may adopt provisions to strengthen and to add to the rights laid down in this Part, which it shall recommend to the Member States for adoption in accordance with their respective constitutional requirements.

28   Article 1(a) of the draft Resolution reads as follows (my translation from the original Italian):
'It is instituted the citizenship of the Union. Citizens of the Union are all citizens of member States.
The Union may establish some conditions for acquisition or loss of the citizenship of member States with the procedures set up for the revision of the Treaty.'

29   See article $X_1.1$ of the Commission's 'Working document', *supra* note 14.

30   The report of the EP Committee for the Institutional Affairs (PE 150.034/def. Or.IT, 23 May 1991, adopted on 14 June 1991) mentions however three main problems which would arise from the fact of leaving the concrete definition of the citizens of the Union substantially to Member States:
       – problems concerning the principle of equality *vis-à-vis* Community law, when a person fulfilling certain requirements acquires the status of citizen 'through' a Member State, whereas another one, fulfilling exactly the same requirements, is prevented from doing so 'through' another Member State;

280 ANTONIO TANCA

criteria on the attribution of citizenship leaves States' freedom in this field totally unimpaired. There are two consequences: the first is that stateless people resident in Europe, refugees and extra-community residents are not included among European citizens; the second is that if any of the above-mentioned people wants to become a European citizen she or he will have to become first of all a citizen of a Member State. This will prove more or less difficult according to the State where this person applies for citizenship. So, for instance, a Chilean person with an Italian grandfather will find it easier to become a European citizen than a Chilean person whose grandparents are English, because the Italian legislation allows the acquisition of Italian citizenship under these conditions, whereas the English law establishes different conditions for the acquisition of English citizenship.

The question which most directly touches gays and lesbians is that of naturalization. Insofar as marriage between persons of the same sex is not allowed by most legislation, acquisition of citizenship by way of marriage is impossible for lesbian and gay couples of different nationalities. Of course, this is not a big problem when both partners have a Community nationality, but it is a big problem indeed when one of the partners is not a Community national. Lesbian and gay couples are therefore in a situation of objective disadvantage *vis-à-vis* heterosexual couples. Admittedly, this is not so much a problem of citizenship as a problem of legislation on marriage. Common European rules on citizenship or on the granting of residence permits could, for instance, encompass the concession of working permits to extra-Community citizens on the basis of a *de facto* relationship with a European citizen (with the possibility of naturalisation after a certain number of years of residence).[31] This solution would avoid touching the thorny problem of marriage between people of the same sex. It would also avoid the blatant discrimination among European lesbian and gay citizens from different States, which would exist if a solution such as that suggested were adopted only by one European State. This is only one of the many reasons for which European rules in this field would be desirable.

- the freedom States maintain to excessively relax the conditions for the concession of their own citizenship (and thus of European citizenship);
- the competence of the Court of Justice to decide upon the citizenship of an individual. What value would such a decision have for the Member State concerned?

31 Some Member States, such as Denmark or, to a certain extent, the Netherlands seem to be going already in this direction. For more details see Chapter Twelve by Jessurun d'Oliveira.

B. Admission to the Union for Lesbian and Gay People from Third States

This problem is only indirectly related to the question of citizenship. It has, in fact, to do with the establishment of common criteria for the *admission* of non-Community persons into the territory of the Community. Besides the aspect, briefly mentioned before, of the admission of lesbians and gay men from third States having a *de facto* relationship with a European citizen, there is the very important question of the admission to Europe of lesbian and gay refugees. By lesbian and gay refugees I do not mean those refugees for political or other reasons who also happen to be gay or lesbian. I rather mean the admission of people who have to flee their country *because they are lesbian or gay* and this fact makes them subject to persecution, imprisonment or worse.

As just said, this question is, as such, connected to citizenship insofar a gay or lesbian person, fleeing her or his own country because of her or his homosexuality, and having a partner who is a Community citizen, may not flee to the Community because homosexual relationships are not recognized as a valid basis to claim citizenship or even a residence permit. Here the recognition of *de facto* relationships could help solve this problem.

But this is only a limited aspect of the question, and it would provide a solution only for a small category of people who are lucky enough to have a partner who is a Community citizen. The problem remains open for all people who must flee their country because of their homosexuality. In my view, a distinction must be made between those who are subject to *de facto* discrimination or risk persecution or imprisonment because of their sexual orientation, and those who, for the same reason may be subjected to inhuman or degrading treatment.

For the latter category (which is by no means a negligible one, if one only looks at countries like Iran), it is believed that at least an implied right to seek asylum in the Member States of the Council of Europe, as a matter of human rights law, already exists.[32]

The other category raises much greater problems. As a matter of fact, all European countries are parties to the 1951 Convention on Refugees and the 1967 New York Protocol. This Convention should also constitute the basis for a relative harmonization of the legislations of the States parties to the

---

32   See Einarsen, 'The European Convention on Human Rights and the Notion of an implied Right to *de facto* Asylum', 2 *International Journal of Refugee Law* (1990) 361. The author's reasoning is mainly based on the European Court of Human Rights case-law, aiming at rendering the protection of the rights granted by the Convention truly effective. This would prevent the expulsion from the European territory of persons at risk of being subjected to inhuman or degrading treatment. It is by no means clear, however, whether a person fleeing his country because of this risk would automatically be granted asylum *only* on this ground.

Schengen agreement under which some European States, namely Belgium, France, Germany, Italy, Luxembourg, the Netherlands and, possibly, Portugal and Spain, are creating a border-check-free space on the European continent.[33]

According to Article 1 of the 1951 Refugee Convention,

> The term 'refugee' shall apply to any person who, owing to well-founded fear of being persecuted for reasons of race, religion, nationality, membership of a particular social group or political opinion, is outside the country of his nationality and is unable or, owing to such fear, is unwilling to avail himself of the protection of that country.[34]

The crucial question therefore becomes whether and to what extent gay men and lesbians may be considered to be covered by the wording of Article 1, as 'members of a particular social group'. I have no access to State practice in this matter, and there is no space here to examine it in detail anyway. It is reasonable to say, however, that there is no stated policy, on the part of States, of considering lesbians and gay men as included within the scope of Article 1 of the Refugees Convention.[35] This is also probably due to the fact that potential refugees on the ground of their homosexuality have difficulties in admitting it to border police.[36]

All EC States are parties to the Refugees Convention. Some of them, however, grant refugees or some categories of them, better treatment than that required by the Convention. With the Schengen agreement, the 1951 Convention will become the lowest common denominator, the basis for the harmonization of the various statutory provisions on the matter. It is therefore crucial that the EC countries expressly include lesbian and gay refugees

---

33   *Convention on the Application of the Schengen Agreement of 14 June 1985 relating to the Gradual Suppression of Controls at Common Frontiers, between the Governments of States Members of the Benelux Economic Union, the Federal Republic of Germany and the French Republic*. Article 28 states: 'The Contracting Parties hereby reaffirm their obligations under the Geneva Convention of 28 July 1951 relating to the Status of Refugees as amended by the New York Protocol of 31 January 1967, without any geo-graphical restriction on the scope of those instruments, as also their commitment to co-operate with the United Nations High Commissioner for Refugees in the implementation of those instruments.' [1991] ILM 68.
     On the Schengen agreement and its implications for legislation concerning asylum see J.L.E. Schutte, 'Schengen: its Meaning for the Free Movement of Persons in Europe', 28 *CML Rev.*, (1991) 549. See also, more specifically, H. Meijers, 'Refugees in Western Europe: "Schengen" affects the entire Refugee Law', 2 *International Journal of Refugee Law* (1990) 428.

34   The Convention was adopted by the UN Conference on the Status of Refugees and Stateless Persons at Geneva, 2-25 July 1951, and entered into force on 22 April 1954. For the full text see UNTS, Vol. 189, at 137.

35   See 'Refugees on the basis of their sexuality', remarks made by Wikström at the conference 'Lesbian, Gay and Bisexual Rights in New Europe', Helsinki, April 4-5, 1992 (mimeogr. text), at 4.

36   Ibid., 5.

in the category covered by Article 1 of the Convention, as members of a particular social group.[37]

C. Freedom of Movement

The 'minimalist' concept which prevailed in the Maastricht Treaty contains an aspect which is particularly relevant for the present purposes. It is the extension of the freedom of movement and establishment within the territory of all Member States to all European citizens. At present, freedom of movement is strictly tied to economic activities (of workers or professionals providing services or seeking to establish themselves in another Member State).. The worker may of course be followed by her or his relatives, who enjoy, to a certain extent, her or his rights in the member State where they settle. The concept of 'relative' or 'family' or 'spouse' does not as yet – at least at Community level – encompass lesbian or gay relationships.[38] Thus a lesbian or gay couple still experiences serious limitations to their freedom to settle in another Member State unless both partners work and manage to find a job in that State. But it is obvious that when freedom of movement is attributed to any European citizen, this problem is solved. The attribution to any European citizen of total freedom of movement and establishment throughout the territory of the Community marks a step forward at least insofar it contributes to the eradication of one of the most blatantly discriminatory aspects of freedom of movement in its traditional sense. It must therefore certainly be welcomed. The practical implications of this 'total freedom of movement' are probably not yet clear (especially its implications upon the social security, health care etc. of Member States). The recognition of *de facto* relationships as mentioned above would certainly be desirable and help to solve some of the problem concerning social security, health care (other questions such as succession rights are probably more complicated).

D. Electoral Rights

The right to vote and be a candidate in local elections and European elections in the State of residence is certainly a very welcome development. Admittedly, this is not a right which particularly characterizes European citizenship, insofar as it is recognized – for local elections – for all foreign residents (extra-Community included) by some Member States. Anyway, it could probably be used as a tool to introduce and fuel the debate about

---

37   Ibid., 9.
38   See Chapter Twelve by Jessurun D'Oliveira and Chapter Fifteen by Emmert.

lesbian and gay issues in Member States where the debate on these issues is not very developed yet, as well as to promote lesbian and gay candidacies.

Interestingly, the text of Article 8b inserted by the Maastricht Treaty makes an explicit reference to Article 138 amended by the same Treaty. This Article concerns the possible adoption, for European Parliament elections, of the same electoral system in every country.[39] The adoption of a common electoral system (presumably involving a certain degree of proportional representation, which seems the best suited for an organ having the characteristics of the European Parliament),[40] would probably facilitate lesbian and gay people or organizations to run for elections, even in countries where the domestic electoral system makes it practically impossible.

E. The Right of Petition

The presence of lesbian and gay representatives in the European Parliament is strictly connected to the right of petition, which is granted to every European citizen by the first part of Article 8d. This right is of course very important to ensure, above all, the effectiveness of the freedom of movement for every European citizen. It could prove crucial to avoid any disguised discrimination against lesbian and gay persons, which might render freedom of movement totally ineffective.

Article 138d inserted by the Treaty on European Union expressly grants a right of petition to every citizen of the Union, *also in association with other citizens or persons*.[41] This provision is drafted in rather generic terms. More specific, and with a somewhat more limited scope (both *ratione personae* and *ratione materiae*) is the parallel right, granted by the second part of Article 8d and in Article 138e, to address complaints to an

---

39   New text of paragraph 3 of Article 138:
         '3. The European Parliament shall draw up proposals for elections by direct univer-
         sal suffrage in accordance with a uniform procedure in all Member States.
         The Council shall, acting unanimously after obtaining the assent of the European
         Parliament, which shall act by a majority of its component members, lay down the
         appropriate provisions, which it shall recommend to Member States for adoption in
         accordance with their respective constitutional requirements'.
40   I am referring to its relative scarcity of effective powers, and to its importance as a fo-
         rum representing as accurately as possible the characters and tendencies present in the
         European peoples.
41   Article 138d:
         Any citizen of the Union, and any natural or legal person residing or having its reg-
         istered office in a Member State, shall have the right to address, individually or in
         association with other citizens or persons, a petition to the European Parliament on
         a matter which comes within the Community's field of activity and which affects
         him directly.

Ombudsman expressly appointed by the European Parliament in relation to cases of maladministration in the activities of Community institutions.[42]

Article 138e inserted by the Treaty is rather detailed. It has both a procedural and substantive content insofar as it defines the competence of the Ombudsman, as well as the subjects entitled to apply to her or him, the procedural rules governing the Ombudsman's activity, and the effects of her or his decisions.

First of all, the activity of the Ombudsman may not encroach on that of other judicial organs of the Union, namely the Court of Justice and the Court of First Instance acting in their judicial role. Thus, any question which is already under examination by any of these two organs, is automatically beyond the scope of the Ombudsman's activity.

The Ombudsman, however, is not obliged to receive a complaint in order to act. According to the second part of Article 138e.1, she or he can start an inquiry on her or his own initiative, or after having received a complaint either directly or through a member of the European Parliament.[43] Obviously his power is limited to instances of maladministration by Community institutions. She or he has no power to inquire into the behaviour of Member States, even when this behaviour is in violation of EC law.

The procedure ends with a report compiled by the Ombudsman and submitted to the European Parliament and the institution concerned. The person lodging the complaint is also informed. The Ombudsman must also submit an annual report to the EP on the outcome of her or his inquiries.[44]

---

42   Article 138e, para. 1, first part:
      1. The European Parliament shall appoint an Ombudsman empowered to receive complaints from any citizen of the Union or any natural or legal person residing or having his registered office in a Member State concerning instances of maladminis tration in the activities of the Community institutions and bodies, with the excep tion of the Court of Justice and the Court of First Instance acting in their judicial role.

43   Article 138e, para. 1, second part:
      In accordance with his duties, the Ombudsman shall conduct inquiries for which he finds grounds, either on his own initiative or on the basis of complaints submitted to him direct or through a member of the European Parliament, except where the al leged facts are or have been subject of legal proceedings. Where the Ombudsman establishes an instance of maladministration, he shall refer the matter to the institu tion concerned, which shall have a period of three months in which to inform him of its views.

44   Article 138e, para. 1, third and fourth parts:
      The Ombudsman shall then forward a report to the European Parliament and the in stitution concerned. The person lodging the complaint shall be informed of the out come of such inquiries.
      The Ombudsman shall submit an annual report to the European Parliament on the outcome of his inquiries.

The remaining three paragraphs of Article 138e deal with the procedure of the Ombudsman's appointment, the characteristics that she or he must have, the duties she or he must perform during his office and so on.

The Ombudsman seems to have, according to Article 138e, rather limited powers. The first limitation, as noted above, is that her or his inquiries are limited to the behaviour of EC institutions and bodies, and not that of Member States. The second limitation is that the actual effects of the Ombudsman's reports are not very clear. It is obvious that they have a hortatory value. This fact, however, taken by itself, may not mean very much. It will be interesting to see to what extent the Ombudsman will really act as an institution totally independent of the European Parliament.[45]

In any case, from the angle of lesbian and gay rights, the creation of an Ombudsman seems to be a very interesting development. As briefly mentioned above, the Ombudsman may receive complaints from individuals as well as from any legal person residing or having its registered office in a Member State. I believe that this expression certainly includes entities such as civil rights associations or lesbian and gay organizations. The limitation in the subject matter of the complaints which may be addressed to the Ombudsman may also be partly overcome by the parallel right of petition to the European Parliament, which is granted by the first part of Article 8d.

The relationship between these two rights is not quite clear from the text. The right of petition to the European Parliament seems to be wider in scope than the right to apply to the Ombudsman. The former may in fact be exercised by groups which are not necessarily organized as a legal person. Furthermore, petitions may concern any matter within the Community's field of activity, and not only maladministration, including, presumably, the behaviour of Member States in violation of the law of the Union. On the other hand, the right of petition may be exercised only by those who are *directly* affected by the activity in question, whereas such limitation does not seem to apply to the right to send complaints to the Ombudsman.[46] Also, while the procedure and effects of the Ombudsman's action are described in detail, the outcome of the procedure dealing with a petition to the European Parliament is not clear at all.

What is relevant for our purposes is that lesbian and gay organizations will be afforded a very useful tool to make their voice heard at European

---

45   Article 138e, para. 3 expressly states:
      The Ombudsman shall be completely independent in the performance of his duties.
      In the performance of those duties he shall neither seek nor take instructions from
      any body. The Ombudsman may not, during his term of office, engage in any other
      occupation, whether gainful or not.
46   This may probably not mean very much. If the right to send complaints to the Om-
      budsman is only limited to cases of maladministration by the European institutions, it
      is obvious that only the 'victims' of such acts may send such complaints.

level. This is not yet something akin to a 'class action' but it certainly represents a good way to check on the actual operation of some of the substantive rights established by the Treaty. Admittedly, the role of the European Parliament is still rather limited. Yet this right, coupled with the freedom of association and the right belonging to every European citizen to vote and run as a candidate for European elections is crucial for the election of a Parliament sensitive to lesbian and gay issues, for the 'europeanization' of these issues and for the defence of lesbian and gay rights at a continental level.

F. Assistance by European Embassies and Consulates

Article 8c sets out, in a somewhat tentative way, the right for every European citizen to be protected by the diplomatic or consular authorities of a State other than her or his own, in the territory of any third State. The term *protection* is somewhat misleading because it is reminiscent of the concept of 'diplomatic protection'.[47] The right of diplomatic protection is the right belonging to every State to bring an international claim against another State which has committed against the former State's nationals acts in violation of international law. The factual condition for the exercise of this right is the existence of a link of citizenship between the individual who has been wronged and the State exercising the right.[48]

Article 8c is certainly not referring to 'diplomatic protection' in this sense. It would be very difficult for a State of which the individual is not a national to espouse a claim on behalf of this individual against a third State. Such State is certainly not obliged to recognize a link which only exists by virtue of a treaty to which it is not a party. Moreover, as is well known, under international law the individual as such has no *right* to diplomatic protection. Such right only belongs to her or his national State which may or may not exercise it according to its own evaluation of circumstances. It would therefore be very strange if, on the basis of Article 8c, an Italian citizen were entitled to obtain from the German government what she or he is not entitled to obtain from her or his own government.

Article 8c must therefore be construed as the right of every European citizen to obtain assistance from embassies or consulates of countries of the Union other than her or his own, in those States where her or his own are absent. It is, in other words, that kind of practical assistance a foreigner may need when in danger or when having problems in a foreign country. In this sense, this norm may certainly fulfil a very useful function, and give

47 This very term was used in the European Parliament texts.
48 *Panevezys-Saldutiskis Railways* case (*Estonia v. Lithuania*) (1939), PCIJ Reports, Series A/B, No.76.

the European citizen a greater sense of belonging to the same political entity. It might also have relevance for present purposes. The main example concerns the difficulties lesbian and gay European citizens might face when travelling in countries where homosexuality is still illegal (and these are still the majority, particularly outside of Europe). The presence of *any* European embassy, especially in small or remote places, is certainly of great practical importance. Admittedly, the importance is only practical: countries which do not have an embassy, usually delegate their functions to other friendly countries at whose embassy the individual may call.

VII. Concluding Remarks

At the end of this chapter I realize that, despite being as cautious as possible, I have in fact been hanging up a few pictures in the air. The complex of acquired rights for lesbians and gay men with reference to European citizenship – provided the Maastricht Treaty comes into force – does not amount to very much. The most important achievement is the development of the concept of freedom of movement, for the reasons I have discussed above. But even that freedom is seriously curtailed by the lack of recognition of *de facto* relationships between people of the same sex. The other aspects relating to citizenship in the 'Maastricht sense': electoral rights, right of petition and right to assistance by the consulates and embassies of foreign States do have, as shown, a certain degree of importance for present purposes. However, the rights of lesbians and gay men are only tangentially affected.

But I have been dealing only with the 'Maastricht conception' of citizenship. Of course I cannot ignore the fact that the term 'citizenship' does in itself evoke a much wider complex of allegiances, rights and duties. Hence, speaking about lesbian and gay people and European citizenship cannot fail to raise the more general question: to what extent are lesbian and gay people European citizens in the real sense of the term. To what extent, in other terms, are they not, from various viewpoints, still second class citizens in European societies?

I have limited my analysis to the technical notion of citizenship and the few rights relating to it. The general answer about what has been acquired and what must still be done will hopefully come from this entire project, of which this chapter is only a small part.

Chapter Twelve
Lesbians and Gays
and the Freedom of Movement of Persons

by

HANS ULRICH JESSURUN D'OLIVEIRA[*]

[*]   Professor, European University Institute, Forence.

Table of Contents

Introduction

This chapter focuses on the status of lesbians and gay men under the Community provisions concerning one of the distinctive and fundamental community freedoms: that of the free movement of persons. Indeed already in Article 3 EEC-Treaty it is stated that 'the activities of the Community shall include [...] (c) the abolition, as between member states, of obstacles to freedom of movement for persons'.[1]

This central principle encompassing 'persons', is elaborated for workers in Articles 48 *et seq.* and in secondary legislation – both regulations and directives – and in the case-law of the European Court of Justice (ECJ). There are also directives for categories of persons not being workers in the strict or normal sense.

Some impact on the freedom of movement of persons issues from the non-discrimination principle found in Article 7 EEC which prohibits discrimination on the grounds of nationality. There is another line of approach which I will include in this chapter because it has some bearing on the freedom of movement of persons: the influence of the right to a family life and to a private life as enshrined not only in several important international conventions such as the European Convention on Human Rights (ECHR) to which all Member States of the European Community adhere, and in various constitutions of the Member States, but which are also integrated into Community Law through a series of decisions of the ECJ.

In the first part of this chapter I will confine myself to a description of the status quo as I see it; in the second part I will draw a picture of some developments which may be produced within the existing framework; in the last part the fetters of this framework will be broken, and some desirable changes will be proposed.

Throughout this report the interplay between the Community legal order and the legal orders of the Member States should be kept in mind: Article 7 EEC, in particular, functions as a valve between those two legal orders. National laws and provisions in conjunction with Article 7 can bring about both restrictions and enlargements of the freedom of movement especially in the area of defining the groups of persons whom the person entitled to freedom of movement under Community law is allowed to have accompanying him/her.

---

1   I will leave aside the important question whether non-community nationals can be considered as 'persons' under Art. 3 EEC Treaty.

I. The Current State of Affairs

A. Independent Right to Freedom of Movement

1. Workers

It may not be wholly superfluous to start this part with a simple syllogism which reads: freedom of movement is granted in Article 3 EEC to persons (workers and others); lesbians and gay men are persons; thus lesbians and gay men enjoy freedom of movement. Article 48, which implements Article 3, is directly effective since the end of the transitional period as the ECJ has repeatedly held.[2]

This freedom of movement includes in the first place the right to be treated on an equal footing with nationals of the host state as regards employment, remuneration and other conditions of work and employment (Article 48(2)); in the second place an autonomous Community regime has been created, independent from the abolition of discrimination on the grounds of nationality: the worker has the rights enumerated in Article 48(3), including the right to accept an actual offer of employment, which right has been extended, in practice, to a certain period[3] in which one may look for a job in another Member State; Article 48 is silent on the point.

These rights of workers are subject to some exceptions, enumerated in Article 48(3): 'limitations justified on grounds of public policy, public security, or public health'. Is the freedom of movement of lesbians and gay men hampered by these exceptions? Are there any provisions in immigration laws or are there any practices of impeding lesbians and gay men from entering a Member State which are legitimized by invoking one of these exceptions? Does there exist in the EC such a thing as the 'gay exclusion' formerly contained in US Immigration Laws?[4]

---

2   Cf. e.g. Kapteyn, Verloren van Themaat and Gormley, 1989, 412.
3   This period varies between 3 and 6 months, and tends to be identified with the period granted to tourists. Cf. e.g. Green, Hartley and Leske, 1991, 112-113; and see Case C-292/89, *Antonissen* [1991] ECR.
4   According to the Immigration and Nationality Act (INA) 8 U.S.C. para. 11 8 2 (a) 'aliens afflicted with psychopathic personality or sexual deviation or a mental defect are excluded from entering the US.' Lundy, 1986, 185-211 (Art. 203) tells us that 'despite the I.N.S. [Immigration and Naturalization Service] protestations to the contrary, evidence suggests that the agency is not committed to effecting a meaningful gay exclusion. In the period 1971 – 1983, the last date for which figures are available, only forty-four of the tens of millions of persons who entered the country were excluded for being 'immoral' and these figures do not indicate how many such persons were so excluded for being gay'. This implies of course a large scale non-disclosure of being gay. 'An alien is excluded from entry as a gay person only if, at the port of entry, he or she makes a 'voluntary, unsolicited, and unambiguous admission of homosexuality and repeats that statement to a second inspecting office' (Art. 192).
See also at 45-49 for more details, including the decision of the US Court of Appeal for the Ninth Circuit, holding that Congress did intend the Immigration and Naturalisation

These exceptions on grounds of public policy, public security or public health, are repeated in regulations and directives concerning the freedom of movement of persons.[5] As these exceptions represent inroads into central and fundamental principles of Community law, they are to be interpreted restrictively, not only by the national authorities and courts, but also by the ECJ. If the ECJ would defer to the judgment of the national authorities, freedom of movement would soon be reduced and would at least show ragged edges; since the ECJ has hedged this freedom by imposing strict conditions on the use of these exceptions by Member States, the margin left to them can always be controlled by the ECJ which has developed quite a number of decisions, not necessarily consistent with each other, in this sensitive area. As Gormley has put it:

> Thus a Member State may not simply determine that because a national of another Member State is, say, a prostitute or a lesbian or has green hair that person may not stay in its territory.[6]

The reason Gormley gives for this statement is, however, less than satisfactory:

> This follows from the requirement of the individual's conduct giving rise to the threat, see e.g. Case 115 & 116/81, *Adoui & Cornuaille*.

In the first place it should be remembered that the case cited concerning prostitution was decided not on the basis of the personal conduct of the individuals in question, but on the basis of the principle of non-discrimination between Belgian prostitutes exercising their trade or profession and prostitutes from other Member States.[7] Indeed in *Rutili*[8] the Court considered that

> restrictions cannot be imposed on the right of a national of any Member State to enter the territory of another Member State, to stay there and to move within it,

---

Service to obtain a 'Class A' certificate as a requisite to excluding even self-declared homosexuals from entering this country because of psychopathic personality, sexual deviation or mental defect. Since 1979 the Public Health Service (PHS) has, however, refused to issue such certificates, one of the reasons being that the American Psychiatric Association had removed homosexuality from its register of mental diseases: *Hill v. INS*, 71 F 2d 1470, 1473 (9th Cir. 1983).

5   I refer to Directive 68/360 on the abolition of restrictions on movement and residence within the Community for workers of Member States and their families (Art. 10); Directive 73/148 on the abolition of restrictions on movement and residence within the Community for nationals of Member States with respect to establishment and the provision of services (Art. 8); Directives 644/221 and 72/194, etc.

6   Gormley in Kapteyn, Verloren van Themaat and Gormley, 1989, 419.

7   In this way the ECJ distanced itself from the earlier *Van Duyn* case (41/74) where the ECJ accepted a difference in treatment between home secretaries and foreign secretaries in the Church of Scientology.

8   Case 36/75, *Rutili v. Minister for the Interior* [1975] ECR 1219.

> unless his *presence or conduct* constitutes a genuine and sufficiently serious
> threat to public policy. (emphasis added)

It does follow then, that Member States are allowed to refuse entrance to
persons whose sheer 'presence' constitutes a qualified threat to public policy, even if there is no further objectionable conduct.[9]

To apply the distinction between 'presence' and 'conduct' to our topic:
sexual preference as presence or condition, and activities stemming from
this preference as conduct, may make a difference. I submit, however, that
lesbian and gay conduct does not amount to:

> the existence, in addition to the perturbation of the social order which any in-
> fringement of the law invokes, of a genuine and sufficiently serious threat to the
> requirements of public policy affecting one of the fundamental interests of soci-
> ety.

This is the general statement by the ECJ[10] concerning the grounds for its
control of the use of the exception by national authorities and courts, and to
which should be added the conditions that there be no discrimination
between treatment by authorities, or law courts, of Community foreigners
and treatment of their own nationals. To the specific question whether
lesbian and gay presence and conduct in the individual case may lead to an
acceptable use of the exception of public policy to freedom of movement of
persons by national authorities, the ECJ has not yet been given the opportunity to express itself. This may be seen as an indication that there are no
problems in this area.

This conclusion should be qualified in view of the variety of perceptions
of the phenomenon of sexual preferences for persons of the same sex by the
Member States and in view of the fact that the lesbian and gay minority
operates less conspicuously on the public scene than eg. the feminist
movement.

I suspect that there still exist practices in Member States which boil
down to discrimination against lesbian and gay workers under various pre-
texts, and which are very difficult to formally attack, because of the *de-
tournement de pouvoir* regularly involved in these practices.[11]

In this respect attention should be drawn to the Resolution of the European Parliament of 22 November 1989 on the Community Charter of

---

9   Wearing green hair is, of course, a matter of individual conduct. The same goes for old
     ladies with blue hair.
10   Case 30/77, *R.v. Bouchereau* [1977] ECR 1999.
11   To bar the entrance of gay or lesbian Member State nationals to the territory of a Mem-
     ber State because of fear of their being HIV positive or of having AIDS, would amount
     to indirect discrimination and would furthermore be an inadequate measure amounting
     to a violation of the rule of reason. Cf. Fernandez, 1991, 87-90; Pais Macedo van Over-
     beek, 1990, 791-824.

Fundamental Social Rights.[12] In this document the European Parliament stresses, with a view to the completion of the internal market and to protecting the interests of all Community nationals, that it considers that priority should be given in the Charter and the action programme to: 'the right of all workers to equal protection regardless of their nationality, race, religion, age, sex, *sexual preference* or legal status.' (emphasis added)

2. Groups of Persons Other than Workers

As stated earlier the Council has bridged some of the gaps between 'workers' and 'persons' by adopting three directives on the right of residence in Community Member States for non-economic purposes. The groups concerned are students, pensioners, and those who have never been economically active.[13] Concerning the right of family members to follow these categories of persons to another Member State, the three directives show some differences. Whereas Directives 90/364 and 90/365 consider that the right of residence 'can only be genuinely exercised if it is also granted to members of the family', Directive 90/366 limits the students' right of residence to 'the spouse and their dependent children', both in the Preamble and in Article 1; in Article 2 however the term 'member of the family' is used again.[14] In all three Directives the term 'spouse' is used as in the earlier Directives and Regulations concerning 'workers'. It is now time to consider the meaning of terms like 'spouse' and 'family'.

B. Family Members of 'Persons' and 'Social Advantages'

Regulations and directives which shape the freedom of movement of persons as guaranteed in primary Community law allow certain categories of persons the right to install themselves with the person whose freedom of movement derives from their primary rules as described above in paragraph I.A.1.

I cite as a practically important example Regulation 1612/68 which sets out 'comparatively generous rules for the admission of members of the

---

12   Doc. A3 – 69/89.
13   Council Directive 90/364 on the right of residence, Council Directive on the right of residence for employees and self-employed persons who have ceased their occupational activity 90/365, and Council Directive 90/366 on the right of residence for students. OJ 1990 L 180/26, 28 and 30. For further commentary on these Directives e.g. O'Keeffe, 1992, 3-19; Van Nuffel, 1990, 887 ff.
14   There is still another annoying variation in the use of terms within the students' Directive, where in the preamble 'the spouse and *their* dependent children' are indicated as entitled to the right of residence. Art. 2(2) mentions 'the spouse and *the* dependent children of a national of a Member State' (emphasis added).

families of migrant workers'.[15] Article 10 of this Regulation is worded as
follows:

> 1. The following shall, irrespective of their nationality, have the right to install
> themselves with a worker who is a national of one Member State and who is em-
> ployed in the territory of another Member State:
> (a) his spouse and their descendants who are under the age of 21 years or are
>   dependents;
> (b) dependent relatives in the ascending line of the worker and his spouse.
> 2. Member States shall facilitate the admission of any member of the family not
> coming within the provisions of paragraph 1 if dependent on the worker referred
> to above or living under his roof in the country whence he comes.

Depending on the category of the persons entitled to freedom of movement
and the right of residence, the group of family members may vary thus.

In order to answer the question whether the partner of a lesbian or gay
man qualifies as belonging to one or more of the above mentioned categories, a survey of the case-law of the ECJ is illuminating. I shall begin
with an analysis of the interpretation of the term 'spouse'.

The key decision of the ECJ concerning this question is *State of The
Netherlands v. Ann Florence Reed*.[16] An English unmarried couple, living
together in a stable relationship for five years came to The Netherlands,
where the man took up a temporary post with a subsidiary of a British undertaking. His companion, being unable to find work, applied for a residence permit as the man's companion, which was rejected. Ms Reed started
several proceedings against this rejection, one being summary proceedings
before the President of the Rechtbank in The Hague against eventual deportation. The President held that Article 10 of Regulation 1612/68 was applicable because in view of modern developments, companions in stable relationships should be treated as spouses. The Court of Appeal in The Hague
based its injunction against deportation on another line of reasoning. It
started from Dutch immigration policy, which provides that a foreigner who
has a stable relationship with a Netherlands national and lives with him in
the same household may as regards the right of residence be treated in the
same way as a spouse, on condition, *inter alia*, that neither of the two is
otherwise married. The Court of Appeal reasoned that it would amount to
discrimination on grounds of nationality prohibited in Article 7 and 48
EEC not to allow the companions of the nationals of other Member States
the same right of residence.

Advocate General Lenz took a negative view on both lines of thought.
He agreed that the word 'spouse' has a specific meaning in Community
law, and that Article 10 does not in this respect refer to national law, either

---

15   Plender, 1989, 193.
16   Case 59/85, [1986] ECR 1283, 17 April 1986.

the law of the host state, or the law of the state of origin. This specific Community meaning of the term 'spouse', at least historically speaking, was in his opinion applicable only to 'a partner to a valid marriage'.

Whether subsequent developments warranted a dynamic approach in this interpretation was another matter. According to AG Lenz the answer should be in the negative, in the first place because of 'the fact that companions can certainly not be treated in the same way as spouses in all Member States in view of the fact that their cultural, social, and ethical conditions vary widely in some respects', and in the second place for reasons of legal certainty.[17]

The ECJ started out with an interpretation of the word 'spouse' in Regulation 1612/68. It rejected here a dynamic interpretation of the word 'spouse', because of what it saw as lack of developments in social and legal conceptions:

> [...] Those developments must be visible in the whole of the Community; such an argument cannot be based on social and legal developments in only one or a few Member States. There is no reason, therefore, to give the term 'spouse' an interpretation which goes beyond the legal implication of that term, which embrace rights and obligations which do not exist between unmarried companions.

As any interpretation by the Court would be directly binding on all Member States, and should take into account the situation in the whole Community, the Court held that:

> in the absence of any indication of a general social development which would justify a broad construction and in the absence of any indication to the contrary of the Regulation, it must be held that the term 'spouse' in Article 10 of the Regulation refers to a marital relationship only.[18]

Having discarded the broad construction of 'spouse' (although the principle of dynamic interpretation had been maintained) the ECJ addressed the non-discrimination issue. Here it resorted to a very broad construction of another term used in the regulation. Article 7(2) provides that in the host state a worker who is a national of another Member State must 'enjoy the same social and tax advantages as national workers'. In earlier cases the Court had emphasized that this phrase should not be interpreted restrictively.[19] Hence fare reductions and the right to use one's own language in court proceedings[20] fall within the concept of a 'social advantage'. The Court went on and expounded:[21]

---

17   Ibid. at 1294.
18   Ibid. at 1300.
19   Case 32/75, *Cristini v. S.N.C.F.* [1975] ECR 1085.
20   Case 137/84, *Ministère Public v. Mutsch* [1985] ECR 2681.
21   *Reed* case, *supra* note 16, at 1303.

In the same way it must be recognized that the possibility for a migrant worker of obtaining permission for his unmarried companion to reside with him, where that companion is not a national of the host Member State, can affect his integration in the host state and thus contribute to the achievement of freedom of movement for workers. Consequently, that possibility must also be regarded as falling within the concept of a social advantage for the purposes of Article 7(2) of Regulation 1612/68.

The upshot of this broad construction is, that Member States which grant foreign unmarried companions of their nationals the right to reside in their territory, cannot refuse the same right to companions of nationals of other Member States under Article 7 and 48 EEC and Article 7(2) of Regulation 1612/68. This is of course a very important decision which may affect companions of workers who are of the same sex, depending on the national legislation of the host country. I will refer to this possibility later.

Although, up until now, the ECJ has refused to revise its rather strict interpretation of the term 'spouse' in Regulation 1612/68, it nevertheless has shown a tendency to broaden its meaning in other respects. In *Diatta*,[22] a Senegalese national, married with her French husband who lived and worked in West Berlin, was refused a prolongation of a residence permit because of her living separately from her husband and of her intention to divorce him. The ECJ considered that the object of the Regulation was to facilitate the freedom of movement of workers under Article 48 EEC, and that Article 10 of Regulation 1612/68 was instrumental to establishing this freedom. It concluded therefore that:

> [17] Having regard to its context and the objectives which it pursues, that provision cannot be interpreted restrictively.

And it went on to say that:

> [18] In providing that a member of a migrant worker's family has the right to install himself with the worker, Article 10 of the Regulation does not require that the member of the family in question must live permanently with the worker [...]. A requirement that the family must live under the same roof permanently cannot be implied.

The ECJ took a formal view concerning the dissolution of the marriage. As long as it had not been terminated by a competent authority, it had to be considered as still existing, even if the spouses lived permanently under different roofs, and even if they intended to divorce. Thus, a marriage, though formally not yet dissolved, which was for all practical purposes dead and buried, can still be the basis for a dependent residence right of the spouse of a worker.

---

22   Case 267/83, *Diatta v. Land Berlin* [1985] ECR 574.

The consequence of *Reed* and *Diatta* is, that the ECJ has retained marriage as a formal condition for being treated as 'spouse' under community law, but that this condition may be devoid of any substance: not only all kinds of arrangements involving living together or apart seem to be allowed, but also marriages of which the existence continues only for the convenience of the advantages of Community law, which are withheld to unmarried couples living in stable relationships under one roof.

C. Family Life and Privacy

An alternative approach to look at the status of lesbians and gay men and their freedom of movement under Community law is through the concept of fundamental human rights. The ECJ has repeatedly held 'that fundamental human rights form an integral part of the general principles of Community law, the observance of which is ensured by the European Court of Justice'.[23] For the identification of these fundamental rights inspiration is sought in the constitutional traditions common to the Member States, international treaties upon which Member States have collaborated or to which they are signatories etc. One of those international treaties is the ECHR.[24] The preamble of the Single European Act (1986) states explicitly that the Member States are:

> Determined to work together to promote democracy on the basis of the fundamental rights recognized in the constitutions and laws of the Member States, in the Convention for the Protection of Human Rights and Fundamental Freedoms and the European Social Charter, notably freedom, equality and social justice.

In this way, through the concept of general principles of law, the observance of which is ensured by the ECJ, the jurisprudence of the European Court of Human Rights becomes relevant to Community law. At the very least such jurisprudence will operate as a guideline for the ECJ when it has to guarantee fundamental rights in the Community legal order. One consequence of this may be that, given that the ECJ guarantees fundamental rights or human rights as an integral part of the Community legal order, it may declare void any Community act which violates such fundamental rights as are enshrined in, for example, the ECHR. In the context of the rights of lesbians and gay men, particular emphasis may be placed on the 'right to respect for private and family life' as laid down in Article 8 of the ECHR, and its

---

23   See, e.g., Case 29/69, *Stauder* [1969] ECR 419; Case 4/73, *Nold* [1974] ECR 491; Case 44/79, *Hauer* [1979] ECR 3727; Case C-260/89, *Elleniki Radiophonia*, judgment of 18 June 1991, not yet published.

24   Cf. e.g. Schermers, 'The European Communities bound by Fundamental Human Rights', *CML Rev.* (1990) 249-257.

impact on Community acts, such as the regulations and directives in the area of the free movement of workers and other persons.

Furthermore the ECJ may scrutinize national legislation and practices as far as these fall within the scope of Community law. This power of scrutiny has been formulated several times in a negative way, and recently also positively. The negative form may be found e.g. in the judgment in *Cinéthèque*.[25]

> Although it is true that it is the duty of this Court to ensure observance of fundamental rights in the field of Community law, it has no power to examine the compatibility with the European Convention of national legislation which concerns, as in this case, an area which falls within the jurisdiction of the national legislator.

This case concerned freedom of expression as laid down in Article 10 of the Convention.

More recently in *Wachauf*[26] the ECJ formulated its view in positive terms and stated in the context of the examination of whether a Community rule was compatible with the requirements of the protection of fundamental rights, that

> those requirements are also binding on the Member States when they implement Community rules.

Still more recently, in *Elliniki Radiophonia,*[27] the ECJ explained the scope of Community law in the area of human rights *vis-à-vis* national legislation as follows:

> In particular, when a Member State invokes the combined principles of Articles 56 and 66 to justify a rule which tends to impede the exercise of the free provision of services, this justification, permitted by Community Law, must be interpreted in the light of the general principles of law, and notably fundamental rights. So, the relevant national rules can profit from the exceptions set out in the combined provisions of Articles 56 and 66 only if they comply with the fundamental rights for which the Court ensures respect.[28]

25   Joined Cases 60 and 61/84, *Cinéthèque and Others v. Fédération nationale des cinémas français* [1985] ECR 2605, at para. 26.
26   Case C-5/88, *Wachauf v. Germany* [1989] ECR 2609.
27   Case C-260/89, *Elliniki Radiophonia, supra* note 23.
28   En particulier, lorsqu'un Etat membre invoque les dispositions combinées des Articles 56 et 66 pour justifier une réglementation qui est de nature à entraver l'exercice de la libre prestation des services, cette justification, prévue par le droit communautaire, doit être interprétée à la lumière des principes généraux du droit et notamment des droits fondamentaux. Ainsi, la réglementation nationale en cause ne pourra bénéficier des exceptions prévues par les dispositions combinées des Articles 56 et 66 que si elle est conforme aux droits fondamentaux dont la Cour assure le respect.

In the area under examination both Regulation 1612/68 and the directives, and also their implementation in the Courts of the Member States must be compatible with such fundamental rights as those of respect for family and private life. Whether national rules implementing Community law are identical with national rules lying within the scope of Community law is an important matter for discussion, but will not be discussed in this chapter. Nevertheless an element in defining the scope of review by the ECJ of national legislation in the area of fundamental rights is formed by the opinion of Advocate General van Gerven in the recent *Grogan* case,[29] concerning the freedom of expression:

> Yet, once a national rule is involved which has effects in an area covered by Community law [in this case Article 59 EEC] and which, in order to be permissible, must be justifiable under Community law with the help of concepts or principles of Community law, then the appraisal of that national rule no longer falls within the exclusive jurisdiction of the national legislature.

In the circumstances of this particular case the Court regrettably considered the Irish prohibition to impart and receive information on abortion as falling outside the field of application of Community law.

The Court referred, however, to its ruling in the Judgment in *Elliniki Radiophonia* of 18 June 1991[30] where it stated that:

> where national legislation falls within the field of application of Community law the Court, when requested to give a preliminary ruling, must provide the national court with all the elements of interpretation which are necessary in order to enable it to assess the compatibility of that legislation with the fundamental rights as laid down in particular in the European Convention on Human Rights – the observance of which the Court ensures.

Are there decisions of the ECJ directly concerned with 'private and family life' or in other ways relevant to this topic?

What we are concerned with here is primarily case-law of the ECJ indicating that the categories of family members and dependents in the regulations and directives concerned are too narrow in the light of the fundamental rights, to protect private and family life.

The case-law concerning Article 8 of the European Convention by the Strasbourg institutions is abundant, and considered in depth in the Chapter by Van Dijk. The autonomous concepts in Article 8 of 'private life' and 'family life', though distinct, show overlapping areas. Within the context of the ECHR it may make no difference whether the object of the provision is to be labelled as private life or as family life, but it may have a certain

---

29   Case C-159/90, *Society for the Protection of Unborn Children Ireland (SPUC) v. Grogan*, (not yet reported) at para. 31.
30   *Supra* note 23, at para. 42. (OJ 1991 C 201/05, 31 July 1991).

impact in the radiation of the case-law concerning Article 8 into the Community legal order. Thus the characterization of a relationship as family life which has to be protected under Article 8 may influence the interpretation of the regulations and Directives which use the same or related terms but which also specify the relationship concerned. It may well be that the definition of categories of persons by Community legislation falls short of what the Strasbourg institutions consider as 'family life' entitled to protection. From the outset it should be made clear that the context of migration which is at stake here is to be considered a special area in which Strasbourg has developed extensive case-law, because here autonomous grounds for interference, allowed and enumerated in Article 8(2) come to the fore which differ from considerations in purely domestic cases.

In most cases the interference with the life of lesbians and gay men has been characterized as interference with the 'private life' of the persons involved. In my view this can be explained primarily by the fact that most cases concerned private sexual behaviour, proscribed by domestic criminal law, and the question raised was whether this interference with 'private life' was acceptable under Article 8(2).[31] In the same way complaints about abortion laws and against interference with the life of transsexuals have been characterized as concerning 'private life', though not exclusively so.[32] Most of the interferences, though not all, have regrettably been accepted by the Strasbourg judges and commissioners under one or more of the headings of Article 8(2).[33] The case of *B. v. France*[34] may herald a more progressive development.

---

[31]   See, e.g., *Dudgeon* case, ECHR Judgment of 22 October 1981, Series A, No. 45 (1982); *Norris* case, ECHR Judgment of 26 October 1988, Series A, No. 142 (1989). See Dubber, 1990, 189-214.

[32]   See Application 6959/75, *Brüggemann & Scheuten v. Fed. Republic Germany*, Yearbook XIX (1976) 382, where the Commission considered 'that pregnancy and the interruption of pregnancy are part of private life, *and also in certain circumstances of family life*' (emphasis added).

[33]   See however the vigorous and fully convincing dissenting opinion of the Dutch Judge Martens in the *Cossey* case, 27 September 1990, Series A, No. 184, 22-41, who holds that the UK 'had violated both Art. 8 and Art. 12 of the Convention'. How strong the feelings of Judge Martens were in this case can be guaged by his statements in an interview, *Nederlands Juristenblad* (1991) 470 seq.:

> The stubborn refusal of the Court to regard the UK law concerning transsexuals as unwarranted interference with respect to private life, family life, and the right to marry, leads to the paradoxical result that e.g. Ms. Cossey can only legally marry another woman: she is forced to a marriage with another woman though not being lesbian (paras. 44 and 45 of the Judgment), as this is what the Court cleverly considers to be 'the traditional marriage between persons of opposite biological sex' (in para. 43) in this particular case. Decisions which lead to this kind of ludicrous results condemn themselves.

[34]   That the Commission and Court are coming round to acknowledging that their position has become untenable can be inferred from the recent decisions in the case of *B. v. France*, judgment of 25 March 1992, Series A, No. 232-C. Following the Commission

As to the elements which play a role in defining the 'family life' in Article 8, it seems to be very difficult to find very definite statements in the case-law. *De iure* and *de facto* elements play a role in different degrees; it is to a large extent *ius in causa positum*. A certain lack of coherence in this area seems to be a permanent feature of the rich case-law.[35] For our topic the following elements are relevant.

Extra-marital relationships can create family life if the persons involved live together on a permanent basis and keep house together.[36] A polygamous family is in principle protected.[37] In some circumstances it is not even necessary for a married couple to live together; in the *Berrehab* case the Court considered:

> It follows from the concept of family on which Article 8 is based that a child born of such a union [a *de iure* and *de facto* marriage] is *ipso iure* part of the relationship; hence, from the moment of the child's birth and by the very fact of it, there exists between him and his parents a bond amounting to 'family life', even if the parents are not then living together.[38]

The case-law concerning lesbians and gay men has been characterized by Henry G. Schermers as 'conservative'.[39] In *X. and Y. v. UK*[40] the Commission gave its opinion that the relationship between homosexual partners:

> despite the modern evolution of attitudes towards homosexuality does not fall within the scope of the right to respect for family life, but may be falling under the heading of the right to respect for private life.

Commenting on this case Van Dijk and Van Hoof pointedly add:

> (seventeen votes to one) the Court decided (by fifteen votes to six) in a landmark decision that Ms B:
>> finds herself daily in a situation which, taken as a whole, is not compatible with the respect due to her private life. Consequently, even having regard to the State's margin of appreciation, the fair balance which has to be struck between the general interest and the interests of the individual [...] has not been attained and there has thus been a violation of Article 8.
> An important success for Judge Martens, who in a succinct separate opinion acclaimed the Court's decision.

35   Cf. Van Dijk and Van Hoof, 1990, 419 seq. See also Van Dijk and Vlasblom, 1991.
36   Applications 7289/75 and 7349/76, *X. and Y. v. Switzerland*, Yearbook XX (1977) 377.
37   Commission, Application 2992/66, *Khan v. UK*, Yearbook X (1967) 478.
38   *Berrehab* case, 21 June 1988, Series A, No. 138, 14.
39   Schermers, 'Verblijfsrecht van buitenlandse vaders', *Nederlands Juristenblad* (1990) 238-240, who in his comments on the *Berrehab* case lists 10 factors relevant for the decision to expel foreigners. See also the important essay by Swart, *Het recht op gezinsleven in het Europees verdrag en het Vreemdelingenrecht*, Report for the Nederlandse Juristenvereniging (1990) reviewed by d'Oliveira, *Nederlands Juristenblad* (1990) 819-822.
40   Appliaction 9369/81, DR 23, 220 (1983). Repeated in Application 14753/89, *X. and Y. v. UK*.

The Commission gives no indication on which criterion it relied for its decision. The difference with an unmarried heterosexual couple is not at all clear, on the contrary there is a clear similarity of interests.[41]

An underdeveloped area concerning the family life of gay men and lesbians in particular is the fact that one of the partners may have a child which is growing up in the household where the other partner may play an important role.[42]

In 1984 an English woman entered into a lesbian relationship with an Australian woman, who became the mother of a child, also of Australian nationality. The three live together. The Australian part of the family was threatened with expulsion and both women lodged a complaint in Strasbourg.[43] The Commission found that 'lesbian partnership involves "private life"', within the meaning of Article 8 of the Convention. However, although lawful deportation will have repercussions on such relationships, it cannot, in principle, be regarded as an interference with this Convention provision, given the right of the State to impose immigration controls and limits. Nonetheless, as the Court found in a British case,[44] if it can be 'shown that the applicants could not live together elsewhere than in the UK, or that their link with the UK was an essential element of their relationship' an interference may still be found.

The problem is, of course, that in itself, according to the case-law of Commission and Court, there is *ipso iure* 'family life' between mother and child, and that this family life can be expanded to include someone who cares for a stepchild. Thus the Commission considered in the case of a mother and a stepchild that:

> it is not necessary to decide whether, in the absence of any legal relationship, the ties between the applicant and the child amounted to 'family' (...). Bearing in mind that the applicant has cared for the child for many years and is deeply attached to him, the separation ordered by the Court undoubtedly affects her 'private life'.[45]

---

41   *Supra* note 35, at 420. What Van Dijk and Van Hoof have in mind when they speak about heterosexual couples should be qualified. Swart, note 39, at 225 tells us, that the considerations of the Commission concerning the complaint about the violation of Art. 14 have not been reported. He reports that the Commission's answer boils down to the statement that, as homosexual relationships do not qualify as family life and heterosexual relationships do, discrimination cannot occur. There is no discrimination, however, between lesbian and gay relationships! No wonder, Swart comments, that this verbal juggling has not been published.

42   Cf. Van Rhee, 'Een bijzonder gezin. De Europese Commissie en homoseksuele relaties' ('A special family'), The European Commission and Homosexual Relationships, *Nederlands Juristenblad* (1990) 1670-1675.

43   Application 14753/89 27 February 1989, *X. and Y. v. UK*.

44   Dec. Adm. Com.t p. 9369/81, para. May 1983, DR 32, 222.

45   Thus Van Rhee, *supra* note 42, at 1674. I agree.

Here the question whether this relationship amounts to family life is left open. In combination with the undoubtedly existent family life of mother and child it would, I submit, be extremely artificial to construe the relationship between child and partner of the mother as something other than family life, and to reduce it to 'private life'.

The case-law in Strasbourg of the European Commission and the Court of Human Rights concerning the persons whose family life or private life is protected under Article 8 is rather restrictive, and sometimes encompasses fewer categories of persons than national legislation and practices do. If one reads the Strasbourg case-law in conjunction with the sometimes ambiguous Community texts – I referred earlier to an example which could play a role in homosexual parenthood[46] – one finds oneself in an confused position when determining the impact of human rights law on Community legislation.

II. Extensions within the Existing Framework

Set out below are some ways in which I consider that Community law may be developed. Such developments may take place in combination with the national laws of the Member States, or by development of case-law under Human Rights instruments.

A. Lesbian and Gay Partners as 'Spouse'

From the perspective of an evolutionary and dynamic interpretation of concepts of Community law such as 'spouse' in the relevant regulations and directives there are two possible lines of development to be traced.

a. In the first place one may consider the reasoning set out in paragraph 15 of the *Reed* case, discussed above:

> In the absence of any indication of a general social development which would justify a broad construction and in the absence of any indication to the contrary in the regulation, it must be held that the term 'spouse' in Article 10 of the Regulation refers to a marital relationship only.

This case involved a companion in a stable heterosexual relationship. There is nothing in the language of the court which would hint at denying this status to companions in stable gay or lesbian relationships, but the issue did not need to be decided in this context of interpretation of Article 10 of

46   See *supra* note 14.

Regulation 1612/68. But it becomes relevant as from the moment that a general social development in the Member States can be traced which would justify bringing stable non-marital relationships under the term 'spouse'. This development can already be said to be visible in many areas of the laws of a number of Member States. This is not the place to give an overview of this evolution, but there are a host of indications which would warrant expanding the construction of this Community term.

A strong indication of the necessity for development in this area is to be found in a recent amendment by the European Parliament to a proposal of the Commission to amend Regulation 1612/68 on the freedom of movement for workers within the Community.[47]

The European Parliament proposed to introduce two new paragraphs in Article 10 of the Regulation in order to include among the categories having the right to install themselves with a worker persons with whom the worker lives in a *de facto* union recognized as such for administrative or legal purposes:

> (2) The right to install themselves referred to in paragraph 1 above shall also cover the person with whom the worker lives in a *de facto* union recognized as such for administrative and legal purposes, whether in the Member State of origin or the host State, and their dependent offspring.[48]

Although I consider that the chances of this amendment being accepted by the Council must not be exaggerated, it shows that Parliament seems to think that the ECJ is acting too slowly in this area and that improvement in the situation of companions is imperative. The proposed provision forms a mix between an equality-based rule and a specific Community right. Its phrasing leaves some doubt about its implications. Similar provisions have been proposed by the European Parliament for directives in the area of restrictions on freedom of movement and residence of workers, such as directive 68/630.[49]

In the meantime the Commission has proposed an amending regulation to Regulation 1612/68, submitted in January 1989.[50] The proposal concerning Article 10 reads:

> The following shall, even if they are not nationals of a Member State, have the right to install themselves with the national of a Member State who is employed in the territory of a Member State:

---

47   OJ 1990 C 68/88, 19 March 1990. The Commission's proposal is to be found in COM (88) 815 final SYN 185.
48   The amendment also introduced a third paragraph to Art. 10 which would improve the status of these family members, including partners in *de facto* unions, after the death of the worker concerned.
49   See Doc. cited in note 47 at 94.
50   COM (88) 81 E final SYN 185, OJ 1989 C 100/6, 21 April 1989.

(a) the spouse and their descendants;
(b) relatives in the ascending line of the worker or the spouse;
(c) any other member of the family dependent on or living under the roof of the worker or the spouse in the country whence they come.

This proposal seems to extend slightly the group of persons with a dependent right of residence with the person entitled to freedom of movement. The discretion of Member States *vis-à-vis* the persons mentioned in the original Article 10(s.2) would be abolished. The age of descendants of the employee would not be relevant anymore. In the Explanatory Memorandum[51] the Commission states as one of the objectives of the revision:

> [the extension of] the categories of persons protected by Community Law, to cover *all* descendants and relatives in the ascending line of the worker and his spouse and to ... *dependent* collaterals.

And the Commission continues quoting *Reed* and *Diatta* to expound:

> Moreover, such an amendment takes account of developments in case-law in the field of the rights of the spouse and the unmarried partner of the Community worker. However, such case-law, although favourable to members of the worker's family, is limited by Articles 10 and 11 currently in force. Hence the need for the amendment.[52]

The purpose of the proposal then seems to be to incorporate the case-law of the ECJ into the existing legislative framework, and thus to strengthen the position of unmarried partners and couples under Community law: it concerns Community-wide harmonization of the categories of persons entitled to follow the worker etc., and thus the incidental use of the equality principle as in the *Reed* case, with varying results depending on national practices is left behind.

It should be noticed that, according to the Commission's proposal, Article 10(3), under which the worker is required to have housing considered as normally available for his family, would be rescinded, because the situation concerning the housing stock as compared with 1964 no longer warrants such a provision.[53] In this way *Diatta* is in part pre-empted in future cases.

b. But there is more. In one Member State, Denmark, lesbians and gay men are allowed to register officially their partnership and this *registered partnership* is assimilated by law in most respects with the marital relationship reserved for partners of different sexes. On October 1, 1989 the law

---

51   COM (88) 815 final SYN 185, 16.
52   Page 19.
53   See also COM (88) 815 Revision final, 29 March 1989, at 22.

on registered partnership entered into force.[54] It may be useful to give some details about the provisions of this law.

First and foremost attention must be drawn to paragraph 3(1) of the law which provides that 'registration of partnership has the same legal consequences as the conclusion of a marriage, except those defined in section 4 of this provision'.

Section 3(2) states:

> Provisions in the Danish law, concerning marriage and the spouses, have analogous application to registered partnership and the registered partners.

As for the exceptions referred to in paragraph 3(1), which are listed in Section 4, these concern primarily adoption and guardianship and the like (not available to registered partners, as the Danish law starts from the principle that children should have parents of different sexes).

Who can apply for registration of their partnership? Relevant factors here are degrees of consanguinity and nationality. As for the first condition that there exist no degree of consanguinity that would prevent a marriage (two cousins may register, two sisters not), it is obvious that the analogy with marriage is very close. This is made explicit in paragraph 2(1) of the Act.

Doubtful is the condition laid down in paragraph 2(2) that 'both partners or one of them (have) his/her/their residence in this country, and possess Danish nationality'. The Act is more restrictive than for the conclusion of marriages in Denmark. This restriction is justified on the basis of potential lack of recognition of the registered partnership in other countries. It is, however, problematic in the light of those treaties which prohibit discrimination on the grounds of nationality. Article 7 of the EEC Treaty may come into play in this respect, given the fact that freedom of movement is at stake.[55]

Furthermore under Articles 8, 12, and 14 of the ECHR, which protect family and private life irrespective of nationality, registered partnerships amount to family life.

And then, insofar as Community law is involved, one may apply the reasoning in the *Reed* case: if Danish nationals are allowed to engage in registered partnerships with persons of another nationality and/or residence, then this should, on the basis of Article 7, also be possible for other Member State nationals. A British national, resident in Denmark on the basis of the

---

54   Law No. 372 of 7 June 1989, JLOV 1263. See on this law e.g. Boele-Woelki and Tange, 'De Deense wet inzake het geregistreerd partnerschap', *Nederlands Juristenblad* (1989) 1537-1543, L. Nielsen, 'Family Rights and the "Registered Partnership" in Denmark', *International Journal of Law and the Family* (1990) 297-307.
55   Cf. Boele-Woelki and Tange, *supra* note 54, at 1538.

Community freedom of movement, should be able to enter into a registered partnership with a non-Danish person. Paragraph 2(2) is not compatible with Community law according to the principle developed in *Elliniki Radiophonica Tileorassi*.[56]

For our present purposes it is necessary also to devote attention to paragraph 4 of the Act. This paragraph reads as follows:

> Provisions in international conventions are not applicable to the registered partnership, unless the other signatories agree to this.

It is not a very clear provision, and it leaves open many questions. In the Memorandum to the Act we find a statement that Denmark is free to unilaterally apply conventional rules concerning marital relationships and spouses to registered partnerships, and that the Danish authorities are even obliged to do so, unless an unjustifiable advantage or disadvantage for registered partner(ship)s compared with marriages would result from this application.

Given the fact that Member States have accepted the jurisdiction of the ECJ and are obliged by Article 5 EEC to uphold the Community legal order, they are bound, I submit, by any decision of the ECJ stating that registered partners like the Danish ones have to be considered as 'spouses' in the sense of Community legislation. This would imply that Danish workers, for example, exercising their freedom of movement under Article 48 of the Treaty, are allowed to be accompanied by their registered partner. The assimilation, brought about by the Danish Act, between registered partners and spouses will in this way be promoted to the level of Community law. The 'marital relationship' referred to in the *Reed* case, even if it will not be construed as encompassing stable (heterosexual) relationships, will nevertheless at least absorb 'registered partnerships'. The intention of the Danish legislature is necessary but as such insufficient for this construction. But if the Court states that 'there is no reason [...] to give the term 'spouse' an interpretation which goes beyond the legal implications of that term, which embrace rights and obligations which do not exist between unmarried companions'[57] one may assert that a well-defined and officially registered partnership, which is in no way hampered by legal uncertainty, has to be considered as on an equal footing with marital relationships, and the partners as 'spouses'.

We may be reminded of the fact that under English law common law marriages were recognized as marriages, although concluded without any intervention of state authorities. If it is true that the 'Home Office have a discretion to enable a common law spouse who has been living in a stable

56   See text to note 28. Cf. Emmert in Chapter Fifteen.
57   *Reed*, para. 10.

relationship with the principal applicant to join him'[58] then this would obviously be a *Reed* lever to permit other Member State nationals on equal footing with UK nationals to settle in the UK with their unmarried partners. In other words: if the Court refers to marital relationships it depends on the law of the Member States whether such a legal relationship exists. It is the combination, the interlocking of Community law and the law of the Member States, including their systems of private international law, which makes the term 'spouse' operational. The autonomy of Community law consists in accepting, for the purposes of Community law, the assimilation between marriage and registered partnerships as brought about by the law of Member States. It is evident that the purpose of the secondary legislation, concerning the family members of those who are 'persons' under Community law who avail themselves of freedom of movement, is the promotion of social integration and the mobility of workers etc. in the Community. The sex of the partner or the sexual preferences of the partners is irrelevant in view of these objectives.

We might now turn to private international law and the Danish registered partnership. Are these partnerships to be recognized elsewhere? Will such a partnership be recognized eg. in The Netherlands and what effects would be the consequence of such recognition? Dutch law attaches in many respects legal consequences to even unregistered relationships, be they partnerships between[59] heterosexuals or between homosexuals. One of the most striking examples, for the comparative lawyer, is Article 8(4) of the Dutch Nationality Act 1985, which allows naturalization of foreign partners of Dutch nationals if they live in a stable non-marital relationship in the Netherlands with an unmarried Dutch person for at least three years. There is no doubt in Dutch practice and literature that the Act includes lesbian and gay relationships in this naturalization procedure.[60]

In this connection – the content of Dutch public policy as a potential barrier to recognition of partnerships registered under Danish law – mention may be made of an administrative practice in a considerable number of Dutch municipalities of registering the partnerships of unmarried persons of the same sex.[61] When two local councillors – appointed by the local

---

58   Fernandez, *supra* note 11, at 90.
59   Cf. the facts of the *Reed* case concerning the Vreemdelingencirculaire (Governmental Policy concerning Immigration).
60   Groot, Tratnik, *Nationaliteitsrecht* (1986) 96.
61   This administrative practice has been taken over to some extent by the Nevabs (Dutch association of civil servants working in the offices of the Registry of Births, Deaths and Marriages), which has issued some guidelines on the matter. The Association of Dutch municipalities (VNG), took the position (1) that marriages between persons of the same sex were not allowed; (2) that the Registries were defined by law and could not be extended with other types of entries; but that local authorities were free to establish a separate register for partnerships. Interestingly a recurrent condition for being registered is the

council as officiers of the Civil Registry (a common phenomenon in the Netherlands), had been prevented by the District Court from being sworn, the Supreme Court (Hoge Raad) declared that the District Court was wrong in so doing provided it was clear that the persons involved fulfilled all requirements of law for this office, including appointment by the local council, and that such a refusal could not be justified by predictions about the way in which the councillor involved would exercise his office.[62] In this particular case, it was indeed the declared wish of the councillors involved to participate in the conclusion of a marriage between two gay men, Messrs Stello and Kuipers.

In a recent letter from the Dutch Minister for Welfare, Health and Culture[63] it is stated that the Minister of Justice has asked the Standing Committee reviewing Legislative Programmes to also answer the question what shape legal regulation could take – independent from that of marriage – for those who desire, by means of a form of registration, governed by public law, to attach legal consequences to the fact that they have accepted reciprocal and enduring responsibility for each other.[64] The Committee handed in its report which was transmitted to Parliament on 14th February 1992.[65] It opted for a system not unlike the Danish one: public registration should entail a number of private and public law consequences, i.e. most of the legal consequences of marriage. It offered as an alternative a less far-reaching form of registration, with fewer consequences involved.[66]

Thus it has become clear that the recognition of Danish partnerships is not to be considered as contrary to Dutch *ordre public*, even if a Dutch partner is involved.[67] In ways analogous to the rules concerning recognition of marriages the registered partnerships may be recognized. This is the case for Dutch private international law, and for other systems of private international law as well.

Depending on similar developments in other Member States the same line of reasoning can be developed.[68] In conclusion one may wonder if the

---

existence of a notarial deed laying down the terms of the living together contract of the partners. See for these developments *Het Personeel Statuut*, 1992, 4-9, and 10-11.

62   Hoge Raad 15 November 1991, *Het Personeel Statuut* 1992, 11.

63   Parliamentary Document 19.504 No. 19, Governmental Policy and Homosexuality, 23 December 1991.

64   Ibid., at 18, para. IV.5.

65   Parliamentary Document TK 1991-1992, 22.300 VI No. 36.

66   Thus Fernandez, *supra* note 11, stating that 'Dutch legislation permits homosexual couples to marry and, therefore, these couples should fall within the definition of "spouse"', seems to be a bit rash.

67   This view is shared by Boele-Woelki and Tange, *supra* note 54, at 1543.

68   One may refer e.g. to the (hesitant) developments in France where legislation concerning 'unions civiles' is considered. See *Le Monde*, 27 April 1992. See in this connection Chapter Three by Waaldijk. See also some data in Waaldijk, *Tip of an Iceberg. Anti-Lesbian and Anti-Gay Discrimination in Europe 1980-1990. A Survey of discrimination and anti-discrimination in law and society*, (1991) ch. 3. Partnerships, 31-38.

time has not come for the ECJ to reconsider its dictum in *Reed*, and to find that – given the evolution in different Member States – the meaning of the term 'spouse' has now (to be) broadened in order to encompass unmarried couples of whatever sex. Given the widespread existence of informal partnerships and relationships both among heterosexuals and among homosexuals, it is time to conclude that to be able to take these partners with one is a powerful incentive to avail oneself of the freedom of movement of workers and others.

In private international law conflicts rules are being developed to allow for finding the applicable law for unmarried couples.[69] This topic has even been put on the agenda of the Hague Conference on private international law.[70]

B. 'Social Advantages'

Even if partners of lesbian or gay workers etc. are denied the status of 'spouse' under Community law, they may invoke the right to follow their partner into another Member State if that State grants this right to such foreign partners of its own nationals. In combination with the principle of non-discrimination laid down in Article 7 EEC, nationals of other Member States in that state have the right to be accompanied there by their partners as well. This has been stated by the ECJ in the *Reed* case, where it was considered to be one of the many 'social advantages' as mentioned in Article 7(2) of Regulation 1612/68.

Everything in this connection depends on the existence, under the law of the Member State concerned, of rules and practices which allow lesbian and gay companions into the country to join their partners who possess the nationality of the country concerned. The nationality of the foreign partner is not relevant in this respect: they may be nationals of Member States or 'extra-communitarians'. What counts, however, is the Member State nationality of the worker etc.

It is to be noted that in the 1990 generation of directives concerning senior citizens, students and others, there is no equivalent of the 'social advantages' criteria on the basis of which companions may reside with the person directly entitled to freedom of movement under these directives. It is submitted that the fact that these categories are deprived of the company of their unmarried partners of the same or opposite sex amounts to discrimination, not on the grounds of nationality this time, but on the grounds of

---

69   See Sarcevic, 'Zur nichtehelichen Lebensgemeinschaft im IPR; unter besonderer Berücksichtigung der jugoslawischen Teilrechte, 81 *StaZ*, 176-182 and further literature in Kegel, *Internationales Privatrecht* (1985).
70   See General Affairs. Preliminary Doc. No. 5 with bibliography.

differences irrelevant to the distinction. Given the fact that the 1990 generation of directives makes the right of residence conditional on a means test –
which in itself would again violate certain non-discrimination provisions –
it is not clear why workers and the self-employed are distinguished from
students and pensioners.

Given the fact that the 'social advantages' of Article 10 of Regulation
1612/68 are not available to the categories mentioned, a revision of the
Reed dictum excluding unmarried partners from the term 'spouse' is indeed
all the more pressing.

C. 'Private and Family Life'

Both the case-law of the European Commission and Court of Human
Rights, and that of the ECJ still have room for development. With changes
in attitude in the group of countries associated in the Council of Europe, or
in the smaller and more closely knit group of Member States of the European Community, these courts may finally see fit to change their artificial
distinction between heterosexual relationships on the one hand, and lesbian
and gay relationships on the other. Such changes may be premised, in the
meantime, by developments concerning the recognition of forms of unmarried family life with legal consequences in the public and private law of the
Member States. Denmark is a model country in this respect, followed by
the Netherlands. In several other countries similar evolutions may be witnessed. They will be instrumental to recognition of lesbian and gay partnerships. The European Community should not wait for the moment that the
Strasbourg institutions see fit to warm their cold feet. The EC has its own
momentum and its own objects, which may allow it to take the lead within
this association of more homogeneous countries.

III. New Developments – Additions

As this section is concerned with the freedom of movement of persons under
Community law I will restrict myself to this legal (dis)order, although I am
quite sure of the fact that an intimate relationship and intertwining is to be
noticed with human rights law as well. This development finds its latest
depository in the Maastricht Union Treaty of which Article F declares that

> (2) The Union shall respect fundamental rights, as guaranteed by the European
> Convention for the Protection of Human Rights and Fundamental Freedoms (...)
> and as they result from the constitutional traditions common to the Member
> States, as general principles of Community law.

Thus the pressure exerted by the ECJ and European Parliament have led to a certain codification of fundamental rights and freedoms in the Community legal order, to be safeguarded by all its institutions.

Equally important is a similar provision in Article K 2.(1) concerning the intergovernmental cooperation in the fields of Justice and Home Affairs, mentioned in Article K.1, which concerns *inter alia* 'immigration policy and policy regarding nationals of third countries'. Here however, control by the ECJ will be missing. This topic may overlap with aspects of the freedom of movement of persons which is without doubt a Community matter. However this may be, it is clear that in the area of freedom of movement of persons generally nothing much is changed in the light of the Maastricht Agreement.

The Commission will have to develop proposals to adapt existing directives or draft new directives to bring them into line with the dynamics which the Maastricht Agreement offers. It is suggested that it would be useful to urge for introduction of a 'social advantage' clause in the directives where this is missing, and, better still, to have the concept of 'family' expanded to include non-married partners and partners in unregistered relationships.

Furthermore there is a need for an organized attempt to uncover forms of direct and indirect discrimination by immigration law and practice in the Member States, which could eventually be used to bring cases before the ECJ. One area which is particularly ripe for consideration is that relating to restrictions on the freedom of movement of nationals and their partners imposed by Member States on the grounds of public policy. By applying existing case-law on public policy restrictions in these situations it may be possible to challenge the practices of Member States as contrary to Community law.

Chapter Thirteen
The Freedom of Movement of Goods and Services

by

BRUNO DE WITTE[*]

---

* Professor of European Law, University of Limburg in Maastricht.

Table of Contents

I. The Scope of the Free Movement of Goods and Services

A. The Common Elements

Separate chapters of the EEC Treaty are devoted to the four so-called Common Market freedoms. The free movement of persons is dealt with in the previous chapter of this report. The free movement of capital is not relevant here. This chapter will deal with the two remaining Common Market freedoms: the free movement of goods (Articles 9 to 37 EEC Treaty) and the freedom to provide services (Articles 59 to 66). Despite the fact that they are treated separately in the Treaty, there are a number of common elements defining the scope of the free movement of goods and of the freedom to provide services: those freedoms protect *economic activities* in which there is an *inter-state element* against *restrictions by public authorities*.

a. To start with the most obvious characteristic of the Common Market freedoms: they do not apply to situations that are purely internal to a particular Member State of the European Community. There must be an *inter-state element* to trigger the applicability of Community law. The importation or exportation of goods must be prevented or hindered; or the cross-border provision of service must be restricted. The existence of such a *prima facie* restriction to inter-state trade is not always easy to establish. An example of a controversy on this point are a few British cases in which plaintiffs argued that the restrictive licensing of sex shops by local authorities amounted to a restriction of the free movement of goods, because it limited the sale of imported sex objects. The European Court of Justice, to which this issue was submitted in the form of a preliminary question, answered that Article 30 of the EEC Treaty did not apply at all because the marketing of imported products was not made more difficult than that of domestic products and because such marketing rules had no connection with intra-Community trade.[1]

b. The free movement of goods and of services are both market freedoms, which means that their role is to regulate and protect *economic activities*.

The free movement of goods applies to commercial transactions about material products; thus, for instance, books, periodicals, films and video-cassettes are all goods in the sense of the EEC treaty.

Service activities are, according to Article 60 EEC Treaty, activities of an industrial or commercial character, of craftsmen and of the professions. The latter category should be taken in a very broad sense: it covers

---

1   Case C-23/89, *Quietlynn Ltd. and Richards v. Southend Borough Council* [1990] ECR I-3059; an almost identical case was decided in the same terms the following year: Case C-350/89, *Sheptonhurst Limited v. Newham Borough Council* [1991] 3 CMLR 463.

professional activities exercised by self-employed persons in all sectors of economic activity, including education, arts and entertainment, health, journalism, broadcasting, etc.

Article 60 of the EEC Treaty specifies that those activities should be 'normally provided for remuneration'. For instance, State education is not a service in the sense of the EEC Treaty because it is, to an overwhelming extent, paid for from State funds.[2] In the *Grogan* case, the European Court of Justice held that information on abortion clinics in Britain by Irish student associations was given on a voluntary basis and independently of the economic activity carried on by the British abortion clinics, and could therefore not be considered as (part of) a service itself.[3] In other words, activities need to be performed for financial reward in order to be protected by EC law. Services rendered gratis are outside the scope of EC law, though it would not seem difficult to put a commercial veneer on basically charitable activities, and bring them within the scope of the EEC Treaty.

c. The third factor defining the scope of the Common Market freedoms is the identity of the addressees of the obligation. The prohibition of any restriction on the trade of goods and the provision of services is directed at public bodies. In its case-law on the movement of goods, the Court of Justice has extended the obligation to private bodies acting under close State supervision or endowed with some form of State authority, but has clearly said that it does not apply to genuine private bodies and individuals.

For services, the situation is slightly different. Interestingly, Article 59 of the EEC Treaty does not designate the source of the restrictions to be abolished; yet, that does not mean that this freedom, in contrast with the free movement of goods, could be invoked against individual firms or individuals. The Court of Justice steered a middle course and held that the Treaty prohibition also applied to rules of non-state bodies (such as sport federations) aimed at collectively regulating employment or services.[4] Restrictions to the cross-border provision of services originating from single business firms or individuals, however, would not seem to be prohibited by the Treaty.

If *some* form of State action is usually required before one can invoke one of the two freedoms, it must also be emphasized that *any* form of State action is covered by the Treaty provisions, ranging from national legislation to simple administrative practices of local authorities and independent agencies. Restrictions against lesbian or gay expression often take place at the local level, in the exercise of the police powers of local authorities; if,

---

2   Case 263/86, *Belgian State v. Humbel* [1988] ECR 5365.
3   Case C-159/90, *Society for the Protection of the Unborn Children Ireland (SPUC) v. Grogan* [1991] 3 CMLR 849, at 891 (paragraph 26).
4   Case 36/74, *Walrave v. Association Union Cycliste Internationale* [1974] ECR 1405.

for instance, a mayor prohibits the projection of a gay or lesbian film from another EC country at the local film festival, there is a restriction of the free movement of goods.

If, however, the same mayor prohibited a performance at a theatre festival, the freedom to provide services would be involved. The reason for this distinction between rather similar activities and restrictions will be explained in the next paragraph.

B. The Distinction Between Goods and Services

In the original structure of the EEC Treaty, there is a clear distinction between the free movement of goods and the freedom to provide services. Whereas the free movement of goods deals with products crossing an intra-Community border, and the producer of the goods is out of the picture, the freedom to provide services was seen as strictly connected with the movement of the provider of a service from one Community country to the other. Freedom to provide service allows self-employed persons to enter the territory of another EC country for a particular activity without fixing their place of abode in that other country. Professionals may thus choose either to set up business in another EC State (in which case they are protected by the right of establishment) or to provide their services on an occasional basis, by moving from their home basis just for the time needed for a particular activity (in which case they are covered by the freedom to provide services). For instance, a Dutch surgeon who has a full-time practice in London but goes regularly to Paris to perform an operation, enjoys the right of establishment in the United Kingdom and the freedom to render a service in France.[5]

This form of providing services, which has clearly inspired the terms of Articles 59 and 60 of the EEC Treaty, has been complemented by two other forms which the Court of Justice has found to be protected as well by the Treaty chapter on services: cross-border provision of services whereby the receiver (and not the provider) of the service crosses the border (e.g. a patient visiting his doctor in another EC country), and provision of services whereby the provider and the receiver remain within their respective countries, while the service itself crosses the intra-Community border.

Only the latter form, which was perhaps not contemplated by the drafters of the Treaty, but has become the most important in economic terms, will be the object of analysis in this chapter. The other forms are covered in the previous chapter of this report, dealing with the free movement of persons. Indeed, whenever the provision of services involves the

---

5   Lasok, 1991, at 48.

crossing of a border and the exercise of economic activities in another country than one's own, the obstacles faced by lesbians and gay men are part of the barriers to the free movement of persons, as they have been described in the earlier chapter. The rest of this chapter therefore deals only with forms of the provision of services that do not involve border-crossing by persons.

This form of economic activity could possibly have been brought under the heading of free movement of goods rather than services. From an economic point of view, the object of those services can be considered as 'immaterial products'. For instance, the Financial Times may choose to export printed copies abroad, or it may instead choose to transmit the data to a printing press abroad; the choice of either of the two mechanisms does not affect the nature of the product, and is a matter of indifference to the consumer. Still, the former operation is qualified as movement of goods under the EEC Treaty, while the latter constitutes provision of services.

The distinction, based on the substance of the product (whether tangible or intangible), was introduced by the European Court of Justice in the *Sacchi* case, dealing with television. The Court held that 'in the absence of express provision to the contrary in the Treaty, a television signal must, by reason of its nature, be regarded as provision of services.' Consequently,

> the transmission of television signals, including those in the nature of advertisements, comes, as such, within the rules of the Treaty relating to services. However, trade in material, sound recordings, films, apparatus and other products used for the diffusion of television signals is subject to the rules relating to freedom of movement of goods.[6]

The Court's approach leads, particularly in the broadcasting sector, to somewhat artificial distinctions. When a programme is carried by Hertzian airwaves across the border, it is considered as a service, and any restrictions on the relay of the programme in the receiving country have to be analysed as restrictions of the freedom to provide services. When, on the contrary, a TV programme produced (and diffused) by a TV channel in country A is acquired by a TV station in country B and transmitted (perhaps simultaneously) by that station, it has crossed the border as a tangible object (a film or tape) and any restrictions on transmission are restrictions on the movement of goods. The use, by the Court of Justice, of the concept of 'services' to cope with the export or import of immaterial things has been called a 'dangerous fallacy' by one commentator.[7] However, the Court has maintained its view ever since and it must now be accepted as established case-law. Broadcasting and electronic data communication are services; the press, books and films are goods.

6   Case 155/73, *Sacchi* [1974] ECR 409, at 432 (operative part, para. 1).
7   Neville March Hunnings, 'Annotation on Case 52/79 and Case 62/79', in *CML Rev.* 1980, 564.

The artificiality of the distinction does not matter so much, as long as the legal regime of services is similar to that of goods. This is the case to a large extent, but not entirely, as will be explained in the next paragraph.

II. The Legal Regime of the Free Movement of Goods and Services

The basic rule of Community law is that goods and services should be able to flow from one Community country to the others without any hindrance by public authorities. But this rule is subject to a number of exceptions, which allow restrictive State measures under specified conditions. As is often the case, freedoms are best defined in a negative way, by considering which are the legitimate limitations to their exercise.

A. Permissible Restrictions

1. Permissible Restrictions of the Trade in Goods

In examining the rights of lesbians and gay men in the context of the free movement of goods, the central notion is that of 'public morality' which is listed in Article 36 of the EEC Treaty among the grounds justifying derogations from the free movement of goods. The concept of public morality has not been specified in Community legislation; its role can be assessed only on the basis of a few British cases that have come to the European Court of Justice for a preliminary ruling. In those cases, the Court has taken a fairly broad view of the discretion of a Member State in defining what are the needs of public morality. It can do so 'in accordance with its own scale of values and in the form selected by it'.[8] There is no attempt, in other words, to define a European standard of public morality. It would therefore seem that all national measures that expressly regulate homosexual activity or expression can be regarded as falling within the definition of public morality, and as allowing, therefore, a prima facie justification of barriers to trade.

Disparities between national legislations seem to be acceptable under Article 36, but discrimination against foreign goods is not. Article 36 has a second sentence according to which measures which by themselves can be justified on one of the grounds listed in the first sentence (for instance, public morality) may 'not constitute a means of arbitrary discrimination or a disguised restriction on trade between Member States'. The role of this second sentence is not easy to understand. It does not rule out the possibility

8   Case 34/79, *Henn and Darby* [1979] ECR 3795.

for States to adopt specific restrictions against imported products; that, after all, is the very purpose of Article 36. But it means that restrictions against imports must be justified by the specific danger caused by imports; for instance, the 'protection of health and life of humans, animals or plants', another of the grounds listed in Article 36, allows the Member States to protect themselves against specific health hazards associated with imported goods (like anti-rabies controls in the UK).

As far as public morality is concerned, it is difficult to imagine specifically foreign 'evils' that would justify import restrictions. It would seem that the State is left with the choice either to prohibit both nationally produced and foreign categories of goods considered to be damageable to public morality, or to allow both; but a dual standard would appear to be an 'arbitrary discrimination' prohibited by the second sentence of Article 36.

Yet, precisely such a dual standard was accepted by the European Court of Justice in the first 'public morality' case coming from the UK, the case of *Henn and Darby*.[9] The Court had to decide whether the application of United Kingdom legislation on pornography to imports of some Danish publications was justified under Article 36. Under UK legislation the importation of 'indecent or obscene' material was prohibited. However, 'indecent' material could be sold throughout the UK (except in Scotland and the Isle of Man) and 'obscene' material of UK origin could normally not be sold, except if it had particular artistic or scientific merit, a defence which was not available for imported products.

The Court of Justice accepted the legitimacy of the British restriction to the free movement of goods by holding that Article 36:

> means that a Member State may, in principle, lawfully impose prohibitions on the importation from any other Member State of articles which are of an indecent or obscene character as understood by its domestic laws and that such prohibitions may lawfully be applied to the whole of its national territory even if, in regard to the field in question, variations exist between the laws in force in the different constituent parts of the Member State concerned.[10]

The Court has given a restrictive reading to most of the other exceptions listed in Article 36. A similar restrictive reading of the public morality exception would have meant that if competing standards of public morality are enforced within a single Member State, the most lenient and not the most stringent one should be applied to goods imported from other EC countries! The Court's attitude was therefore singularly permissive *vis-à-vis* UK legislation on pornography.[11]

9   Ibid.
10   Ibid., at 3813-14.
11   See the analysis by Kommers and Waelbroeck, 1986, at 207-209.

In the later *Conegate* case, also brought before the Court of Justice through a preliminary question by a British court, the European Court took a slightly different view from that in *Henn and Darby*.[12] In *Conegate*, the UK customs authorities had seized consignments of inflatable dolls from Germany, on the grounds that they were indecent or obscene. So far as these articles were concerned and, by contrast with obscene publications, there was hardly any restrictive domestic legislation, except for a prohibition of transmission by post and a restriction on their public display. The European Court decided that those very limited restrictions did not prevent inflatable dolls from being manufactured and marketed freely in the United Kingdom. Hence, the exception in Article 36 could not be invoked to prohibit the import of similar goods from other EC countries. It is disputable whether *Conegate* confirms or partly overrules the earlier *Henn and Darby* ruling of the Court.

In a later British case, which was directly relevant for the rights of gay men, the Customs had seized a number of gay books imported from Holland on the grounds of their obscenity. The applicant, the bookshop Noncyp Ltd., trading under the name 'Gay's the Word', pointed once more to the fact that the special defence in the Obscene Publications Act of 1959 allowed a domestic obscene publication to be 'justified as being for the public good on the ground that it is in the interests of science, literature, art or learning', whereas such justification was not available for imported books. The Court of Appeal decided that the role of Article 30 and 36 of the EEC Treaty as regards obscene publications had been conclusively settled in *Henn and Darby*, and refused to examine the present case in the light of *Conegate*, because the latter case did not deal with publications. The Court of Appeal did not even see the need for a preliminary reference to the European Court of Justice on the issue of Community law and dismissed Noncyp's appeal.[13] An opportunity was thereby lost to allow the European Court to clarify its case-law on the public morality exception.

2. Permissible Restrictions of the Trade in Services

(a) The regime of the EEC Treaty

In assessing the acceptability of restrictions to the trade in services, a basic distinction must be made between two categories of restrictions: discrimination against services coming from abroad, and disparities, i.e. obstacles to trade resulting from the application of national rules that do not distinguish between national and foreign services.

12   Case 121/85, *Conegate Limited v. Her Majesty's Customs and Excise* [1986] ECR 1007.
13   Court of Appeal, *Noncyp Limited v. Bow Street Magistrates' Court* [1989] 1 CMLR 634.

The first category of restrictions are allowed only for very good reasons that are enumerated in the EEC Treaty itself. The second category of restrictions are more readily acceptable, namely whenever they serve a broadly defined public interest. This is known as the 'Cassis de Dijon' test, from the famous case in which it was first formulated by the Court of Justice. It has been consistently applied in a large number of cases, first on the free movement of goods, and, more recently, also in cases relating to the movement of services.[14]

The grounds justifying restrictions on the trade in services (that is, of 'immaterial things') are not identical with those justifying restrictions of the trade in goods. There is no comprehensive list of heads of justification comparable to that of Article 36. The chapter on services simply allows for the application by analogy of derogation grounds listed in the chapter on the right of establishment. Those grounds, as listed in Article 56(1) of the Treaty, are: public policy, public security and public health.

Public morality is not among them, and one may wonder whether 'public policy' might encompass public morality. In the absence of relevant case-law of the European Court of Justice, there is a textual argument against that view. Article 36 mentions 'public policy' alongside 'public morality' as one of the permissible grounds of restriction of the movement of goods; therefore, one would think that when Article 56 of the same Treaty mentions 'public policy', this concept must be exclusive of 'public morality'. This would have the important consequence that State action specifically directed at imported services cannot be justified by the need to protect the moral values of the country.

The situation is different with regard to the measures that are indistinctly applicable to domestic and imported services. Such measures can also constitute restrictions in the sense of Article 59 of the EEC Treaty, but as they usually serve some domestic public interest, there is a much wider range of justifications available. A large number of such public interests have already been accepted by the Court in its case-law on services, and the list is not exhaustive. Although the Court of Justice was never called to decide it, there is no doubt that 'public morality' would also qualify as one of those grounds. Yet, it must be emphasized again that, as a ground of public interest, morality could only justify restrictions that do not discriminate against services originating from other EEC states; if there is any, direct or indirect, discrimination, the Court will revert to the much stricter (and almost fatal) standards laid down in Article 56(1). In this respect, the legal

---

14   See the judgments of 26 February 1991 on the services of tourist guides: Case C-154/89, *Commission v. France*, para.15; Case C-180/89, *Commission v. Italy*, para.18; and Case C-198/89, *Commission v. Greece*, para.19.

regime of the trade in 'immaterial things' might well be more liberal than that of the trade in goods.

(b) The Television Directive

There is a paradox here. The Treaty chapter on free movement of goods mentions public morality as a possible exception to the freedom, but the Community political institutions have never tried to define the contours of this exception in the form of a directive or a communication. In the chapter on the free movement of services, by contrast, public morality is not mentioned as a possible exception, and yet the Community has adopted legislation harmonizing public morality standards for one category of services, namely broadcasting services. This Community definition of public morality standards can be found in the EEC *Directive on 'Television Without Frontiers'* adopted in 1989;[15] the Commission and Council thought that liberalization of the transfrontier diffusion of television programmes had to be accompanied by a minimum amount of common regulation on a number of issues, including the 'protection of minors'. Article 22 of the Directive states the following:

> Member States shall take appropriate measures to ensure that television broadcasts by broadcasters under their jurisdiction do not include programmes which might seriously impair the physical, mental or moral development of minors, in particular those that involve pornography or gratuitous violence. This provision shall extend to other programmes which are likely to impair the physical, mental or moral development of minors, except where it is ensured, by selecting the time of the broadcasts or by any technical measure, that minors in the area of transmission will not normally hear or see such broadcasts.

In its original proposal for the Directive, the Commission had accompanied this substantive rule with a strong procedural obligation for the States, holding that those States:

> shall ensure that internal broadcasts are checked prior to transmission and broadcast only if they comply with the requirements under paragraph 1 above [i.e., the requirements for the protection of minors]. The Member States shall ensure that, in the case of broadcasts that do not respect these requirements, appropriate remedies to secure compliance with the rules are imposed on the broadcasters concerned.[16]

---

15   EEC Directive 89/552 of 3 October 1989 'on the coordination of certain provisions laid down by law, regulation or administrative action in Member States concerning the pursuit of broadcasting activities', OJ 1989 L 289/23.

16   Proposal for a Council Directive concerning broadcasting activities of 30 April 1986, OJ 1986 C 179/4, Article 15.

This provision called for the institution of a form of prior restraint, which is regarded with particular hostility in most legal systems,[17] and it was therefore replaced in the final text of the Directive by the more cautious words of the opening sentence of Article 22, which impose on the States the general obligation to 'take appropriate measures' in order to ensure respect for the requirements. Such a general obligation need not have been expressed, as it is inherent in the Member States' obligation to implement all EC Directives.

It should be noted that the Directive constitutes only a partial harmonization of broadcasting activity. There is an express clause, in Article 3, paragraph 1 of the Directive, to the effect that:

> Member States shall remain free to require television broadcasters under their jurisdiction to lay down more detailed or stricter rules in the areas covered by this directive.

This means that the standard of Article 22 is the minimum standard with which all television programmes have to comply if they want to benefit from free movement in the Community; but in addition, States can still impose stricter morality standards on their own television stations.

B. Community Control on National Restrictions

1. The Proportionality Test

This is the single most important test in the judicial practice of the European Court of Justice in cases involving a restriction of one of the Common Market freedoms. Even if the restrictive State measure was adopted in order to reach one of the legitimate aims mentioned above, there is a further hurdle to be taken before the measure is acceptable under EC law; it must stand the test of proportionality, which the European Court has borrowed from German administrative law. Proportionality means that the means and the end must be closely related. In order for a national rule to pass the proportionality test, it must be objectively necessary in order to help achieve the aim sought by the rule. The necessity requirement means that if the objective could have been achieved in another way, which does not hamper interstate trade to the same extent, then that other way should have been chosen, and the national measure becomes illegitimate. Finally, even if the measure is really indispensable in order to achieve the aim, it may nevertheless be unlawful if it causes restrictions that are out of proportion with the benefit which the States achieves.[18] For instance, the UK would

17   See Barendt, 1987, 114 ff.
18   See, in the context of the movement of goods, Kapteyn, VerLoren van Themaat, 1989, 395 (and the European Court cases cited in their note 199); and see, in the context of the

not be allowed to ban completely the import of animals from the continent, even if this were the only effective way of preventing the spread of rabies.

The constitutive elements of the proportionality test may seem rather technical, but what it really means in daily judicial practice is that all restrictive measures of States are subject to a test of reasonableness performed by the judiciary (both national courts and the European Court). Only in recent years has the test been systematically used by the European Court of Justice, and one may think that the *Henn and Darby* case, which is more than twelve years old, would no longer be decided so smoothly in favour of the United Kingdom's authorities.

2. Respect for Fundamental Rights

For a number of years now, the European Court of Justice has developed a doctrine about the implied protection of fundamental rights in the Community legal order. It has moved to fill the gap in legal protection left by the Community treaties (that do not contain a list of fundamental rights) by deciding that fundamental rights are part of the unwritten general principles of law which *Community institutions* have to respect in the course of their activities. The sources from which the Court derives its 'unwritten Bill of Rights' are the constitutional traditions common to the Member States, and the international treaties for the protection of human rights which those Member states have signed and ratified. The likelihood of Community measures directly affecting the fundamental rights of lesbians and gay men may seem rather remote, but there is the example of the television Directive, described above, to show that the Community's legislative activity may impinge upon their rights and interests. The provision of the Commission's first proposal for a directive, which imposed on the Member States the duty to create prior restraints of television programmes, might well have been contrary to the fundamental right of freedom of expression. Many of the remaining provisions of the Directive, although less obviously questionable, are also restrictions on broadcasting activity, and are therefore subject to review on the basis of Article 10 of the European Convention on Human Rights and similar national constitutional provisions.

The 'general principles' doctrine was developed by the European Court of Justice in order to fill what it perceived to be a gap in judicial protection against possible violations of fundamental rights by Community action. There is no such obvious gap as regards the protection of fundamental rights against action by the Member States. All those States have their own domestic system for the protection of fundamental rights, and are

movement of services, the opinion of Advocate-General Van Gerven in *SPUC v. Grogan*, judgment of 4 October 1991 [1991] 3 CMLR 849, at 874.

signatories of the European Human Rights Convention. So the European Court of Justice could rightly conclude that it did not have the task, nor the power, to impose a fully-fledged fundamental rights system upon the Member States.

Yet, recent developments in case-law have made it clear that general principles of Community law (including fundamental rights) also bind the *Member States* whenever they act within the scope of Community law.

It is not easy to decide when a measure falls 'within the scope' of Community law,[19] but it would seem to be the case whenever the State is restricting one of the Common Market freedoms (like the free movement of goods or services). When they restrict one of those freedoms, the States act within a margin of discretion attributed to but also constrained by the Treaty, and therefore within the 'scope' of that Treaty. Restrictions on the free movement of goods and services are therefore, as a matter of Community law, subject to review of their compatibility with fundamental rights.[20] As one of the main sources of those fundamental rights, the European Convention of Human Rights is made indirectly applicable to the Member States through the mediation of EC law. Restrictions on lesbian or gay activities, whenever they constitute at the same time restrictions to the free movement of goods or services (or, for that matter, persons) under EC law, are subject to the European Convention standards through the prism of Community law.

It then remains to be seen whether, in substance, the ECHR imposes on the States any stricter standards of behaviour than the EEC Treaty's own requirements which were examined above. A full answer to this question is given in Chapter Six by Van Dijk dealing with the European Convention for Human Rights. On first view, though, the Convention would seem to be important because it offers specific protection to certain types of activities, particularly to activities that are forms of 'expression' in the sense of its Article 10. The protection of freedom of expression, in combination with the non-discrimination clause of Article 14 of the ECHR, provides a standard by which to judge restrictive State measures which is clearer than the rather indeterminate public morality, public interest and proportionality standards used in EC law on goods and services. The ECHR rules imply at the very least that transnational forms of lesbian and gay speech, be they in print or in television, may not be subject to more severe restrictions than other forms of speech. If, for instance, the censor board of a particular country treated lesbian or gay films in a particularly rigid way, the distributor

---

19   See the analysis by Temple Lang, 1991, 23.
20   The clearest statement of this rule was made by the European Court of Justice in case C-260/89, *Elliniki Radiophonia ERT v. DEP* (the 'Greek television case'), judgment of 18 June 1991, not yet reported, paragraph 43; see summary and annotation by Chalmers in *ELR* (1992) 248.

importing such films from other EC countries could invoke the free movement of goods in conjunction with Articles 10 and 14 of the European Convention.[21]

The incorporation of the ECHR in EC law is interesting not only for substantive but also for procedural reasons. First, the Convention is not applied as such but subsumed within the autonomous concept of general principles of Community law. The interpretation which the European Court of Justice gives of that autonomous concept need not be identical with the interpretation of the Convention by the European Court of Human Rights. There are no clear indications, up until now, as to whether the Court in Luxembourg will give a more expansive interpretation of Convention rights than the Court in Strasbourg.

Second, the mediation through EC law allows European Convention arguments to be pleaded before national courts in any Community country. This is particularly useful in those countries, like the United Kingdom or Ireland, where the European Convention is not part of the law of the land.[22] Yet, it should be emphasized once more, that this possibility of bringing in the European Convention 'by the back door' of EC law is only available in cases that come within the scope of the EEC Treaty. Purely internal situations may well raise equally compelling issues under the European Convention, but will not at the same time be issues to be pleaded on the basis of EC law before a national judge.

21   Examples from Britain in the 1980's (which were not challenged in the European Court) include the ban on the importation of a book 'The Joy of Gay Sex' on grounds of public morality while the importation of its companion volume 'The Joy of [heterosexual] Sex' was permitted, and the occasional ban on importing a French newspaper for homosexuals, 'Gai Pied', and a Dutch journal 'Sek'. Bans based on a distinctive treatment of homosexual forms of expression can be challenged as violations of the free movement of goods (or the free movement of services, as the case may be), in combination with the fundamental rights of the European Convention.
22   See Grief, 1991, 555.

Chapter Fourteen
Rights in the Workplace

by

LAMMY BETTEN[*]

*   Department of International, Social and Economic Public Law, University of Utrecht.

Table of Contents

I. Introduction

Discrimination against lesbians and gay men endangers not only their right to earn a living in an occupation freely entered into;[1] it also affects a number of other fundamental rights, such as the right to freedom of expression, the right to a family life, the right to freedom of association, etc. Indeed, a number of examples have demonstrated that, as soon as a lesbian or a gay worker exercises these rights, her or his job can be in immediate danger. Even if homosexual workers abstain from actively exercising their rights their jobs may still be put in jeopardy. If others (for instance, fellow workers) start a rumour that a worker is a homosexual, the chances are considerable that this worker will be harassed or even dismissed because of this sexual orientation. Workers in some categories of professions are extremely vulnerable, such as teachers, social workers, nurses and, in general, everyone who works with children. There seems to be a – totally unfounded – fear that homosexuals will assault children, or the – equally unfounded – fear that the children will immediately imitate the teacher and become lesbian or gay themselves. The process of discriminatory action against homosexuals obviously starts even before they are in work. Many of them are rejected when applying for a job for the sole reason of their – obvious or suspected – sexual orientation.

The poignant examples of unjust treatment of homosexuals in their professional life demonstrate the need for immediate action. The question in this paper is whether there is any legal justification for the European Community (EC) to act in this area. The moral justification is obvious. The obligation of any legislature to abolish all forms of discrimination and to give victims of discrimination any kind of legal protection (which is all a legislature can do) is so obvious, that the starting point for discussion is how this can best be achieved, not analyzing whether it should be undertaken.

In this paper I will examine possible legal bases for the EC to act. The underlying question is whether the creation and functioning of the internal market and, in particular, the achievement of the free movement of persons on that market necessitate specific Community action to abolish discrimination against homosexuals in the workplace.

Two questions will be at the core of this contribution.

Question 1: How far does discrimination against homosexuals in the workplace *at the national level* affect the functioning of Community law and, consequently, become a matter of concern for the EC?

---

1   As defined, e.g., in Art. 1, para. 2 of the European Social Charter.

If there were no longer any discrimination against homosexuals in the Member States, and if there were firm protection of the rights of lesbians and gay men, it would be hard to argue that there was a need for Community action, for instance, in the context of the free movement of persons, as there would be no obstacle to lesbian or gay workers moving from one Member State to the other. This leaves the question whether the Community should act on another basis than the free movement of persons, for instance in the framework of the so-called 'social dimension', or in the context of its often repeated commitment to the protection of fundamental rights within Community law. I will deal with these questions as follows: in section II, I will present a number of examples of discrimination against homosexuals in the workplace in the national contexts, in order to illustrate the problems with which they are confronted. In section III, I will put these problems into the Community context, and argue that there is a need for Community action. In section IV the legal bases for Community action will be analyzed.

Question 2: Are gay men and lesbian women discriminated against *in EC law?*

At first sight there seems to be no reason to suggest that EC law as it stands and is developed is not applicable to homosexuals. I will examine though, whether rights and benefits given to the partners and family members of workers apply also to same-sex partners and their children. If that proves to be the case, the question that arises is how far EC law is directly or indirectly discriminatory with regard to homosexual workers (section V)? As this question refers to the intrinsic functioning of EC law and not to the effect of national discriminatory practices on the functioning of EC law the quest for legal bases for EC action is obviously a different one (section VI). Some concluding observations will be made in section VII.

II. Discrimination against Gay Men and Lesbians in the Workplace[2]

The ways in which homosexuals are discriminated against in the workplace are manifold. The common factor, however, is always prejudice. In other words, there is no proof whatsoever that lesbians and gay men are less capable of carrying out any profession than heterosexual persons. This may seem rather self-evident, but practice shows a very different picture. Even worse, it seems that the judiciary, notably in the United Kingdom,

2   Although the examples of national cases of discrimination against lesbians and gay men may also appear in other chapters of this report, they are mentioned here as well

sometimes views prejudice against homosexuals as acceptable and representing no bar to dismissal. An example of this judicial 'reasoning' is provided in the case of *Burman v. Trevor Page and Co. Ltd.*[3] Mr. Burman was a furniture delivery driver for a company which served the 'top end of the market'. He was dismissed following a conviction of taking part in gay group sex, a 'crime' for which he was fined £25. An industrial tribunal judged the dismissal to be fair on the grounds of a) the risk to his colleagues and b) the risks to the business if it became known that the company employed someone with this kind of conviction. Mr. Burman had admitted that since his conviction he had not sought to change his lifestyle and he did not want any treatment. The tribunal then proceeded to comment that the 'gravity of the matter is established by the words of revulsion with which the fellow employees both male and female spoke of it'. The bottom line was that to the members of the tribunal 'it seems misconceived that long-serving and loyal employees should be expected (...) to overcome their hostility'. The customers, too, had to be protected against this dangerous individual as Mr. Burman might make use 'of his opportunities when visiting customers' houses to interest members of the customers' families in homosexual activities with him', even though there had not been the slightest evidence of such behaviour in the past.

Prejudice against homosexuals played an important role also in the judgment of the famous case of *John Saunders v. Scottish National Camps Association Ltd.*[4] John Saunders was employed as a maintenance worker by the Scottish National Camps Association at a camp for teenage school children. He had been working for more than two years when it became known (from a 'trustworthy' source) that he was gay. He was dismissed. The industrial tribunal did not consider this dismissal unfair, a judgment which was confirmed by the Employment Appeal Tribunal, and the Court of Session (the final appellate court in Scotland). Even though the tribunal had admitted that being a homosexual was not in itself sufficient for dismissal, the fact that he was working in close proximity to children was. The tribunal held that the employer's decision to dismiss was fair with the following words: 'In this case the substance of the employers' case was that the applicant was a homosexual; that he was required to work daily with children of ages 10 to 18; that the employers considered that to be a risk to the children; *that there is a body of opinion which takes that view*

---

because it is essential to establish the nature of discriminatory practices before the question of a Community 'answer' to such practices can be examined.

3   Norwich Tribunal, April 1977, unreported. Mentioned by Crane, 1982, 114. See also a report on the mechanics of discrimination in the workplace by Beer, Jeffery and Munyard, 1981.

4   (1980) IRLR, 174 et seq.

(emphasis added); and that the probable views of many parents was a legitimate matter to take into consideration'.[5]

The main reasons for dismissing homosexuals can be summarized as follows:[6] medical reasons (on the grounds of a medical report they are declared to be homosexual, and therefore 'ill'), fear of corruption (homosexuals are often seen as wildly uncontrolled persons who make sexual advances at any time towards any person nearby, especially when that person is a child), actual or imagined pressure from clients or from other staff, presumed inadequacy at work (based on the prejudice that homosexuals are unreliable, inefficient, etc), the fear that they may be HIV positive (as homosexuals in Europe, the Americas and Australia have been one of the groups most affected by HIV).

The list of examples of discrimination against homosexuals in the workplace can be extended endlessly. The above quoted cases are British. This is not to suggest that homosexual workers face more discrimination in Great Britain than in other Member States. There are, however, far more widely reported cases of discrimination against homosexuals in Great Britain than in any other EC-Member State. This is probably because most of these cases are based on discriminatory provisions in British penal law. Under these provisions only homosexual men can be convicted of committing the crime of 'gross indecency' which suggests something terrible, but which is no more than a minor offence, usually attracting a fine of a few pounds. The offence consists of a sexual intimacy between men (a) in a public place or (b) in a private place with one man under 21, or with more than two men present. Another offence is contained in Section 32 of the 1956 Sexual Offences Act under which it is unlawful for a man to 'persistently solicit or importune in a public place for an immoral purpose', the immoral purpose in the above mentioned cases being homosexual behaviour. To have sexual relations in private is legal, but to make arrangements for them in a public place is a criminal offence. Very active use is made of this provision: in 1989 462 men were convicted.[7]

As mentioned in section I, it is not only in the workplace itself that homosexuals have to suffer discriminatory treatment. They are confronted also with particular difficulties in obtaining a job. Cases in which they are rejected solely on account of their sexual orientation are hard to prove and it is, therefore, equally hard to find examples of such cases in reported case-law. In some countries, however, it is the legislature itself which makes it difficult for homosexual men to apply successfully for jobs, e.g. in those countries in which homosexuals are considered to be unfit for military

5   (1981) IRLR, 277.
6   See the report by Beer and others, *supra* note 3.
7   See paragraph II.F.3 of Chapter Three by Waaldijk.

service. This can impede the person's job chances in a number of ways, not only with the army itself but also afterwards if they have been dismissed from the army because of homosexual behaviour (on or off duty).[8]

It should also be recognized that there is a hidden form of economic discrimination in that most lesbian and gay workers cannot include their partners in public or private pension and other work-related benefit schemes, e.g. private health insurance. As there is rarely a lower rate of contribution for such workers, the effect is that they receive a lower real rate of pay for work of equal value.

III. EC Action to Abolish Discrimination against Lesbians and Gay Men in the Workplace

Evidence of Community action to combat discrimination against homosexuals at the national level is apparent only in respect of the free movement of workers and the development of a European social area. The actions, so far mainly undertaken by the European Parliament, have received very little positive comment from the Commission.

The most comprehensive document is the Squarcialupi Report on *Sexual Discrimination at the Workplace*.[9] A Resolution based on this Report was, adopted by the European Parliament on the 13th of March 1984.

In the report, the Italian MEP Vera Squarcialupi noted that although most European legislatures are now more tolerant with regard to homosexuality between adults, they do not provide any protection against discrimination. With regard to discrimination in the workplace, Squarcialupi observed that even though, in theory, homosexuality does not conflict with any type of employment nor does it jeopardize an individual's career prospects, in practice systems of security checks used in hiring, particularly in public administration, provide the means to reject people with homosexual tendencies. Another obstacle to a person's career development is dismissal from military service because of homosexuality. Every time such a person has to provide proof of good conduct in order to get a job, this dismissal, and the reason for it, will come to the surface. She notes reports of cases in Member States of dismissals of persons because of their homosexuality, and concludes that these reports show that homosexuals are systematically excluded from certain professions.[10]

---

8   For a number of examples of ways in which a person's chances of employment or promotion (in and outside the army) are frustrated by laws prohibiting homosexuality in military service, see *The Iceberg Report, anti-homosexual discrimination in Europe 1980-1990*, 1991, University of Utrecht.

9   EP Doc. 1-1358/83, 13 February 1984, PE 87.477 def., 9 et seq.

10 Ibid., at p. 12.

The Resolution based on the Squarcialupi Report requested the EC-Commission to submit proposals to ensure that no cases arise in the Member States of discrimination against homosexuals with regard to access to employment and working conditions; to take steps to induce the World Health Organization (WHO) to delete homosexuality from its International Classification of Diseases;[11] to invite Member States to provide a list of all provisions in their legislation which concern homosexuals; to identify, on the basis of such lists, any discrimination against homosexuals with regard to employment, housing and other social problems by drawing up a report, pursuant to Article 122 EEC Treaty.[12] In the same Resolution, the EP requested its own Legal Committee:

> to examine in which way differences between the laws of the various Member States with regard to the ban on homosexuality or the minimum age of consent constitute barriers to the right to freedom of movement and to freedom of establishment as an employee or self-employed person and, in so doing, also to indicate what EC measures might be applied to remove such barriers.[13]

In the preamble to this Resolution, the EP refers to Articles 100 and 118 EEC Treaty, to the Preamble and Article 117 of the Treaty, to Article 8 of the European Convention on Human Rights (ECHR) (protection of family life) and to Articles 12 and 13 of the Universal Declaration of Human Rights. It also refers to Regulations 1612/68 and Directive 68/360 to argue that these documents point out that the free movement of persons not only implies that citizens have the right to be protected from discrimination on the basis of nationality, but that the free movement of persons is a fundamental right with an independent meaning.

A proposal for EC action in general terms in an draft EP resolution designed by the Dutch MEP Ien van den Heuvel with regard to legal and illegal discrimination against homosexuality[14] had not provoked any reaction by the Commission. The Squarcialupi Resolution with better argued and more detailed proposals received a reaction, which, however, did not lead to any action. Commissioner Richard (who said he had found the debate on the Squarcialupi report 'extremely useful, interesting and sometimes fascinating') expressed the opinion that the EEC Treaty does not contain any provision which would authorize legal measures to abolish discrimination with regard to access to the working place and working conditions. Article 117 would not provide sufficient legal basis; any measure would have to be

---

11   The WHO decided in 1991 that from 1993 onwards homosexuality will no longer be listed in the disease classification manual as a mental disorder. For comments, see the *Washington Blade* of 17 January 1992, 1 and 12 and *Gai Pied Hebdo* 503 of 16 January 1992, 10.
12   OJ 1984 C 104/46-48.
13   Ibid.
14   EP Doc. 1-1072/82, PE 87.477 def.

based on Article 235, which would require that the Council be convinced that such a measure is necessary to attain a Community objective. Although the Council had accepted this as a basis for the 1976 *Directive on Equal Treatment of Men and Women in the Workplace*, the Commissioner thought that similar measures would be unlikely in the future, not because of technical legal problems, but because of the serious financial problems of the EC (!). Because of those problems the Commissioner could not grant the request of the EP to conduct a research into the treatment of homosexuals in the Member States.[15]

With regard to the problem of dismissals because of sexual orientation, the Commissioner was somewhat more positive. He said that the Commission was considering proposing a Directive on the grounds for dismissals of individuals. It would have to be based on Articles 100 and 117 of the Treaty. The aim of the Directive would be to approximate dismissal procedures at the national levels and to limit the grounds for dismissal. Sexual orientation would not be one of the permitted grounds for dismissal and such dismissals would, therefore, be illegal. The Commissioner promised the Directive would be published as soon as the economic situation in general and the labour market in particular improved.[16]

In his concluding remarks the Commissioner suggested that the Council of Europe might be a better forum to aim for protection of homosexuals against discrimination. He was not trying, he said, to shift the responsibility to another organization, but, in view of the administrative and financial obstacles, he foresaw little possibility for EC action in the future.[17]

This last conclusion of Mr. Richard proved to be right. Since these Resolutions which date from the early 1980s hardly any evidence can be found of concern for discrimination against homosexuals in EC documents. The European Parliament did urge that priority be given to equal protection of workers 'regardless of ... sexual preference' in its Resolution on the *Community Charter of the Fundamental Social Rights of Workers* (the 'Social Charter').[18] However, the proposal to include prohibition of discrimination on the grounds of sexual orientation in the EP *Charter on Fundamental Rights and Freedoms of EC Citizens* was rejected.[19]

15   EP Debates, 13 March 1984, No. 1-311/1, at 19.
16   Ibid., at 18.
17   Ibid., at 19
18   OJ 1989 C 323/46, 29 December 1989.
19   PE 132.563 Minutes of Proceedings of 12 April 1989.

IV. Legal Bases for EC Action

The question whether it is the task of the EC legislature to interfere in the
area of discrimination against homosexual workers should not be limited
solely to the aspect of free movement of persons. The argument that the EC
has no basis for legislative action in the area outside the freedom of movement of persons as the issue does not affect the functioning of the EC
labour market is too narrow. From the time when the social aspects of the
Common Market came into focus, the EC has committed itself to taking
the social effects of the Common Market into account. In the 1974 Council
resolution to initiate the Social Action Programme, the following were
stated to be the main objectives of that programme: full and better employment at EC, national and regional levels as an essential condition for
an effective social policy; improvement of living and working conditions so
as to make possible their harmonization while improvement is being maintained; and increased involvement of management and labour in the economic and social decisions of the EC.[20] The aim to achieve an accelerated
raising of the standard of living by means of approximating (economic)
laws as stated in Article 2 of the EEC Treaty in itself provides a basis for
EC action to abolish all forms of discrimination in living and working
conditions. Finally, the changes in the status of fundamental rights in EC
law provide prospects for further action.

Therefore, the question of providing legal bases for EC action in the
area of discrimination against homosexual workers will be approached
from three different angles:
– the free movement of persons;
– the social dimension of the internal market;
– the protection of fundamental rights.

A. The Free Movement of Persons

The question whether discrimination against lesbians and gay men is an
obstacle to achieve free movement of persons was put to the Commission
by MEP M. Ford in April 1990. Mr. Ford formulated his question in the
following way:

> Given that the free movement of people, the creation of a barrier-free internal
> market, and the harmonization of regulations between the Member States are
> three of the principal objectives of the European EC (as set out in Articles 48,
> 49, 100, 100a and 101 of the Treaties), will the Commission not accept that dis-
> crimination against lesbians and gay men is a disincentive and an obstacle to the

---

20   OJ 1974 C 13/1, 12 February 1974.

achievement of these objectives and is therefore contrary to Articles 48, 49, 100, 100a and 101 and that, furthermore, these Articles provide a legal basis for outlawing discrimination against lesbians and gay men in the workplace?[21]

The answer of the Commissioner was disappointingly clear. The Commission cannot take measures against any form of discrimination against sexual minorities in the Member States. According to the EEC Treaty it can only act against discrimination on the basis of nationality or to enforce equal treatment of men and women in the workplace and in social security.[22]

From the ECJ case-law it has become clear that Article 48 of the Treaty, which forms the basis of the EC's law on free movement of persons, covers not only visible, but also disguised and minor forms of discrimination and that it prohibits discrimination in working and employment conditions in a broad sense, such as military service, education facilities and all forms of social advantages.[23] The term 'discrimination' refers here to discrimination on the basis of nationality. The question is whether discrimination against homosexuals because of their sexual orientation can be brought under this heading. In other words, should (penal) laws condemning only homosexual behaviour be challenged in EC law because of their alleged affects on the free movement of persons? The EP Legal Committee expressed the opinion that:

> the relevant provisions in the EEC Treaty and secondary legislation limit the rights provided where such limitations are 'justified on grounds of public policy, public security or public health' and that, in any case, the actual or potential effect of the existence of such laws on the freedom of movement of persons is so minimal as to not, without more, give good grounds for EC action in this area.[24]

It seems that the Committee does not deny that discrimination on the basis of sexual orientation is an obstacle to the free movement of lesbians and gay men throughout the EC. Its argument is that the existence of discrimination against homosexuals in criminal law can only marginally affect the free movement of workers.

It is submitted that the question whether such discrimination constitutes a major or minor obstacle to the free movement of persons, is hardly relevant. If, in a given situation, such discrimination affects the free movement of only one individual, it constitutes a violation of the Treaty. For instance, a worker from a Member State who wants to look for or accept a job in Great Britain and who is known to have had many homosexual

---

21 Oral Question, H-549/90, 30 April 1990 EN.
22 WD EP 16 May 1990, No. 3-390/296.
23 Kapteyn *et al.*, 1989, 413-414. The authors quote a substantial list of cases in which the Court has defined the scope of the free movement of persons.
24 *Supra* note 22, at 29.

relations which he has solicited in public places (which is not a crime in other Member States) may be considered to constitute a present threat to the requirements of public policy in Great Britain, and, for that reason, be denied access to the British labour market, or be deported. Although this has to do, in the first place, with his being gay, it has also to do with his nationality, because under his own national laws he has no criminal past, and has, therefore, not had any reason to avoid behaviour which is considered to be criminal in Great Britain. *Vice versa*, a British gay worker with a record of repeated offences under the Sexual Offences Act may theoretically not be considered a 'present threat' to the requirements of public policy in another Member State, but may in practice be looked upon with some suspicion by officials or potential employers who do not understand what these 'gross indecencies' consist of.

In general, it may be argued that the free movement of homosexual workers between Member States is hindered by the existence of less liberal policies in some Member States by comparison with more liberal policies in others. The reverse could also be the case, in particular as regards workers from Great Britain, if their 'criminal' record is misunderstood, or with regard to those workers from countries in which they were dismissed from military service because of homosexual behaviour (e.g. Italy).

The difference in attitude in the various Member States towards homosexuals causes a considerable problem for lesbian and gay workers and is an obstacle to their free movement in the internal market. Such obstacles should be removed by EC action. This can be supported by the argument that, as the EP remarked in its above-mentioned Resolution, Regulation 1612/68 and Directive 68/360 state that the free movement of persons is a fundamental right of all workers in the EC. That right is violated by any Member State which discriminates against workers for any other reason than their nationality or which does not protect workers against such discrimination. I would argue that the existence of such differences in treatment does constitute a sufficient basis for EC action.

A counter-argument could be that the rules of free movement of persons as laid down in EC law were not meant to be used as instruments to abolish certain discriminatory provisions in criminal or other national laws. It could also be argued that the continuing large differences between Member States as regards their levels of wages or social security benefits also constitute obstacles for the free movement of persons. EC law provides for a system guaranteeing that workers will not actually lose the benefits to which they are entitled in their own or another Member State upon moving from one to the other Member State. It does not provide for a system, however, to compensate losses if a worker moves from a State with higher social security benefits to a State with lower benefits. Neither does the system compensate workers who move from a higher wage-level Member State to a lower wage-level one. It could be argued that this encourages one-way migration (obviously from the lower to the higher wages or benefits), but it does not promote the full free movement of persons on the internal market. Therefore, these differences, too, are obstacles to the free movement of persons, not prohibited by EC law. In fact they are recognized in the system of the rules on free movement of persons.

The 1992 euphoria has caused certain Member States to review what they consider to be their generous social security system. The Netherlands, for instance, is in the middle of an operation to cut back social security benefits. Even though the main reason for this was primarily economic (the system was simply too expensive), there was a firm eye on the day (1 January 1993) on which the internal market was intended to have its final barriers removed. In other words, the fear that the system might attract many workers from 'less generous' Member States, played a considerable role in the arguments for cutting back the system. This shows that Member States themselves recognize the effect of the differences of social security benefits on their competitiveness. The same goes, of course for the differences in wage levels, one of the oldest incentives for creating common international norms at a time when wage levels and other working conditions are thought to be too low and poor to be justifiable for the economic good of the countries concerned.

Can these differences be considered in the same light as differences in penal laws which constitute obstacles to the free movement of persons? In other words, if the Member States recognize that differences in wage levels and social security systems may cause distortion of competition and the EC treaty system recognizes that such differences are obstacles to the free movement of persons, but these are not considered to be such important violations of the free movement of persons that they should be removed by EC action, how can one argue that this should be done with regard to provisions in penal law which may affect the right of free movement of homosexual workers? I would argue that such discrimination cannot be viewed in the same light as differences in wage levels and social security systems. First, the fact that the rules of free movement of persons were not meant to 'attack' certain provisions in penal and other national laws is no reason to suggest that such provisions should not be removed where they are, in fact, an obstacle to the free movement of persons. Second, there is a marked difference between legal provisions in a Member State discriminating against a category of persons and between economically determined wage levels and social security systems. Third, the acceptance of the effects of differences in the economic systems cannot be a justification for accepting other differences in national laws once it is established that such differences constitute an obstacle to the free movement of persons because that would make any and all discriminatory differences – with the sole exception of discrimination on grounds of nationality – acceptable under EC law. If these are not sufficiently convincing arguments to lead to a conclusion that there is a necessity for legislative EC action in this area, there is only one possibility left which is that of bringing a case before the ECJ, possibly under a 177 EEC Treaty procedure.

B. The Social Dimension of the Internal Market

After the initial declarations in the early 1970s on the importance of EC intervention in the area of social policy, progress has not exactly been steady. After the initial steps forward, in particular in the area of equal treatment of men and women workers, a period of stagnation followed, influenced by major economic problems and the aversion of some Member States' governments to any EC intervention beyond the strictly economic powers of 'Brussels'. In the course of the discussions on the Single European Act and the '1992' euphoria or nightmare (depending on one's views) the subject of widening the EC's powers in the social area never gained the same impact as the economic aspects of the internal market. Yet, some concessions were accepted. The Preamble to the Single European Act proclaims the determination 'to improve the economic and social situation by extending common policies and pursuing new objectives, and to ensure a smoother functioning of the Communities by enabling the Institutions to exercise their powers under conditions most in keeping with EC interests'. Articles 118a and b were added to the Social Policy chapter (Title III) of the Treaty and a new Title V was added which contains provisions on economic and social cohesion.

Article 2 of the 1992 Maastricht Agreement on Social Policy, signed by eleven of the twelve Member States, specifies a number of areas of social policies in which decisions can be taken by a qualified majority.[25] This in itself is no reason to expect that this treaty will improve the chances of a broader interpretation of responsibilities of the Member States with regard to homosexuals. The increased influence of trade unions and employers' organizations on the decision making process under the Maastricht Treaty provides even less reason for increased optimism. These 'social partners' as they are called in EC terms are not well known for their sympathy to homosexual workers whose situation certainly has never been high on their list of priorities and cannot be expected to gain that place in the European context in the near future.

Articles 117, 118 and 122 of the EEC-Treaty currently provide a basis for carrying out studies, arranging consultations etc. to discuss further the

---

25   The qualified majority for decisions taken under the new Article 189c being 44 and not
      54 votes. See Article 2 of the Maastricht *Protocol* on Social Policy.

problem of discrimination against homosexual workers. A more interesting prospect would be offered, however, if a basis could be found for issuing directives to abolish this type of discrimination. It is submitted that such action would fall within the aim stated in Article 117, and can be achieved by the functioning of the Common Market, the procedures provided for in the Treaty and the approximation of legislative and administrative provisions. As the Court of Justice pointed out in the *second Defrenne* case[26] the EC is not merely an economic union, but is intended, by common action, to ensure social progress and seek the constant improvement of living and working conditions.[27] The instruments provided by the Treaty are Articles 100 – 102 as well as Article 235. The question is whether action in this field would involve the functioning of the Common or Internal Market, in which case Articles 100 – 102 should be used. If that is not the case, then a directive should be based on Article 235 EEC Treaty. Directives based on Article 100 (and now 100a), referring expressly to Article 117 are not uncommon. This is so, for instance, in the Directives regarding collective redundancies,[28] safeguarding of rights of employees in the event of transfers of undertakings[29] and, the protection of employees in the event of the insolvency of their employer.[30] One of the considerations which these directives have in common is that 'differences still remain between the Member States' in the area covered by the directive, which is stated to be one of the incentives for adopting the directive. The effect on the Common Market is not stated, but it is suggested that these differences 'can have direct effect on the functioning of the Common Market'. This is a rather broad formula which creates possibilities for further legislative action in the area of social policy, if the political will is there. The latter is obviously the crucial factor as was suggested by the Commission as well as the European Parliament's Legal Committee.[31]

Another option which should be seriously considered is to use Article 118a introduced by the Single European Act. It should not be too difficult to argue that harassment and discrimination against homosexual workers falls under the safety and health of employees, the protection of which is stated as the aim of this provision. Article 118a itself offers a basis to adopt directives in this area. In this context note should be taken of the Recommendation on the *Protection of the Dignity of Women and Men at Work* and the *Code of Practice on Measures to Combat Sexual Harassment*

26 Case 43/75, *Gabrielle Defrenne v. Sabena* [1976] ECR 455.
27 Ibid., at 572.
28 Directive 75/129 of 17 February 1975, OJ 1975 L 48/29.
29 Directive 77/187 of 14 February 1977, OJ 1977 L 61/26.
30 Directive 80/987 of 20 October 1980, OJ 1980 L 283/23.
31 See section III *supra*.

both adopted by the EC Commission on 27th November 1991.[32] The Recommendation seeks to promote awareness that conduct of a sexual nature or other conduct based on sex affecting the dignity of women and men at work is unacceptable and may, in certain circumstances, be contrary to the provisions of the Equal Treatment Directive.[33] In providing the basis for a definition of such unwanted conduct, the Recommendation should help to ensure that the problem is effectively dealt with at national level and under existing law.[34] The Code of Practice aims to provide practical guidance to employers, trade unions and employees on means of ensuring that sexual harassment does not occur in the workplace and, if it does, to ensure that adequate procedures are in place to deal with the problem and prevent its recurrence.[35] The Code of Practice, but not the Recommendation, explicitly states that harassment of lesbians and gay men falls within the definition of sexual harassment or the protection of dignity of men and women. Whatever the practical impact of this Recommendation and the Code of Practice may be, it is important to remark here that the Commission considers that not only is sexual harassment 'an obstacle to the proper integration of women into the labour market', but also that it can have 'a devastating effect upon the health, confidence and morale of those affected by it'. The Commission further commented:

> it is undeniable that harassment on the grounds of sexual orientation undermines the dignity at work of those affected and it is impossible to regard such harassment as appropriate workplace behaviour.[36]

C. The Protection of Fundamental Rights in EC Law

The alleged protection of fundamental rights in EC law, also supports the argument in favour of EC action aimed at abolishing discrimination against homosexual workers. Before the Single European Act, the ECJ has stated repeatedly that fundamental rights are protected in EC law. Although it has had some trouble in finding a legal basis for such protection,[37] it has repeatedly referred to the ECHR as forming part of the general principles of EC law.[38] After the adoption of the Single European Act, the Court consolidated the reference to the ECHR as a source of EC law in its

---

32   The final text of the Recommendation and the Code of Practice has been published twice: OJ 1992 C 27/04 and OJ 1992 L 79. The Recommendation is based on a Council Resolution of 29th May 1990 (OJ 1990 C 157/02) and has been endorsed by a Council Declaration of 19th December 1991 (OJ 1992 C 27/01).
33   Directive 76/207 of 9 February 1976, OJ 1976 L 39/40.
34   Press Release IP(91) 1082 of the Commission, Brussels, 4 December 1991.
35   Ibid.
36   Introduction to the Code of Practice.
37   Betten, 1985, 25-45.
38   This happened for the first time in Case 4/73, Nold [1974] ECR 491.

judgment of 18 May 1989 in Case 249/86, *Commission v. Federal Republic of Germany*.[39] In this judgment the Court stated that

> Regulation No. 1612/68 must also be interpreted in the light of the requirement of respect for family life set out in Article 8 of the Convention for the Protection of Human Rights and Fundamental Freedoms. That requirement is one of the fundamental rights which, according to the Court's settled case-law, restated in the Preamble to the Single European Act, are *recognized* by EC law.[40]

This judgment suggests that citizens of the Member States can rely on the ECHR to form part of EC law. It is unfortunately less clear, how far homosexual workers who are discriminated against can rely on the ECHR before the ECJ with regard to either discrimination in the workplace or their free movement in the Internal Market. The prohibition of discrimination in Article 14 ECHR is an accessory provision, that is to say, that it can be relied upon only in connection with other rights protected in the Convention. Neither the right to access to a workplace nor the right to just and fair working conditions are included in the Convention, so it seems unlikely that applications of discrimination in the workplace will be declared admissible.

It is different with regard to liberty of movement, which does form part of the Convention. Article 2 of the Fourth Protocol to the Convention recognizes the right to liberty of movement within the territory of a Contracting State, to choose one's residence and to leave it. Allegations of discrimination against homosexuals in their right to liberty of movement as protected in the ECHR are, in principle, admissible. There are, however, considerable differences as regards the contents as well as the effects of liberty of movement under the European Convention on the one hand, and the freedom of movement in EC law, on the other. The Convention provides a general right for citizens of Contracting States who have lawfully entered another Contracting State to liberty of movement and freedom to choose a residence, as well as the freedom to leave that country again. Freedom of movement in EC law goes much further and is far more detailed. In the first place, it actually creates the right to enter another Member State on the basis of the Treaty and not on the basis of national laws. Moreover, it entails the right to be given assistance in looking for a job, as well as the right not to be discriminated against in any way on the basis of nationality with regard to rights connected with work, housing, taxes and so on. In other words, allegations of discrimination under the ECHR seem to be limited to the above quoted three rights, and do not seem to cover the rights connected with labour law, which are covered by Article 48 EEC Treaty and the regulations and directives based on Article 48.

---

39   Case 249/86, *Commission of the European Communities v. Federal Republic of Germany (Re Migrant Workers)* [1986] ECR 1263.
40   Ibid., at 1290 (emphasis added).

This leaves us with the question whether, proceeding from the assumption that the ECJ has now recognized the rights of the ECHR to form part of Community law, the protection of Article 14 ECHR can be applied to the freedom of movement *as recognized in Community law*. In other words, will the ECJ be prepared to extend the protection of Article 14 ECHR to the freedom of movement in Community law, or will it reason that Article 14 can be applied only in connection with the rights protected under the Convention and cannot, therefore, be relied upon in connection with all aspects of the free movement of persons in Community law? The question is complicated by the fact that as yet, not all Member States have ratified the Fourth Protocol.[41] Since the Court's formula in the abovementioned case of the Federal Republic of Germany against the Commission, it may no longer be important whether all Member States have ratified a certain provision regarding fundamental rights before it is recognized in Community law. The Court no longer adds this proviso.

Another instrument to be considered in this context is ILO Convention No. 111 as well as Recommendation No. 111 (1958). Both instruments define the term 'discrimination' to include:

> any distinction, exclusion or preference made on the basis of colour, sex, religion, political opinion, national extraction or social origin, which has the effect of nullifying or imparing equality of opportunity or treatment in employment or occupation

as well as:

> such other distinction, exclusion or preference which has the effect of nullifying or imparing equality of opportunity or treatment in employment or occupation as may be determined by the Members concerned after consultation with representative employers' and workers' organizations, where such exist, and with other appropriate bodies. [42]

There is no explicit reference to discrimination against homosexuals and there is no indication that this is considered to be implicit in the term 'sex' mentioned in Article 1, but there is some ground to suggest that the ILO accepts the inclusion of discrimination against homosexuals in the Convention, as some Member States included in their reports on the implementation of Convention No. 111 measures to protect homosexual workers. The ILO-Committee of Experts 1988 General Survey mentions from the reports in Canada: the Quebec Charter of Human Rights and Freedoms in Canada; from the United States: the District of Columbia Human Rights Act 1977, stating that sexual orientation includes male or female homosexuality,

---

41 Of the EC Member States, Spain, the United Kingdom and Greece have not yet ratified the Protocol (1 July 1991).
42 ILO Convention No. III Article 1(a) and (b); ILO Recommendation No. III (1958).

heterosexuality and bi-sexuality by preference or practice; from France the
Penal Code as amended by the Act of 25 July 1985, prohibiting discrimination in employment and occupation on grounds, in particular, of the habits
of the employee; and from Sweden: an amendment to the Penal Code,
which came into force on 1 July 1987 and which includes homosexuality
among the prohibited grounds of discrimination[43]

This could be a guideline for a direction to be taken by the Community
legislature, although it can be no more than a guideline, as no less than
three EC-Member States have not ratified this Convention, for reasons,
however, which are not connected directly to the aspect of discrimination of
homosexuals. Ireland has not ratified the Convention, because of the fact
that race, colour, religion, political opinion, national extraction and social
origin are not grounds of discrimination which are subject to national legislation. The Government of Luxembourg has reported that its legislation
contains discriminatory measures concerning foreign workers with regard to
their participation as representatives of employees in the enterprise. The
United Kingdom indicated that it did not intend to alter the legislation to
give full effect to the Convention, because of difficulties in certain areas,
such as qualifications concerning the manner in which the 1976 Race Relations Act is applied to members of the armed forces, restrictions on the employment of foreigners in the public service and distinctions in wages paid
to seafarers employed on board UK vessels according to whether they are
domiciled in the United Kingdom.[44]

V. Discrimination against Homosexual Workers in EC Law

The question whether EC law itself discriminates against homosexual
workers will be discussed from two perspectives: the law on free movement
of persons and the directives with regard to equal treatment of men and
women.

The major question with regard to the position of homosexuals under
the rules of free movement of persons is whether homosexual migrant workers and their partners are granted the same facilities as heterosexual migrant
workers. This was dealt with in the *Reed* case,[45] in which the unmarried
companion of a British worker migrating to the Netherlands claimed a residence permit as the man's companion, the Court held that the term 'spouse'
in Article 10 of Regulation 1612/68 referred to a marital relationship only.
The main reason the Court gave for this restrictive interpretation of the term

43   *Equality in Employment and Occupation, General Survey by the Committee of Experts on
      the Application on Conventions and Recommendations*, Geneva, 1991, 65 (footnote 191).
44   Ibid., at 10-11.
45   Case 59/85, *State of the Netherlands v. Ann Florence Reed* [1986] ECR 1283 et seq.

was that there is no general development in the whole of the EC to the effect that non-marital relationships could be regarded as equally to marital relationships. In the end, Ann Florence Reed succeeded with her claim because the Court referred to Article 7, paragraph 2 of the regulation which prescribes that migrant workers must be treated equal to national workers.[46] If a State grants foreign unmarried companions of national citizens the right to reside in the territory, that same right cannot be refused to a non-national citizen. This is an important decision in more that one sense. First of all, it seems to promote the differential treatment of unmarried couples in the EC. Indeed, married couples basically enjoy the same rights everywhere in the EC. Some Member States, however, take a much more positive attitude towards equalizing the position of non-married to married couples than other Member States. The above mentioned recent review of the social security system in the Netherlands has by and large brought about equality in the treatment of married and unmarried couples (which is not, by the way always favourable for the unmarried couples). It means that the Netherlands could become an attractive country for unmarried migrant workers (as would be, for instance, Denmark). It may be questioned how far this is more than theory. So far, there is little proof that labour mobility in Europe is affected by these considerations. Still, in a changing society, where in some countries economic and political climates become particularly unfavourable to certain categories of workers, this may become a reason to move to a 'friendlier' country. As information about differences in treatment become more widespread, it can reasonably be assumed that more people will take advantage of beneficial circumstances.

A more important argument however, is that, whereas unmarried heterosexual couples have the choice to get married, homosexual couples do not have this choice (although in Denmark the registered partnership law grants most of the same rights of marriage to same sex couples). So, where this argument of 'its your own choice' can be used against heterosexual unmarried couples, this cannot be the case with homosexual couples. Parity with married couples where their social rights and duties are concerned is, therefore, of crucial importance to homosexual migrant workers in order to move freely from one State to another, without having to suffer separation from their partners and if such should be the case, children. However, the arguments brought forward by the ECJ for a restrictive interpretation of the term 'spouse' in Article 10 of Regulation 1612/68 apply even more strongly in the case of unmarried, homosexual couples. Even though some Member States may be moving in the direction of treating unmarried heterosexual couples in the same way as married couples (also because this may be economically advantageous for the State concerned), there is still a long way

46   But see note 32 in Chapter Fifteen, and accompanying text.

to go before this will apply to unmarried homosexual couples. In view of this, the prohibition on treating foreign homosexual couples differently from national homosexual couples (Article 7, paragraph 2 Regulation 1612/68) does not provide any solution because in most Member States homosexuals are not treated in a way that will attract homosexual workers from other Member States.

With regard to 'social' directives, issued by the EC so far, it is submitted that no express evidence of provisions which are discriminatory *vis-à-vis* homosexuals can be found. On the other hand, there is no evidence of positive measures aimed at protecting the position of lesbians and gay men in the workplace either. Particularly interesting in this context are of course the equal treatment and sexual harassment measures. The equal treatment directives were clearly meant to deal with equal treatment of men and women only. So far no one has invoked them in a case of alleged unequal treatment of homosexual workers. I have already argued that in its *Code of Practice on Protecting the Dignity of Women and Men at Work*, the Commission offers ample opportunity for homosexuals to find support for their case in these measures. With regard to the equal treatment directives I agree with Angela Byre's arguments in this volume for bringing test-cases before the ECJ to test if the Court is 'ready' to include discrimination on the basis of sexual orientation in the principle of non-discrimination on grounds of sex.

VI. Legal Bases for Fighting Discriminatory EC Law

If EC law itself is discriminatory with regard to the treatment of homosexual (migrant) workers, there are few opportunities to fight this in court. Indeed, if the ECJ itself accepts only restrictive interpretations of terms such as 'spouse' and does not include in the principles relating to equal treatment the unequal treatment of homosexuals, it is not possible to take the case further. In section IV.C *supra* I have already pointed out the difficulties of fighting allegedly discriminatory EC law in the context of the ECHR. It should be added here, that if the ECJ rejects claims of violation of the right of equal treatment by homosexual workers, the case cannot be brought to the European Commission of Human Rights, even though the EC Commission concedes that the European Commission and Court of Human Rights are best equipped to protect sexual minorities against discrimination.[47] As early as 1978, the European Commission of Human

---

47   *Supra* note 22, ibid.

Rights made it clear in the *CFDT* case[48] that it cannot declare such cases admissible for the obvious reason that the EC is not a party to the ECHR. This situation shows again the problem of the lack of express incorporation of fundamental rights in EC law. It is not to be expected this time that the national constitutional courts will rebel against the ECJ's restrictive interpretation of EC law in this regard as they did with regard to the lack of protection of fundamental rights in the early seventies.[49]

VII. Concluding Remarks

EC action in the field of discrimination between men and women in employment and social security has had a major impact, at least in some Member States. The so-called 'Equal Treatment Directives' forced national laws in which inequalities were still occurring to be changed and the ECJ has played a significant role in promoting the practical application of the principle.

In spite of this major effort to abolish discrimination between male and female workers, much statistical and other research data suggest that many inequalities still exist in the EC. This is mentioned here to indicate that any action taken in the field of discrimination at large, even a determined one like the EC Equal Treatment Programme, requires a lot of stamina to achieve even a little. This will be even more so in the field of discrimination against lesbians and gay men. The experience with actions to promote equal treatment of male and female workers has shown that the removal of cultural and social prejudices regarding the role of a man or a woman in society is an uphill battle. This battle will be even harder when it comes to changing prejudices about lesbians and gay men. Indeed, even though it may be difficult for a woman to follow a 'career-path' in the same way as a man, she will not be considered an outcast because she is a woman. She may be judged for wanting a career instead of or together with raising a family, she will not be considered a socially undesirable or unacceptable being, as is still very often the case with gay men and, probably even more so, lesbians.

This is obviously not an argument for advocating that the EC abstain from action to abolish discrimination against lesbians and gay men. I have

---

48   *Confédération Française Démocratique du Travail v. The European Communities, the member States of the European Communities Collectively and Individually*, 10 July 1978, 16 *CML Rev.*, 501 et seq.

49   I am, of course, referring to the judgment of the Italian Corte Costituzionale in the *Frontini* case (reported in [1974] 14 CMLR 389 et seq.) and, in particular, the judgment of the German Bundesverfassungsgericht in the *Solange I* case (reported in [1974] 14 CMLR 551 et seq.).

argued that discrimination against lesbian and gay workers is an obstacle to the free movement of persons in EC law, and that the EC should remove these obstacles by making full use of the possibilities of Articles 48, 49, 100, 100a and 101 of the EEC Treaty. As regards other forms of discrimination, which do not fall directly within the scope of free movement of persons, it was argued that in creating directives regarding the equal treatment of workers (including the abolition of sexual harassment) the EC legislature should not limit itself to male and female workers in general, but should take the particular position of lesbian and gay workers into account. Such action may not be immediately based on the economic aspects of the functioning of the Common or Internal Market; it is an aspect that belongs to the social dimension of that market as well. It may be clear from this contribution that alleged legal difficulties are not so hard to overcome; it is the presence of the political will to protect homosexual workers within the EC context that is essential. If, however, a Common European Market is to be created in which human dignity, personal freedom and social justice are essential aspects, EC action to abolish any form of discrimination against lesbians and gay men is a dire necessity and the political will must be found.

Chapter Fifteen
The Family Policy of the European Community

by

FRANK EMMERT[*]

*   Executive Director, Academy of European Law, Florence.

Table of Contents

Introduction

The traditional family with married partners of opposite sex and their own two or three children is not exactly dying out. However, it seems fair to ask whether this 'normal' family situation should continue to be considered as *the norm*, the standard used to measure all other forms of human relationships in a world where unmarried cohabitation, divorces, children born out of wedlock, single-parenting, and same-sex relationships have become widespread.[1] Whether one welcomes these evolutions or rejects them, they are a fact of life and have developed in spite of many legal and social disadvantages. All three branches of public authority have to deal with these developments in some way or another. Up to now there has been a reluctance in the Community as well as in the Member States to take any measures which might be seen as supporting and contributing to these developments. Often this has resulted in a reluctance to take any measures at all. This 'sit and wait-strategy' is putting the burden on those who are disadvantaged and discriminated against. These persons are thus marginalized. They see that discriminatory and unfair conditions are ignored by the Community and the Member States and become alienated and disillusioned with the authorities and laws.

---

1   It is difficult to give statistical data on these developments. To give two examples: a) The Member States use slightly different criteria as to what constitutes a lone- or single-parent family. If a separated/divorced-parent has a stable relationship with a new partner who does not adopt the child and thus does not become a parent, will this still be considered a lone-parent family? What is a 'stable relationship'? b) Especially in countries where homosexual relationships between consenting adult males have been prohibited until recently and where stigmatization is (still) widespread, lesbians and gay men tend to hide their sexual orientation and will not appear in statistical surveys.
The following data can thus be considered only as rough estimates: Over the decade from 1970 to 1980 the total number of marriages in the Community declined by 20%; the number of divorces tripled between 1964 and 1982 (source: *Communication from the Commission on Family Policies*, COM (89) 363 final, at 4 and 5); births outside marriage in 1989: Belgium 11%; Denmark 45%; France 28%; Germany 10%; Greece 2%; Ireland 13%; Italy 6%; Luxembourg 12%; Netherlands 11%; Portugal 15%; Spain 10%; United Kingdom 27%; total divorce rate in 1985: Belgium 32.0%; Denmark 49.1%; France 39.9%; Germany 35.1%; Greece 11.9%; Italy 5.3%; Luxembourg 33.9%; Netherlands 41.1%; Portugal 13.1%; Spain 9.5%; United Kingdom 44.6% (source: Eurostat; taking into account the very pronounced trends from 1960 to 1989, respectively 1985, these figures are definitely higher today).
In Germany ('old' eleven federal states) the number of single mothers has risen between 1979 and 1990 from 88.000 to 220.000 according to government statistics (source: *Frankfurter Allgemeine Zeitung*, 14 May 1992, 7).
In studies in the USA 20.3% of the men and 13% of the women have admitted sexual encounters with same sex partners to the point of an orgasm. 28% of the women and 50% of the men have acknowledged sexual arousal by members of their own gender (source: Note, 'Sexual orientation and the Law', *Harvard Law Review* (1989) 1508 1671 (at 1511, footnote 1) – in Europe these figures may be lower due to the still prevailing hostility in many Member States; see also note 2 in Chapter Three by Waaldijk.).

By contrast, the respect for human dignity, equality and individuality and the effective guarantee of the free movement of persons in Europe would demand an active role of the authorities on the Community and Member State level. They should do their share to bring about a situation where the fundamental freedoms are best guaranteed for all members of society.

The task of this chapter is to examine 'the family policy' of the Community. Several intertwined issues have to be dealt with: The topic suggests first of all that there is a clear concept of what can be called a 'family'. This implies that there is a sufficiently unambiguous definition of 'family' in Community law. And if there is, does the definition rely on the traditional concept of 'blood families'?[2] Or does it (could it?) include other forms of human relationships which have otherwise been called 'non-traditional relationships' or 'alternative lifestyles'?

Furthermore, the topic suggests that there is a 'policy', a strategy, an action plan, a concept of what should and what should not be done with and for families. The legal, economic and social privileges granted to traditional families by their mere existence could already be called a policy, albeit only a policy of preference for some form of human relationships over others. However, most if not all of those privileges are granted by the Member States. They could therefore be considered national family policies but would not qualify for the supranational concept to be examined here, applied in a more or less uniform way throughout the Community by its supranational organs. The question will be, whether an independent family policy of the Community can be identified.

The first part of this report will thus examine past and present declarations and actions of the Community which may be taken as expressions of a family policy. This part could be called common ground or the established legal situation of families in Community law and policy. The question will be whether there is a sufficiently homogeneous concept of the various Community organs, making it fair to speak of 'a Community policy'. Otherwise there may be only a list of contradictory and diffuse efforts which do not deserve to be called policy.

In the second part, the focus will be on the question, whether the expressions of family policy identified in the first part can be applied to relationships of lesbians and gay men. This is clearly the case if Community norms expressly include lesbians and gay men in their field of application. More likely, however, the measures will have to be interpreted, as they will not define their range in such clear terms. Finally, some actions may be found to be hostile to same-sex relationships, specifically excluding them. This section is embarrassingly short which is, in the main, a reflection of

---

2   Under the traditional concept family relations can only be established via blood relationship, marriage, and adoption.

the fact (made plain elsewhere in this report) that the Community has paid little attention to the needs of lesbians and gay men.

The third part will then examine whether the existing legal situation in its treatment of same-sex relationships can be found to be satisfactory from a Community point of view; or, to say it differently, whether the Community should be satisfied with *its* existing family policy and leave the improvement of the situation of lesbians and gay men to the Member States.

The report will conclude by proposing *de lege ferenda* action by the Community wherever it may be necessary or at least useful, to end unjustified differences in the treatment of same-sex relationships.

I. The Present Community Treatment of 'Families'

A. Primary and Secondary Community Law and its Interpretation by the Court of Justice

The word 'family' is contained neither in the EEC-Treaty nor in the Maastricht Treaty. However, there is a reference to 'dependents'. According to Article 51 of both treaties, migrant workers *and their dependents* benefit from the two fundamental principles of Community social security law, namely the principle of aggregation of all insurance periods acquired in any of the Member States and the principle that payments shall be made irrespective of the place of residence in the Community. It is generally accepted that the Treaty never envisaged a freedom of movement restricted to the workers themselves and excluding their families.[3]

In the present context the Treaty's equal treatment provisions are also important. Article 7 paragraph 1 of the EEC Treaty (Article 6 paragraph 1 in the Maastricht Treaty) generally prohibits any discrimination on grounds of nationality. More specific equal treatment clauses, which take precedence over Article 7 within their proper field of application,[4] are included in Article 48 paragraph 2 (no discrimination on grounds of nationality 'as regards employment, remuneration and other conditions of work and employment') and Article 119 ('equal pay for equal work' for men and women).

Council Directive 64/221 on the co-ordination of special measures concerning the movement and residence of foreign nationals which are justified on grounds of public policy, public security or public health[5] is expressly

---

3   Cf. Wölker in Groeben, Thiesing, Ehlermann (eds.), *Kommentar zum EWG-Vertrag*, 4th ed. 1991, Vorb. Arts. 48 to 50, para. 40.
4   Established jurisprudence of the Court of Justice, cf. most recently: Case 305/87, *Commission of the European Communities v. Hellenic Republic (Re Acquisition of Immovable Property)* [1989] ECR 1461 (Rec. 12 f.) and AG Jacobs in that case, Rec. 14, at 1472.
5   JOCE, 4 April 1964, 850; special English edition 1963-64, 117.

applicable to 'any national of a Member State who resides in or travels to another Member State of the Community, either in order to pursue an activity as an employed or self-employed person, or as a recipient of services' (Article 1 paragraph 1) and to 'the spouse and to members of the family' (Article 1 paragraph 2). It protects these persons from excess Member State restrictions under the guise of public policy-, security- or health-measures.[6] However, it does not define 'members of the family'.

Article 10 of *Council Regulation 1612/68 on freedom of movement for workers within the Community*[7] contains the following definition of a worker's family:

> 1. The following shall, irrespective of their nationality, have the right to install themselves with a worker who is a national of one Member State and who is employed in the territory of another Member State:
>   (a) his spouse and *their* descendants who are under the age of 21 years *or* are dependants;
>   (b) dependant relatives in the ascending line of the worker and his spouse.
> 2. Member States shall facilitate the admission of any member of the family not coming within the provisions of paragraph 1 if dependent on the worker referred to above or living under his roof in the country whence he comes.
> 3. For the purposes of paragraphs 1 and 2, the worker must have available for his family housing considered as normal for national workers in the region where he is employed; [...][8]

Subsequent secondary legislation refers to this definition of Regulation 1612/68. For example, *Council Directive 68/360 on the Abolition of Restriction on Movement and Residence within the Community for Workers of Member States and their families*[9] requires Member States to abolish restrictions previously applied against nationals of other Member States *and* 'members of their families to whom Regulation (EEC) No. 1612/68 applies' (Article 1). Article 4 paragraph 4 of that same Directive also makes it clear that the family members do not have to be nationals of any Member State of the Community to benefit from the Directive. It is sufficient that the worker be a Community national.

Commission Regulation 1251/70 on the right of workers to remain in the territory of a Member State after having been employed in that State[10] gives the right to remain permanently in another Member State also to the members of the family of the worker 'as defined in Article 10 of Regulation (EEC) No. 1612/68' (Article 1). They retain this right even after the death of the worker (Article 3).

---

6   Cf. for example Case 67/74, *Carmelo Angelo Bonsignore v. Oberstadtdirektor der Stadt Köln* [1975] ECR 297.
7   JOCE 1968 L 257/2; special English edition 1968-69, 475.
8   Ibid., emphasis added.
9   JOCE 1968 L 257/13; special English edition 1968-69, 485.

Thus, the definition of Regulation 1612/68 gains importance beyond its immediate field of application.

In the field of self-employed establishment and the provision of services *Council Directive 73/148 on the abolition of restrictions on movement and residence within the Community for nationals of Member States with regard to establishment and the provision of services*[11] provides its own, slightly different definition of members of the family which benefit from the same freedoms:

> 1. The Member States shall, acting as provided in this Directive, abolish restrictions on the movement and residence of:
> (a) nationals of a Member State who are established or who wish to establish themselves in another Member State in order to pursue activities as self-employed persons, or who wish to provide services in that State;
> (b) nationals of a Member State wishing to go to another Member State as re-cipients of services;[12]
> (c) the spouse and *the* children under twenty-one years of age of such nationals, irrespective of their nationality;
> (d) the relatives in the ascending and descending lines of such nationals and of the spouse of such nationals, which relatives are dependent on them, irrespective of their nationality.
> 2. Member States shall favour the admission of any other member of the family of a national referred to in paragraph 1 (a) or (b) or of the spouse of that national, which member is dependent on that national or spouse of that national or who in the country of origin was living under the same roof.[13]

Finally, for the area of social security law, Article 1(f) of *Council Regulation 1408/71 on the application of social security schemes to employed persons, to self-employed persons and to members of their families moving within the Community*[14] contains the following definition:

> 'member of the family' means any person defined or recognized as a member of the family or designated as a member of the household by the legislation under which the benefits are provided or [...] by the legislation of the Member State in whose territory such person resides; [...]

---

10   JOCE 1970 L 142/24; special English edition 1970, 402.
11   OJ 1973 L 172/14; this directive has replaced Dir. 64/220, JOCE 1964 56/845.
12   Recipients of services who are privileged under this directive are *inter alia* tourists, cf. Case 186/87, *Ian William Cowan v. Trésor public* [1989] ECR 195.
13   Ibid., emphasis added. By contrast to Reg. 1612/68, which speaks of the worker, his spouse and *their* descendants, para. 1(c) of Dir. 73/148 speaks only of *the* children of the professional. This may seem to exclude the children of his/her spouse whom he/she has not adopted (e.g. children from a previous marriage of the spouse). However, contrary to para. 1(b) of Reg. 1612/68, para. 1(d) of Dir. 73/148 goes on by giving the right of movement and residence not only to dependant relatives in the *ascending line* of worker and spouse, but to those relatives in the *ascending and descending lines* of professional *and* spouse. Thus, children related only to the spouse are included after all.
14   Originally published in JOCE 1971 L 149/2; revised current version in OJ 1983 L 230/8.

All three definitions do not purport to contain final and complete lists or criteria for the determination of 'members of the family'. Other persons than those expressly listed can be members of the family according to national law and will benefit from the quoted articles and norms. Furthermore, the definitions refer to relatives in the descending line, i.e. children and grand-children, without any statement as to how the relationship was established. In particular this means that it is immaterial from a Community-law point of view whether the children were conceived 'naturally', through artificial insemination or were adopted and are thus not biologically related at all. Again, Community law relies on the national requirements as to who is and who is not recognized as a descendent.[15]

The Court of Justice has been called upon a number of times to interpret the personal range of the freedom of movement and the social security provisions. Indirectly these judgments are also delimiting the Community's regulatory competence concerning the definition of 'members of the family' and 'spouse' and thus the Community's powers to adopt what could be called an independent family policy.

A rather restrictive view was expressed by Advocate General Trabucchi in Case 21/74.[16] Trabucchi stated that discrimination against married women may result from the fact that,

> when he gets married, a man does not automatically acquire the nationality of the wife and would, therefore, never be in the position of losing the privileges associated with the status he had before the marriage [while the opposite will frequently be the case]. But, as I have already indicated, *Community law cannot remould from its own point of view the whole world of social and human relationships*. Where the national legislation provides for a method of acquiring nationality [...], those responsible for drafting the Community legislation rightly accept the situation as they find it as a point of reference, and they will do so long as it is not in itself repugnant to a fundamental human right, as discrimination based on sex alone would be. *Community law cannot object to the fact that, in the management of its internal relationships, each State pays regard to the principle of family unit in accordance with its own conception of it and without in social terms conflicting with the public policy of the Community.* [...][17]

At first glance the Advocate General seems to reject a Community competence concerning family policy entirely, and rather to leave the field to the Member States. A second look will show, however, that Trabucchi is

---

15   The view expressed by Steiner, 1990, on page 168, that it 'would be in keeping with the Court of Justice's approach to take a broad view of the rights of children of the family' and that it may suffice that persons have been 'treated as children of the family even though they were not, strictly speaking, descendants', thus focusses too much on the Court's side, i.e. Community law, and neglects the decisiveness of national law on this question.
16   *Jeanne Airola v. Commission of the European Communities* [1975] ECR 221.
17   Ibid., at 233, emphasis added.

making two reservations: the Member States must not obstruct the public policy of the Community and they may not violate fundamental human rights. These reservations shall be examined more closely below.

Some interesting observations on the concept of 'spouse' are contained in Advocate General Mancini's opinion on Case 149/82[18] concerning child benefits for divorced parents:

> Various interpretations of the concept of 'spouse' [in Article 10 of Regulation 574/72[19]] have been put forward: According to the [British] Insurance Officer, the question is to be resolved on the basis of the law applied by the social security institution which seeks to rely upon Article 10. Under United Kingdom law, only persons whose marriage subsists are regarded as spouses; thus a divorcee is a former spouse and not a spouse. [...] By contrast with that interpretation of the expression 'spouse', which I would describe as restrictive, the Commission and the Council expressly ask the Court to interpret it widely. The Commission submits that, *in the interpretation of Community social security legislation*, emphasis should be placed on the position of the worker as regards his professional trade activity rather than on his status familiae. The Council points out that there is a lacunae in the regulation. It therefore proposes that the Court should fill that lacunae by regarding as a 'spouse' any person having legal custody of and residing with the children in respect of whom the benefits are payable. The view of the Insurance Officer is to be rejected. In the first place it overlooks the fact that the reference made in the regulation to national legislation concerns the definition of 'member of the family' and not that of 'spouse'. [...] *As regards the Council's proposal that any person having custody of and residing with the children in respect of whom the benefits are payable should be regarded as 'spouse', I do not consider it acceptable in the context of the proceedings before this Court. It is a matter for legislature. That does not mean that it is not valid as a matter of legal policy.* [...][20]

On the one hand the Advocate General is rejecting the narrow British definition of 'spouse' with the argument that only the definition of 'members of the family' is left to national law. On the other hand he rejects the very wide definition proposed by the Council by saying that such a wide definition could not be introduced by the Court but only by Community legislature. The Court followed the Advocate General by not endorsing the Council's very wide concept of 'spouse', but still included divorced parents amongst those entitled to child benefits as spouses:

> [19] However, the task assigned to the Court by Article 177 of the EEC Treaty is not that of delivering opinions on general or hypothetical questions [namely whether a 'spouse' can also be a third person which was never married to either parent] but of assisting in the administration of justice in the Member States. In this case, therefore, the interpretation of the provision in question should be

18   *Stephanie Robards v. Insurance Officer* [1983] ECR 171, 189.
19   Regulation of the Council of 21 March 1972 fixing the procedure for implementing Regulation (EEC) No. 1408/71, OJ English Special Edition 1972 (I), 159.
20   Case 149/82, *supra* footnote 18, at 194 and 195, emphasis added.

confined to the case which is before the national court, namely that of a divorced spouse who has not remarried and is carrying on a professional or trade activity. *It would be for the Commission and the Council to take the necessary measures in order to amend the provision in question* if it appeared that such an amendment were necessary in order to enable other cases to be satisfactorily resolved. [20] The reply to be given [...] to the Social Security Commissioner is that the second sentence of Article 10(1)(a) of Regulation No. 574/72 must be interpreted as meaning that it applies to a divorced spouse. [...][21]

While it remains unclear, why 'members of the family' was left to the competence of the Member States' to define and 'spouse' not,[22] it must not be forgotten that all this interpretation was done in the context of a very specific application of a very specific regulation and may not be valid in other contexts.

The definition of 'spouse' had very severe consequences for a non-Community national in Case 267/83:[23] The plaintiff of the main proceedings was a Senegalese national, married to a French migrant worker and living in Berlin. After the marriage had broken up and the couple had separated, but before the divorce, the German authorities refused to renew the plaintiff's residence permit on the grounds that she was no longer a 'member of the family' of a Community national. Upon reference for preliminary ruling the Court of Justice rejected this interpretation of Regulation 1612/68 but only on the ground that the marriage, at the point of time in question, had not yet been dissolved. The Court thus established two principles: a) the right of the family members to install themselves with the migrant worker in another Member State does not require that they live permanently with him or her under the same roof; b) once the family bond is legally dissolved through divorce or otherwise, the persons who had derived their rights from the migrant worker cease to be family members and may be expelled.[24]

---

21   Ibid., at 187, emphasis added.
22   AG Lenz, in Case 59/85, *State of the Netherlands v. Ann Florence Reed* [1986] ECR 1283, held it to be unacceptable that the term 'spouse' were left to be defined by national law because in that case 'there would be divergence in the application of the law on an issue important for freedom of movement, which would be just as unacceptable as divergence with regard to the term "worker" was held to be in the judgments in Cases 75/63 [*Mrs M.K.H. Hoekstra (née Unger) v. Bestuur der Bedrijfsvereniging voor Detailhandel en Ambachten* [1964] ECR 177] and 53/81 [*D.M. Levin v. Staatssecretaris van Justitie* [1982] ECR 1035].' (at 1293). However, is the same not also true for the term 'members of the family'?
23   *Aissatou Diatta v. Land Berlin* [1985] ECR 567.
24   For a very critical discussion of this result see Weiler, 'Thou Shalt Not Oppress a Stranger: On the Judicial Protection of the Human Rights of Non-EC Nationals – A Critique', 3 *EJIL* (1992) 65 (at 85 to 91). In a parallel case which had come before the British courts, High Court Judge Comyn had struck down the expulsion order arguing that if an EEC worker could remove the 'cloak of protection' from a non-EEC spouse by deserting or divorcing him [or her], or by leaving the country, 'this would add a new terror to marriage'. Unfortunately, this view was shared neither by the Court of Appeals

As Weiler has pointed out,[25] the Court, in deviating from the guidelines set up by Advocate General Trabucchi[26] failed to even consider whether these results might violate fundamental human rights of the plaintiff, e.g. her right to human dignity (by giving the husband the *de facto* power to have her expelled) or her right to family life (had there been children).

At least as far as Community nationals are concerned, the Court is however sensitive to discrimination by a Member State on grounds of nationality.

In a case which came before the Court as a preliminary reference from the Hoge Raad[27] a British national had come to the Netherlands to work there for a subsidiary of a British company. His girl-friend had accompanied him. She first applied for a residence permit on the basis that she was looking for work and after she had been unable to find work she based her application on her relationship with the migrant worker. Under Dutch law at that time, a foreigner was entitled to be treated as a spouse for purposes of immigration law, if he or she had a stable relationship *with a Dutch citizen*, was not otherwise married and appropriate accommodation and sufficient means of existence were provided. Thus, the Hoge Raad asked for interpretation of Community law on two different lines: (a) should Article 10(1)(a) of Regulation 1612/68 nowadays be interpreted to include not only 'spouses' but equally unmarried companions? (b) was the Dutch law a discrimination on grounds of nationality prohibited by Article 7 or 48 EEC?

On the first question, the Dutch government argued

[when], in support of a dynamic interpretation, reference is made to developments in social and legal conceptions, those developments must be visible in the whole of the Community; such an argument cannot be based on social and legal developments in only one or a few Member States.[28]

The Commission concurred that in 'the Community as it now stands it is impossible to speak of any consensus that unmarried companions should be treated as spouses.'[29] And the Court agreed, arguing that such a wide interpretation of Article 10 of Regulation 1612/68 would be binding and directly applicable in all Member States according to Article 189 and therefore 'any interpretation of a legal term on the basis of social developments must take into account the situation in the whole Community, not merely

---

nor by the House of Lords and a reference to the Court of Justice was not made on the ground that the matter had already been settled in Diatta; cf. Steiner, 1990, 167.

25   *Supra* footnote 24, at pp. 87-88.
26   Cf. *supra* footnote 17 and accompanying text.
27   Case 59/85, *State of the Netherlands v. Ann Florence Reed* [1986] ECR 1283.
28   Ibid., Rec. 10.
29   Ibid., Rec. 11.

in one Member State.'[30] This finding of the Court is evidently based on the *absence of laws* in most Member States to the effect that unmarried couples must (under certain conditions such as long standing stability, exclusivity, etc.) be treated equally to married couples. The Court is evidently not looking at the *presence of millions of unmarried couples* in all Member States.

On the second question, however, the Court did not follow the suggestion of the Dutch Government and the Advocate General. Relying on Article 7(2) of Regulation 1612/68 rather than Article 10, the Court held:

> [24] Article 7(2) [...] provides that in the host State a worker who is a national of another Member State must 'enjoy the same social and tax advantages as national workers'.
> [25] The Court has emphasized, in particular in its judgment of 30 September 1975 in Case 32/75 (*Cristini v. SNCF* [1975] ECR 1085), that the phrase 'social advantages' in Article 7(2) must not be interpreted restrictively.
> [26] As the Court has repeatedly held, the purpose of Article 7(2) of Regulation No. 1612/68 is to achieve equal treatment, and therefore the concept of social advantage, extended by that provision to workers who are nationals of other Member States, must include all advantages 'which, whether or not linked to a contract or employment, are generally granted to national workers primarily because of their objective status as workers or by virtue of the mere fact of their residence on the national territory and the extension of which to workers who are nationals of other member countries therefore seems suitable to facilitate their mobility within the Community' (judgments of 31 May 1979 in Case 207/78 *Ministère public v. Even* [1979] ECR 2019, and 20 June 1985 in Case 94/84 *Office national de l'emploi v. Deak* [1985] ECR 1873). [...]
> [28] *In the same way it must be recognized that the possibility for a migrant worker of obtaining permission for his unmarried companion to reside with him, where that companion is not a national of the host Member State, can assist his integration in the host State and thus contribute to the achievement of freedom of movement for workers.* Consequently, that possibility must also be regarded as falling within the concept of a social advantage for the purposes of Article 7(2) of Regulation No. 1612/68.[31]

Understandably, the Court chose what could be called the minimalist solution, helping the plaintiffs in question[32] by freely interpreting the Community-law term 'social advantages' instead of redefining the Member State-law term 'spouse' and risking harsh criticism for judicial activism.

30   Ibid., Rec. 12-13; to a limited extent the Court was in agreement with AG Lenz, who had proposed to reject the wide interpretation of Article 10 on grounds of legal certainty: 'if companions are to be treated in the same way as spouses it is imperative to lay down limits, criteria and conditions (in particular with regard to the duration and nature of the relationship). These are certainly a matter for the legislature, and can hardly be determined by the Court of Justice in the course of interpretation of a regulation intended to cover other cases.' (at 1294).
31   Ibid., at 1302-1303, emphasis added.
32   Or rather not helping them as Ms Reed and her partner had given up before the judgment was handed down and had gone back to the UK.

Another famous example where the Court in fact interfered with Member State legislation concerning family rights on the grounds of discrimination based on nationality is Case 249/86.[33] Germany had made the right of the relatives and dependants of migrant workers to stay with him or her conditional upon him or her continually providing adequate housing for the entire family. This had resulted in the expulsion of previously admitted family members after a deterioration of the housing situation, for example through the birth of another child or the arrival at the age of majority of a child. At the same time, German nationals in a comparable position did not have to fear any consequences. The Court rejected the German interpretation of Regulation 1612/68:

> [10] Regulation No. 1612/68 must [...] be interpreted in the light of the requirement of respect for family life set out in Article 8 of the Convention for the Protection of Human Rights and Fundamental Freedoms. That requirement is one of the fundamental rights which, according to the Court's settled case-law, restated in the preamble to the Single European Act, are recognized by Community law.
> [11] [...] Article 10(3) of Regulation No. 1612/68 must be interpreted in the context of the overall structure and purpose of that regulation. [...] in order to facilitate the movement of members of workers' families the Council took into account, first, *the importance for the worker, from a human point of view, of having his entire family with him*, and, secondly, the importance, from all points of view, of the integration of the worker and his family into the host Member State without any difference in treatment in relation to nationals of that State.[34]

In all cases where the Court of Justice is referring to Articles of the European Convention of Human Rights, it does so only in the fairly general manner exemplified *supra* in recital 10, i.e. to the Convention text itself and the text of the additional protocols. In no case has the ECJ ever referred to or otherwise discernably taken into account the interpretation of those texts by Convention organs in individual cases. Thus, the established practice of the ECJ to refer to the Convention as a source of human rights to be respected in Community law does not necessarily mean that the Human Rights Commission's restrictive interpretation of 'family' as excluding stable gay male[35] and lesbian[36] partnerships is also valid in Community Law. On the other hand, this established practice may become very significant for Community Law if and when the *Draft Protocol to the Convention for the Protection of Human Rights and Fundamental Freedoms Concerning the Elimination of Discrimination Based on Sexual Orientation*[37] is adopted

---

33   *Commission of the European Communities v. Federal Republic of Germany (Re Housing of Migrant Workers)* [1989] ECR 1263.
34   Ibid., at 1290, emphasis added.
35   *X. and Y. v. UK*, 32 DR 220 (1983).
36   *S. v. UK*, 47 DR 274 (1986).
37   For a critical appraisal of the Draft see Helfer, 1991, (especially 188-191).

by the Council of Europe and ratified by the majority of the Member States of the EC.

A second observation is of more immediate relevance: The Court is subscribing to Advocate General Trabucchi's view and the limitation on Member States' family policy drawn by Community legislative acts which have to be interpreted in taking into account (Community) human rights.[38] It is just not always consistent in applying those standards.[39]

B. Non-Binding Recommendations, Resolutions and Reports

A complete list of all the occasions on which any Community organ has ever had to deal in one way or another with family matters would not only be very hard to compile but also very long and fairly meaningless. Thus, the following examples are a rather random selection which attempts to cover those family related matters which represent significant developments also for lesbians and gay men.

1989 saw a *Communication from the Commission on Family Policies.*[40] The findings of the Communication were based on a seminar on the implications of Community family policies, held in Frankfurt from 18-19 April 1989. They concern primarily the implications of demographic changes in the Member States, in particular the declining birth rate. However, as the name already suggests, the Communication deals with family *policies* in the plural, i.e. above all those of the Member States. Section II on 'Recognition of the Role of the Family and Action in its Favour by the Public Authorities' does contain a chapter 3 on action at Community level. But it previews only the gathering of information, drawing up of an inventory on measures and provisions in effect (at the national levels), long-term population studies and 'concertation at senior national level'.[41] There is no intention of establishing an independent Community family policy.

Of its own motion the Economic and Social Committee decided on 25 April 1991 to draw up an *Opinion on Lone-Parent Families.* The Opinion was adopted on 31 October 1991.[42] After analysing the overall disadvantaged situation of lone-parent families, the Opinion suggests modifications in the national welfare systems, a new social housing strategy, improved

---

38   Cf. *supra* footnote 17 and accompanying text. For a general discussion of Community human rights protection cf. Cassese, Clapham, Weiler (eds.), 1991; and in particular therein the contributions by Vila Costa, Les droits des femmes dans la Communauté européenne (Vol. III, 177), and Castillo, Les droits des enfants dans la Communauté (Vol. III, 225).

39   Cf. Weiler, *supra* footnote 24.

40   COM (89) 363 final; cf. also EP *Resolution on Family Policy*, OJ 1983 C 184 (17 November 1983).

41   Ibid., at 14.

42   CES (91) 1266, Rapporteur: Ms Slipman.

access to child-care resources and improved access to education and training. What the report does not explicitly say is that all measures required to
implement these suggestions would, at the present stage of development of
European integration, have to be effected by the Member States, who are in
no way bound by the Opinion.

In its *Proposal for a Council Recommendation on Child Care*[43] the
Commission found *inter alia* 'a clear need for closer approximation in
levels of support for employed parents, including services providing care for
children, in order to eliminate imbalances in the labour market and facilitate mobility between Member States'.[44] Thus the Commission asked the
Council to *recommend* 'that Member States develop measures in order to
enable women and men to reconcile their occupational and their family
obligations, arising from the care and upbringing of children'.[45]

Concerning rights of lesbians and gay men, the European Parliament
took the lead in 1982. Following motions for resolutions by Mr Glinne and
others on sexual discrimination[46] and by Mrs van den Heuvel on statutory
and other discrimination against homosexuals[47] it requested an opinion on
sexual discrimination at the workplace from the Committee on Social
Affairs and Employment. The result was the so-called Squarcialupi
Report[48] which formed the basis for the adoption by the Parliament on 13
March 1984 of the *Resolution on Sexual Discrimination at the Workplace*.[49]
In that resolution the European Parliament

> 4. Urges the Member States to:
>   (a) abolish any laws which make homosexual acts between consenting adults
>   liable to punishment,
>   (b) apply the same age of consent as for heterosexual acts, [...]
> 5. Calls on the Commission to:
>   (a) renew its efforts with regard to dismissals to ensure that [...] certain indi-
>   viduals are not unfairly treated for reasons relating to their private life,
>   (b) submit proposals to ensure that no cases arise in the Member States of dis -
>   crimination against homosexuals with regard to access to employment and
>   working conditions, [...]
> 6. Also calls on the Commission to:
>   (a) invite Member States to provide, as soon as possible, a list of all provi-
>   sions of their legislation which concern homosexuals,

---

43   Com (91) 233 final, 28 August 1991.
44   Ibid., Explanatory Memorandum, para. A.7.
45   Ibid., Article 1; the Opinion of the Economic and Social Committee on the Commission
      proposal was adopted on 28 November 1991, CES (91) 1390, Rapporteur: Mrs
      Guillaume.
46   EP Doc. 1-172/82.
47   EP Doc. 1-1072/82.
48   *Report on Sexual Discrimination at the Workplace*, EP Working Doc. 1-1358/83, 13
      February 1984.
49   OJ 1984 C 104/45.

(b) to identify, on the basis of such lists, any discrimination against homosexuals with regard to employment, housing and other social problems by drawing up a report, pursuant to Article 122 of the EEC Treaty;

On the basis of a mandate provided by *Council Resolution of 29 May 1990 on the Protection of the Dignity of Women and Men at Work*[50] the Commission elaborated a *Commission Recommendation on the Protection of the Dignity of Women and Men at Work* and, annexed to it, a *Code of Practice on Measures to Combat Sexual Harassment.*[51] The purpose of the Code is

> to give practical guidance to employers, trade unions, and employees on the protection of the dignity of women and men at work. [...] The aim is to ensure that sexual harassment does not occur and, if it does occur, to ensure that adequate procedures are readily available to deal with the problem and prevent its recurrence.[52]

The Code explicitly identifies lesbians and gay men amongst those groups of employees particularly vulnerable to sexual harassment.[53]

On 30 October 1991 the Economic and Social Committee adopted its Opinion on the *Draft Commission Recommendation on the Protection of the Dignity of Women and Men at Work.*[54] It welcomed the initiative and generally endorsed the findings and proposals of the Commission, regretting however, that they were limited to a recommendation instead of a more binding EC instrument.[55]

Finally on July 1992 Parliament adopted the Resolution on *Rights of the Child* which provides for the rights of children to grow as full members of society, including their freedom of conscience and right to self determination. Paragraph 8.5. specifically outrules discrimination of children on the basis of sexual orientation.[56]

C. Results of Part I

Two results should be obvious from the foregoing analysis: Firstly, the Community has clearly not taken over the main responsibility for family matters from the Member States. All binding acts of Community law are without exception closely related either to migrant workers and thus the fundamental freedom of movement, provision of services and establish-

---

50   OJ 1990 C 157/3.
51   OJ 1992 L 49/1.
52   Ibid., para. 1, at 3.
53   Ibid. For a further discussion on sexual harassment at work and employment protection and controls for lesbians and gay men in the workplace, see Chapter Fourteen by Betten.
54   C (91) 1397 final.
55   CES (91) 1253, Rapporteur: Ms Maddocks (30 October 1991), para. 1.3.
56   EP Document A 30172/92, Rapporteur: Mr Bandres Molet (Report dated 27 April 1992).

ment, or the equality of the sexes as explicitly provided for in Article 119 of the EEC Treaty and what may be called the catalogue of fundamental human rights respected by the Community. Wherever Community organs have become active outside of the context of free movement of persons, the results were without exception non-binding resolutions and recommendations in rather general language.[57]

Secondly, for any person to come within reach of Community regulatory competence there are only two possibilities *de lege lata*: either the person becomes a migrant worker or a member of what is accepted as the family of a migrant worker under Article 10 of Regulation 1612/68, or the person claims a right against a Member State which is guaranteed by the Community *and has to be respected by the Member States.*[58] Most Community nationals and the larger parts of family life of all Community nationals remain under the exclusive competence of the Member States. Even where binding Community 'family law' does exist, it is not independent from Member States' law. The definition of 'family' depends to a large extent on the definitions of the Member States. Immediate result of this interdependence are differences in the level of personal freedom and the extent of protection from Member State to Member State.

The latter is evident in particular as far as the right of 'members of the family' other than spouses and dependent parents or children are concerned, to migrate with a worker to another Member State. Today there is no legal obligation on the Member States to admit unmarried partners or non-dependent or less close relatives even if they have been living with the migrant worker in the State of origin. Some Member States will have more restrictive policies than others in this area. And the Court of Justice has made it quite clear that it will not 'legislate' new definitions of 'spouse' or 'members of the family' to extend existing Member States' legal obligations of admission, residence, work permits, etc. before a clear majority of the Member States has enacted national legislation in the same direction.

More far-reaching legal obligations have been proposed by Parliament in its *Proposal for a Regulation Amending Council Regulation (EEC) No. 1612/68 on Freedom of Movement for Workers within the Community.*[59] The European Parliament has suggested the following addition to Article 10:

---

57 Even in those non-binding acts the Community organs have frequently attempted to establish a connection to the safe-haven of the fundamental freedoms, cf. the *Child Care Recommendation, supra* footnotes 43-45 and accompanying text.

58 On the question whether and to what extent Community human rights are binding not only on Community organs but also on the Member States, when the latter are acting within their own area of competence and not implementing Community legislation cf. Chapter Two by Clapham and Weiler, and Chapter Eight by Snyder *et al.*

59 OJ 1990 C 68/88.

2. The right to install themselves referred to in paragraph 1 above shall also cover the person with whom the worker lives in a de facto union recognized as such for administrative and legal purposes, whether in the Member State of origin or in the host Member State, and their dependent offspring.
3. The death of the worker, dissolution of the marriage or ending of the de facto union shall not prejudice the rights acquired under paragraphs 1 and 2 of this Article.

A somewhat less far reaching amendment on similar lines was proposed by the Commission two months later in its *Modified Proposal for a Council Regulation (EEC) Amending Regulation (EEC) No. 1612/68 on Freedom of Movement for Workers within the Community.*[60] The Commission proposed to rephrase Article 10 subparagraph (a) as follows: '(a) the spouse *or any person with similar status under the system of the host country* and their descendants;'.[61]

However, these proposals have not been taken up so far by the Council and given the resistance of some Member States against further obligations concerning admission of 'aliens' a positive vote of the Council does not seem likely for some time to come either.[62]

II. Lesbians and Gay Men under Exisitng 'Family Law' of the Community

All Community-law documents that refer to lesbians and/or gay men are without exception non-binding recommendations, resolutions and reports. They merely 'urge' Member States to abolish discriminatory legislation, 'invite' them to cooperate by providing information on their laws and practices, etc. Their effect has been virtually zero.[63]

Lesbians and gay men are not mentioned in one single binding norm of the Community. Thus, the regulations and directives dealing with family law in one way or another have to be interpreted to find out if and to what

---

60 OJ 1990 C 119/10.
61 Ibid., at 11, emphasis added.
62 However, Regulation No. 1612/68 is based on Article 49 EEC. Thus, amendments used to require that the Council is 'acting on a proposal from the Commission and after con-sulting the Economic and Social Committee' (pre-Single Act), have been altered to the requirement now that the Council is 'acting by a qualified majority on a proposal from the Commission in co-operation with the European Parliament and after consulting the Economic and Social Committee' (current EEC Treaty as amended by the Single Act), and in the future is 'acting in accordance with the procedure referred to in Article 189b and after consulting the Economic and Social Committee' (Maastricht Treaty). These amendments have brought and will bring an increased influence of Parliament and re-duced possibilities of individual Member States to block legislation in this area.
63 Tatchell, 1990, 6-7.

extent they would be applied to lesbians and gay men *under the present jurisprudence of the Court of Justice.*

As has been shown *supra*, Community norms as interpreted by the Court leave the definitions of 'spouse' and 'members of the family', which usually decide the personal range of application of the norms, largely to the Member States. How free are the Member States, therefore, in their definition of 'members of the family'? Where is the line beyond which they begin to obstruct the public policy of the Community or the enjoyment of fundamental human rights?

The question whether a lesbian or gay partner of a migrant worker can claim benefits under Community law has not come before the Court thus far. However, the most likely answer is not hard to predict. One might even go so far as to saying that the Court would accept a Member State's (non-discriminatory) exclusion from 'the family' of all persons, except the spouse (of a traditional marriage) and genetically related children. Advocate General Trabucchi once expressed the Member States' competence to define the term 'family members' as follows:

> [...] although there may be problems of definition in this matter, they will never relate to the worker's children, whose membership of the family could not be contested even on the narrowest acceptation of the concept of 'member of the family'.[64]

A major 'benefit' offered to lesbians and gay men under existing Community law becomes visible upon application of the Court's decision in the *Reed* case[65] on a Danish registered partnership. The *Danish Registered Partnership Act of 1989* permits lesbian or gay couples to enter into an institutionalized partnership if (at least) one of the partners is of Danish nationality. The registered partnership has similar legal consequences as marriage. However, the couple cannot adopt children, nor can there be common custody of children, they cannot demand a church wedding and, most importantly, the partnership is not recognized in other countries.[66]

If the Court held in *Reed* that 'the possibility for a migrant worker of obtaining permission for his unmarried [opposite sex] companion to reside with him [...] can assist his integration in the host State' and consequently 'must be regarded as falling within the concept of a social advantage for the purposes of Article 7(2) of Regulation No. 1612/68',[67] the same must be true of the possibility of a migrant worker to register a same-sex partnership in Denmark the way Danish nationals can.

---

64   Case 7/75, *Mr and Mrs F. v. Belgian State (Re Handicapped Child)* [1975] ECR 679, at 697.
65   Cf. *supra* footnote 27 and accompanying text.
66   See also paragraph II.B.2.c of Chapter Three by Waaldijk.
67   *Supra* footnote 27, Rec. 28 of the judgment.

Thus, the limitation of the *Danish Registered Partnership Act* to situations where at least one of the partners is of Danish nationality, cannot be upheld against migrant workers who have come to Denmark from other Member States.

III. Evaluation and Proposals

A. What Should the Optimal Situation Be Like?

A convincing presentation of the 'optimal situation' requires first of all an agreement on the moral judgment concerning sexual preference for same-sex partners. It is submitted that homosexuality should be considered as part of someone's personality like blue eyes or left handedness. It is not helpful to look for the reasons of homosexuality when considering how lesbians and gay men should be treated. It seems irrelevant whether or not the reasons are of a genetic nature, stem from early childhood experiences or can be wholly or partially subject to personal decision. The fact is that some persons will have preferences for same-sex lovers. This is not good or bad, it is just different. Moral or legal condemnation will not do away with the factual situation. It has been recognized that homosexuality is not a disease. There are forms of homosexual behaviour which are undesirable in any society but this is equally true for certain forms of heterosexual behaviour (for example rape, seduction of children, incest, etc.).

The sight of lesbians and gay men openly displaying affection in a manner accepted between heterosexual couples such as holding hands or kissing in public is simply unfamiliar. It is no more or no less detestable than heterosexual intimacy in public, merely less common. This is likely due in part to the real threat of violence (physical and verbal) or public censure which remains socially acceptable behaviour in most Member States. We should all be reminded that heterosexual public displays of affection – whilst being considered perfectly normal in modern Western societies – were legally and morally censured until not very long ago. A classification of the one as natural, the other as unnatural is based on prejudice and custom rather than fact.

To support this assertion, some observations concerning a very sensitive area, namely the access of lesbians and gay men to jobs as school teachers, shall be cited. They unmask the shaky foundations of most arguments given in defence of a real or presumed need to discriminate:

> The state might argue that because teachers serve as role models for their students and interact with them during adolescence, permitting gays to teach would influence some students to become gay themselves. A common response to this assertion is that it is simply not true: teachers have no influence on the future

sexual identity of their students. This view often relies on the belief that sexual orientation is genetically determined or formed in the early years of childhood. But because we have not yet determined the origins of sexual orientation with any certainty, a response to the state's articulation of its goal must assume that the states's fear is to some degree justified – that some students who would not otherwise have done so would engage in gay sexual activity or even identify themselves as gay. [...] The state would probably argue that an increase in the incidence and acceptability of homosexuality would pose a threat to the institutions of marriage and family – institutions protected in many other contexts. The flaw in this argument is not that the goal is invalid, but that the means are unaccountably underinclusive. Spinsters, bachelors, and divorced people are permitted to teach without challenge, and even unwed mothers and single pregnant women have won constitutional protection for their right to teach, despite their possible encouragement of untraditional lifestyles. [...] The underinclusiveness of discrimination against gay teachers for the purpose of protecting marriage and family suggests that perhaps another principle motivates the singling out of gay teachers. The difference between divorced and gay teachers is not that the latter pose a greater threat to the institutions of marriage, but that homosexuality is today considered immoral, just as divorce once was. [...][68]

Once the basic claim to equal treatment regardless of sexual orientation is established, the focus will have to shift to the question whether equality can and should be granted in all aspects of traditional family life. Total equality would mean the granting of all rights thus far reserved to heterosexual couples to same-sex partnerships. This would include the right to sexual relationships among adults and teenagers, the right to marry (in church), to have children (through adoption or artificial insemination), etc. and all benefits and responsibilities related to these social institutions.

It is submitted that the decisions to grant equality can and must be limited to a relatively small number of fundamental questions. All other present forms of discrimination – and there are many[69] – have to disappear by necessity as a natural and just consequence of the fundamental decisions. For example, if the right to marriage or marriage-like status is recognized, it has to entail the right to free movement as a dependent, the right to equal

---

68   Note, 'The Constitutional Status of Sexual Orientation: Homosexuality as a Suspect Classification', 98 *Harvard Law Review* (1985) 1285, at 1306-1308, footnotes omitted.

69   Examples of discriminatory laws in the United Kingdom which have come before the European Commission on Human Rights: *Desmond v. UK*, Appl. No. 9721/82, 7 May 1984 (unpublished) and *X. and Y. v. UK*, 19 DR 66 (1978) on 21 year age of consent requirement for gay men as compared to 16 year age of consent requirement for heterosexuals (and lesbians); *Johnson v. UK*, 47 DR 72 (1986) on criminalization of sexual acts in private where more than two consenting adult males are present; *B. v. UK*, 34 DR 68 (1983) on prohibition from service in the armed forces; *S. v. UK*, 47 DR 274 (1986) on the denial to the surviving lesbian partner of protection under rent control laws if the deceased partner was the only tenant of record (see also *infra* footnote 77); *X. and Y. v. UK*, 32 DR 220 (1983) on deportation on one homosexual partner due to foreign nationality; cf. Helfer, 1991, (at 174). For a general guide to the legal situation of lesbians and gay men in Europe, see the publications listed in note 5 of Chapter Three by Waaldijk.

treatment for social and health insurance, equality concerning intestate inheritance, taxation, divorce or separation, etc. If the right to have children is recognized, it has to entail the right to tax benefits, custody and visiting rights. The one without the other would be abusive, discriminatory and violative of fundamental human rights to equal treatment and respect of human dignity, because after a fundamental opening of these institutions to same-sex couples, there are no justifiable reasons for discrimination in ancillary rights. Half-hearted solutions in this area would only calm the conscience of the majority and take the impetus out of the presently discernable movement towards fair treatment for lesbians and gays.

Thus, the policy decisions will have to be whether or not to allow homosexual relationships between teenagers (age of consent), whether or not to guarantee full equality in the workplace (including employment in traditionally sensitive areas such as school teaching, military and secret services, etc.), whether or not to give same-sex couples the right to traditional marriages (and to make this right enforceable even against religious organizations), whether or not to create an alternative but legally equal status (so-called 'registered partnerships'), whether or not to allow lesbians or gay men to adopt children with both partners becoming 'parents', whether or not to allow artificial insemination of lesbian women with recognition of the equal parenthood of their partner.

It is further submitted that a 'Stufentheorie' should be applied in the process of these policy decisions. Interference must be minimal and protection at a maximum where no third party rights are involved. Once the rights and interests of third persons may be or will be infringed, regulatory intrusion on the rights of lesbians and gay men will gradually become more easily justifiable and protection less comprehensive. Finally, where certain forms of (homosexual) behaviour must by necessity violate overriding rights of others, regulatory prohibition will be mandatory and protection cannot be granted.[70]

At the highest level, where legislative and administrative interference should be totally excluded, would be sexual relationships between consenting adults in private. As the European Court of Human Rights stated in *Dudgeon v. UK*:

> Although members of the public who regard homosexuality as immoral may be shocked, offended or disturbed by the commission by others of private

---

70   This approach is also known as strict, intermediate and minimal scrutiny. If a criterion for different treatment, in our case sexual orientation, is held to be a 'suspect classification' because it should normally not be relevant for legitimate regulatory purposes, any different treatment on the basis of this criterion will be subject to strict scrutiny. In that case the differentiation can only be upheld, if 'pressing public necessity' can justify burdening the suspect class (*Korematsu v. United States*, 323 U.S. 214, 216 (1944)).

homosexual acts, this cannot on its own warrant the application of penal sanctions when it is consenting adults only who are involved.[71]

In this respect it has to be irrelevant, whether the private sexual acts are taking place between two or more consenting adults. A situation still existing in the United Kingdom[72] where the presence of a third person ends 'privacy', making the sexual acts between men unlawful, is clearly untenable.

General public safety in terms of relatively accepted social behaviour (holding hands, kissing etc.) should also be placed on a very high level of protection, where legislative and administrative interference would only be acceptable in the face of 'pressing public necessity'. In this respect a useful parallel can be drawn to German Freedom of Assembly law (*Versammlungsrecht*). The free exercise of their rights by minorities has to be protected by the German State (the police, if necessary). Restrictions on peaceful assemblies of minorities are only possible in case of a public emergency, e.g. if police forces protecting a minority group-assembly are grossly outnumbered by a hostile and violent counter-group.

The full equality of lesbians and gay men in 'normal' jobs should also be given a high level of protection. Ordinary labour law is fully capable of treating any problems that might arise in the context of access to employment, remuneration, promotions, termination of work contracts, and working conditions in general. If a person is not performing on his or her contractual obligations, the (private) reasons for this are of little relevance. If the employer and the colleagues cannot remedy the situation in cooperation with the person concerned he or she will have to face consequences such as delayed promotions, or, in extreme cases, termination of the employment. Lesbians and gay men do not deserve and do not demand any discriminatory or preferential treatment in this respect.

However, if a person does fulfil her contractual obligations 'in spite' of his or her non-traditional private- or sex-life, there must not be any discrimination as compared to his or her colleagues. Quite to the contrary, his or her employer may well be obliged to protect him or her against harassment and abuse by colleagues; in extreme cases this may involve a duty to sanction the behaviour of certain colleagues. Just as an employer must not remain indifferent to sexual harassment of a female employee by her male colleagues, the same must be true in the case of harassment due to sexual orientation.

Somewhat lower protection levels may be guaranteed concerning employment in so-called 'sensitive' jobs. However, the State should observe two limitations before discriminatory interferences become permissible:

71   Series A 1981, 24.
72   Cf. *supra* footnote 69 and accompanying text.

firstly, any action against lesbians or gay men should be limited to individual cases where problems have actually arisen. There should be no group-discrimination simply on the basis of sexual orientation. Secondly, the burden of proof should always be on the state or employer who wants to interfere with equality rights. The common argument of the fear of blackmail of lesbian or gay employees in 'sensitive' posts can be countered by the removal of that potential threat i.e removal of any social stigma from lesbian or gay lifestyles.[73]

The more third party rights can be or are affected, the lower the protection afforded to sexual orientation minorities. This has to be true in particular where the third parties cannot or not fully protect their rights. Thus, a certain age of consent-limit is required to protect minors. However, it seems difficult to justify a differentiation between the age of consent for heterosexual acts and the one for same-sex acts. If a state has such a low age limit for heterosexual acts (e.g. 12 in Spain) that it may argue that persons of that age 'are not fully responsible for what they are doing', those states should rather consider raising their general age of consent instead of discriminating against lesbians and gay men.

An area which has been subject to very restrictive laws in all Member States is the adoption of children by lesbian and gay couples. Usually, the only way for such couples to adopt children is adoptions by only one partner who is hiding his or her sexual orientation and cohabitation with a same-sex partner from the authorities in charge of the adoption. In most Member States 'single' men are practically excluded from adopting children altogether, whereas it is generally easier for 'single' women to adopt children.

As a result of this policy, whenever one partner of a same-sex couple does succeed with an adoption, the other partner does not become mother/father or otherwise legally responsible for the child.[74] Thus, although factually the child is raised by two 'parents', it is denied legally equal status and protection. This can have severe consequences e.g. if the adopting partner dies. In this situation, the child will usually be taken away by the authorities from the other partner as well (maybe after many years of 'happy family life') and may well end up in an institution. If the other partner dies, the child will not be entitled to intestate inheritance. This result is all the more serious if the other partner was the only bread-winner and a will does not exist or is successfully contested by relatives of the de-

---

73   A circular argument has been generally used to restrict lesbians and gay men from assuming top jobs in many civil service departments: If they admit their homosexuality, they will not be hired – although they cannot be blackmailed. Yet, if they hide their homosexuality to get the job, they are open to blackmail only because they were forced to lie in the first place.

74   See paragraph II.C.2 of Chapter Four by Van der Veen and Dercksen.

ceased, because not only will there be no inheritance for child and surviving partner, but the surviving partner (and parent) will then also be left without pension or other income.

Member States' reservations against legalization of adoptions by same-sex couples are increasingly incomprehensible in the light of the growing body of research on the possible effects of growing up in such a 'family' on the children. The care and attention actually given to the children clearly outweighs the gender of the 'parents'. Also, the question arises as to whether the States can remain blind to the fact that all over Europe hundreds of thousands of children are in fact growing up either in 'families' of lesbian or gay couples or often in homes shared by same-sex house mates who may live together for many years just like a family but without having sexual relationships with each other. Last but not least, one might ask whether children are not better off in a 'family' of same-sex lovers rather than in an institution.

The latter question leads directly to the question whether artificial insemination should be made available to lesbians. By contrast to children adopted by same-sex couples, those not yet conceived are not in need of help. Thus, the desires of the prospective parent(s) concerning artificial insemination are decisive. This area of 'family law' may, pending further investigation, be on a very low level of protection for lesbians and gay men.

B. How Can the Optimal Situation Be Achieved?

There are three fundamentally different approaches to the notion of 'family' and the rights and responsibilities attached to family relationships.[75] The traditional approach has been called 'formal' approach. It refers to traditional statutory language when definitions for 'family' or 'spouse' are needed for example in the context of immigration rights, various social benefits, child-care and custody, etc. Alternative relationships without ties of blood, adoption or marriage do not qualify under this concept for the rights and advantages reserved to families and spouses.

In recent times a 'functional' approach has developed in some contexts and has been applied by some decision-making organs. This approach recognizes the nuclear or formal family definition as the norm but then looks for functional resemblances in non-traditional relationships when

---

75 The terminology used here is loaned from American doctrinal discourse. For a summary of the American situation see Note, 'Looking for a Family Resemblance: The Limits of the Functional Approach to the Legal Definition of Family', 104 *Harvard Law Review* (1991) 1640-1659.

deciding whether or not they should be treated on an equal footing in a certain context.[76] Thus, if an alternative relationship

> shares the essential characteristics of a traditionally accepted relationship and fulfils the same human needs [...] such as economic cooperation, participation in domestic relationships, and affection between the parties [...][77]

it is granted certain social benefits otherwise reserved to traditional families. This approach is frequently the answer of progressive courts to changes in society in the face of unchanged legislation:

> For functionalist courts, the value of marriage and parenthood derives from positive societal effects, such as encouragement of stable, affectionate, and economically efficient human relationships. Because some non-traditional families produce similar beneficial effects, the restriction of benefits to traditional families under the formal approach is underinclusive.[78]

Legislative organs with their inherent tendency to avoid controversial decisions which might alienate voters like to leave the matter at that, i.e. to leave the search for just and fair rules to the courts on a case by case basis. However, some severe disadvantages result from the legislative inactivity:

First of all, the question whether equal treatment will be granted in a certain respect will depend on the individual administrative body or court which is handling the case in question. In the absence of statutory regulation there will always be more conservative and more progressive administrative and judicial organs. This makes it unforeseeable and arbitrary for the parties concerned. Case-law will probably develop some guidelines over time but these will always be limited to certain court districts and instances and will usually be little known outside the sphere of specialized lawyers.[79]

---

76   For examples see the Council's submission in the *Robards* case, *supra* footnote 18 and accompanying text, or the Dutch treatment of unmarried couples as described in the *Reed* case, *supra* footnote 27 and accompanying text.

77   See Note, *supra* footnote 75, at 1646. Other criteria for functional parallelism: 'exclusivity and longevity of the relationship, the level of emotional and financial commitment, the manner in which the parties have conducted their everyday lives and held themselves out to society and the reliance placed upon one another for daily family services,', ibid. at 1648-1649, quoted from the New York Court of Appeals' examination of a homosexual relationship which had lasted for 11 years and ended with the death of one partner who happened to be the only tenant of record. The surviving partner was claiming protection under rent control laws which prohibit the dispossession of the surviving spouse (74 N.Y. 2d 201 543 N.E. 3d 49, 544 N.Y. 2d 784 (1989).

78   See Note 76, *supra* footnote 75, at 1647-1648 (footnote in the original omitted in this quotation).

79   In a number of cases the ECJ has held it unacceptable if directives are transformed merely by (internal) administrative regulations of the Member States, precisely because these will be little known to the individuals concerned, may be subject to creeping modifications and may not be adequately enforceable against the state organs, cf. most recently: Case C-361/88, *Commission of the European Communities v. Federal Republic of Germany (Re Air pollution with sulphur dioxide)* and Case C-59/89, *Commission of*

Secondly, the comparative nature of the functional approach will lead to discrimination against non-traditional partnerships. Whereas traditional families will be accepted as eligible for benefits, etc. as such, non-traditional families will have to prove their eligibility each time they claim a benefit. This will subject them and only them to investigations concerning such private matters as sexual activity, degree of exclusivity, distribution of tasks and responsibilities in the family and management of finances.

Finally, it cannot be denied that legislative disregard and the subsequent legal uncertainty will further stigmatization within a society against non-traditional relationships and adversely affect their stability and longevity.

The only solution to this dilemma is the 'legislative' approach, i.e. action by the legislature in an effort to create for non-traditional relationships an institutionalized basis for equal treatment. The opening up of traditional marriages to lesbian and gay couples is an obviously problematic area, however, as it will meet with widespread resistance from conservative parts of society, churches, etc. and may thus be counterproductive to the efforts for improved recognition and acceptance of lesbians and gay men in everyday life. The best approach is most likely the creation of a new status, as has been done in Denmark,[80] which may be called 'registered partnerships' and will grant equality before the law to certain alternative partnerships. In an effort to check abuse and disintegration of stable human relationships, this new status may be reserved to certain forms of partnerships and a, once and for all, demonstration of certain criteria.

C. Why Should the Community Take an Active Role Rather Than Leaving it to the Member States?

There are two main reasons why the Community should take a more active role: Firstly, there is the Community's alleged commitment to the protection of fundamental rights and freedoms. If the Community wants to deliver upon the promises made in this respect it cannot go on to ignore the widespread discrimination against lesbians and gay men and the foot-dragging of many Member States when it comes to ameliorating the situation. Secondly, diverging Member State laws on lesbian and gay rights are severely inhibiting the free movement of these persons as migrant workers, providers and users of services and professionals seeking to establish themselves in other Member States.

---

the European Communities v. Federal Republic of Germany (Re Air pollution with lead), judgments of 30 May 1991, not yet published in the ECR.
80   Cf. *supra* footnote 66 and accompanying text.

The EEC-Treaty deals with 'workers' more or less on a par with goods, services and capital, i.e. primarily considers them factors of production, and does not as such contain a catalogue of human rights. The families of the workers are mentioned neither in Article 3(c) nor in Article 48. However, the Court of Justice has begun as early as 1969 to glean independent Community human rights and freedoms for migrant workers, their families, and all other Community citizens, from sources such as the 'constitutional traditions common to the Member States'.[81] It was again Advocate General Trabucchi who said:

> The migrant worker is not regarded by Community law [...] as a mere source of labour but is viewed as a human being. In this context the Community legislature is not concerned solely to guarantee him the right to equal pay and social benefits in connection with the employer-employee relationship, it also emphasized the need to eliminate obstacles to the mobility of the worker, *inter alia* with regard to the 'conditions for the integration of his family into the host country'.[82]

And more specifically:

> [In] order to attain real freedom of movement for workers within the territory of the Community they must be accorded real equality of treatment with the nationals, at least in regard to economic matters and social benefits in particular. In this context it is not important [...] that the legislation in question was not expressly conceived for workers as such and members of their families, but applies generally to the entire resident population.[83]

This jurisprudence has been endorsed by Parliament, Council and Commission in their Joint Declaration of 5 April 1977:

> 1. The European Parliament, the Council and the Commission stress the prime importance they attach to the protection of fundamental rights, as derived in particular from the constitutions of the Member States and the European Convention for the Protection of Human Rights and Fundamental Freedoms.
> 2. In the exercise of their powers and in pursuance of the aims of the European Communities they respect and will continue to respect those rights.[84]

and by an express mention in the Preamble of the Single Act:

> [The Heads of State of the Member States] Determined to work together to promote *democracy on the basis of the fundamental rights* recognized in the constitutions and laws of the Member States, in the Convention for the Protection of Human Rights and Fundamental Freedoms and the European Social Charter, notably freedom, equality and social justice. [...]

---

81 Cf. in particular Case 4/73, *J. Nold, Kohlen- und Baustoffgroßhandlung v. Commission* [1974] ECR 491, at Rec. 13.
82 Case 7/75, *Mr and Mrs F. v. Belgian State (Re Handicapped Child)* [1975] ECR 679, at 696.
83 Ibid.
84 OJ 1967 C 103/1.

Aware of the responsibility incumbent upon Europe *to aim at speaking ever increasingly with one voice and to act with consistency and solidarity* in order more effectively to protect its common interests and independence, in particular to display the principles of democracy and compliance with the law and with *human rights* to which they are attached, so that together they may make their own contribution to the preservation of international peace and security in accordance with the undertaking entered into by them within the framework of the United Nations Charter.[85]

and most recently in the Preamble of the Maastricht Treaty on European Union and in its Article F:

2. The Union shall respect fundamental rights, as guaranteed by the European Convention for the Protection of Human Rights and Fundamental Freedoms signed in Rome on 4 November 1950 and as they result from the constitutional traditions common to the Member States, as general principles of Community law. [86]

On the basis of these declarations, the Community would seem *obliged* to take an active role and to stand up against discrimination by any Member State in a field of Community competence.[87] The Community cannot accept violations of the fundamental rights to human dignity, equality, family life, freedom of opinion, and privacy, where it has a possibility to stop them.

Moreover, diverging Member State laws on lesbian and gay partnerships are inhibiting the free movement of this significant group in the Community. Some of these problems have always been there: if homosexuality is punishable in some states (e.g. Ireland; also in the UK, when more than two consenting adult males are taking part in sexual acts), or different ages of consent are applicable (the range in the Community is from 12 years in Spain to 21 years in the UK[88]), migrant lesbians or gay men will either avoid restrictive States or risk criminal prosecution for something which is totally lawful in their own State of origin (and most other Member States).

One very interesting problem has been added in 1989 with the *Danish Registered Partnership Act.*[89] Lesbian and gay couples who enter into such a registered partnership – and as has been shown above, the right to do so

---

85 Bulletin of the EC, Suppl. 2/86, 5, emphasis added.
86 Other acts of Community organs pertaining to human rights are documented in Clapham, 1991, in particular in Annex II; cf. also Hummer, Simma, Vedder and Emmert, 1991, 144.
87 On the problem whether and to what extent Community human rights are binding as such on Member State organs, when the latter are acting in their own area of competencies and not implementing Community law, cf. Chapter Eight by Snyder, Somsen and Hoyer on subsidiarity and competence.
88 *ILGA Pink Book*, and *supra* footnote 69.
89 Cf. *supra* footnote 66 and 80 and accompanying text.

must be open not only to a Danish national and his or her partner but also to any other Community national who has lawfully migrated to Denmark – cannot leave Denmark without losing the benefits of their special status. For them, the free movement of persons under Community law is practically not available, unless they agree to leave their 'family' behind.[90]

The only fully satisfactory solution to this dilemma would be a Community directive obliging all Member States to create a status for lesbians and gay men comparable to the Danish registered partnerships.

D. Legal Basis for Community Action

In the so-called Squarcialupi Report, drawn up on behalf of the Committee on Social Affairs and Employment of the European Parliament, one of the conclusions is that

> the fact remains that [discrimination against] male and female homosexuality is a real problem and there is thus every justification for raising it in a supranational political body such as the European Parliament, as proof of genuine respect for personal freedom and individual difference. [...][91]

However, as has been shown in the preceding sections, the protection of human rights and an effective guarantee of free movement for all Community citizens require more than a 'raising' of the problems in Parliament.

Nevertheless, Community law is first of all based on the principle of enumerated competence.[92] By contrast to sovereign states, the only born subjects of international law, the Communities were created by the Member States through the Treaties of Rome and Paris. The creators have chosen in these treaties not to transfer all their inherent rights as states (which would have ended their own existence as independent sovereigns and would immediately have formed a federation), but have chosen rather to transfer only those rights expressly listed in the treaties. Thus, while the Community institutions are certainly not prevented from 'raising' topics of family law

---

90 A pragmatic solution to this dilemma is the 'establishment' of the partner as a self-employed professional. If the same-sex or opposite-sex but not-married partner cannot find employment to establish his or her independent right of residence, he or she may gain this right e.g. by declaring to be a self-employed private language- or music teacher. However, this opportunity may not always work, is unsatisfactory as to rights beyond mere residence and is unavailable to partners who are not nationals of a Member State of the Community.

91 *Report on Sexual Discrimination at the Workplace*, EP Working Documents 1983/1984, Doc. 1-1358/83, 13 February 1984, at 16; cf. also *supra* footnote 48 and accompanying text.

92 Cf. Art. 4 para 1 of the EEC-Treaty: 'The tasks entrusted to the Community shall be carried out by the following institutions: an Assembly, a Council, a Commission, a Court of Justice. *Each institution shall act within the limits of the powers conferred upon it by this Treaty.*' (emphasis added).

and discussing them, they can only take legally binding measures if a competence of the Community can be found in the treaties.[93]

It has been argued that Article 117 in combination with Article 119 EEC would provide a legal basis sufficient for a redefinition of *Council Directive 76/207 on the implementation of the principle of equal treatment for men and women as regards access to employment, vocational training and promotion, and working conditions*[94] to prohibit also discrimination based on sexual orientation.[95] However, that approach seems unnecessarily shaky and inadequate. If Community action is necessary for an effective guarantee of the fundamental freedom of movement of persons, Article 100a (together with Article 7a(2) and/or Article 117) provides a solid foundation for such an action. It also has the advantage that the measures to be adopted do not require unanimity in the Council and thus cannot be blocked by one or two hesitant States.

IV. Summary

Whilst the European Community has no single defined 'family policy', a summation of resolutions, statements, directives and articles indicates the existence of a certain 'fluid' policy.

This 'policy' accepts the competence of the Member States to the definition of 'members of the family' whilst retaining some elements of supranational definition of 'spouse' which is narrow in scope.

Until now the Community organs have accepted that Member States have different levels of legislative regulation of homosexuality. However, in terms of family policy and the free movement of workers, any narrow definition of family which excludes lesbian and gay 'family' units will restrict the free movement of this significant percentage of the population.

There is a strong argument that there is no justification for the high level of regulation of the lives of lesbians and gay men by Member States.

---

93 As to the effects of the principle of subsidiarity as spelled out in the Maastricht Treaty on European Union on the principle of enumerated competences, see Chapter Eight by Snyder *et al.*

94 OJ 1976 L 39/40. The relevant Article 2 of the Directive reads as follows:
1. For the purposes of the following provisions, the principle of equal treatment shall mean that there shall be no discrimination whatsoever on grounds of sex either directly or indirectly by reference in particular to marital or family status.
2. This directive shall be without prejudice to the right of Member States to exclude from its field of application those occupational activities and, where appropriate, the training leading thereto, for which, by reason of their nature or the context in which they are carried out, the sex of the worker constitutes a determining factor. [...].

95 Opinion of the EP Legal Affairs Committee on discrimination against homosexuals (25-26 January 1984, draftsman: Ms Hooper), reproduced in EP Working Document 1-1358/83 (the Squarcialupi Report, cf. *supra* footnote 48 and accompanying text), at 26.

The protection of the rights of the individual must be paramount where there is no infringement on the rights of third parties or the state. This must be true also for lesbians and gay men. Prejudice by certain parts of the population is no excuse for denying same-sex couples social recognition. On the contrary, legal equality and recognition is likely to contribute to the elimination of prejudice and would thus benefit not only the homosexuals but the Member States and the Community as a whole.

Chapter Sixteen
A Call for a Nine Point Community Action Plan to Combat Discrimination Against Lesbians and Gay Men

by

ANDREW CLAPHAM* and J.H.H. WEILER**

* Formerly Executive Director of the Academy of European Law, European University Institute, Florence.
** Professor of Law, Harvard Law School; Director, Academy of European Law, European University Institute, Florence.

The European Parliament, in Article 6 of its Declaration of Fundamental Rights and Freedoms, which codifies the Community's legal commitment in this field, has affirmed that everyone has the right to respect and protection for their identity. Sexual orientation is a fundamental dimension of human identity. And yet, it is evident, that in Europe as elsewhere, lesbians and gay men are subjected in all spheres of social relations, often from an early age, to ridicule, intimidation, discrimination and outright physical assault. They are subjected to this not because of what they do but because of who they are. Homophobia is an extreme expression of contempt towards people merely on the basis of their identity. Eradicating this form of bigotry is a task which has to be the concern of everyone in the so-called private and public spheres.

The darkest aspects of recent European history act as a constant reminder, in the words of Richard von Weizsäcker, of the '... many ways of not burdening one's conscience, of shunning responsibility, looking away, keeping mum.' And yet, it is also evident that whereas other forms of bigotry and hatred towards individuals and groups based on their identity, such as racism and anti-semitism, have been the concern of public authorities in statements and legislative and administrative action, no corresponding attention, in kind and degree, has been given to the position of lesbians and gay men. This disparate treatment is so conspicuous as to become, in and of itself a form of toleration of, complicity in, and even tacit encouragement of insidious homophobia.

The European Community, in its sphere of activities and within its proper jurisdiction, cannot go on shunning responsibility, looking away, keeping mum. Commissioners and Presidents-in-Office of the Council can no longer appear in public fora and shift the burden to the Council of Europe, to the Member States, to private organizations.

The Community cannot continue its inaction because this would compromise principal objectives of the Treaty: to illustrate, unequal treatment in the workplace of lesbians and gay men which is not yet interdicted by the EC is as much a problem for the Community as is unequal treatment of men and women which is already interdicted.

The Community cannot continue its inaction because this would also compromise its commitment that in the field of its activities human rights will not be compromised.

All Community institutions have a role to play in addressing this problem, but it is, naturally, the Commission, as Guardian of the Treaties which must give the lead.

This, then, is a call for a Commission-led Community Action Plan to combat discrimination against lesbians and gay men.

Institutional aspects – Commission Responsibility

1. Combatting homophobia and ensuring the protection of fundamental
    human rights of lesbians and gay men should become officially part of
    the portfolio of a Member of the Commission with corresponding re-
    sponsibility within the Commission Administration and the Budget.

An Ad-Hoc Task Force

2. The Commissioner responsible should set up an ad-hoc Task Force
    composed of internal and external members to prepare a detailed plan
    and monitor its implementation. Such a plan may include the follow-
    ing elements:

Community Declaration

3. Preparation of a Community Declaration, modelled on the Declaration
    against Xenophobia and Racism, spelling out the commitment to com-
    batting discrimination against lesbians and gay men within the proper
    jurisdiction of the Community.

The Commission as Employer

4. The Task Force should review the current Staff Regulations with a
    view towards amendments which would visibly eradicate all forms of
    discrimination against lesbians and gay men in all aspects of the
    workplace. The Commission should be a model in this respect. This
    should then be pressed in all other Community institutions.

Equal Treatment Amendment

5. As a priority item, the Task Force should prepare the ground work for a
    proposal which would amend the current Equal Treatment Directive
    and extend it from gender discrimination to discrimination based on
    sexual orientation.

Legislative Agenda – Internal Market and Social Europe

6. As a longer term project the Task Force should review existing legisla-
    tion and planned legislation in the internal market and social and

labour policy areas with a view to inclusion of language which would ensure the protection of rights of lesbians and gay men in these areas.

Liaison with Member States and Private Organizations

7. The Task Force should review ways by which the Commission may encourage Member States and private organizations to combat discrimination against lesbians and gay men within their respective spheres of competence. This should be performed in liaison with lesbian and gay groups at the national and transnational level.

Study and Monitoring

8. The Commission should, itself and through decentralized means, put in place mechanisms to study and monitor the forms of discrimination against lesbians and gay men, in particular in the sphere of economic activity, with a view to enhancing awareness and where necessary taking action.

    In particular the Commission should consider the recommendations for further research set out as recommendations in the legal, social and economic chapters of this report.

Bill of Rights

9. The Commission should promote the inclusion of the prohibition of discrimination on grounds of sexual orientation in the list of prohibited grounds which might be adopted in any future Community Bill of Rights or Treaty.

Annex 1: Selected Bibliography

Armitage, G., J. Dickey and S. Sharples, *Out of the Gutter: A Survey of the Treatment of Homosexuality by the Press*, London: Campaign for Press and Broadcasting Freedom, 1987.

Arnull, A., 'The Incoming Tide: Responding to Marshall', in *Public Law*. London (1987) 383.

Ashman, P., 'Background of the Proposal for a Protocol to Amend the European Convention on Human Rights', in *Study-Conference on the Possibilities of Expanding the European Convention on Human Rights to Eliminate Discrimination Based on Sexual Orientation* (CSCE Parallel Activity, Copenhagen 26-27 May 1990), Conference Report. Copenhagen: LBL-F48, 1990.

Barendt, E., *Freedom of Speech*. Oxford: Clarendon Press, 1987.

Bayer, R. *Homosexuality and American Psychiatry: The Politics of Diagnosis*. New York: Basic Books, 1981.

Beer, C., R. Jefferey and T. Munyard, *Gay Workers, Trade Unions and the Law*. London: National Council for Civil Liberties, 1981.

Bercusson, B., 'The European Community's Charter of Fundamental Social Rights for Workers', in 53 *Modern Law Review*. London (1990).

Betten, L., *The Right to Strike in Community Law*. Amsterdam: Elsevier Science Publishing, 1985.

Boele-Woelki, K. and P. Tange, 'De Deense wet inzake het geregistreerd partnerschap', in *Nederlands Juristenblad*. 1989.

Boisson, J., *Le triangle rose. La déportation des homosexuels (1933-1945)*. 1988.

Bonfrère, L., *Homoseksualiteit en bedrijfscultuur*. Den Haag: Vuga, 1992.

Bos, M., M. Pot and E. Willems, 'Grensverlegging of grensversperring? Vreemdelingenrecht en homoseksualiteit', in M. Moerings and M. Mattijssen (eds), *Homoseksualiteit en recht*. Arnhem: Gouda Quint, 1992, 163-184.

Boutet, A., *La position du droit face à l'homosexualité en France*, Mémoire de licence en Droit Public, Université de Perpignan, année 1987-1988.

Brennan G. and J.M. Buchannan, *The Reason of Rules*. Cambridge: Cambridge University Press, 1985.

Burrows, F., *Free Movement in European Community Law*. Oxford: Clarendon Press, 1987.

Cameron, S., 'Marriage and the Distribution of Employment Incomes', in *Applied Economics*. Oxford, 1985.

Carlier, B., *et al.*, *Homostudies in Vlaanderen*. Antwerpen: Federatie Werkgroepen Homofilie, 1985.

Casey, J. *Constitutional Law in Ireland*. London: Sweet & Maxwell, 1987.

Cassese, A., 'The Self-Determination of Peoples' in Henkin, Louis (ed.), *The International Bill of Rights; The Covenant on Civil and Political Rights*. New York: Columbia University Press, 1981, 92-113.

Cassese, A., A. Clapham and J.H.H. Weiler (eds), *European Union – The Human Rights Challenge* (Vol. I: Clapham, *Human Rights and the European Community: A Critical Overview*; Vol. II: *Human Rights and the European Community: Methods of Protection*; Vol. III: *Human Rights and the European Community: The Substantive Law*). Baden-Baden: Nomos Verlagsgesellschaft, 1991.

Cavailhes, J., P. Dutey, G. Bach-Ignasse, *Rapport Gai, enquête sur les modes de vie homosexuels en France*. Paris: Editions Persona, 1984.

Clapham, A., *Human Rights and the European Community: A Critical Overview* Volume I of *European Union – The Human Rights Challenge*. Baden-Baden, Nomos Verlagsgesellschaft, 1991.

Crane, P., *Gays and the Law*. London: Pluto Press, 1982.

Colvin, M., *Section 28 – A Practical Guide to the Law and its Implications*. London: National Council for Civil Liberties, 1989.

Daly, M., 'At work', in B. Galloway (ed.), *Prejudice and Pride – Discrimination Against Gay People in Modern Britain*, London: 1983, 35-61.

Delpérée, F., *Droit constitutionnel. Tome 1. Les données constitutionnelles*. Bruxelles: Larcier, 1980.

Diez-Hochleitner, J., 'Conferencia intergubernamental sobre la union politica: propuesta sobre ciudadania europea', in 43 *Revista Espanola de Derecho Internacional*. Madrid (1991).

Dercksen, A., *Vetrouwenspersonen en homoseksualiteit in arbeidssituaties*. Den Haag: VUGA, 1992.

De Witte, B. (ed.), *European Community Law of Education*. Baden-Baden: Nomos Verlagsgesellschaft, 1989.

Dijk, P. van and G.J.H. van Hoof, *Theory and Practice of the European Convention on Human Rights*, 2nd edition. Deventer: Kluwer, 1990.

Dijk, P. van and G.J.H. van Hoof, *De Europese Conventie in Theorie en Praktijk*. Deventer: Kluwer, 1990.

Dijk, P. van et al., 'Human Rights and the Freedom of Movement of Persons in Europe; The Role of the National Judiciary in the Netherlands', in *T.M.C. Asser Institute Colloquium Freedom of Movement of Persons in Europe*, September 1991. [forthcoming]

Dose, R., 'Der § 175 in der Bundesrepublik Deutschland (1949 bis heute)', in *Die Geschichte des § 175 – Strafrecht gegen Homosexuelle*. Berlin: Verlag rosa Winkel, 1990, 122-143.

Dubber, M.D., 'Homosexual Privacy Rights Before the U.S. Supreme Court and the European Court of Human Rights. A Comparison of Methodologies', in *Standford Journal of International Law*. Stanford (1990).

Durrell, A., 'At home', in B. Galloway (ed.), *Prejudice and Pride – Discrimination Against Gay People in Modern Britain*, London: 1983, 1-18.

Dworek, G., and R. Kühn (eds), *Selbstbestimmt Schwul – § 175 ersatzlos streichen*. Bonn: Die Grünen im Bundestag 1989.

Dworkin, R., *Taking Rights Seriously*. London:, 1979.

Einarsen, T., 'The European Convention on Human Rights and the Notion of an Implied Right to *de facto* Asylum', in 2 *International Journal of Refugee Law*. Eynsham, 1990.

Ellerman, R., (ed.), *Soziale Diskriminierung Homosexueller*. Königswinter: Friedrich Naumann Stiftung, 1987.

Ellin, J. 'The Rights of Homosexuals and the Principles of Liberalism', in Arnaud, A.j., R. Hilpinen and J. Wroblewski, *Rechtstheorie* Suppl. 8. 1985, 305.

Elmer, M., and M. Lund Larsen, 'Explanatory Article on the Legal Consequences etc., of the Danish Law on Registered Partnership', translated from the Danish law journal *Juristen* (1990) No. 3.

Elsen, C., *Report on the Legal Situation of Homosexual Men & Women in the Armed Forces*. International Lesbian and Gay Association – Information Pool on Gays and Lesbians and the Military. Brussels, 1987 (plus later updates).

Emborg, M., *The Danish Law on Registered Partnership. How it Works*, discussion paper, 1989 (unpublished).

Emmert, F., 'Horizontale Drittwirkung von Richtlinien', in *Europäisches Wirtschafts- und Steuerrecht*. München: European Law Press, 1992, 56-67.

Enkelaar, C.C.M., and M. Rood-de Boer, 'Family Relations and Modern Medicine', in P.H.M. Gerver *et al.* (eds), *Netherlands Reports to the Twelfth International Congress of Comparative Law Sydney-Melbourne 1986*. The Hague: T.M.C. Asser Instituut, 1986, 137-158.

Evans, A. and H.U. Jessurun D'Oliveira, 'Nationality and Citizenship', in A. Cassese, A. Clapham and Joseph Weiler (eds), *European Union – The Human Rights Challenge,* Vol. II., Baden-Baden: Nomos Verlagsgesellschaft, 1991.

Fernandez, M., 'AIDS: The Immigration Perspective', in *Immigration and Nationality Law and Practice*, Vol. 5, No. 3. 1991.

Finer, S.F. and B.A. Morgan, 'Women and Minorities in Introductory Economics Textbooks 1974-1984, in 18 *Journal of Economic Education*. New York, 1987.

Frowein, J.A., and T. Stein (eds), *Die Rechtsstellung von Ausländern nach staatlichem Recht und Völkerrecht – The Legal Position of Aliens in National and International Law*. Berlin: Springer Verlag, 1987.

Gabel, 'The Phenomenology of Rights. Consciousness and the Pact of the Withdrawn Selves, in *Texas Law Review*. Austin (1984) 1563.

Gaja, G., 'Aspetti problematici della tutela dei dritti fondamentali nell'ordinamento comunitario', *in Rivista di diritto internazionale*. Milano (1988).

Galloway, B., 'The police and the courts', in B. Galloway (ed.), *Prejudice and Pride – Discrimination against gay people in modern Britain*, London: Routledge, 1983, 102-124.

Geelhoed, L.A., 'Het subsidiariteitsbeginsel: een comunautair principe?' in 39 *Tijdschrift voor Europees en economisch recht*, No. 7/8. *SEW,* Gent (1991) 422-435.

Geerlings, J., and M. van der Meer, *Lesbisch Moederschap, praktijk en theorie. Een onderzoek.* Utrecht: Interfacultaire Werkgroep Homostudies, Rijksuniversiteit Utrecht, 1989.

Geerlof, J., 'Ouders met beleid', in A. Dercksen *et al.* (ed.), *Tolerantie onder NAP. 20 essays over homosexualiteit voor Rob Tielman,* Utrecht: Interfacultaire Werkgroep Homostudies, Rijksuniversiteit Utrecht, 1992, 29-37.

Geerlof, J., and R. Tielman, *Hebben homo's ouders?.* Utrecht: Interfacultaire Werkgroep Homostudies, Rijksuniversiteit Utrecht, 1986.

Geurtsen, W., A. Hofmeijer, and T. Zondervan, *Homo of hetero, gezegend ben je! Remonstranten over huwelijk en andere relatievormen.* Utrecht: Interfacultaire Werkgroep Homostudies, Rijksuniversiteit Utrecht, 1991.

Gibson, P., 'Gay Male and Lesbian Youth Suicide', in *Report of the Secretary's Task Force on Youth Suicide.* US Dept. of Health and Human Services. Washington, 1989.

Golombok, S., A. Spencer and M. Rutter, 'Children in Lesbian and Single-Parent Households: Psychosexual and Psychiatric Appraisal', 24 *Journal of Child Psychology and Psychiatry.* Oxford (1983) 551-572.

Gonsiorek, J.C., and J.D. Weinrich, 'The Definition and Scope of Sexual Orientation', in J.C. Gonsiorek and J.D. Weinrich (eds), *Homosexuality. Implications for Public Policy.* Newbury Park: Sage, 1991, 1-12.

Green, N., T.C. Hartley and J.A. Usher, *The Legal Foundations of the Single European Market.* Oxford: University Press, 1991.

Grief, N., 'The Domestic Impact of the European Convention on Human Rights as Mediated Through Community Law', in *Public Law.* London, 1991.

Groot, G.-R., and M. Tratnik, *Nationaliteitsrecht.* Zwolle: Willink, 1986.

Groot, G.-R. de, *Staatsangehörigkeitsrecht im Wandel – Eine rechtsvergleichende Studie über Erwerbs- und Verlustgründe der Staatsangehörigkeit.* The Hague: T.M.C. Asser Instituut, 1988 (also published by: Carl Heymans Verlag).

Harris, D. and R. Haig (eds), *AIDS: A Guide to the Law.* London: Routledge, 1990.

Haveman, R., and M. Moerings, 'De homogeniteit van het strafrecht', in M. Moerings and M. Mattijssen (eds), *Homoseksualiteit en recht.* Arnhem: Gouda Quint, 1992, 39-62.

Hay, R., *The European Commission and the Administration of the Community.* European Documentation. Brussels: Office for Official Publications of the European Communities, 1989.

Heger, H., *The Men With the Pink Triangle.* London: Gay Men's Press, 1980.

Helfer, L.R., 'Finding A Consensus on Equality: The Homosexual Age of Consent and the European Convention on Human Rights', in *New York University Law Review New York* (1990).

Helfer, L.R., 'Lesbian and Gay Rights as Human Rights: Strategies for a United Europe', in *Virginia Journal of International Law*. Charlottesville (1991).

Hekma, G., *Homoseksualiteit, een medische reputatie. De uitdoktering van de homoseksueel innegentiende-eeuws Nederland*. Amsterdam, SUA, 1987.

Hendriks, A., and L. Markestein, 'Recht als medicijn', in A. Hendriks and E. van der Veen (eds), *Homoseksualiteit en recht*. Arnhem: Gouda Quint, 1992, 185-214.

Hepple, B., 'The Implementation of the Community Charter of Fundamental Social Rights', in 53 *Modern Law Review*, No. 5, London (1990).

Hofmeister, H., 'Austria', in Kohler, P.A. and H.F. Zacker (eds), *The Evolution of Social Insurance 1881-1981*. London: Pinter, 1982.

Hoogenboom, T., 'The Position of Those Who Are Not Nationals of a Community Member State', in A. Cassese, A. Clapham and J.H.H. Weiler (eds), *European Union – The Human Rights Challenge*, Vol. II., Baden-Baden: Nomos Verlagsgesellschaft, 1991.

Hoogma, M., 'Een lesje politiek', in A. Dercksen *et al* (ed.), *Tolerantie onder N.A.P.: 20 Essays over homoseksualiteit voor Rob Tielman*. Utrecht: Interfacultaire Werkgroep Homostudies, Rijksuniversiteit Utrecht, 1992, 63-70.

Hooker, E., 'The Adjustment of the Male Overt Homosexual', 21 *Journal of Projective Techniques*. Glendale (1957) 18.

Horowitz, C.F., 'Homosexuality's Legal Revolution', in *The Freeman*. May 1991, 173-181.

Hummer, W., B. Simma, C. Vedder and F. Emmert, *Europarecht in Fällen*. Baden-Baden: Nomos Verlagsgesellschaft, 1991.

Hurwitt, M., and P. Thornton, *Civil Liberty: the Liberty/NCCL Guide*. London: Liberty / National Council for Civil Liberties, 1989 (fourth edition).

Jeffery-Poulter, S., *Peers, Queers & Commons – The Struggle for Gay Law Reform from 1950 to the Present*. London: Routledge, 1991.

Kapteyn, P.J.G., P. Verloren van Themaat and L.W. Gormley, *Introduction to the Law of the European Communities after the Coming Into Force of the Single European Act*. Deventer-Boston: Kluwer, 1989.

Khayatti, D., 'Proper Schooling for Teenage Lesbians', in A. Hendriks and E. van der Veen (eds), *The Third ILGA Pink Book*. Boston: Prometheus Books, 1993 (in print).

Kommers, D. and M. Waelbroeck, 'Legal Integration and the Free Movement of Goods: The American and European Experience', in M. Cappelletti, M. Seccombe and J.H.H. Weiler (eds), *Integration Through Law. Europe and the American Federal Experience*, Vol. 1, Book 3. Berlin: de Gruyter, 1986.

Koopmans, T., *Vergelijkend publiekrecht*. Deventer: Kluwer, 1986 (tweede druk).

Koopmans, T., 'Constitutionele toetsing', in 122 *Handelingen Nederlandse Juristen-Vereniging*. (1992), I, 35-84.

Lasok, D., 'The Professions in the European Community; The Treaty Framework', in 29 *Columbia Journal of Transnational Law,* No. 41, New York (1991).

Lautmann, R., *Seminar Gesellschaft und Homosexualität.* Frankfurt am Main: Suhrkamp, 1977.

Laurent, F., *E/CN.4/Sub.2/1988/31.* New York: United Nations, 1988.

Lonbay, J., 'Education and the Law: The Community Context', in *European Law Review.* London (1989).

Lundey, S.E., 'I DO BUT I CAN'T: Immigration Policy and Gay Domestic Relationships', in *Yale Law and Policy Review.* New Haven (1986).

Macdonald, R.St.J., 'The Margin of Appreciation and the Case-Law of the European Court of Human Rights', in *Collected Courses of the Academy of European Law 1990.* Volume I, Book 2, Dordrecht: Martinus Nijhoff Publishers, 1992.

Mackenzie-Stuart, L., *The European Community: Catchwords and Reality,* Josephine Onoh Memorial Lecture, 26 February 1991. Hull: Hull University Press, 1991.

Malt, M., '... *ist unstreitig homosexuell' Diskriminierung von Lesben und Schwulen in Arbeits- und Zivilrecht.* Hamburg: Frühlings Erwachen, 1991.

Mancini, F., 'Robert Schuman Lecture on Community Law, in *Collected Courses of the Academy of European Law 1990.* Volume I Book 1, Dordrecht: Martinus Nijhoff Publishers, 1991.

Marks, J.D., 'A Victory for the American Family', in *New York Times,* 21 February 1992.

Martens, C., and J. van Straaten, 'Juridische en fiscale gevolgen van ongehuwd samenwonen', in M. Moerings and M. Mattijssen (eds), *Homoseksualiteit en recht.* Arnhem: Gouda Quint, 1992, 145-162.

Mattijssen, A., 'Wie niet waagt, die niet wint. Homodiscriminatie en het civielrecht', in M. Moerings and M. Mattijssen (eds), *Homoseksualiteit en recht.* Arnhem: Gouda Quint, 1992, 11-38.

Meer, T. van der, *De Wesentlyche sonde van sodomie en andere vuyligheden. Sodomietenvervolging in Amsterdam 1730-1811.* Amsterdam, Schorer Imprint, 1984.

Mohr, R., *Gays/Justice.* New York: Columbia University Press, 1988.

Morris, P.E. and P.W. David, 'Directives, Direct Effect and the European Court: The Triumph of Pragmatism – Pt II', in *Business Law Review* (1987).

Nielsen, L., 'Family Rights and the Registered Partnership in Denmark', in *International Journal of Law and the Family.* 1990.

Nuffel, P. van, 'Een bijna algemeen verblijfsrecht in de Europese Gemeenschap. Commentaar op de verblijfsrechtrichtlijnen van 28 juni 1990', in *SEW,* No. 12. Gent (1990).

Oort, D. van, 'Sexuelle Gewalt gegen Lesben und bisexuelle Frauen aller Altersgruppen', in C. Nachtwey (ed.), *Gewalt gegen Schwule / Gewalt gegen Lesben. Ursachenforschung und Handlungsperspektiven im internationalen Vergleich.*

Berlin: Referat für Gleichgeschlechtliche Lebensweisen, Senatsverwaltung für Jugend und Familie, 1992.

Odijk, F. van, *Tolerantie tot een bepaalde grens. Homoseksuele vrouwen en mannen bij de gemeente Amsterdam*. Utrecht: Interfacultaire Werkgroep Homostudies, Rijksuniversiteit Utrecht, 1988.

O'Keeffe, D., 'The Free Movement of Persons and the Single Market', in 17 *European Law Review*, No. 1, London, February 1992.

Pais Macedo van Overbeek, J., 'AIDS/HIV Infection and the Free Movement of Persons within the European Economic Community, in 27 *CML Rev.* (1990).

Philip, C. (ed.), *L'enseignement supérieur et la dimension européenne*. 1989.

Pius XI, Pope, *Quadragesimo Anno*, Actae Apostolicae Sedis 23. Rome, 1931.

Plender, R., *International Migration Law*. Rev. 2nd ed. Dordrecht: Nijhoff, 1988.

Polikoff, N.D., 'This Child Does Have Two Mothers: Redefining Parenthood to Meet the Needs of Children in Lesbian-Mother and Other Non-Traditional Families', in 78 *Georgetown Law Journal*. (1990).

Posner, R.A., *Sex and Reason*. Harvard University Press, Cambridge 1992.

Ranjault, P., 'On The Principle of Subsidiarity', in 2 *Journal for European Social Policy*, No. 1 (1992).

Rhee, R. van, 'Een bijzonder gezin (A Special Family), The European Commission and Homosexual Relationships, in *Nederlands Juristenblad*. Ned. Zwolle (1990) 1670-1675.

Schelter, K., 'La Subsidiarité: Principe directeur de la future Europe', in 344 *Revue du Marché Commun*. Paris (1991).

Schermers, H.G. and D. Waelbroeck, *Judicial Protection in the European Community* (5th ed.) Deventer: Kluwer, 1992.

Schippers, J., *Voorkeur voor mannen*. Amsterdam: Schorer Imprint, 1989.

Schwarze, J., 'Article 235 and Law-Making Powers in the European Community', in 27 *International and Comparative Law Quarterly*. London (1978).

Sell, R.L., *et al.*, *Homosexual and Bisexual Behavior in the United States, the United Kingdom and France*. Paper presented at the Sixth International Conference on AIDS, San Francisco, June 1990.

Snyder, F., *The Effectiveness of European Community Law: Institutions, Processes, Tools and Techniques*. Florence: European University Institute, 10 February 1992 (Public Lecture); and in 55 *Modern Law Review*. London (1993) 19.

Snyder, F., J.-P. Jacqué and J.H.H. Weiler, *On the Road to European Union – A New Judicial Architecture. An Agenda for the Intergovernmental Conference*. *CML Rev*. London (1990) 185.

Solbes-Mira, P., 'La citoyneneté européenne', in 345 *Revue du marché commun et de l'union européenne*. Paris, Mars 1991.

Spicker, 1 *Journal of European Social Policy*, Vol. 1 (1991).

Steenbeek, J.G., 'Het Koninkrijk Denemarken', in L. Prakke and C.A.J.M. Kortmann (eds), *Het staatsrecht van de landen der Europese Gemeenschappen*. Deventer: Kluwer, 1988, 67-111.

Steiner, J., *Textbook on EEC Law*, 3rd edition, 1992.

Tasker, F. and S. Golombok, 'Children Raised by Lesbian Mothers: The Empirical Evidence', *Family Law*. Bournemouth, May 1991.

Tatchell, P., *Out In Europe: A Guide to Lesbian and Gay Rights in 30 European Countries*. London: Channel 4, 1991.

Tatchell, P., *Europe in the Pink. Lesbian & Gay Equality in the New Europe.* London: GMP Publishers, 1992.

Temple Lang, J., 'The Sphere in Which Member States Are Obliged to Comply With the General Principles of Law and Community Fundamental Rights Principles', in 2 *Legal Issues of European Integration*. Amsterdam, Europa Instituut (1991).

Thill, J., 'Het Groot-Hertogdom Luxemburg', in L. Prakke and C.A.J.M. Kortmann (ed.), *Het staatsrecht van de landen der Europese Gemeenschappen*. Deventer: Kluwer, 1988, 607-672.

Thinius, B., 'Verwandlung und Fall des Paragraphen 175 in der Deutschen Demokratischen Republik', in *Die Geschichte des § 175 – Strafrecht gegen Homosexuelle*, Berlin: Verlag rosa Winkel, 1990, 145-162.

Thomas, P., and R. Costigan, *Promoting Homosexuality – Section 28 of the Local Government Act 1988*. Cardiff: Cardiff Law School, 1990.

Tielman, R., *Homoseksualiteit in Nederland. Studie van een emancipatiebeweging.* Amsterdam/Meppel: Boom, 1982.

Tielman, R., 'Homoseksualiteit in de Nederlandse pers', in E. Bakker and J. Schuyf (eds), *Homoseksualiteit en de Media*. Utrecht: Interfacultaire Werkgroep Homostudies, Rijksuniversiteit Utrecht, 1985.

Tielman, R., and T. de Jonge, 'Country-by-Country Survey. A Worldwide Inventory of the Discrimination and Liberation of Lesbians and Gay Men', in *The Second ILGA Pink Book. A Global View of Lesbian and Gay Liberation and Oppression.* Utrecht: Interdisciplinary Gay and Lesbian Studies Department, University of Utrecht (published for the International Lesbian and Gay Association, with a grant of the Ministry of Welfare, Health and Culture), 1988.

Tielman, R., and H. Hammelburg, 'World Survey', in A. Hendriks and E. van der Veen (eds), *The Third ILGA Pink Book*. Boston: Prometheus Books, 1993 (in print).

Tielman, R., A. Kersten, and D. van der Ploeg, *Homoseksualiteit in het onderwijs*. Utrecht: ISOR, Rijksuniversiteit Utrecht, 1990.

Tielman, R., A. Hendriks, and E. van der Veen (eds), *The third ILGA Pink Book.* Boston, USA: Prometheus Books, 1993 (in print).

Trenchard, L., and H. Warren, *Something to Tell You: The Experiences and Needs of Young Lesbians and Gay Men in London*, London Gay Teenage Group, 1984.

Udding, E., and M. Ramakers, *The Legal and Social Situation of Lesbians and Gay Men. A Country-by-Country Survey*. Brussels: International Lesbian and Gay Association, 1991.

Veen, E. van der, and A. Dercksen, *Onderzoeksverslag deel I. Een analyse van antihomoseksueel en antilesbisch geweld en discriminatie wegens homoseksualiteit in de periode 1974-1989 door de overheid en politiek, justitie en politie, levensbeschouwelijke organisaties, familie en gezin*. Utrecht: Interfacultaire Werkgroep Homostudies / Centrum Anti-discriminatie Homoseksualiteit, Rijksuniversiteit Utrecht, 1990.

Veen, E. van der, 'Homoseksualiteit en politie', in E.A. van der Veen, E.L.A.M. de Kerf, Th. A. Stallmann, and H. in 't Veld (eds), *Homoseksualiteit en politie*. Lochem: Van den Brink, 1992, 13-30.

Veen, E.van der, 'Queerbashing across Europe: police strategies for catching the perpetrators', in P. Derbyshire (ed.), *Safer cities: Police and Sexuality* (in print).

Vliet, F. van, 'Waar een wil is is een wet! Een bijdrage over de positie van lesbische moeders en homoseksuele vaders in het afstammingsrecht', in M. Moerings and M. Mattijssen (eds), *Homoseksualiteit en recht*. Arnhem: Gouda Quint, 1992, 97-124.

Vrooman, J.C., *Een leefvormregistratie in de sociale zekerheid?* in PS, 1992, 1396-1404.

Waaldijk, K. 'Constitutional Protection Against Discrimination of Homosexuals', in 13 *Journal of Homosexuality*. USA: Hayworth Press (1986/1987) 57-68.

Waaldijk, K., 'De heteroseksuele exclusiviteit van het huwelijk na Hoge Raad 19 oktober 1990', in *Ars Aequi*, jrg. XL, 1991, 47-56.

Waaldijk, K., 'Zó niet getrouwd: hetero-huwelijk en bovenwettelijk discriminatieverbod', in M. Moerings en M. Mattijssen (eds), *Homoseksualiteit en recht*. Arnhem: Gouda Quint, 1992, 63-97, (a).

Waaldijk, K., 'De paradox van het homohuwelijk: een politiek paradigma', in A. Dercksen *et al.* (ed.), *Tolerantie onder N.A.P.: 20 Essays over homoseksualiteit voor Rob Tielman*. Utrecht: Interfacultaire Werkgroep Homostudies, Rijksuniversiteit Utrecht, 1992, 207-214, (b).

Waaldijk, K., 'Vrij samen. Over het advies van de commissie-Kortmann inzake de vrijwillige registratie van leefvormen', in *RegelMaat*. Lelystad, The Netherlands (1992) 43-49, (c).

Weiler, J.H.H., 'The Transformation of Europe', in 100 *Yale Law Journal*. New Haven, 1992, 2403-2483.

Weiler, J.H.H., 'Methods of Protection: Towards a Second and Third Generation of Protection', in A. Cassese, A. Clapham and J.H.H. Weiler (eds), *Human Rights and The European Community: Methods of Protection* Volume II of *European Union – The Human Rights Challenge*. Baden-Baden: Nomos Verlagsgesellschaft, 1991.

Westerveld, M., 'Sociale zekerheid en homo-emancipatie: via gelijkberechtiging naar roze kostwinnerschap', in M. Moerings and M. Mattijssen (eds), *Homoseksualiteit en recht*. Arnhem: Gouda Quint, 1992, 145-162.

410

Wilke, M. and H. Wallace, *Subsidiarity: Approaches to Power-Sharing in the European Community*, RIIA Discussion Papers No. 27. London, 1990.

Wit, J. de, 'De zaak Haenen-Vincineau. Homoseksualiteit also wettelijk strafbare ontucht in België', in *Recht en Kritiek*. Nijmegen (1987) 243-258.

Wong, C., *Immigration rights for lesbians and gays*, paper, Stockholm: ILGA, 1988.

Young, O.R., 'The Politics of International Regime Formation: Managing Natural Resources and the Environment', in 43 *International Organization*, No. 3. Boston, 1989.

Zillich, N., *Homosexuelle Männer im Arbeitsleben*. Frankfurt: Campus, 1988.

Aspectos jurídico-legales de la homosexualidad. Barcelona: Instituto Lambda (Temas Monográficos de sexologia 4), 1988.

Equality Now for Lesbians and Gay Men. Dublin: Irish Council for Civil Liberties (ICCL), 1990.

Iceberg 1991: Kees Waaldijk, *Tip of an iceberg. Anti-gay and anti-lesbian discrimination in Europe 1980-1990. A survey of discrimination and anti-discrimination in law and society*. First report, draft version 16.12.1991. Utrecht: Department of Gay and Lesbian Studies, University of Utrecht, 1991.

ILGA Bulletin. 4/91. Brussels: International Lesbian and Gay Association, October 1991.

Looking for a Family Resemblance: The Limits of the Functional Approach to the Legal Definition of Family, in 104 *Harvard Law Review*. Cambridge (1991).

A National Survey of Anti-Discrimination Laws: A Listing of Legal Protections for Lesbians and Gay Men Regarding Employment, Housing, and Public Accommodation. New York: Lamda Legal Defense and Education Fund, 1990.

Out for Ourselves. The Lives of Irish Lesbians & Gay Men. Dublin: Dublin Lesbian and Gay Men's Collectives, 1986.

Recht schwul – Rechtsratgeber für Schwule, SchwIPs – Schwule Initiative gegen den Paragraphensumpf (ed.). Berlin: Verlag rosa Winkel, 1982.

Resource Material on Lesbian/Gay Law Reform. Dublin: Gay & Lesbian Equality Network, 11 April 1992.

La situation juridique et social de l'homosexualité au Portugal. Lisboa: Ministério da Justiça, 23 June 1992 (report prepared at the request of the Department of Gay and Lesbian Studies of the University of Utrecht, for the benefit of the study funded by the Commission of the EC into the rights of lesbians and gay men in the internal market of the EC).

Schwule im Recht – Rechtsratgeber für homosexuelle Menschen, SchwIPs – Schwule Initiative gegen den Paragraphensumpf (ed.). Bamberg: Palette Verlag, 1992.

Sociaal en Cultureel Rapport 1992, Rijswijk: Sociaal en Cultureel Planbureau, 1992.

'The Constitutional Status of Sexual Orientation: Homosexuality as a Suspect Classification', in 98 *Harvard Law Review*. (1985).

Annex 2: Index of Transnational Law Provisions

A.   EEC Treaty and Maastricht Treaty on European Union

B. European Convention of Human Rights

Annex 3: Index of Decisions of Transnational Courts

A. Judgments and Opinions of the European Court and Commission of Human Rights (alphabetical order)

414

Van Oosterwijck; *201*

X. v. Belgium (Application 9484/81); *195*

X. v. Belgium (Application 11389/85); *112; 200*

X. v. FGR (Application 10040/82); *203*

X. v. United Kingdom (Application 16106/90); *43; 52; 59*

X. v. United Kingdom; *43*

X. and Y. v. Switzerland (Applications 7289/75 and 7349/76); *190; 305*

X. and Y. v. United Kingdom (Application 9369/81); *189; 191; 197; 305; 375; 383*

Zukrigh v. Austria (Application 17279/90); *195*

B. Judgments of the European Court of Justice (arranged by case number)

Case 8/55, Fédéchar; *229*

Case 26/62, Van Gend en Loos; *53; 230*

Case 15/63, Lassalle; *257*

Case 75/63, Hoekstra; *257; 372*

Case 29/69, Stauder; *42; 301*

Case 41/69, ACF Chemiefarma NV; *229*

Case 11/70, Internationale Handelsgesellschaft; *231*

Case 22/70, ERTA; *229*

Case 4/73, Nold; *301; 352; 390*

Case 155/73, Sacchi; *324*

Case 21/74, Airola; *370*

Case 36/74, Walrave and Koch; *53*

Case 41/74, Van Duyn; *34; 38; 295*

Case 67/74, Carmelo Angelo Bonsignore v. Oberstadtdirektor der Stadt Köln; *368*

Case 7/75, Mr and Mrs F. v. Belgian State: *381; 390*

Case 32/75, Cristini v. SNCF; *299; 374*

Case 36/75, Rutili; *39; 42; 49; 235; 295*

Case 43/75, Defrenne v. Sabena II; *55; 211; 351*

Case 48/75, Royer; *235*

Cases 3, 4, 6/76, Kramer et al.; *229*

Case 117/76, Ruckdeschel; *27*

Case 30/77, Bouchereau; *39; 235; 296*

Joined Cases 87 and 130/77 and 22/83 and 9 and 10/84, Vittorio Salerno; *251*

Cases 103 and 145/77, Royal Scholten-Honig Holdings; *37*

Case 149/77, Defrenne v. Sabena III; *211*

Case 120/78, Cassis de Dijon; *49; 328*

Case 207/78, Even; *374*

Annex 4: Analytical Subject Index[1]

---

1   For the purposes of this index lesbians and gay men are addressed as homosexuals, without distinction of gender, wherever possible.

International Studies in Human Rights

International Studies in Human Rights

This series is designed to shed light on current legal and political aspects of process and organization in the field of human rights.

MARTINUS NIJHOFF PUBLISHERS – DORDRECHT / BOSTON / LONDON